GW00838395

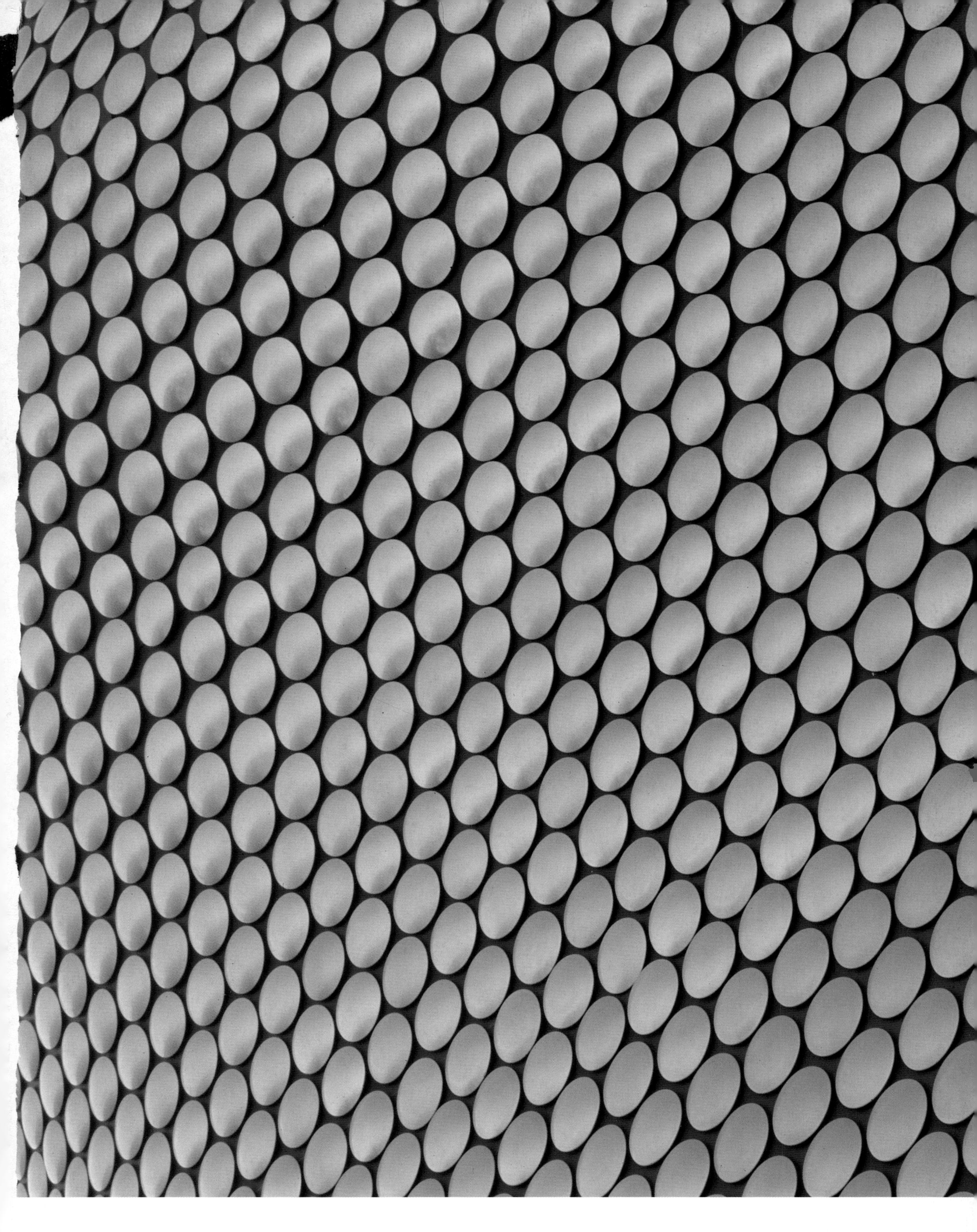

SKIN + BONES

Organized by BROOKE HODGE
Essays by BROOKE HODGE and PATRICIA MEARS   Afterword by SUSAN SIDLAUSKAS

The Museum of Contemporary Art, Los Angeles

Thames & Hudson

SKIN + BONES

Parallel Practices in **Fashion** and **Architecture**

azzedine**ALAÏA**
shigeru**BAN**
hussein**CHALAYAN**

prestonscott**COHEN**
COMMEdes**GARÇONS**
neil m.**DENARI**ARCHITECTS

DILLER SCOFIDIO+**RENFRO**
winka**DUBBELDAM**/ARCHI-TECTONICS
peter**EISENMAN**
alber**ELBAZ**FOR**LANVIN**

foreignoffice**ARCHITECTS**
futuresystems

frank**GEHRY**
tess**GIBERSON**
zaha**HADID**
HERZOG&**DE MEURON**
yoshiki**HISHINUMA**

toyo**ITO**
JAKOB+**MACFARLANE**
greg**LYNN**FORM
elena**MANFERDINI**
martin**MARGIELA**
alexander**MCQUEEN**
enric**MIRALLES** benedetta**TAGLIABUE**/EMBT ARQUITECTES
MIYAKEissey
MORPHOSIS
NEUTELINGS RIEDIJKARCHITECTEN
jean**NOUVEL**
OFFICEdA
OMA/rem**KOOLHAAS**
narciso**RODRIGUEZ**

ralph**RUCCI**
kazuyo**SEJIMA**+ryue**NISHIZAWA**/SANAA
nanni**STRADA**
yeohlee**TENG**

TESTA&**WEISER**
olivier**THEYSKENS**FOR**ROCHAS**
isabel**TOLEDO**

bernard**TSCHUMI**
dries van**NOTEN**
VIKTOR&**ROLF**
junya**WATANABE**

vivienne**WESTWOOD**
WILKINSON EYREARCHITECTS

yohji**YAMAMOTO**
j.meejin**YOON**/MYSTUDIO

contents

6 FOREWORD

8 ACKNOWLEDGMENTS

262 PROJECTS in the EXHIBITION

265 selected BIBLIOGRAPHY

10 **SKIN + BONES: PARALLEL PRACTICES in FASHION and ARCHITECTURE** Brooke Hodge

22 **CREATIVE PROCESS:** NARCISO RODRIGUEZ Jacky Marshall

30 **FRAYING the EDGES: FASHION and DECONSTRUCTION** Patricia Mears

38 **DECONSTRUCTION and ARCHITECTURE: CONFLICTING INTERPRETATIONS** Brooke Hodge

50 **PARALLEL PRACTICES:** ARCHITECTS and DESIGNERS in the EXHIBITION

260 **AFTERWORD** Susan Sidlauskas

6

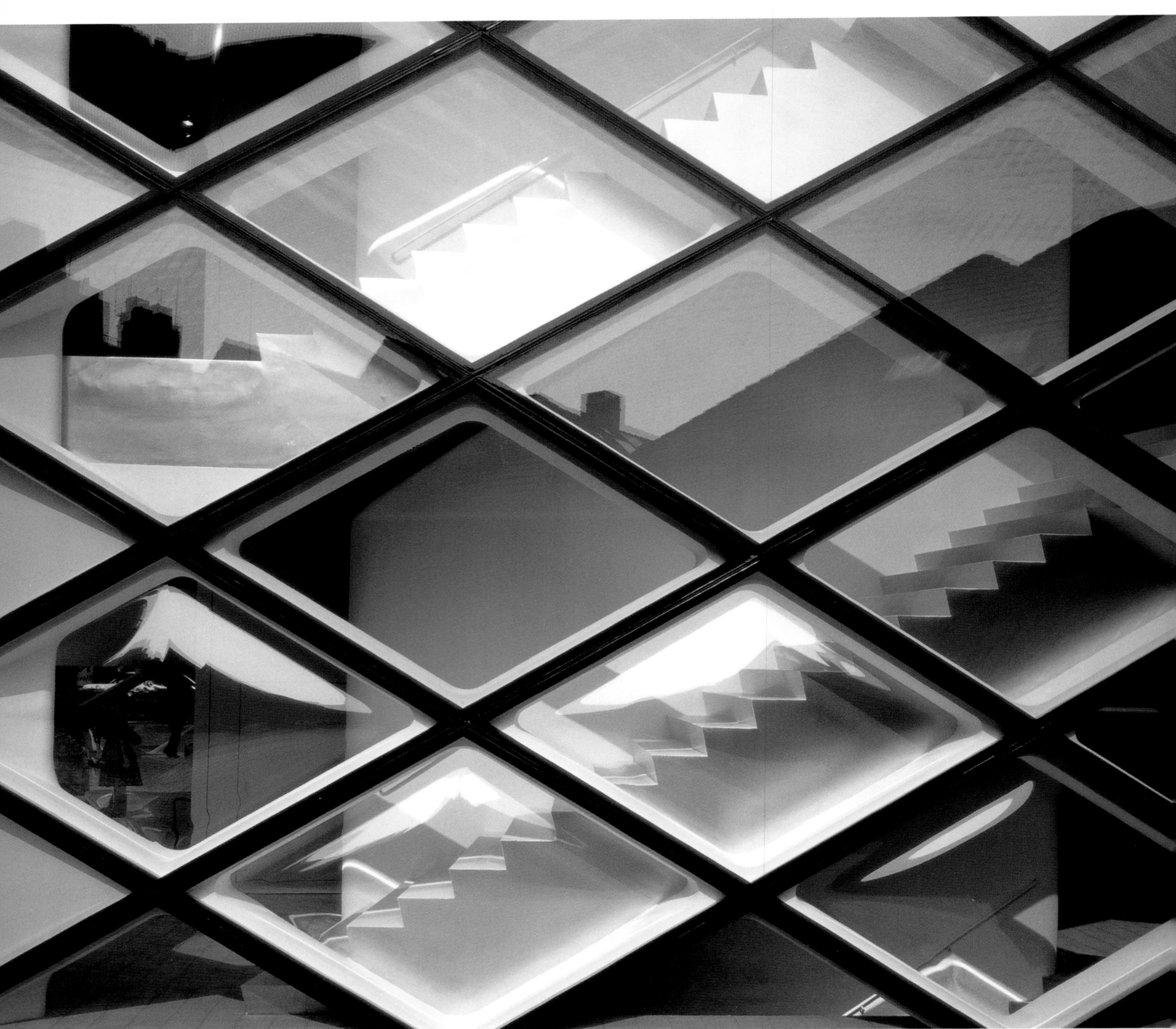

FOREWORD Jeremy Strick DIRECTOR

The Museum of Contemporary Art, Los Angeles (MOCA), is pleased to present the first major museum exhibition devoted to fashion and architecture. While a number of recent exhibitions have explored the relationship between art and fashion, less attention has been paid to the relationship between architecture and fashion, despite the increasing overlap in strategies and techniques shared by the two disciplines. Since the 1980s, a growing number of avant-garde fashion designers have approached garments as architectonic constructions, while architecture has boldly embraced new forms and materials—thanks to numerous technological advancements that have revolutionized both the design and construction of buildings and made techniques like pleating, stitching, folding, and draping part of the architectural vocabulary. Garments of increasing conceptual sophistication and structural complexity can be seen on runways and in the streets, just as buildings of unparalleled fluidity and innovation have come to grace major urban centers around the world.

Taking full advantage of its location in a city renowned for its innovative buildings, MOCA has established a long and distinguished history of engagement with architecture through exhibitions such as "Blueprints for Modern Living: History and Legacy of the Case Study Houses" (1989), "At the End of the Century: One Hundred Years of Architecture" (2000), "The Architecture of R. M. Schindler" (2001), "What's Shakin': New Architecture in L.A." (2001), "Frank O. Gehry: Work in Progress" (2003), and "Jean Prouvé: Three Nomadic Structures" (2005). In addition, MOCA has presented exhibitions featuring some of the most important designers of our time, including Ronan and Erwan Bouroullec, J Mays, and Roy McMakin. "Skin + Bones: Parallel Practices in Fashion and Architecture" extends MOCA's commitment to design by embracing the most intimate of designed objects: clothing.

Organized by MOCA Curator of Architecture and Design Brooke Hodge, "Skin + Bones" charts new terrain by highlighting common ground and suggesting fertile potential for the future development of each discipline. Brooke's vision for the exhibition was supported early on by Audrey Irmas, through the Sydney Irmas Exhibition Endowment. She also received important encouragement from Board of Trustees Chair Cliff Einstein and his wife Mandy, Trustees Gil Friesen and Carol Appel, as well as from Chair of the Architecture & Design Council Deborah Irmas. I extend my gratitude to MOCA's entire Board of Trustees for their foresight and commitment—without them, MOCA's reputation for innovation would be unthinkable. We are also grateful to exhibition sponsors The Ron Burkle Endowment for Architecture and Design Programs; the Sydney Irmas Exhibition Endowment; The MOCA Architecture & Design Council; Mondriaan Foundation, Amsterdam; Étant donnés: The French-American Fund for Contemporary Art; Dwell; Elise Jaffe + Jeffrey Brown; The Japan Foundation; the Consulate General of the Netherlands; Ralph Pucci International; and Yellow Book USA. This publication is made possible through a generous grant from Carol and Jacqueline Appel.

Lastly, I thank the architects and fashion designers in "Skin + Bones" for showing us the future, now.

HERZOG & DE MEURON, **PRADA AOYAMA TOKYO EPICENTER**, TOKYO, 2000–03, DETAIL OF FAÇADE

ACKNOWLEDGMENTS Brooke Hodge CURATOR OF ARCHITECTURE AND DESIGN

"Skin + Bones: Parallel Practices in Fashion and Architecture" was first conceived in late 2000 as I was interviewing for my position at The Museum of Contemporary Art, Los Angeles (MOCA). My interest in the intersection of fashion and architecture had been piqued by previous work on "Structure + Expression: Comme des Garçons," an exhibition I organized for Harvard University's Graduate School of Design in 2000. Rei Kawakubo's clothes, furniture, and retail spaces for her company Comme des Garçons inspired me to look more closely at relationships between the disciplines and the way in which their cross-fertilization has led to new design processes, fabrication methods, and even aesthetics in both garments and buildings.

"Skin + Bones" has benefited from the contributions, insight, and sheer hard work of many people. I extend thanks to MOCA Director Jeremy Strick and Chief Curator Paul Schimmel for their unflagging support of this project from the start. I am grateful to the museum's Board of Trustees, including former Chairman Bob Tuttle, current Chairman Clifford J. Einstein, and President Willem Mesdag, for their encouragement. I also thank Geri and Hal Alden, Carol and Jacqueline Appel, Mandy Einstein, Gilbert B. Friesen, Audrey M. Irmas, Deborah Irmas, and Dallas Price-Van Breda for their support and friendship. The generosity of the exhibition's sponsors has made this project possible, and warmest thanks go to The Ron Burkle Endowment for Architecture and Design Programs; the Sydney Irmas Exhibition Endowment; The MOCA Architecture & Design Council; Mondriaan Foundation, Amsterdam; Étant donnés: The French-American Fund for Contemporary Art; Dwell; Elise Jaffe + Jeffrey Brown; The Japan Foundation; the Consulate General of the Netherlands; Ralph Pucci International; and Yellow Book USA. In preparing the tour, it has been a pleasure to work with Chief Curator Osamu Fukunaga, Curator Yusuke Minami, and Assistant Curator Yayoi Motohashi at The National Art Center in Tokyo, and I am grateful for their support and enthusiasm for the exhibition.

The architects and fashion designers featured in the exhibition have my deepest gratitude not only for their extraordinary work, but also for their enthusiastic and generous participation in this endeavor. I am grateful to Azzedine Alaïa and Caroline Fabre-Bazin; Shigeru Ban and Hiroko Kusunoki; Hussein Chalayan, Milly Patrzalek, Leila Barstow, and Polona Dolzan; Preston Scott Cohen and Tobias Nolte; Rei Kawakubo, Adrian Joffe, and Chigako Takeda at Comme des Garçons; Neil Denari and Paola Vezzuli; Elizabeth Diller, Ricardo Scofidio, Charles Renfro, Denise Fasanello, Gaspar Libedinsky, and Kathryn Crawford; Winka Dubbeldam at Archi-Tectonics; Peter Eisenman, Cynthia Davidson, and Mathew Ford; Benedetta Tagliabue, Elena Rocchi, and Mireia Fornells at EMBT Arquitectes; Farshid Moussavi, Alejandro Zaera-Polo, and Eduarda Lima at Foreign Office Architects; Future Systems; Frank Gehry and Keith Mendenhall; Tess Giberson; Zaha Hadid, Roger Howie, Sarah Schuster, and Woody Yao; Jacques Herzog, Pierre de Meuron, and Esther Zumsteg; Yoshiki Hishinuma, Tetsuko Kitayama, and Kaori Yoshikawa; Toyo Ito and Miki Uono; Dominique Jakob and Brendan MacFarlane; Alber Elbaz, Hania Destelle, Isabelle Tasset, and Stéphanie Albinet at Lanvin; Greg Lynn, Jackilin Bloom, Brittney Hart, and Chris Kabatsi; Elena Manferdini; Martin Margiela and Emilie Thang; Alexander McQueen, Amie Witton-Wallace, and Myriam Coudoux; Miyake Issey, Fujiwara Dai, Jun Kanai, Yuko Kawai, Nancy S. Knox, and Masako Omori; Thom and Blythe Mayne, Anne Marie Burke, John Carpenter, and Emily Waugh at Morphosis; Willem Jan Neutelings, Michiel Riedijk, and Dianne Beukema; Jean Nouvel and Charlotte Kruk; Monica Ponce de Leon, Nader Tehrani, Jozefien Lerou, and David Dahlbom at Office dA; Rem Koolhaas, Joshua Prince-Ramus, and Jan Knikker at Office for Metropolitan Architecture; Olivier Theyskens and Nicolas Frontière at Rochas; Narciso Rodriguez, Casey Cadwallader, and Jacky Marshall; Ralph Rucci and Vivian Van Natta; Kazuyo Sejima, Ryue Nishizawa, Florian Idenburg, Sam Chermayeff, and Etsuko Yoshii at SANAA; Nanni Strada and Clino Castelli; Peter Testa and Devyn Weiser; Isabel and Ruben Toledo; Bernard Tschumi and Meredith Collins; Dries Van Noten, Bache Jespers, and Jan Van Hoof; Viktor Horsting, Rolf Snoeren, and Bram Claassen; Junya Watanabe; Vivienne Westwood, Kathryn Dale, and Murray Blewett; James Eyre, Chris Wilkinson, and Emma Keyte; Yeohlee Teng and Jason Morrison; Yohji Yamamoto, Nathalie Ours Choussat, Carla Wachtveitl, Coralie Gauthier, and Sarah Brown; and J. Meejin Yoon and Eric Höweler.

I am extremely indebted to the many lenders who have graciously shared their riches, including The British Broadcasting Company; Centre Canadien d'Architecture; Heinz Architecture Center, Carnegie Museum of Art; FRAC Orléans; Groninger Museum; Museum für Angewandte Kunst, Vienna; The Museum of Modern Art, New York; The Costume Institute of The Metropolitan Museum of Art; Musée d'art moderne, Luxembourg; Netherlands Architecture Institute; Centre Georges Pompidou; Seattle Public Library; Judith Clark; Todd Eberle; Burçu Gokcek; Jacky Marshall; and Marcus Tomlinson. I am indebted also to Ron Arad and Tokujin Yoshioka for making their wonderful chairs available for the exhibition. I am grateful as well to Ralph Pucci, Maria Pucci, Stephen Allen, and Ed Schilling of Ralph Pucci International for generously lending the stylish mannequins.

As always, it has been my great pleasure to work with the very capable and dedicated staff at MOCA. Manager of Exhibition Programs and Curatorial Affairs Susan L. Jenkins and her predecessor, Stacia Payne, provided collegial support and invaluable administrative counsel. I am grateful for the support of my curatorial colleagues, including Senior Curator Ann Goldstein, Associate Curator Alma Ruiz, Curatorial Associate Rebecca Morse, and former curators Connie Butler and Michael Darling. Warmest thanks go to Librarian Lynda Bunting for her assistance in obtaining key research materials and her cheerful patience regarding many overdue books. I also extend my appreciation to Emily Bishop, assistant to the chief curator, and Cara Baldwin, Cory Peipon, and Gabriel Ritter, curatorial assistants. This project could not have been realized without the dedication of my current and former MOCA curatorial assistants Cynthia Pearson, Ragan Cole-Cunningham, Theeng Kok, and Beth Rosenblum. Sincere thanks also go to research assistants Ellen E. Donnelly and Po-Wen Shaw for their insightful contributions and expertise.

It has been my great pleasure to once again work with Tracey Shiffman who, together with Jenny Yee and Ari Young, handled the formidable task of transforming a vast amount of text and images into this beautiful and elegant catalogue. I am grateful to all of the contributing photographers, especially Todd Eberle, Jacky Marshall, and William Palmer. Special thanks also go to essayists Patricia Mears and Susan Sidlauskas for taking time from busy schedules to draw on their vast knowledge of fashion and architecture for the book. Such an ambitious publication could not have been accomplished without the extraordinary dedication of MOCA's editors. The perceptive advice, keen eye, and intelligence of Director of Publications Lisa Mark cannot be underestimated. I am also very grateful for the care, professionalism, and commitment of Senior Editor Jane Hyun and Editor Elizabeth Hamilton. Former Publications Assistant Theeng Kok handled the mountain of images with grace and good humor. When the going got tough, the editorial staff pitched in to help on aspects above and beyond what was expected of them.

A project of this size would not have been possible without the tireless commitment of many individuals who work behind the scenes. Rosanna Hemerick, senior associate registrar, managed the myriad details and complexities of loans and shipping with great expertise and humor. Director of Exhibition Production Brian Gray, Exhibition Production Coordinator Sebastian Clough, Chief Exhibition Technician Jang Park, and Exhibition Technical Manager David Bradshaw have been key collaborators from the outset. MOCA's installation team, as always, deserves resounding thanks for its professionalism and care. Tsao & McKown Architects, New York, gave us an elegant exhibition design and helped make sense of a vast quantity of material, and I am especially grateful to Calvin Tsao, Zack

McKown, Richard Rhodes, and Andrew Tripp. Sam Gainsbury and Deepika Patel of Gainsbury and Whiting, London, advised us on the installation of Alexander McQueen's pyramid, and Greg Lynn's "bubble" wall from his Slavin House (2004–projected 2008) was made possible with the advice and fabrication skills of Emmanuelle Bourlier and Andreas Froech of Panelite, Los Angeles.

I am grateful to MOCA's development department for raising funds for this project. Sincere thanks go to Director of Development Jennifer Arceneaux, Grants Officer Elizabeth Jordan, and Events Manager Vanessa Gonzalez. I would also like to acknowledge the efforts of Paul Johnson, Thom Rhue, and Laurie McGahey, key former members of the development staff. Thanks go to Chief Financial Officer Jack Wiant and his team in the finance department. Invaluable media support was cultivated by Director of Public Affairs John Hindman and Public Relations Coordinator Rebecca Taylor. Additionally, I thank Katherine Lee, former director of public relations and marketing, for her enthusiasm and advice in the project's early stages. I also extend appreciation to the Creative Services team. Greater understanding of this subject matter is made possible by MOCA's renowned education department. I am especially grateful to Director of Education Suzanne Isken and Education Program Coordinators Aandrea Stang, Jeanne Hoel, Catherine Arias, and Denise Gray for their enthusiasm and dedication.

I also wish to extend my gratitude to other valued colleagues for their contributions: Ari Wiseman, assistant director; Angie Duncan and Shannon Ernster in the director's office; Grant Breding, director of retail operations; Nancy Duggan, director of human resources; Randall Murphy, director of administration; Robert Hollister, director of collections and registration, and Amy Via, former assistant registrar; Mimi McCormick, Cari Abrams, and Breanne Chappell, operations; Gemma Beristain, Sergio Ramirez, and Frank Ramirez, facilities and security; Gary Castro, Walter Lopez, and John Byers, information technology; Patricia Cross Bell, receptionist; and Aldo Espina, logistics associate.

Over the past twenty years, I have been fortunate to work with remarkable individuals who have profoundly influenced my thinking about architecture in its many guises. I especially thank Phyllis Lambert, Peter Eisenman, Jorge Silvetti, and Rei Kawakubo. Their rigorous, visionary, and often unconventional work continues to challenge my own. Holly Brubach, Harold Koda, Matilda McQuaid, Susan Sidlauskas, Mark Wigley, and the late Amy M. Spindler made early invaluable contributions to research on fashion and architecture. Eric Owen Moss, Hsin-Ming Fung, and Chris Genik made it possible for me to teach seminars and studios at the Southern California Institute of Architecture (Sci-ARC) that advanced my research. I also thank my Sci-ARC students for their invaluable insights. Patricia Mears, Miki Higasa of Kaleidoscope, Pierre Rougier of PR Consulting, and Calvin Tsao have provided invaluable assistance and advice on numerous fronts.

My research travel has taken me to many places, and I have benefited from the hospitality and friendship of Matilda McQuaid, Craig Konyk, and Alex and Ana Konyk; Ab Rogers and Sophie Braimbridge; Deborah Irmas; Mark Lewis and Janice Kerbel; Elspeth and Nick Norden; Amale Andraos and Dan Wood; Henry Urbach and Stephen Hartman; Jean-François Bédard and Olivier Gouteix; Gotscho; Petra Blaisse; Matthijs Bouw; Stijn Roodnat and Marleen Kaptein; Gilian Schrofer; Agnes Wijers; Georg Kochi; Mariko Gordon and Hugh Cosman; Momoko and Tad Sano; Kozo Fujimoto; Masako Ban; Yoshiko Yoneyama; the Tamura family; and Yumiko Shimizu and Masamichi Katayama. Over my five years of work on this project, many individuals have been generous with their time, encouragement, and wisdom: Roman Alonso; Dana Bauer; Colleen Coughlan; Sylvie Christophe; Lisa P. Darling; Sonia Eram; Silvia Gaspardomoro; Jennifer and Randy Green; Karin Higa; Barbara Jakobson; Elisa Jimenez; Steven Johanknecht; Geri Kavanaugh; Christopher Kennen; Robert Kloos; Didier Krzentowski; Cara McCarty; Colette Mullan; Jamie Norden; Jennifer Parker; Tita and Lisa Ponti; Joseph, Louise, and Hugo Rosa; Jason Schmidt; Cameron Silver; Paulette Singley; Ellen Steel; Christopher Tandon; Ali Tayar; Pilar Viladas; Kevin West; Jeanne C. Wikler; and Tim Williams.

Finally, I would like to thank my family for their patience and encouragement over the years. They have not seen much of me during my work on this project.

SKIN + BONES: PARALLEL PRACTICES in FASHION and ARCHITECTURE

Brooke Hodge

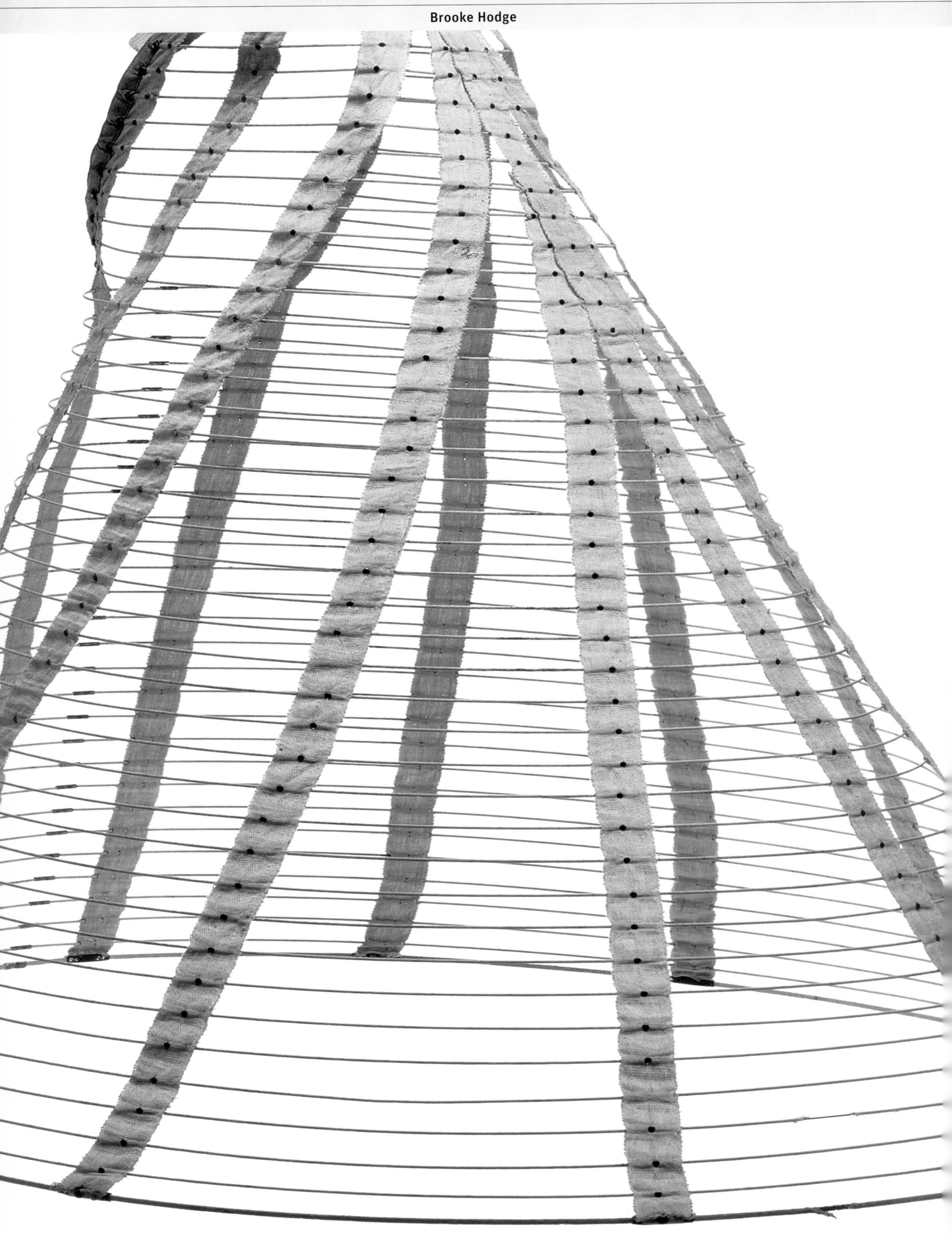

That fashion and architecture have a great deal in common may be surprising, given the obvious differences between the two disciplines. Fashion is thought of as ephemeral and superficial, using soft, sometimes fragile, materials, whereas architecture is considered monumental and permanent, using rigid, highly durable materials. Their scales of production, too, are wildly different: fashion designers create garments for the human body, while architects create buildings large enough for many bodies to inhabit simultaneously. Regardless of scale, however, the point of origin for both practices is the body. Both protect and shelter, while providing a means to express identity—whether personal, political, religious, or cultural.

While the fashion designer and architect create objects that differ in size and materials, their creative processes can be strikingly similar. Both begin with a flat two-dimensional medium, transforming it to create complex three-dimensional forms. The same prevailing aesthetic tendencies, ideological and theoretical foundations, and technological innovations have influenced each, resulting in garments and buildings that share stylistic or structural qualities or derive from common creative impulses. And, over time, designers in both fields have drawn from each other for inspiration as well as certain technical strategies. Vocabulary derived from architecture has been applied to garments ("architectonic," "constructed," "sculptural," etc.). And architects have also borrowed and adapted sartorial strategies and vocabulary from the fashion world, draping, wrapping, weaving, folding, printing, and pleating surfaces and materials. The significant and manifold parallels manifested in the skin and bones of both garments and buildings are the subject of this exhibition and catalogue.

My own interest in the parallels between fashion and architecture developed from work on a 2000 exhibition devoted to the avant-garde Japanese fashion house Comme des Garçons, headed by Rei Kawakubo.[1] During the course of my research, I was struck not only by visual similarities between clothing design and architectural structure, but also by how her garments can be more aptly described using architectural terminology. I was also impressed by Kawakubo's desire to create a total environment for her work—one that embraces not only the clothes but also the design of retail spaces, graphics, and furniture, much in the same way members of the Wiener Werkstatte or the Bauhaus strove to create a *Gesamtkunstwerk*.

"Skin + Bones" takes as its point of departure design from the beginning of the 1980s. In both fashion and architecture, the early 1980s were marked by significant design events and advances that have contributed to cultural shifts in each field. Japanese fashion designers Kawakubo and Yohji Yamamoto first presented their work during the Paris ready-to-wear collection shows in April 1981. The oversized, often asymmetrical black clothing they showed featured intentional holes, tatters, and unfinished edges that stood in stark contrast to the elegantly decorative, crisply tailored, and formfitting looks being shown by the majority of designers and, as a result, challenged accepted ideas of fashion, femininity, and beauty. The following year, architect Bernard Tschumi won the international competition to design Parc de la Villette in Paris (completed in 1998). His project, and the resulting collaboration between architect Peter Eisenman and philosopher Jacques Derrida, served to introduce ideas of deconstruction to a much larger audience. For designers in both fields, the early 1980s were characterized by a struggle for liberation from convention that involved experimentation with new forms and an openness to ideas and techniques from other disciplines to inspire radically different approaches to design.

A critical event with reverberations for both fashion and architecture occurred in 1982, when Susan Sidlauskas organized an exhibition for the Massachusetts Institute of Technology's Hayden Gallery (now List Visual Arts Center) called "Intimate Architecture: Contemporary Clothing Design," which examined the formal aspects of the work of eight fashion designers from an architectural point of view. While multiple historical connections can be drawn between fashion and architecture, Sidlauskas's influential exhibition was the first public presentation to illuminate and analyze the architectural aspects of contemporary clothing design to make a formal connection between the two practices. In many ways, "Skin + Bones" follows the threads of investigation laid down by "Intimate Architecture."[2]

While Sidlauskas's exhibition made it clear that fashion designers were conversant with architectural forms and principles and, indeed, with the work of particular architects, it is only recently that a true cross-fertilization has developed, as architects have in turn begun to pay closer attention to fashion design. This is largely due to two developments that have taken place during the last ten or so years. First, the practice of major fashion houses commissioning

1 The exhibition "Structure + Expression: Comme des Garçons" was presented at Harvard University's Graduate School of Design in May 2000 on the occasion of awarding Harvard's Excellence in Design Award to Rei Kawakubo.

2 "Intimate Architecture: Contemporary Clothing Design" featured the work of Giorgio Armani, Gianfranco Ferré, Krizia, Stephen Maniello, Miyake Issey, Claude Montana, Ronaldus Shamask, and Yeohlee Teng. It was shown at Massachusetts Institute of Technology's Hayden Gallery in Cambridge, Massachusetts, 15 May–27 June 1982. A small illustrated catalogue accompanied the exhibition. Roughly coincident with the opening of "Intimate Architecture," the February 1982 issue of *Artforum* magazine featured on its cover a rattan corset designed by Miyake in collaboration with bamboo artist Koshuge Shochikudo, marking the first time fashion was featured so prominently by an art magazine.

opposite:
Crinoline skirt, 1865; forty steel-wire hoops and eleven white linen tapes; left to right diameter: 37 1/2 inches; back to front diameter: 38 1/2 inches; hem circumference: 119 1/8 inches; collection Kyoto Costume Institute

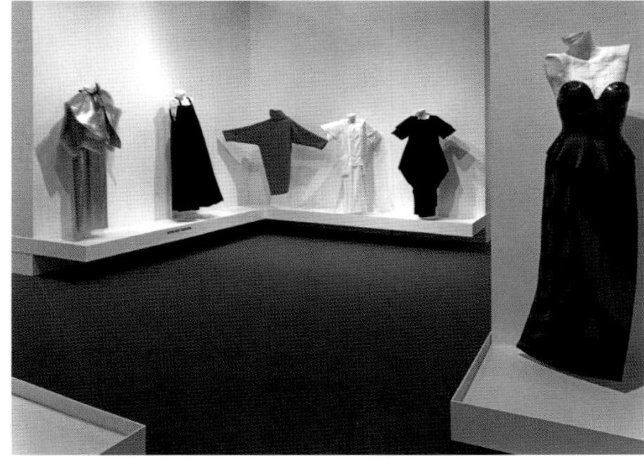

1
"Intimate Architecture: Contemporary Clothing Design," installation at Hayden Gallery, Massachusetts Institute of Technology, Cambridge, 1982

2
OFFICE FOR METROPOLITAN ARCHITECTURE/REM KOOLHAAS
Prada vs. GDP, 1999, informational graph for Prada stores design development

well-known architectural firms—such as Office for Metropolitan Architecture (OMA)/Rem Koolhaas, Herzog & de Meuron, and Future Systems, among others—to design their retail spaces has demanded that the architects carefully study the work of their clients. In the case of Koolhaas's designs for Prada, his firm's exhaustive research covered everything from clothing construction to mechanisms of display and even global distribution and branding.[3] Second, as architects have moved away from freehand drawing and model-making toward increasingly sophisticated design software to generate more complex architectural forms, they have looked to fashion for inspiration—in particular, its methods of construction and its manipulation of flat, almost two-dimensional cloth. Indeed, fashion has a long history of dealing with the kinds of complex forms and constructions that architects are now able to confront thanks to advancements in software and building materials.

The work of each of the forty-six international designers and architects featured in "Skin + Bones" is characterized by a strong well-articulated aesthetic and consistent conceptual vision largely unaffected by the vicissitudes and rapid pace of the fashion calendar or prevailing commercial trends. While the majority of the designers in this exhibition emerged or gained prominence during the early 1980s, some, like Italian fashion designer Nanni Strada, have been practicing for much longer. Among the architects, many received their first commissions or had their work featured in prominent museum exhibitions during those years. All have made or show the promise of making significant contributions to their fields, and their achievements have shaped conventional thinking about design and architecture. Interpreting strategies from each other's work and engaging with issues of body, shelter, and identity, they have forged new connections between disciplines.

HISTORICAL PRECEDENTS and STYLISTIC PARALLELS

Environmental and cultural conditions influence fashion designers and architects alike. When viewed as part of a historical continuum, both garments and buildings are invaluable anthropological artifacts that mark important cultural and economic conditions, stylistic preferences, and new developments in technology and materials. Moreover, the designers and architects of today continue to be influenced by such artifacts, reinterpreting them for a contemporary context.

The connection between clothing and shelter dates as far back as the Ice Age, when people used animal skins to cover themselves and to fashion exterior walls for crude structures. In ancient Greece, the flutes of columns were echoed in the drapery folds and cylindrical form of the *chiton*—the iconic woolen tunic made from a single length of fabric draped over the bodies of both men and women. Both classical Greek dress and architecture were conceived in harmony with the proportions of the human figure. In fact, different types of *chitons* were named for the Doric and Ionic architectural orders. A number of contemporary architects looking to create façades with more visual interest have begun to explore folding and draping.[4] In Casa La Roca (unbuilt, 1995) by Office dA, the building's brick façade is manipulated to create a cascade of folds resembling fabric draped on a human body.

The Medieval propensity for extreme verticality can be seen in both Gothic dress and architecture. Sharply pointed shoes, sleeves, and *hennins* (conical headdresses) relate directly to the ogival arches and soaring spaces of Gothic structures such as the thirteenth-century cathedrals at Amiens, France, and Salisbury, England. Recently, the Gothic arch was the inspiration for a dress designed by Yeohlee Teng for autumn/winter 1999–2000, in which pattern pieces in the shape of ogival arches were sewn together to form its skirt.

Certainly, deeper and more complex parallels have developed between the two disciplines as a result of new industrial technologies and manufacturing processes. In the 1850s, prefabrication of building materials and advancements in steel construction resulted in light, open architectural spaces, as fewer structural elements were required to engineer buildings. The Crystal Palace, an open web of cast-iron girders covered with glass designed by Joseph Paxton for the Great Exhibition of 1851 in London, had one of the most open and expansive building interiors of its time. A similar approach to construction was applied to women's wear: as a practical solution for heavy layers of petticoats or crinolines, designers developed armatures of metal hoops to support the wide dome-shaped skirts of the 1850s. Notably, this period also marks the emergence of the sewing machine as we know it today, making precise forms and mass production possible in the garment industry.

The sensuous, organic curvilinear shapes made popular by Art Nouveau in the late nineteenth century could be seen in fashion at the time in the work of Paul Poiret, among

3 For further details of the OMA/Rem Koolhaas research on the Prada brand, see OMA/Koolhaas, *Projects for Prada Part 1* (Milan, Italy: Fondazione Prada, 2001). Helen Castle's *Fashion and Architecture* issue of *Architectural Design* 70, no. 6 (December 2000), provides a comprehensive overview of the numerous fashion/architecture retail collaborations initiated in the late 1990s/early 2000s. The most prominent built examples of this trend are Koolhaas's Beverly Hills, California (2000–04), and SoHo, New York (2000–01), epicenters for Prada; Herzog & de Meuron's seven-story Prada Aoyama flagship in Tokyo (2000–03); and Future Systems's work with Marni in Milan (1999); Selfridges in Birmingham, England (1999–2003); and Comme des Garçons in New York's Chelsea district (1998).

4 For an extensive discussion of folding in fashion, see *Ptychoseis=Folds + Pleats: Drapery from Ancient Greece to 21st Century Fashion*, exh. cat. (Athens: Hellenic Culture Organization, 2004). The exhibition was held at the Benaki Museum,Athens, 22 June–17 October 2004.

3
YEOHLEE TENG
Gothic Arch Dress, autumn/winter 1999–2000

4
YEOHLEE TENG
Bronze Top and Pewter Skirt with bronze Gothic arch detail, autumn/winter 1999–2000, design sketch

5
OFFICE dA
Casa La Roca (unbuilt), Caracas, 1995, model

6
JOSEPH PAXTON
Crystal Palace, London, 1851

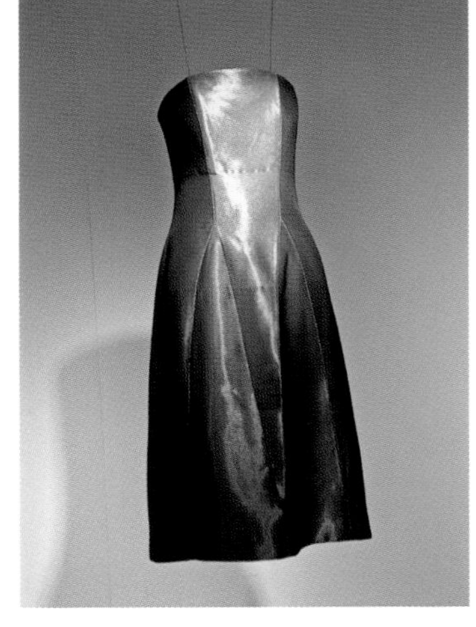

3

4

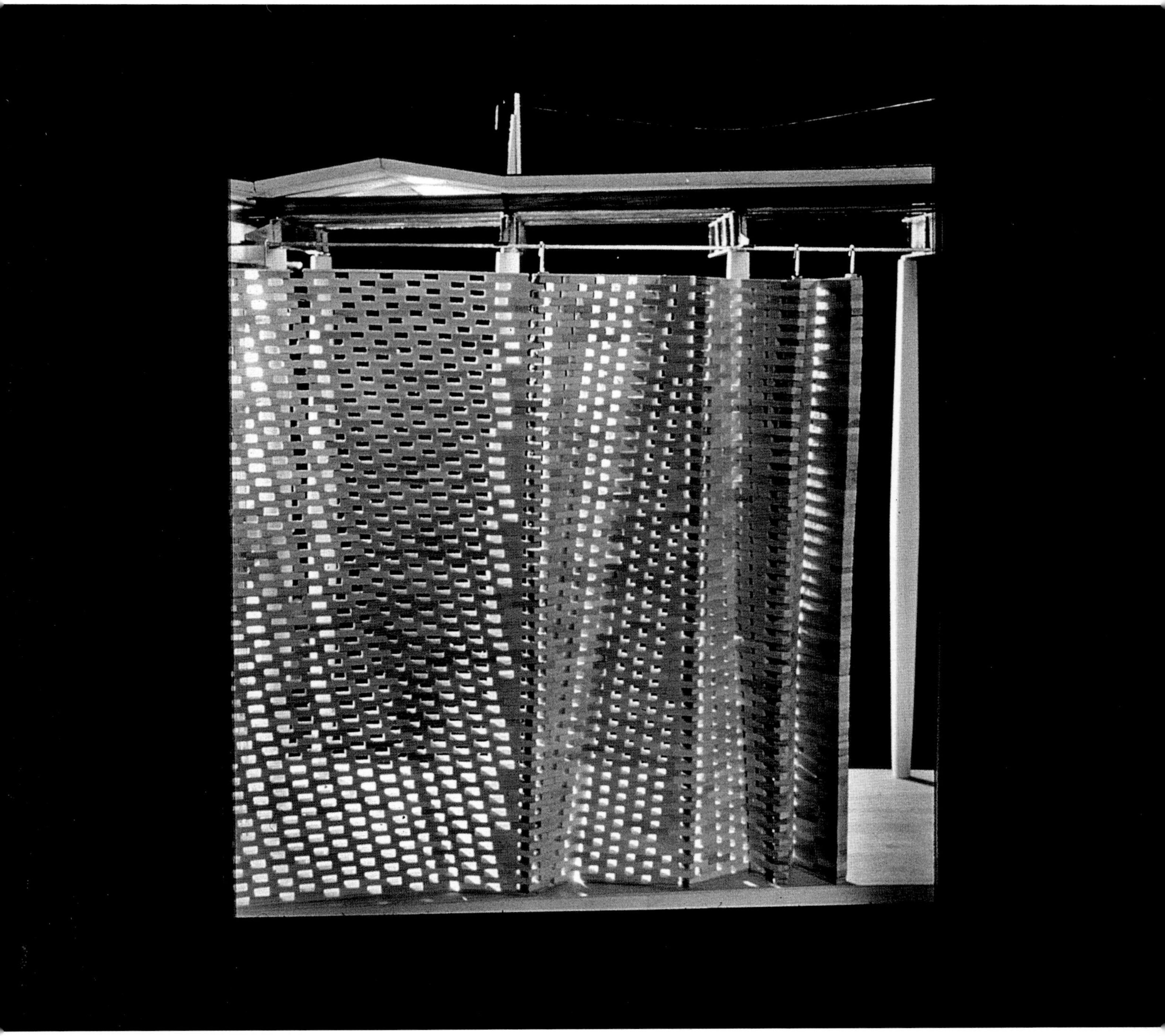

5

6

5 "Lord of the Space Ladies," *Life* (24 May 1965): 57.

others, as well as in the sinuous natural forms incorporated into architecture by practitioners like Hector Guimard and Louis Sullivan. In the work of this period, simplicity of form and fluid ornamentation were paramount, and shapes derived from nature were critical sources of inspiration. Later, in keeping with the emerging ideals of modernism, both fashion and architecture moved toward greater simplicity during the early to mid-twentieth century as ornament was stripped away, forms were pared down, and structure began to be exposed. This is particularly evident in the work of architects such as Le Corbusier and J. J. P. Oud and fashion designers such as Coco Chanel and Cristobal Balenciaga. In particular, the Bauhaus school—including architects like Walter Gropius and textile designers like Annie Albers—emphasized practicality and the idea that buildings and garments alike should be expressive of their function. Fashion designer André Courrèges, who began his career as an engineer and whose clean futuristic clothes were profoundly influenced by Le Corbusier, summed up the aspirations of fashion and architecture in the 1960s: "My problem is...to harmoniously resolve function problems—just like the engineer who designs a plane, like the man who conceives a car."[5]

Over the past twenty-five years, fashion and architecture have followed ever more similar aesthetic directions due in part to an increasing cross-disciplinary dialogue between the two fields. To a large degree, globalization and information technology have led to the quick and easy dissemination of the latest developments in both practices. In the 1980s, the application of classical motifs—the Greek fret or key pattern, column capitals, or the acanthus leaf—to women's wear and accessories in the designs of Gianni Versace and Hermès occurred contemporaneously with architecture's embrace of postmodernism's stylized neoclassical elements. However, among the most striking parallels in recent years has been the adoption of minimalist and deconstructivist aesthetics by practitioners in both fields. Calvin Klein is acknowledged as the contemporary master, if not originator, of minimalist fashion, albeit with a substantial debt to designers including Halston, Yves Saint Laurent, Giorgio Armani, Miuccia Prada, and Helmut Lang. Neutral in color, streamlined in shape, and virtually devoid of ornament, his garments of the 1970s and 80s possess a clean and modern simplicity that in many ways reflects the International Style architecture of Le Corbusier, Richard Neutra, and Ludwig Mies van der Rohe of the 1920s and 30s and the crisp

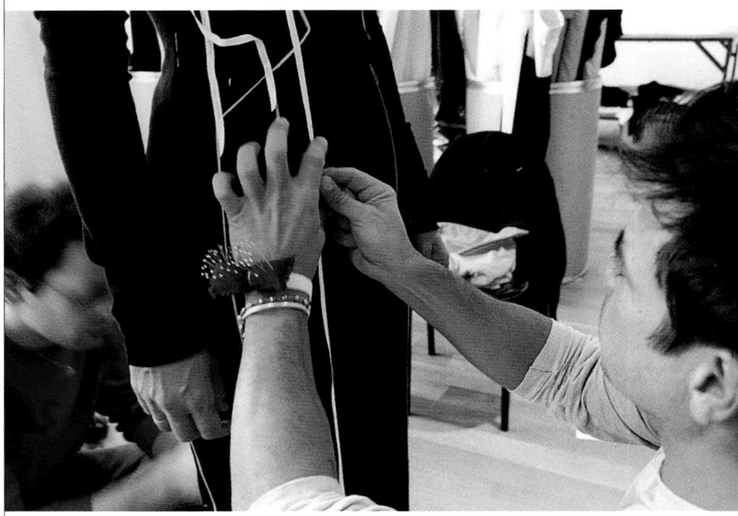

7
LUDWIG MIES VAN DER ROHE Seagram Building, New York, 1954–58

8
NARCISO RODRIGUEZ at work in the studio on his autumn/winter 2004–05 collection, New York, 2004

7

8

glass curtain wall buildings of the 1950s and 60s. Klein has further advanced the minimalist aesthetic in the designs of his stores, recognizing a vast market for his particular brand of modernism.[6]

Prada has also designed severely reductive minimalist collections, but these do not represent an ongoing tendency in her work. Instead, as she once explained, her adoption of a palette restricted to brown, navy blue, and black in the early 1990s was a reaction to the excesses of the 1980s.[7] Narciso Rodriguez, however, has developed a sophisticated and recognizable minimalist sensibility for his high-end women's wear that owes a great and acknowledged debt to the work of Mies van der Rohe. Like Mies, Rodriguez is concerned with the inherent beauty of structure and construction. The majority of Rodriguez's elegant formfitting clothes are made with a precision that allows them to fluidly follow the curves of the female body without relying on drape or volume to give them form.[8] In the suite of photographs by Jacky Marshall elsewhere in this volume, Rodriguez can be seen taping and retaping seams and fit lines and making minute adjustments by pinning to achieve a precise fit. Eschewing applied or extraneous decoration, he allows the beauty of seams and darts to serve as his garments' only decoration.

Deconstruction in fashion and architecture is a more complex subject and is addressed by two parallel texts in this volume. Patricia Mears traces the adoption of deconstructive strategies and devices by fashion designers in her essay "Fraying the Edges: Fashion and Deconstruction." Mears shows that while fashion's obsession with deconstruction is not as theoretically influenced as that of architecture, deconstructed garments with frayed edges, exposed seams, and deliberate holes and cuts began to appear in high fashion in the influential early collections of Comme des Garçons and Yohji Yamamoto, which were shown in Paris around the same time deconstructivist theories were being discussed and debated by architects. Interestingly, "deconstruction" was not a term used by designers to describe their work, but was applied later by fashion writers. Bill Cunningham first applied the term in the March 1990 issue of *Details*, and Amy M. Spindler's 1993 *New York Times* article "Coming Apart" cemented it in the fashion lexicon through her discussion of the lineage and influence of the Japanese designers on a younger generation of Belgians including Ann Demeulemeester, Martin Margiela, and Dries Van Noten.[9] Spindler also noted that—in an example of the cyclical nature of fashion—for his 1993 haute couture collection for Chanel, Karl Lagerfeld borrowed from deconstruction, "leaving the ladies feeling breathlessly avant-garde with a bit of tattered tulle."[10] Margiela's work with deconstruction is arguably the most conceptual and complex in fashion, and his method of appropriating and taking apart vintage clothes and reassembling them results in garments that seem completely new. Similarly, Frank Gehry's remodeling of his own residence in Santa Monica, California (1977–78/1991–94), began with a conventional structure and, using readily available materials, ended with something utterly innovative and unexpected. Gehry dismantled parts of the exterior envelope of a 1920s bungalow and integrated off-the-shelf industrial materials like plywood and chain link to transform the house into a complex new spatial volume. [See my essay "Deconstruction and Architecture: Conflicting Interpretations" for other examples.] While fashion designers and architects may not have adopted ideas of deconstruction for the same reasons or from the same sources, it is telling that these tendencies emerged in both practices at about the same time.

6 See Cathy Horyn, "The Calvinist Ethic," *The New York Times Magazine* (14 September 2003): 64–69.
7 Miuccia Prada in American *Vogue*: "At one point, in the early Nineties, people wanted only simple clothing to cancel everything out. After Lacroix zero. So there was minimal: Calvin Klein, Jil Sander. But after zero, we have to go on, to do something else." This quotation (without exact citation) appears in James Sherwood, "The Nineties Utility Movement: Prime Suspect in the the Death of Designer Fashion," in Francesco Bonami, et al, eds., *Uniform: Order and Disorder* (Milan, Italy: Charta, 2000), 177.
8 Narciso Rodriguez introduced volume in the form of flowing skirts to his women's wear in his autumn/winter 2004–05 collection, having mastered the art of precise minimal construction in his preceding collections.
9 See Amy M. Spindler, "Coming Apart," *The New York Times*, 25 July 1993, sec. 9, 1.
10 Ibid.

9
MAISON MARTIN MARGIELA
Dress from **O Artisanal** collection, spring/summer 2005

10
FRANK GEHRY
Gehry Residence,
Santa Monica, California, 1977–78/1991–94

9

10

SHELTER and IDENTITY

If the earliest examples of cladding for the human body were not "designed" but rather devised out of necessity, contemporary practitioners in both fields have continued to address the human imperative for shelter in ingenious ways. Teng has developed a series of collections based on ideas of nomadism, designing cloaks and other garments specially suited for travel. Dutch designers Viktor & Rolf addressed the idea of shelter in a more conceptual way with their seminal Russian Doll haute couture collection of autumn/winter 1999–2000. This collection comprises nine garments that, during the runway show, were gradually layered on the body of a model standing on a revolving platform. Beginning with a simple unornamented dress woven from coarse fibers, the designers layered the additional garments so that by the end of the show, the model was enclosed—almost hidden—inside a dense volume, similar to the way the smallest Russian doll is nested in her bigger sisters' bodies.

Architecture is predicated on the need for structures that house and protect inhabitants from the elements. Japanese architect Shigeru Ban addresses this programmatic necessity in interesting and unusual ways. In his Tokyo Curtain Wall House (1993–95), Ban played on the idea of the glass curtain-wall construction by making an enormous retractable fabric curtain the exterior surface of two sides of the building to provide the residents with shelter and privacy. More recently, Ban has explored other light construction materials—such as inexpensive paper tubes and bamboo—to create both high-end architecture and emergency shelters. The temporary housing he designed for victims of the Kobe earthquake (1995) and for Rwandan refugees (1995–99)—in which structures are built from paper tubes and covered with the plastic sheets issued to refugees by the United Nations—represents an aspect of his practice that has become increasingly important to him.

11
HUSSEIN CHALAYAN
Afterwords collection, autumn/winter 2000–01, views of presentation

12
SHIGERU BAN ARCHITECTS
Paper Emergency Shelters for the United Nations High Commissioner for Refugees, Byumba Refugee Camp, Rwanda, 1995–99

Hussein Chalayan became known in the 1990s in both fashion and architecture circles for the conceptual direction of his work. For his Afterwords collection (autumn/winter 2000–01), which debuted during the women's ready-to-wear shows in Paris, Chalayan designed a simple white and vaguely domestic stage set. Four chairs and a round coffee table were grouped together near the front of the stage. The presentation culminated in a brief performance in which four models, dressed in simple slips, appeared on stage as a Bulgarian women's choir sang. Each approached a chair, removing its slipcover and, in a few moves, transforming it into a dress. After putting on the dresses, they folded up the chairs, which became carrying cases. A last model entered and, after removing a circular piece from the center of the coffee table, stepped into the opening and transformed the table into a skirt of ever fuller concentric circles by attaching the innermost ring to her waist. Finally the five models exited, leaving behind an empty room. With this presentation, Chalayan addressed issues related to his personal identity as a London-based Turkish Cypriot and his identification with refugees of the 1990s Balkan conflict. The collection suggested the necessity of leaving behind one's home "with nothing but the clothes on your back" and rebuilding one's life elsewhere. Allusions to identity, the fragility of life, and the importance of creative expression are evident in much of Chalayan's work.

Uniforms also reflect collective identity; for example, children's school uniforms signify an affiliation with an educational institution, a relationship to learning, compliance with certain rules, and even connections to a particular social or economic class. These same uniforms may be appropriated and altered by groups seeking to subvert those associations, such as Japanese teenagers who wear them as a type of costume, bringing a different meaning altogether.

Just as dress can be adopted and adapted as a means of personal expression, architecture has been used to express

11

12

collective identity, values, and status. For example, nineteenth-century bank buildings were invariably built of stone and featured classical columns and a pediment; the timelessness of these classical architectural elements and the solidity of the materials reassuringly suggested the security and permanence of the institution to its clients. In the Giardini di Castello in Venice, Italy, where important international biennial exhibitions of art and architecture have taken place since 1895, a collection of national pavilions stands. Each country's pavilion is intended (in ways sometimes subtle, sometimes obvious or even clichéd) to express a connection to its indigenous or vernacular architecture: the U.S. Pavilion is neoclassical and resembles Thomas Jefferson's Monticello; the Canadian Pavilion, designed by the Italian firm BBPR, resembles a teepee or wigwam, referencing indigenous Canadian architecture; and the French, British, and German Pavilions are sober and classical in character, asserting the stature of those countries in the history of art and architecture.

Today such stereotypical representations of identity seem antiquated and even politically incorrect, but architecture continues to serve as an assertion of identity or place in the world. For instance, Prada's commissioning of OMA/Koolhaas and Herzog & de Meuron to design major retail spaces underscores the company's identity as a purveyor of sophisticated cutting-edge design in both fashion and architecture.

CREATIVE PROCESS

Both fashion designers and architects begin by taking an idea and, working out its practical requirements, translating it into a three-dimensional structure using flat materials. In both disciplines it is common to explore initial ideas about form and materials by sketching. From early sketches, study models are made, since it is imperative to study the evolving designs in a form that more closely resembles that of the finished product. In the case of fashion, mock-ups of a garment are made of muslin and are often fitted and draped directly on a dressmaker's form or a fit model. Rodriguez, in particular, places great emphasis on working with a model at this stage, spending hours making minute adjustments to the shape of a garment and marking and re-marking the placement of its seams to achieve a precise fit. Some architects and fashion designers use a responsive or intuitive process to translate their ideas into three-dimensional models and patterns. For example, both Gehry and Kawakubo have used materials at hand—a rumpled pillowcase, a crinkled paper bag, a crumpled piece of velvet—to assist in communicating their concepts to colleagues who then work out the often complex technical issues required to actualize the design. While fashion designers have the luxury of being able to work directly on the body fairly early on, due to the sheer scale of a building and the expense and time required to construct it, architects use a series of scale models to develop and communicate design. Only rarely, and often in the case of small or temporary structures, do they fabricate full-scale mock-ups or prototypes.

The types of notations or instructions found in a standard set of architectural drawings—plan, section, and elevation, as well as drawings of details—are also found in a dressmaker's pattern. Graphic devices indicate the placement of seams, darts, and fastenings as well as the shapes of the various components that are cut and assembled into a finished garment. Architects develop floor plans to show the disposition of a building's rooms, the location of walls, doors, and windows, as well as the placement of plumbing fixtures and sometimes even furniture. Increasingly, computers are being used in both fashion and architecture to generate patterns and plans, which benefit from greater precision and ease of revision than can be achieved via freehand methods.

13
VIKTOR & ROLF
Second, fifth, and final preparation dresses from **Russian Doll** haute couture collection, autumn/winter 1999–2000, collection Groninger Museum

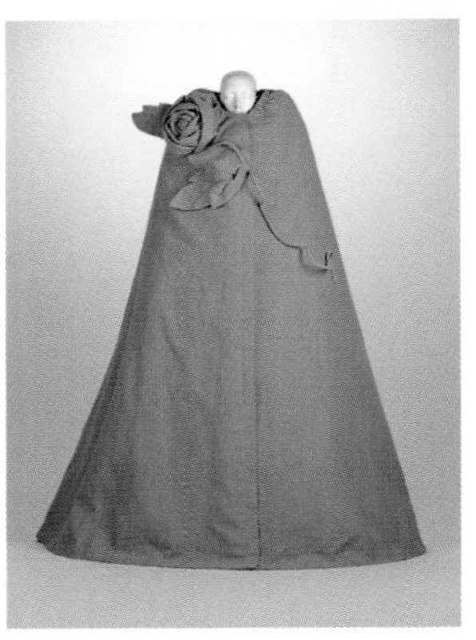

13

In fact, many young architects are now using digital means exclusively to generate ideas, drawings, and three-dimensional computer models.

Elena Manferdini is a young architect, also trained as an engineer, who has recently incorporated fashion design into her interdisciplinary practice. Since 2004, she has generated several collections of one-of-a-kind, or couture, garments that she has designed using three-dimensional rendering software such as Maya by Alias Wavefront, which was originally created for animation, video, and game development, as well as architectural applications. She fabricates her clothes by using Surfcam machining software to laser-cut the individual pieces of a garment as well as to create a decorative pattern on its surface. However, the computer can not do everything and, in the end, a combination of hand- and machine-sewing is needed to complete each design. Manferdini's work is a good example of architects looking to fashion and emphasizes the way the two practices can draw on and influence each other.

TECTONIC STRATEGIES

The strategies each fashion designer and architect in this exhibition has developed to shape the envelope, spatial volume, and surface of individual garments and buildings are highlighted in the individual designer profiles in this volume. The strategies discussed there are among the most original, advanced, and evocative examples in both contemporary practices.

Geometry has long been employed to generate form in architecture. Preston Scott Cohen's work with descriptive and projective geometry in his early drawings has resulted in intricate and complex work as he has explored ways to use unusual forms such as the torus to create extraordinary spatial effects. Eisenman and OMA/Koolhaas have experimented with the convoluted twist and continuous form of the Möbius strip to generate buildings. Eisenman's Max Reinhardt Haus (unbuilt, 1992–93) and Koolhaas's CCTV Tower (2002–projected 2008) in Beijing are examples of the employment of the Möbius strip in tall vertical buildings. Like Manferdini, architect J. Meejin Yoon drew on her dual interests in fashion and architecture to create her Möbius Dress (2005), in which a large Möbius strip is looped over and around the body to create a tent-shaped garment.

In fashion design, rigid geometrical forms appear less often, since conventional garments are made of multiple pieces of fabric that are cut and assembled to complement and conform to the shape of the body. However, explorations of geometry have appeared frequently in the practices of both Teng and Isabel Toledo. Teng, who has always been interested in making the most efficient and economical use of a length of fabric, has created garments made up of precise geometric forms that can be reassembled like puzzle pieces back into the original piece of cloth. When these garments are worn, however, their geometry is invisible; each takes on a completely different shape due to gravity, which causes it to hang or drape, and the body, which fills out its form. Toledo is also inspired by geometry, but of a more organic, less rational variety. She takes a reductive approach to pattern-making—what she calls "romantic mathematics"[11]—by paring each garment down to its simplest geometric form (cylinder, cone, etc.). On the body, her clothes undergo a transformation as well, as pieces cut from squares, circles, and triangles lose their flatness and become delicate, flowing organic shapes. Toledo has studied the properties of different fabrics and how they perform on the body, calling the results "liquid architecture." This describes "the way fabrics of different weights (in particular, matte jersey) cascade into folds, skim the body, and fall like water to the ground."[12] Her Pedestal Dress (autumn/winter 1993–94) and Suspension Dresses (1997–98) are examples of the way she adapts architectonic principles to explore and manipulate the structure and volume of her garments.

In addition to Toledo's work, garments incorporating the principle of suspension have also appeared in the collections of fashion designers as varied as Ralph Rucci, Junya Watanabe, and Teng. Rucci's suspension garments, such as the black wool-crepe dress from his spring/summer 2005 haute couture collection, are less about gravity than they are about the complex engineering that goes into the composition and finishing of a garment, some of which comprise more than eighty-five pattern pieces.[13] "Suspension" refers to the way the pieces of fabric seem to hang in the final garment, held together by almost indiscernible layers of hand-stitching. Watanabe's spring/summer 2003 Objet collection featured floral-printed and white dresses whose delicacy belies the fact that they are made of a sturdy, rather stiff nylon fabric that can be ruched by either tightening or lengthening a series of nylon webbing straps deployed in various locations on the garment, similar to the way the shape of an open parachute can be manipulated by its straps.

11 Isabel Toledo, cited in Alix Browne and Anne Bissonnette, *Toledo Toledo*, exh. cat. (New York: Visionaire Publishing, 2000), n.p.
12 Ibid.
13 Bissonnette gives a detailed description of the construction of these pieces in *Chado Ralph Rucci* (Kent, Ohio: Kent State University Museum, 2005), 38. "In his 'suspension' garments, made of double-faced cashmere, each pattern piece is sliced at the edges between the two faces of the cloth and the seam allowances are folded inside the space between the two faces. This creates pattern pieces that have no raw edges. All edges are closed and topstitched by hand. The pieces are then transferred to their final configuration on a piece of muslin and placed one eighth of an inch apart. They are basted by hand on the muslin and the pieces are joined with worms [a modified French knot developed by Rucci's staff]. Once the assembly is complete, the muslin is removed. Multiple levels of hand stitching seem to vanish."

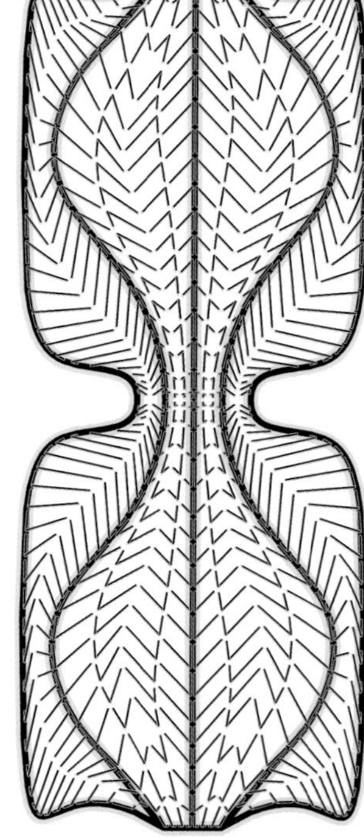

14
left to right:
ELENA MANFERDINI
Laser cutting **Leaf Scarf** for **Clad Cuts** collection, spring/summer 2005; and **Leaf Scarf**, details of digital pattern drawings

14

In her spring/summer 2006 collection, Teng presented several different dresses with cables that hoist fabric in a way that recalls the engineering of suspension bridges.

In 2004, a major section of "Metamorph," the vast international exhibition organized by Kurt W. Forster for the Venice Architecture Biennale, explored the properties of building "skins," which can be defined as the continuous exterior surface that covers the structural framework, or "bones," of a building. Several of the architects included in "Skin + Bones" are remarkable for the sophistication and innovation that they bring to their thinking about skin. Toyo Ito's Tod's Omotesando Building in Tokyo (2002–04) features a surface made of glass and crisscrossed load-bearing concrete beams that appears at once light and strong, a marriage of skin and bones that creates a pattern that references the trees that face the building's site. In their Seattle Central Library (1999– 2004), Koolhaas and Joshua Prince-Ramus of OMA stretched a diamond-patterned structural mesh skin over the cantilevered and vertical volumes of the building, much like a fishnet stocking stretched over a leg. In fashion, the garment itself serves as a metaphorical skin, but the products of the innovative computer-programmed industrial-knitting machine developed by Miyake Issey draw a direct parallel to the structural skins being developed for contemporary architecture. With A-POC (A Piece of Cloth) technology, a whole garment is cut from a woven or knitted tubular piece of fabric rather than assembled from many pieces sewn together.

Folding and pleating may be the tectonic strategies shared most frequently by fashion and architecture. In folding, one flat piece of material becomes a volumetric form through the introduction of creases; pleating is a subset of folding, in which regularly spaced folds or creases occur at close intervals. Morphosis's Sun Tower in Seoul (1994–97) features a perforated aluminum surface wrapped around the building, culminating in origami-inspired folds at the top. Since the early 1990s, folding has been used by architects as a device to create greater visual interest through dramatic effects of light and shadow on a building's exterior and to manipulate the volumetric forms of the interior. Eisenman's unbuilt projects for Rebstockpark in Frankfurt, Germany (1990–91), and the Emory Center for the Performing Arts in Atlanta (1991) are remarkable early explorations into the development of folded architectural skins. Winka Dubbeldam/Archi-Tectonics's Greenwich Street Project in New York (2000–04) makes use of a sophisticated skin of folded glass for its principal façade. Architects Elizabeth Diller and Ricardo Scofidio explored these ideas in their project *Bad Press: Dissident Housework Series* (1993–98), which debuted at the Richard Anderson Gallery in New York in 1993. The installation featured abnormally folded men's shirts ironed into different configurations and displayed in Plexiglas cases resembling shelves.

In his groundbreaking Pleats Please Issey Miyake line, the Japanese designer was able to introduce new textures and sculptural volumes thanks to his pioneering work with pleating techniques. Traditionally, flat fabric is pressed and pleated before being sewn, but Miyake reversed this process, creating oversized garments that shrink after pleats are applied. The sculptural forms of these pleated garments have inspired a number of architects, including Gehry.

In their respective fields, Gehry and Kawakubo have taken the idea of wrapping the body further. Gehry encased the complex steel skeleton of Los Angeles's Walt Disney Concert Hall (1987–2003) in a skin of stainless-steel panels to create expressive curved forms reminiscent of a ship's sails. Kawakubo's seminal Body Meets Dress, Dress Meets Body collection of spring/summer 1997 presented exaggeratedly mutated female forms created by pads of various shapes and sizes placed in unexpected places, forcing the fabric to stretch around them.

The translation of drapery folds into rigid building skins is seen in two projects by Boston-based architects Office dA. For Zahedi House in Weston, Massachusetts (unbuilt, 1998), the architects wrapped a taut skin of corrugated metal around a wood-frame house. On one façade, the skin becomes looser and more evocative of domestic interiors as it is distorted and manipulated into gentle curtainlike folds to reflect the shifts in program that occur on the interior and the need for openings on the exterior. In their design for Casa La Roca, the architects combined a brick skin with the idea of drapery. Varying from solid and taut to "perforated" and folding, the skin's terra-cotta blocks, bricks, and tiles weave together. The skin signals the domestic function of the building as well as provides enclosure, privacy, and ventilation.

The idea of incorporating printed textiles into clothing designs is not new, but the way Van Noten has developed, layered, and combined multiple colorful printed patterns is fresh and unconventional. Taking his inspiration from the elaborate patterns developed by cultures such as the

15
CHADO RALPH RUCCI
Suspension Dress from haute couture collection, spring/summer 2005

16
ISABEL TOLEDO
Packing Dress, from collection, spring/summer 1988, on mannequin and laid flat to show its geometry

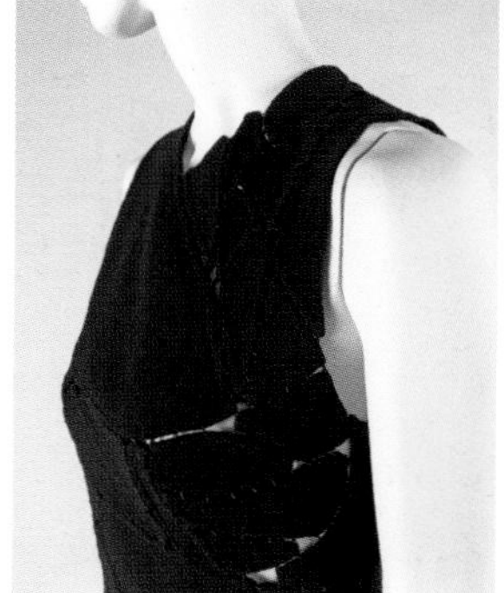

15

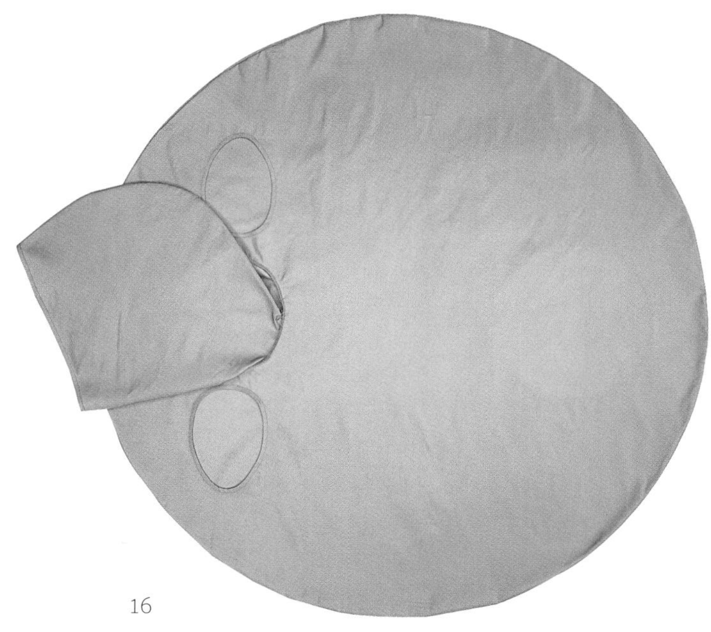

16

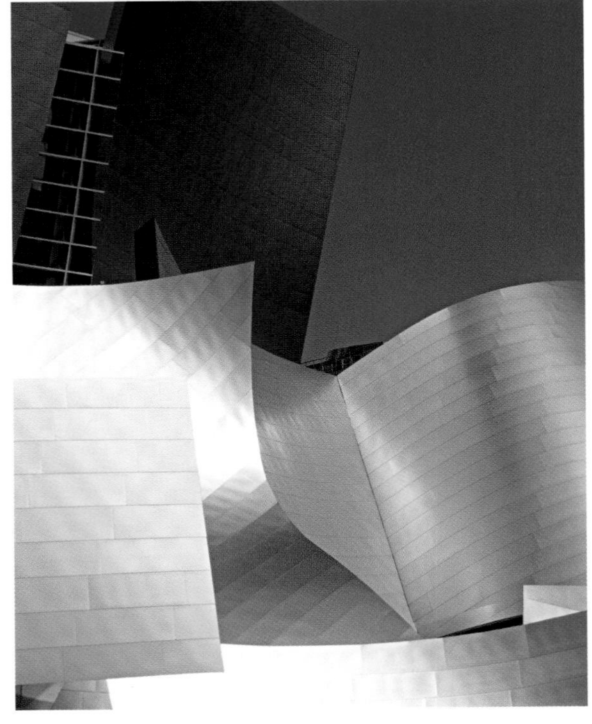

17

18

Ndebele tribe of Africa as well as from folkloric motifs, Van Noten developed his own contemporary prints. In architecture, applying a pattern to a building's façade is often redundant since repeating surface patterns and textures are created by functional and structural elements such as fenestration, apertures, posts and beams, etc. In the printed skins of two buildings—the Ricola-Europe SA Production and Storage Building (Mulhouse-Brunstatt, France, 1992–93) and the Library of the Eberswalde Technical University (Eberswalde, Germany, 1997–99)—Herzog & de Meuron seem to have taken their cue directly from textiles and fashion.[14] Ricola's façade comprises translucent panels printed with a repeating plant motif based on a photograph by Karl Blossfeldt that references the building's corporate identity as the manufacturer of herbal cough lozenges. In descriptions of the building, Herzog & de Meuron explicitly refers to the façade's relationship to textiles: "The effect the panels have on the interior can be compared to that of a curtain—textile-like—that creates a relationship to the site's trees and shrubs."[15] At Eberswalde, seventeen horizontal bands of images are silkscreen-printed on glass and concrete panels. The images come from photographs selected by artist Thomas Ruff from magazines he has collected over the years. The source of the printed images not only alludes to the building's function as a library but also serves to unify the entire structure by diminishing the material differences between glass and concrete.

In what may be the closest relationship of architecture to fashion, architects Peter Testa and Devyn Weiser are conducting extensive research into new technical textiles—such as carbon fiber and prepreg tape[16]—that can be adapted for construction using traditional techniques, such as braiding, weaving, and knitting. Their intensive study is coupled with a close examination of the work of contemporary fashion designers such as Yoshiki Hishinuma, whose Inside Out 2Way Dress (spring/summer 2004) prompted an investigation into taping building pieces together, and Olivier Theyskens for Rochas, whose garments' volumes and shapes are particularly influential.

CONCLUSION

As the boundaries between fashion and architecture continue to blur, further parallels along with an increasingly rich and vital dialogue are sure to develop between the two disciplines. Architects who have experimented directly with the design of garments will begin to translate their investigations into the realm of architecture. Fashion designers will continue to look at the materials and methods of architecture to create ever more ingenious garments. And this cross-fertilization may result in the development of increasingly hybrid practices. A deep interest in the dialogue between the disciplines can be seen in the practices of the designers featured here, in classes being offered at architecture and fashion schools, and in books and exhibitions that explore the manifold relationships of fashion and architecture to other creative practices. The work featured in "Skin + Bones" reveals the interweaving of fashion and architecture. One can only imagine the promise that lies in those threads that have yet to be connected.

14 Interestingly, Jacques Herzog's mother was a tailor, and he grew up surrounded by textiles. See interview with Herzog by Jeffrey Kipnis in *El Croquis*, no. 84 (1997).

15 "Ricola Europe Factory and Storage Building," in ibid., 94.

16 Prepreg tape is a high-performance composite material that can be made of carbon fiber or a filament structure that is impregnated with a stiff, rigid epoxy resin. It is most commonly used in sports equipment such as tennis racquets as well as in the aerospace industry, where it is used to create airplane wings and fuselages. Testa & Weiser's use of these materials in an architectural context is unique.

17
HERZOG & DE MEURON
Ricola-Europe SA Production and Storage Building, Mulhouse-Brunstatt, France, 1992–93, view of main façade from inside

18
FRANK GEHRY
Walt Disney Concert Hall, Los Angeles, 1987–2003

19
COMME DES GARÇONS
Garments from **Body Meets Dress, Dress Meets Body** collection, spring/summer 1997

20
DRIES VAN NOTEN
Garments from collection, spring/summer 1997

19

20

overleaf:
NARCISO RODRIGUEZ at work in his studio, New York

pages 22–23: Collection, autumn/winter 2004–05

pages 24–25: Collection, autumn/winter 2005–06

pages 26–29: Collection, spring/summer 2005

CREATIVE PROCESS: NARCISO RODRIGUEZ Photographs by Jacky Marshall

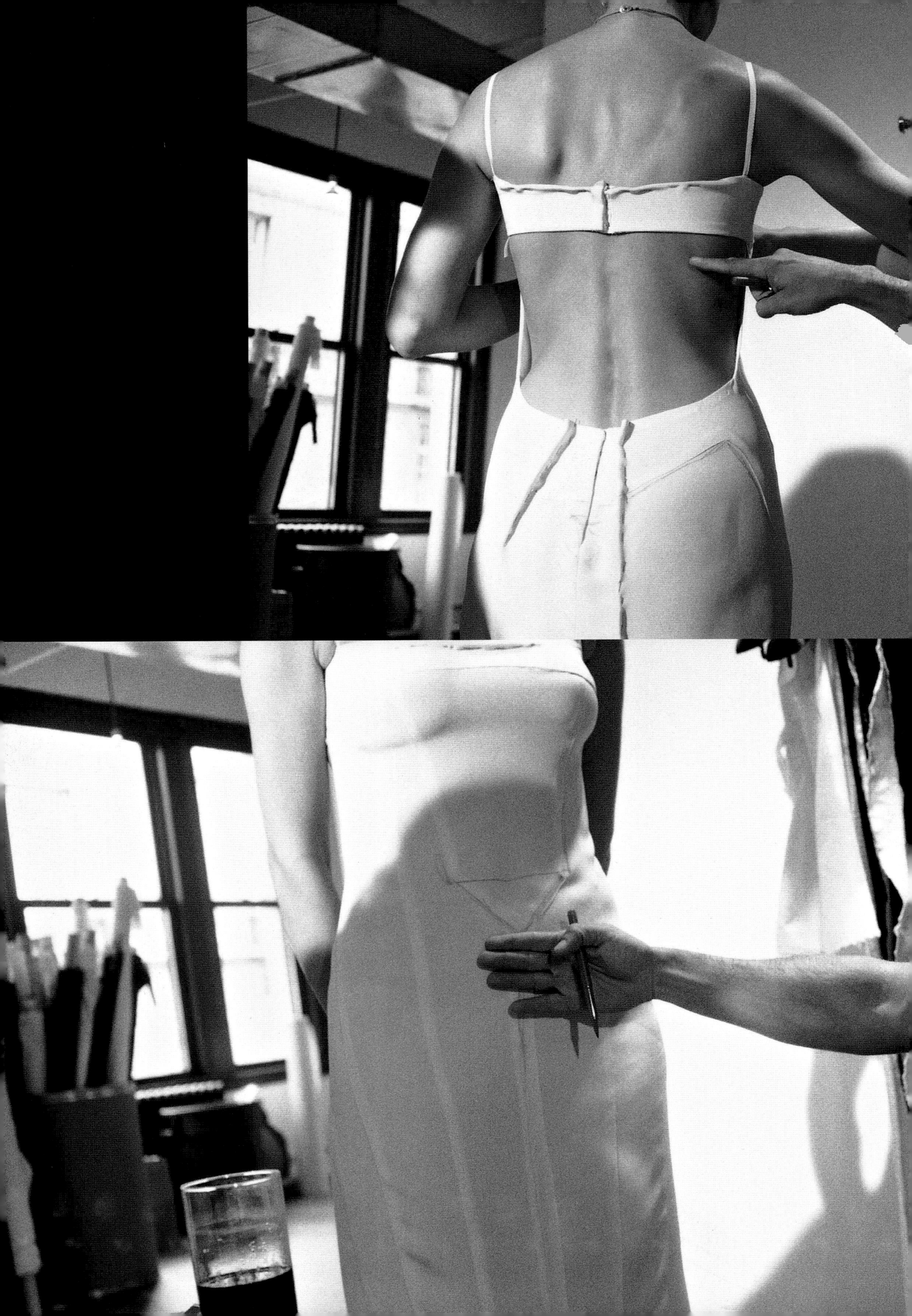

777
1
4

6 7 8

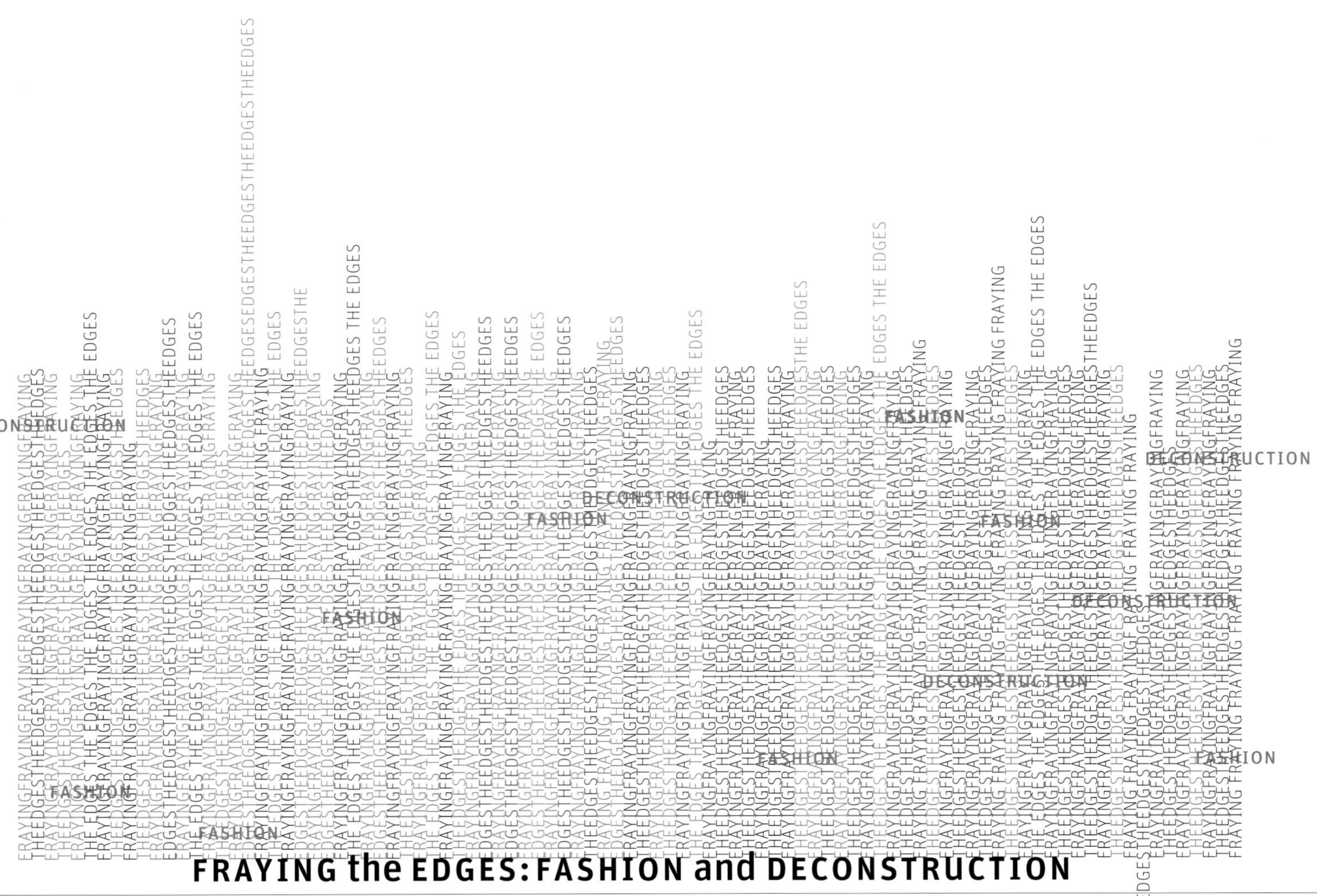

FRAYING the EDGES: FASHION and DECONSTRUCTION

Patricia Mears

The term "deconstruction" has been applied in a wide range of artistic disciplines—including art, architecture, design, and music—for nearly thirty years. In fashion, it shook the very foundations of clothing creation; the aesthetic of deconstruction differed dramatically from the polished and finely finished garments that were dominant during the 1970s and 80s. Deconstructed garments are often unfinished-looking, with loose frayed hems and edges; they sometimes appear to be coming apart or look recycled or made from composite parts. These fashions are frequently dark in color, suggesting poverty, devastation, and/or degradation, while their silhouettes tend to obscure the body and lack a clear frontality.

Originating in the writings of French philosopher Jacques Derrida in the 1960s, deconstruction's relationship to contemporary fashion design has yet to be fully explored by theorists, critics, and curators. However, there is no reason to believe that Derrida's ideas were the motivating force behind the pioneering designs of Zandra Rhodes—specifically her Conceptual Chic collection of 1977—or those of Rei Kawakubo or Yohji Yamamoto. Nor can one assume that punk, the radical countercultural movement that emerged in Britain during the 1970s, had any direct relationship to Derrida.

Introduced to fashion in the early 1980s, the aesthetics associated with deconstruction were initially met with disdain, but have since undergone a remarkable and ironic reversal as they have been rapidly appropriated by both mainstream and high fashion during the past decade. Though it emerged from the streets of London roughly thirty years ago in the uniform of the punks, it can be argued that its official birth occurred in 1981 with the Paris debut of Comme des Garçons and Yamamoto.

THE ROOTS of DECONSTRUCTION in FASHION

It should be noted that although deconstruction in fashion is relatively new, numerous historical precedents exist, including the opulent silks deliberately woven with slits and slashes that were the rage in fashion during the sixteenth-century German Renaissance. Considered one of the strangest fashion phenomena of the Renaissance, slashing supposedly originated in 1477 when Charles the Bold was slain in battle and Swiss and German mercenaries patched their torn garments with opulent textile scraps looted from the wealthy Burgundians. True or not, by the early 1500s aristocratic men throughout many Western European courts had adopted this flashy new style. Their deliberately slashed sleeves and hose revealed under-layers of cloth, thus displaying several splendid fabrics simultaneously.[1]

Another precedent for the degraded appearance of deconstructed fashion emerged from those who made their living selling discarded clothing and textiles. In the nineteenth and twentieth centuries respectively, writers Charles Baudelaire and Walter Benjamin were fascinated by these "ragpickers" who, as Caroline Evans explained, scavenged cloth for recycling, thereby "recuperating cultural detritus cast aside by capitalist societies."[2] The ragpicker of yore utilized the waste that was created by the frivolity of fashion at its most extreme.

It can be argued that the first contemporary manifestations of deconstruction appeared in the clothing worn by punks beginning in 1976. The youth of Great Britain, long-time leaders in counterculture fashion,[3] had come to dominate the creation of street styles during the post–World War II era. Among those of the mods and the teddy boys, the clothes worn by the punks stand out as particularly aggressive and menacing. The self-crafted aesthetic often involved day-glo colored hair coifed into spiked mohawks, used or vintage clothing obviously ripped and torn then reassembled, spike-studded leather, black Dr. Martens boots, and jewelry made from safety pins, which pierced both cloth and skin. Punk fashion also contained elements of fetishism, particularly the work of the punk movement's "official" designers, London-based Malcolm McLaren and Vivienne Westwood, whose fashions were often inspired by bondage gear.

In 1977, Rhodes, another London designer (of both textiles and clothing), created her Conceptual Chic collection. Though she is credited with designing the first high-fashion

1 The irony of expensive silks being deliberately distressed by the wealthiest members of society has been a sporadically recurring theme in fashion history.

2 Caroline Evans, *Fashion at the Edge: Spectacle, Modernity and Deathliness* (New Haven, Connecticut: Yale University Press, 2003), 36.

3 The "Macaronis" of the eighteenth century are an early example of British counterculture style. Young men of means were often sent to the Continent for the Grand Tour, especially to Italy, as part of their cultural education. There they adopted an ultra-modish form of dress—noted for its outré and scandalously tight fit—as well as a taste for foreign cuisine, thus the derogatory name Macaroni. The Macaronis in their plumed hats are mentioned in the song "Yankee Doodle Dandy." The backwardness of the poorly dressed American troops fighting for independence was disparagingly compared to these fashion trendsetters in London.

21
HANS HOLBEIN THE YOUNGER
Charles de Solier, Sieur de Morette, 1534
Oil on oak panel; $36\frac{7}{16}$ x $29\frac{3}{4}$ inches; Gemaeldegalerie, Staatliche Kunstsammlungen, Dresden, Germany

22
YOHJI YAMAMOTO
Garments from collection, spring/summer 1983

23
VIVIENNE WESTWOOD in her Destroy T-shirt, 1974

21

22

23

punk collection, Rhodes was no anarchist—she was inspired by a decidedly non-punk source, the late 1930s Surrealist designs of Italian-born couturier Elsa Schiaparelli.[4] Specifically, Rhodes was inspired by Schiaparelli's Tear Dress from 1938, itself a wearable version of garments depicted in Salvador Dalí's painting *Three Young Surrealist Women Holding in Their Arms the Skins of an Orchestra* (1936). The dress's visual potency comes from the fact that this most formal of evening costumes is presented in a "deteriorated" state, its fabric printed with trompe l'oeil rips of garment and flesh.[5] Rhodes did her own "tear" prints on chiffon for garments that were carefully decorated with safety pins and silver chains.

PARIS, 1981

While precedents for deconstruction existed in fashion by 1981, Japanese designers Kawakubo and Yamamoto are credited with formalizing its elements in their first Paris collections. The French referred to this look as "Le Destroy," as its distinguishing features included deliberate holes, ragged edges, irregular hemlines, crinkled fabrics, and loose-fitting layers that fell aimlessly over the body. For some, the clothes resembled the garb of homeless people or survivors of an apocalypse. The press was virulent in its condemnation of this aesthetic, calling it everything from "ragged chic" to "Hiroshima bag lady." With these early collections, Kawakubo and Yamamoto simultaneously severed connections with the sartorial past and led the way for the future. As Kawakubo declared, "We must break away from conventional forms of dress for the new woman of today. We need a new strong image, not a revisit to the past."[6]

Following the success of earlier Japanese designers who presented their collections in France (first Hanae Mori and, later, Kenzo Takeda and Miyake Issey), Yamamoto convinced Kawakubo to take the financial and critical risk of showing their collections. Fashion sociologist Yuniya Kawamura explained the reasons Japanese designers found Paris an attractive outpost:

> The younger generation of Japanese designers follows the methodology of Kenzo and others, taking advantage of the French fashion system and "Paris" as their symbolic capital which will eventually result in their economic capital.... These designers share a lack of concern about satisfying the Japanese market, the critics or the public because acceptance in Paris will automatically bring acceptance elsewhere.[7]

4 Elsa Schiaparelli is one of the most important and original figures of twentieth-century fashion. While her career spanned forty years, beginning in 1926, she became best known for her Surrealist-inspired designs of the late 1930s. Despite the fact that Schiaparelli worked in the traditional method of applying decorative, two-dimensional images to the surface of her clothing rather than employing innovative construction techniques, she was a revolutionary designer who became the first couturier to integrate sophisticated and complex artistic concepts into highly wearable material. Schiaparelli viewed the creation of clothing in terms of artistic inspiration and regarded fashion as much more than a craft.

5 Though the Tear Dress was not torn at all; it, like all couture garments of the era, was beautifully cut and constructed.

6 Rei Kawakubo, quoted in "The New Wave from Japan," *The New York Times Magazine* (30 January 1983): 40.

7 Yuniya Kawamura, *The Japanese Revolution in Paris Fashion* (Oxford, England: Berg, 2004), 111.

8 Ibid., 125–26.

9 The governing body of the French fashion system is La Fédération Française de la Couture, du Prêt-à-Porter des Couturiers et des Créateurs de Mode.

10 Claire Mises, "Prêt-à-Porter 1982: Du sectarisme grace aux formes adoucies," *Libération*, 17–18 October 1981, 8. Editor's translation. "Ils puisent leur inspiration à la meme source: on se croirait au Moyan-Âge dans un film de Mizogushi [*sic*]. Peut-être y a-t-il plus de rigueur dans le travail de Comme des Garçons, cela donne une image complètement intemporelle à ses vêtements. Ils ont l'air d'avoir longtemps été portés...Ohji [*sic*] Yamamoto arrive à peu près au même raffinement, en un peu plus évident...ces deux stylistes poussent le côté complètement déstructuré des vêtements, la souplesse des matières et la simplicité des formes."

At the Intercontinental Hotel in Paris in early April 1981, they presented their collections to a small audience of about one hundred people, who witnessed "a new style characterized by monochromatic, asymmetrical, and baggy looks":

> They set the stage for the beginning of the postmodern interpretation on the part of those who design clothes breaking the boundary between the West and the East, fashion and anti-fashion, and modern and anti-modern.... these designers placed great significance on clothing inherited from the past, including Japanese farmers' clothes designed through necessity and adapted textile and quilting from ancient Japan, which Japanese would not consider fashionable.[8]

This first showing was not particularly well attended and contradicts the widely held notion that they were immediately recognized as revolutionaries. The designers themselves confirmed the assertion that few journalists and even fewer retailers attended their debut. But, by the next fall and with the help of a French publicist, Kawakubo and Yamamoto were officially added to the roster of the Fédération,[9] the reigning body of the French fashion system.

With the exception of a few journalists, such as Claire Mises of *Libération*, they were all but ignored by the press for the entire year of 1981. In October of that year, Mises wrote:

> They derive their inspiration from the same source: the Middle Ages in a Mizoguchi film, I believe. There may be more severity in the work of Comme des Garçons, which gives a sense of timelessness to their clothes. Yohji Yamamoto comes with about the same level of refinement, a bit more in evidence...these two designers push the limits completely through deconstructed garments, flexibility of materials, and simplicity of forms.[10]

No reports of the Kawakubo and Yamamoto 1981 collections were published in either the *New York Times* or *Women's Wear Daily*. The only Japanese designers who received media coverage that year were Kenzo (professionally referred to by his first name) and Miyake; the reviews were most often complimentary, though some remained uncertain about the flowing and oversized clothes.

Other journalists from *Libération*, such as Michel Cressole and Serge Daney, increased their coverage of Kawakubo's and Yamamoto's subsequent collections, thus setting a trend for other French publications such as *Le Nouvel Observateur*, *Le Figaro*, and *Dépêche Mode* to do likewise. The relationship between the Japanese designers and the French fashion system had the potential to be mutually beneficial, and many journalists recognized it. Though Paris has long been the

world's fashion capital, it has traditionally relied on the influx of foreign talent to infuse its own culture with new artistic influences and to foster radical change. It can be argued that the deconstructed aesthetic of Kawakubo and Yamamoto would never have become an international phenomenon had they not decided to show their collections in Paris.

The overall critical assessment of Kawakubo and Yamamoto by the French occurred earlier and was generally more nuanced and analytical than that in the United States. Despite the inflammatory titles of articles such as "L'Àpres troisième guerre du feu" (After World War III); "Le Bonze et la kamikaze" (The monk and the kamikaze); "Les Japonais jouent 'Les Misérables'" (The Japanese do *Les Misérables*); "L'Offensive japonais" (the Japanese offensive); "Fripe nippone" (Japanese secondhand); and "Yohji Yamamoto: Brut et sophistication" (Yohji Yamamoto: Brutal sophistication), many in France understood that Kawakubo and Yamamoto were presenting a new kind of fashion that, while not conventional to their eyes, was nonetheless worthy of comment.

With the exception of a few, most serious journalists in the United States and Europe were both perplexed and occasionally angered by clothes they viewed as antiestablishment as well as antifemale. Ironically, some of the more reactionary journalists betrayed a certain sexism in their reviews: "Japanese fashion star Yohji Yamamoto is correct in his assessment of his own work. His designs are definitely 'for the woman who stands alone.' Who would want to be seen with her? Yamamoto's clothes would be most appropriate for someone perched on a broom."[11] Because of her gender, Kawakubo received particularly harsh criticism from mainstream fashion journalists and editors, many of them working women who considered themselves feminists. Holly Brubach, in an article on Yves Saint Laurent, expressed sentiments felt by many:

> The dread and hopelessness that pervade so many of the recent clothes by Japanese designers, notably Rei Kawakubo, are nowhere to be found in Saint Laurent's collections. Japanese fashion in its more extreme forms prefigures a world that no one is looking forward to. The woman who wears Comme des Garçons (Kawakubo's label) is well off but not proud of it, unwilling to dress herself up so that other people have something pleasing to look at, and overburdened by the news she reads everyday in the paper.[12]

While these critics focused on the supposedly joyless and unflattering look of the clothes, Kawakubo expressed her feminism with a rebellious spirit reminiscent of 1970s punk:

> When I was young, it was unusual for a female university graduate to do the same job as a man. And of course women didn't earn the same. I rebelled against that. And when my fashion business started running well, I was thought of as unprofessional because I was not a fashion school graduate. Then, when I went to Paris... I rebelled against that as well. I never lose my ability to rebel. I get angry and that anger becomes my energy for certain. I wouldn't be able to create anything if I stop rebelling.[13]

Interestingly, as early as 1982, fashion trade journals like *Women's Wear Daily* began to mention, albeit briefly and tepidly, the fact that a handful of American buyers were in fact taken by the new Japanese looks. The first article devoted exclusively to the Comme des Garçons and Yamamoto collections, appearing in the 15 October 1982 issue, noted that they possessed a kind of poignant beauty. Journalists Patrick McCarthy and Jane F. Lane wrote that Yamamoto's pants were original, with "paper-bag gathers and loop fastenings" and plain and rough-hewn fabrics that were made to look rich and daring.[14] But the aggressive nature of Kawakubo's presentations and the "Flintstone Age" primitivism of the footwear were also described in equal measure.

American retailers were among the first to bring deconstruction fashion from Japan to the West. While touring Tokyo in 1979, Alan Bilzerian—Boston-based owner of the eponymous boutique—came across a pair of extraordinary trousers made by Yamamoto. After much effort, Bilzerian made contact with the designer and imported these first garments to the United States prior to Yamamoto's Paris debut. Likewise, Barbara Weiser, co-owner of Charivari, the New York boutique that reigned as the spot for cutting-edge fashion during the 1970s and 80s, discovered Yamamoto serendipitously while in Paris on a buying trip in 1981. She remarked how the allure of his garments came both from their austerity and complexity; unable to understand how they were meant to be worn at first sight, she found herself mesmerized by their mysterious folds and sweeping volumes.

By 1983, Miyake had joined Kawakubo and Yamamoto in defining the Japanese avant-garde. In the United States, their collective identity was largely due to a pair of editorial spreads that appeared in American *Vogue* in April and July of 1983. In the first, the work of the three designers appeared together in photographs by Irving Penn.[15] *Vogue*'s second editorial, which included the Japanese triumvirate among other designers, was even more daring and evocative. The photographs by Hans Feurer were taken outdoors (as opposed

11 Mary L. Long, "Yohji Yamamoto," *People* (1 November 1982): 7.
12 Holly Brubach, "The Truth in Fiction," *The Atlantic Monthly* (May 1984): 96.
13 Kawakubo, in Kawamura, *The Japanese Revolution in Paris Fashion*, 129–30.
14 Patrick McCarthy and Jane F. Lane, "Paris: Japanese Show Staying Power," *Women's Wear Daily*, 15 October 1982, 5.
15 Certain readers found somewhat backhanded ways of expressing their disdain. "Allow me...to express my admiration for your wonderful magazine and its continuing crusade to elevate the standards of American fashion. This...in no way diminishes my long-standing regard for the fine work you have been doing in bringing culture to Middle America." George M. Gaither, "Seeking 'Redress,'" letter to the editor, *Vogue* (July 1983): 70.

24
ELSA SCHIAPARELLI
Tear Dress, printed silk crepe evening dress and veil, 1938; Philadelphia Museum of Art, gift of Mme Elsa Schiaparelli, 1969

25
SALVADOR DALÍ
Three Young Surrealist Women Holding in Their Arms the Skins of an Orchestra, 1936
Oil on canvas; 21¼ x 25⅝ inches; collection of The Salvador Dalí Museum, St. Petersburg, Florida

26
COMME DES GARÇONS
Lace Sweater from collection, 1982

27
YOHJI YAMAMOTO
Garments from collection, autumn/winter 1983–84

26

27

to the sterile studio of Penn's images) and featured models, solo and in groups, as well as details of the clothing. The models' odd eye makeup (ombréd masks made from a gradation of blue shadow, or a solid horizontal line across closed eyes and continuing across the face) and windblown manes evoked a sense of boundless freedom as they moved briskly by the camera. The details, especially a pair of woven leather booties by Comme des Garçons, conveyed a poignant sense of humble simplicity.

The earliest clients of Kawakubo and Yamamoto understood that the two designers were not actually "deconstructing" fashion by making very precious objects look worn or used, but carefully "constructing" clothes using specially made textiles and design techniques. Rather than follow the punks—who chose to cut and slash inexpensive, readily available clothing to achieve a pauper aesthetic—Kawakubo and Yamamoto maintained a healthy respect for craft. Referring to one of her best-known designs—the infamous Lace Sweater of 1982, a black knitted top deliberately woven with holes—Kawakubo noted:

> The machines that make fabric are more and more making uniform, flawless textures. I like it when something is *off*—not perfect. Hand weaving is the best way to achieve this. Since this isn't always possible, we loosen a screw of the machines here and there so they can't do exactly what they're supposed to do.[16]

Their garments were as carefully made and beautifully executed as any high-end ready-to-wear object in the West; Kawakubo and Yamamoto demonstrated a basic respect for textiles by minimizing cutting and sewing—emphasizing the inherent quality of the materials rather than cleaving fabric to the body. This totemic draping makes their work unique in the modern fashion lexicon.

One of the ways Kawakubo and Yamamoto distinguished their work from typical body-conscious clothing was to produce garments that were almost exclusively unfitted or oversized. This "one-size-fits all" look flew in the face of the then-current taste for the kind of aggressive and highly sexualized silhouettes associated with the 1980s. Though their clothes have changed a great deal over the past two decades—becoming more formfitting and evoking historic Western modes—Kawakubo and Yamamoto are still more likely to create versions of fashion that subvert notions of gender. While both embrace distinct versions of feminism (specifically within Japan), Kawakubo's intellectual approach stands in stark contrast to the highly sexualized body that figures into many European and American designers' work, while Yamamoto embraces a dual mix of historic modes and incorporates elements from men's garments into the feminine vernacular. As he stated:

> Men's clothing is more pure in design. It's more simple and has no decoration. Women want that. When I started designing, I wanted to make men's clothes for women. But there were no buyers for it. Now there are. I always wonder who decided that there should be a difference in the clothes of men and women. Perhaps men decided this.[17]

Both designers' visions of gender presentation were misunderstood in the West as asexual or unisexual.

Just as important to the work of Kawakubo and Yamamoto is the color black. Their early unrelentingly black-on-black aesthetic—in combination with loose silhouettes and ragged finishings—earned their devotees the nickname *karasuzoku*, or "crow gang." For journalists, the ubiquitous presence of black carried centuries' worth of weighty symbolism, which they presumed had been processed through a kaleidoscope of self-conscious modernism or postmodernist theory by the designers. Black conveyed a plethora of culturally influenced meanings, including poverty, devastation, sobriety, asceticism, intellectualism, chicness, self-restraint, and nobility.

For Kawakubo and Yamamoto, one of the most important expressions of the role of darkness in contemporary society comes from writer Junichiro Tanizaki's seminal essay *In Praise of Shadows* (1933). Tanizaki mused about how darkness affects the way in which a woman's body is seen or not seen. Despite the fact that Tanizaki published his essay before Kawakubo and Yamamoto were born, there is a similarity between his description of women in their kimonos during the Taisho and early Showa periods and those who donned avant-garde Japanese fashion in the late twentieth and early twenty-first centuries. He wrote:

> The body, legs, and feet are concealed within a long kimono...to me this is the very epitome of reality, for a woman of the past did indeed exist only from the collar up and the sleeves out; the rest of her remained hidden in darkness. A woman of the middle or upper ranks of society seldom left her house, and when she did she shielded herself from the gaze of the public in the dark recesses of her palanquin. Most of her life was spent in the twilight of a single house, her body shrouded day and night in gloom, her face the only sign of her existence.... women dressed more somberly. Daughters and wives of the merchant class wore astonishingly severe dress.

16 Kawakubo, cited in Leonard Koren, *New Fashion Japan* (Tokyo: Kondansha, 1984), 117.

17 Yamamoto, in Kawamura, *Japanese Revolution in Paris Fashion*, 133.

Their clothing was in effect no more than a part of the darkness, the transition between darkness and face.[18]

Tanizaki articulated a moment in Japanese history—between old Japan and its modern incarnation—that paved the way for Kawakubo's and Yamamoto's presentations of the female form, making explicit their connection to the role of darkness in traditional Japanese clothing. In this way, their work can be seen as an allusion to the rusticity, simplicity, and unselfconscious restraint of preindustrialized Japan. Historically, black dyes connoted rural life as well as the noble warrior. Yamamoto noted:

300 years ago black was the color of the farmer and the lower-class samurai. It wasn't exactly black but an indigo blue dyed so many times it's close to black. The samurai spirit is black. The samurai must be able to throw his body into nothingness, the color and image of which is black, but the farmers liked black or dark, dark indigo, because the indigo plant was easy to grow, and the dye was good for the body and kept insects away.[19]

During the mid- to late 1980s, Kawakubo and Yamamoto remained the preeminent figures in the world of avant-garde fashion, and their influence began to permeate the hallowed halls of culture. In 1987, for example, Comme des Garçons was prominently featured in an important exhibition highlighting the work of three of the twentieth century's most important female fashion talents. Curators Richard Martin and Harold Koda organized "Three Women: Madeleine Vionnet, Claire McCardell, and Rei Kawakubo" for the Museum at the Fashion Institute of Technology, New York. They argued that Vionnet, the greatest couturier of the golden age of modern fashion; McCardell, the leading innovator of mid-century design; and Kawakubo, the postmodern visionary, were equally important figures. The exhibition not only illustrated the regard these curators had for Kawakubo's work but was also evidence of her lofty ascent while only at the midpoint of her career.

BELGIAN DECONSTRUCTION

By the end of the 1980s, however, the novelty of Kawakubo's and Yamamoto's aesthetic began to wane, usurped by new talent from Antwerp, Belgium. A contingent of young designers including Ann Demeulemeester, Dries Van Noten, and especially Martin Margiela created a new kind of deconstructed fashion. Margiela, for example, began by creating a typical Western high-fashion garment, but then pulled it apart and inverted certain components like sleeves and pockets. The garment was then reconstructed with the interfacings and raw edges deliberately on view. Though Margiela's clothes were new, they reflected his appreciation for reclamation: "I love the idea of recuperation. I believe that it is beautiful to make new things out of rejected or worn things."[20] Margiela's work was first seen by an international audience in 1989, several years after his graduation from the Royal Academy of Fine Arts in Antwerp. His garments—as refined as that of any tailor on Savile Row—appropriate the vocabulary and exacting standards of couture. His inversion of traditional construction elements displays the integrity and honesty of the dressmaker's craft. Interior elements—such as linings, shoulder pads, interfacings, and padding—that are normally carefully hidden became both structure and ornament for Margiela. Even small details like snap closures, sewn on with raw basting stitches, are a form of applied ornament.

While Margiela's particular brand of deconstruction was new and unique, it was built upon a language that had already been established by Kawakubo and Yamamoto. However, it was Margiela's designs that brought the term "deconstruction" into the fashion lexicon. More specifically, Bill Cunningham, a photographer and one the world's foremost commentators on and archivists of fashion trends, noted his garments:

Realized a brash new spirit exploding out of rap music and deconstructivist architectural impulses...those present were witness to an event unique in the annals of fashion history...the deconstructivist impulse of the clothes and the manner in which they were shown—tops of dresses falling down over the hips, intriguing undergarments revealed, plastic dry-cleaning bags serving as tops. Jackets were hardly recognizable, the sleeves tied about the waist like a schoolchild's sweater.[21]

Margiela and his Belgian contemporaries—known collectively as the Antwerp Six—made biannual pilgrimages to Paris and were apparently familiar with the work of the older Japanese designers: "Antwerp's fledgling designers would scurry to Paris during runway seasons, begging, borrowing and copying invitations to get into the shows and see what the future held for them. They witnessed the rise...of Rei Kawakubo and Yohji Yamamoto."[22]

Though he was not the first fashion designer to embrace deconstruction, Margiela remains its most catholic practitioner. From his first seminal runway show, held inside a crumbling building in a Parisian ghetto in 1989, to his recent

18 Junichiro Tanizaki, *In Praise of Shadows* (1933), trans. Thomas J. Harper and Edward Seidensticker (Stony Creek, Connecticut: Leete's Islands Books, 1977), 28.
19 Yamamoto, cited in Koren, *New Fashion Japan*, 157.
20 Martin Margiela, quoted in Luc Derycke and Sandra Van de Veire, eds., *Belgian Fashion Design* (Antwerp, Belgium: Ludion, 1999), 292.
21 Bill Cunningham, "Fashion de Siècle," *Details* (March 1990): 180.
22 Amy M. Spindler, "Coming Apart," *The New York Times*, 25 July 1993, sec. 9, 9.

28
Garments by **MARTIN MARGIELA** in "9/4/1615," installation at Brooklyn Anchorage, New York, 1999

28

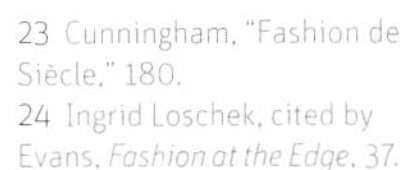
23 Cunningham, "Fashion de Siècle," 180.
24 Ingrid Loschek, cited by Evans, *Fashion at the Edge*, 37.

29
Garments by **MARTIN MARGIELA** in "9/4/1615," installation at Brooklyn Anchorage, New York, 1999, details

jewelry made from the crystal drops of old chandeliers, he stands as the preeminent master of redefining beauty through an aesthetic that suggests ragpicking and recuperation. Indeed, Cunningham credited him with the "overthrow of the old regime of fossilized elegant taste."[23]

A 1997 exhibition of Margiela at the Museum Boijmans Van Beuningen in Rotterdam, The Netherlands, may arguably be the closest thing to conceptual art undertaken in the realm of fashion—drastically different from the vanity exhibitions fashion designers have mounted over the past several decades. Clothing from Margiela's previous collections was covered with mold and bacteria and displayed outdoors where it could decay—drawing a comparison between "the natural cycle of creation and decay [and] the consumer cycle of buying and discarding."[24]

THE 1990S

From the late 1980s to the mid-90s, Kawakubo and Yamamoto continued to show work but to less fanfare, as they began to be perceived as rehashing the innovations of earlier collections. Yet, their appropriation of historical fashions from the New Look (c. 1947–48) period—which is itself a historical revival of the Belle Époque (c. 1895–1914)—never merely mimicked vintage clothing, as had so many other designers since the 1970s. The polish of French 1950s couture was deliberately tarnished in their hands. Their impact remained low-key until autumn/winter 1995–96, when they came out with a fresh approach that distinguished them even from the designers they inspired.

Yamamoto, for example, integrated the highly sculptural and architectonic elements of Christian Dior and Cristobal Balenciaga, who often created day suits and coats, ball gowns, and opera coats devoid of any applied ornament. They, like Yamamoto, understood that monochromatic or tone-on-tone use of black (or other neutrals) is often the most effective in expressing the dynamic three-dimensional possibilities of rending dramatic form through garment construction. They crafted severely beautiful couture creations with oversized collars cut like enormous wings, ample melon-shaped sleeves, and full swinging skirts billowing away from corseted waists and resting upon padded hips. Yamamoto's New Look versions of these dresses were often made without the requisite padding and beautiful silk linings. He chose to make ball gowns out of black and white wool felt, the same fabric used to cover billiard tables. His coats were sometimes

29

made from wool batting sandwiched between black netting, their sleeves hinged with synthetic webbing.

Kawakubo, on the other hand, designed brocaded coats and cocktail dresses with sheer insets that revealed the body and demonstrated a lack of support materials. Cocktail dresses and evening gowns were often asymmetrical and gave the appearance of having been taken apart and reassembled backwards, deliberately askew. Dresses made from what appeared to be silk slips dating to the 1950s were cut in half and attached to other slips before being wrapped and tied around the body. Both collections—Yamamoto's industrial couture and Kawakubo's deranged socialite look—led to a resurgence of interest in deconstruction, resulting in some of the most beautiful and intellectually moving fashions seen in the late 1990s. Their popularity reemerged along with an interest in formalwear, and their poetic approach paved the way for subsequent generations of creators.

While Kawakubo, Yamamoto, and Margiela brought deconstruction to the realm of high fashion, those who attempted to move it into the mainstream were less successful. One of the best known examples was the Grunge collection of spring/summer 1993 by Marc Jacobs for Perry Ellis. His last for that company, the collection sought to draw a connection between contemporary youth culture (in this case grunge, the punk-influenced rock-music style that emerged in Seattle) and high fashion, but it was not well received. Models donned expensive silk dresses made from patterned fabrics that were criticized for being deliberately mismatched and loosely constructed, though some found their twisted and matted hair tucked under knitted stocking caps, combat boots and Birkenstock sandals, and nose rings more offensive.

Though the runways were largely bereft of deconstructed elements throughout the 1990s, many young independent designers of that time utilized them so fluidly that deconstruction became a hallmark of their work. Susan Cianciolo, for example, was celebrated for her naïve and gentle New Age, neo-folk approach, which emphasized handwork and small-scale business operations over the machine-made, multinational approach favored by other designers. Hers was a contemporary vision of hippie ideology that, while formally influenced by deconstruction, flew in the face of its roots in a more violent antiestablishment style. Ironically, clothing such as Cianciolo's labor-intensive garments or T-shirts by Project Alabama, a cooperative of quilters-turned-couturiers under the direction of designer Natalie Chanin, would have been financially out of reach for the originators of punk street style.

The incorporation of deconstruction by the world's leading purveyors of high-end ready-to-wear and haute couture lines signals a far more profound shift in fashion. A younger cadre of designers who have taken over other venerated Parisian firms (such as Olivier Theyskens at Rochas and Alber Elbaz at Lanvin) are so versed in the elements of deconstruction that the finest and most coveted examples of their work consistently utilize that aesthetic. From protest to poetry, deconstruction remains one of the most important design elements in fashion today.

30
SUSAN CIANCIOLO
Garments from **RUN 7** collection, spring/summer 1998

31
ALBER ELBAZ FOR LANVIN
Dress from collection, autumn/winter 2003–04

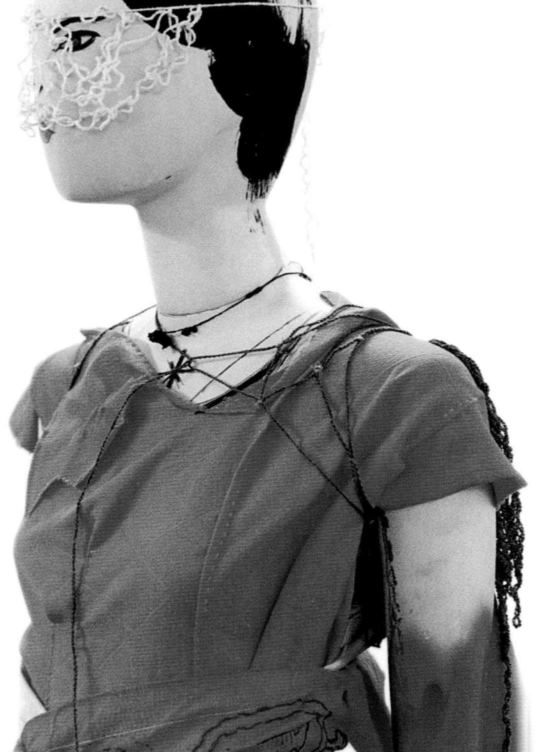

30

31

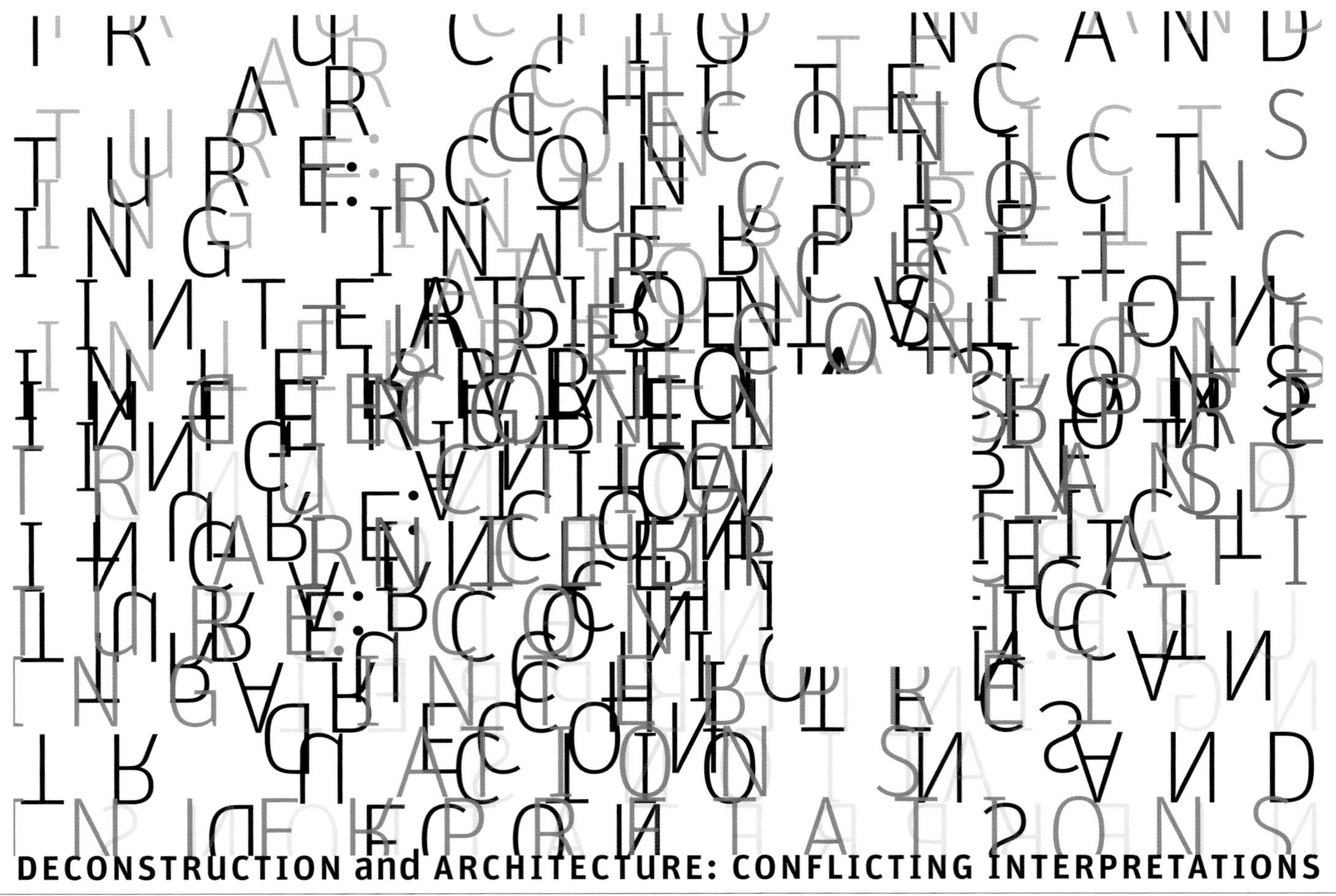

DECONSTRUCTION and ARCHITECTURE: CONFLICTING INTERPRETATIONS

Brooke Hodge

The 1988 exhibition "Deconstructivist Architecture" at the Museum of Modern Art, New York (MOMA), was a major event in the architecture world for practitioners, critics, and students alike. Not since the museum's seminal 1932 "Modern Architecture" exhibition introduced the term "International Style" into the design lexicon had MOMA signaled a new stylistic tendency by grouping current architectural projects under a single title.[1] "Deconstructivist Architecture" was eagerly anticipated and much talked about, even before it opened. From its inception, it was surrounded by speculation and conjecture as to who was in, who was out, what "deconstructivism" might be, where it might have come from, and how it was related to "deconstruction."

"Deconstruction" was, and still is, most closely associated with French philosopher Jacques Derrida, though he himself resisted defining the term. Introduced in his books *Writing and Difference* (1967) and *Of Grammatology* (1966), deconstruction eludes definition because—as a critical methodology predicated on the continual shifting and uncovering of language and meaning—any definition can, in theory, be "deconstructed." Derrida was interested in the formal devices of language; his reading or unraveling of textual objects or linguistic structures is, essentially, a process that consists of breaking a text down to identify binary oppositions (male/female, black/white, etc.) in order to reveal and undermine the established hierarchy that exists between them. Derrida challenged the notion that every text has a single unified meaning and asserted that a complete understanding of a text is impossible, as it can be opened up to reveal different, even conflicting, interpretations or voices.

In his writings, Derrida often seized on a fragment within an existing text, analyzing it tenaciously to the point where ruptures would appear that threatened to dismantle the established meaning. Breaking down its ruling system or logic, he challenged the very meaning of what had been seen or known as familiar.[2] The rhetoric of deconstruction—"dismantling," "disjunctive," "rupture," "layers"—was picked up by a number of other disciplines, including art, film, fashion, literature, and architecture. Interestingly, the language with which Derrida wrote about deconstruction often made use of architectural terms (such as "construct," "structure," "foundation," and "dwelling"), though he was not the first philosopher to employ architectural metaphors in his writing and openly acknowledged a debt to Martin Heidegger in this regard.

Some connection between "Deconstructivist Architecture" and Derridean deconstruction would have been understandable, even expected, given the background of those involved in the exhibition. Curator and architect Philip Johnson's collaborator on the project, architecture theorist and critic Mark Wigley, was one of the earliest scholars to bring a reading of Derrida to bear on architectural discourse and to study in depth his use of architectural metaphor. Wigley's doctoral dissertation "Jacques Derrida and Architecture: The Deconstructive Possibilities of Architectural Discourse" (1986)[3] made him an ideal candidate to explore such a connection, though he had no practical experience with exhibitions. (Wigley is now dean of Columbia University's Graduate School of Architecture, Planning, and Preservation.) The selection of architects and projects was made following a series of meetings and conversations between the curators and among a number of prominent professionals.

MOMA's deconstructivist exhibition featured seven participants—Coop Himmelb(l)au, Peter Eisenman, Frank Gehry, Zaha Hadid, Rem Koolhaas, Daniel Libeskind, and Bernard Tschumi—all practicing in different parts of the world. Even though Coop Himmelb(l)au, Eisenman, Gehry, and Tschumi had built work to their credit, the projects in the show were, for the most part, theoretical or unbuilt. Nonetheless, the curators maintained that all the work in the exhibition represented buildings that could or would be built. For many of the participants, the MOMA exhibition marked the first occasion that their work was shown in the United States; however, Gehry coincidentally was the subject of a retrospective exhibition, organized by the Walker Art Center in Minneapolis, that was concurrently on view at New York's Whitney Museum of American Art.

Other than Tschumi and Eisenman, the architects in "Deconstructivist Architecture" for the most part denied a direct connection to Derrida's theories and even to one another. In his catalogue essay, Wigley attempted to clarify some of the misconceptions about what linked the work of these architects:

> Deconstruction itself...is often misunderstood as the taking apart of constructions. Consequently, any provocative architectural design which appears to take structure apart—whether it be the simple breaking of an object or the complex dissimulation of an object into a collage of traces—has been hailed as deconstructive.... On the contrary, deconstruction gains all its force by challenging the very values of harmony, unity, and stability, and proposing instead a different view of structure: the view that flaws are intrinsic to the structure. A deconstructive architect is therefore not one who dismantles buildings, but one who locates the inherent dilemmas within buildings.[4]

The MOMA show, then, served to highlight some elements common to the architects it put forward as "deconstructivist." Wigley achieved this not by linking the projects to Derridean deconstruction, but to early twentieth-century Russian Constructivism, a period when "traditional thinking about the nature of the architectural object was placed in doubt"[5]:

> The projects...draw from Constructivism and yet constitute a radical deviation from it.... Irregular geometry is again understood as a structural condition rather than as a dynamic formal aesthetic. It is no longer produced simply by the conflict between pure forms. It is now produced within those forms. The forms themselves are infiltrated with the characteristic skewed geometry, and distorted. In this way, the traditional condition of the architectural object is radically disturbed.[6]

This "distortion of form" was achieved through rotated grids, warped planes, diagonal elements, shifted or displaced functions or features, perforation of the building envelope, exposed structural elements, and use of industrial materials:

> The form is distorting itself. Yet this internal distortion does not destroy the form. In a strange way, the form somehow remains intact. This is an architecture of disruption, dislocation, deflection, deviation, and distortion, rather than one of demolition, dismantling, decay, decomposition, or disintegration. It displaces structure instead of destroying it.[7]

Since few projects in the exhibition were built, the drawings and models were left to suggest how each architect's work fit into the curatorial thesis. Two of the hallmarks of deconstructivist architecture—the displacement of building elements and crudely assembled structural members—were evident as much in the way the drawings and models were approached aesthetically as from the buildings' actual construction, underlining the fact that an exhibition can be valuable in generating a dialogue to garner mainstream acceptance of new ways of thinking. In the case of "Deconstructivist Architecture," the currency of ideas—rather than the realization of buildings—was of critical importance.

Included in the exhibition was Hadid's project for The Peak in Hong Kong (unbuilt, 1982–83), which is remarkable for its proposed transformation of the site's natural topography through excavation and for the thrusting and slicing

1 Though the two exhibitions were separated by fifty-six years, they shared a common curator; Philip Johnson was involved in the organization of both. Johnson, together with Henry-Russell Hitchcock, was responsible for bringing modern architecture to America in the form of MOMA's 1932 International Style exhibition. Also a practicing architect, he worked closely with Ludwig Mies van der Rohe on New York's Seagram Building (1954–58), one of the acknowledged masterpieces of modern architecture. The tireless promoter of modernism went on to build one of the icons of postmodernism (AT&T Building, New York) and, less than five years later, was a key player in facilitating the rise of deconstructivism through the "Deconstructisvist Architecture" exhibition.

2 For a concise discussion of deconstruction, see Terry Eagleton, *Literary Theory: An Introduction* (Minneapolis: University of Minnesota Press, 1983). "Deconstruction is [for Jacques Derrida] an ultimately *political* practice, an attempt to dismantle the logic by which a particular system of thought, and behind that a whole system of political structures and social institutions, maintains its force. He is not seeking, absurdly, to deny the existence of relatively determinate truths, meanings, identities, intentions, historical continuities; he is seeking rather to see such things as the effects of a wider and deeper history—of language, of the unconscious, of social institutions and practices" (148).

3 Mark Wigley's doctoral dissertation on the topic was subsequently expanded and published as *The Architecture of Deconstruction: Derrida's Haunt* (Cambridge, Massachusetts: The MIT Press, 1993).

4 Wigley, "Deconstructivist Architecture," in Johnson and Wigley, *Deconstructivist Architecture* (New York: The Museum of Modern Art, 1988), 11.

5 Ibid.

6 Ibid., 16.

7 Ibid., 17.

32

32
"Deconstructivist Architecture," installation at The Museum of Modern Art, New York, 1988

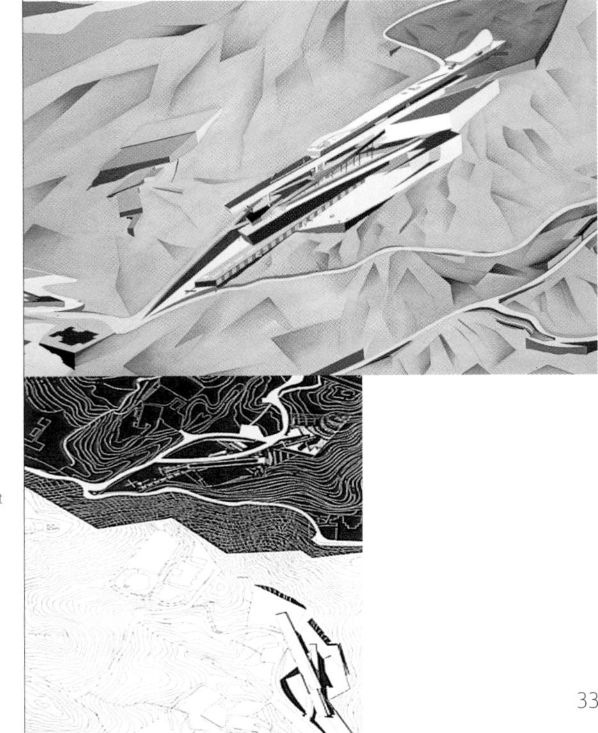

33

33
ZAHA HADID ARCHITECTS
The Peak (unbuilt), Hong Kong, 1982–83, contextual rendering (top) and site-plan painting (bottom)

beams that are its major architectural elements. Building elements seem to float; the forms of the building are repositioned to confront each other, twisting and disrupting the traditional parallel planes of modernism. Hadid's project had won first prize in a design competition for a private club in the hills above Hong Kong's Victoria Harbor and brought her work to international attention. A student of Koolhaas at the Architectural Association School of Architecture in London, she is renowned for the drawings and paintings she produces to represent her projects. Of all the work in "Deconstructivist Architecture," Hadid's is most closely related to the angular cubistic forms and intersecting planes of Russian Constructivism—something that was emphasized by the graphics she presented.

Gehry, whose work for some time had been concerned with forms more often linked to art or sculpture, was represented in the exhibition by two residential projects—one of which was for his own house in Santa Monica, California, which he had been transforming since 1977. Closer in spirit to the work of artist Gordon Matta-Clark[8]—who operated on existing architecture by cutting, splitting, and exposing its structural elements—than to any of the other architects in the exhibition, Gehry used the existing Dutch Colonial bungalow in which he and his family lived as the staging ground for his architectural interventions.

The initial project evolved in several stages, during which he subtracted from and added to the existing structure to create new forms and spaces. Gehry stripped away the outer skin of the house in some places, punctured the roof, and removed portions of the façade in order to introduce twisted protruding forms, let in light, add space, or reveal the structure's framework. These new forms seem to push through the existing building envelope as if they had been trapped inside and were suddenly free to grow through the walls and roof. He placed glass over some parts of the interior structure and left windows hanging in front of a wall. He also layered industrial off-the-shelf materials such as chain-link mesh and corrugated metal over some of the building's apertures and on parts of its façade. One aspect of Gehry's architectural practice at that stage of his career was characterized by taking buildings apart (literally and figuratively) and reassembling their elements in unconventional ways. Though this has often been regarded as deconstructivist, his work with form and typology was not engaged with either deconstruction or Russian Constructivism.

8 In Frank Gehry's office, the process of taking apart elements of a building and reconstituting them in new ways was sometimes actually referred to as "Matta-Clarking."

34–35
FRANK GEHRY
Gehry Residence, Santa Monica, California, 1977–78/1991–94, first-stage axonometric projection (left) and exterior and interior views

36–37
OFFICE FOR METROPOLITAN ARCHITECTURE/ REM KOOLHAAS
Apartment Building and Observation Tower (unbuilt), Rotterdam, The Netherlands, 1982, isometric triptych showing overall site (top) and axonometric projection from city side (bottom)

38
COOP HIMMELB(L)AU
Rooftop Remodeling, Vienna, 1983/1987–88

39
EISENMAN ROBERTSON ARCHITECTS
Biocenter (unbuilt), University of Frankfurt, Germany, 1987, site model

Coop Himmelb(l)au's Rooftop Remodeling (1983/1987–88), a renovation of the attic space of a traditional apartment building in Vienna, showed another aspect of deconstruction. Interested in the idea that a new structure could feed like a parasite on an existing one, the architects designed a skeletal structure that slices through the roof and a corner of the building and appears to land on it like a fantastical insect. The addition is a metal and glass construction whose chaotic form is based on an analysis of the existing building's structure much in the way that deconstruction promotes analysis of existing texts to generate new readings.

Eisenman, who at the time was a principal in the firm Eisenman Robertson Architects, was represented by his proposed design for the Biocenter for the University of Frankfurt, Germany (unbuilt, 1987). The design, for a center for advanced biological research, organizes the distribution of laboratories along a central spine. While the units branching out from the spine were initially based on basic modernist blocks, the shape of each was derived from those of the four nucleotides that constitute DNA and RNA. The dialogue between man-made modernist forms and natural biological code works to distort the framework of the project by adding new shapes that clash with each other, disturbing and displacing the original forms and the spine.

Eisenman's approach is always tied to his research on the program, site, and typology of each project, which provide a conceptual foundation that determines the massing and building form. His projects are thus organized according to esoteric systems that are indiscernible to the casual observer but that afford them a certain internal logic. At the time of the exhibition, he was better known for his writings about architecture than for his relatively small body of built work.

Koolhaas and his Office for Metropolitan Architecture, based in Rotterdam, The Netherlands, were represented in the exhibition by a 1982 unbuilt project for an apartment building and observation tower in Rotterdam. The complex, which functioned primarily as a high-rise apartment building, also contained communal facilities such as a school, hotel, health center, and swimming pool. It is difficult to classify Koolhaas's project as either a single, monolithic horizontal slab or a row of five discrete towers, since the building can be read as both and neither simultaneously. The monolith is distorted by the towers, which tilt and project from its volume, and the towers are distorted by the monolith, which appears to slice through them. Only at the far end of

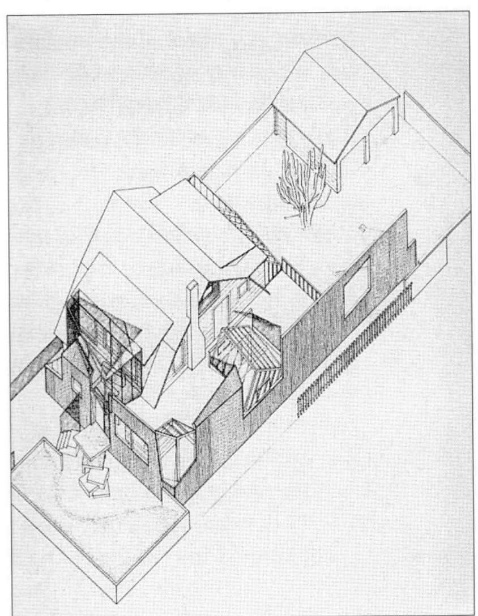

the compound does a whole, rather modernist tower form seem to detach itself from the somewhat chaotic overall composition. Koolhaas's axonometric projection of the building, like Hadid's representations, also reveals a debt to the drawings of the Russian Constructivists, with its fragmented forms and its simultaneous relaying of various types of information—parts, whole, plan, elevation, set—in a hybrid representational strategy. Koolhaas's work has been less about violent fragmentation and sharp forms than that of some of his colleagues in the exhibition. Like Eisenman, Koolhaas has given equal weight in his practice to writing and theoretical speculation.

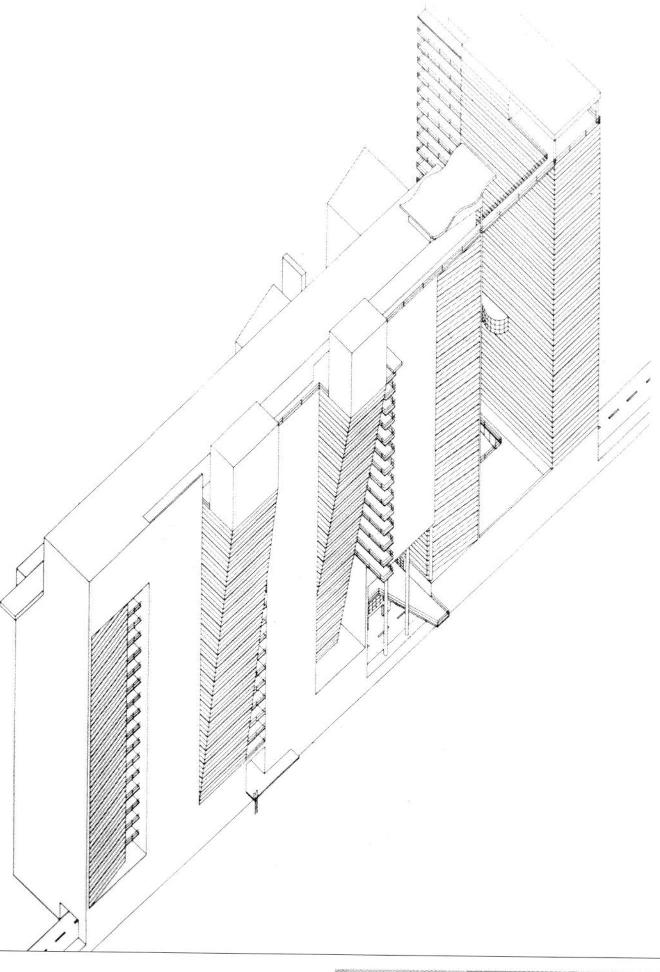

36

37

38

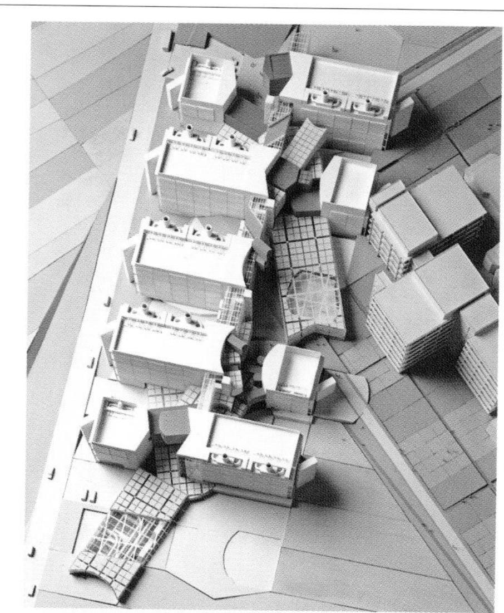

39

Libeskind, a Polish-born architect whose practice at the time was based in Milan, Italy, was represented by City Edge (unbuilt, 1987), an office and residential development project for the Tiergarten section of Berlin. The major element of Libeskind's scheme was a gigantic horizontal bar, elevated at an angle by slender supports so that at one end it hovers ten stories above ground, overlooking the Berlin Wall. The basic "dumb" form of the Berlin Wall is exploited and its very existence and authority are contested by Libeskind's thrusting beamlike building, which slices through the site. Both symbolically and formally evocative, Libeskind's project confronts the Wall and its physical and psychosocial effects on the city. Wigley and Johnson displayed several different architectural models designed by Libeskind to represent the project, with each model exploring a different aspect of the dialogue between building and city. Libeskind's drawings and models are jarring and evoke a sense of conflict and chaos. The building is almost impossibly long and operates on the city fabric in an aggressive way. The drawings, hybrids of collage and other representational strategies, are so densely layered and composed that the content is at times indecipherable, almost seeming deliberately obscured.

Finally, Swiss-born architect Bernard Tschumi was represented by his elaborate plan for Parc de la Villette in Paris, which is discussed in depth later in this essay.

As well as opening the door for architects (and the public) to begin thinking about form in new ways, the exhibition served to legitimize something that had been in the air for some time already. By grouping mostly unrelated projects and presenting them within a cohesive and legitimizing framework, the exhibition sanctioned the work on display and granted acceptance to what had previously been thought of as radical. "Deconstructivist" architecture—and, surreptitiously, architecture that was influenced by deconstruction—was officially introduced to the mainstream in a way that belied its inherent fragmentation. It could now officially be adopted, translated, and diluted.

Several months prior to the opening of MOMA's exhibition, a symposium organized by Andreas Papadakis—the publisher of Academy Editions, a series of books on architecture—was staged at the Tate Gallery in London. The symposium gathered a diverse group of practitioners, critics, and academics, including Catherine Cooke, Eisenman, Hadid, Charles Jencks, Tschumi, and Wigley, to talk about deconstruction in architecture. The papers presented at this symposium were published by Rizzoli in *Deconstruction: Omnibus Volume* (1989), which also featured a review of the symposium by David Lodge, a critical essay on the "Deconstructivist Architecture" exhibition by James Wines, and other projects by architects and firms such as Coop Himmelb(l)au, Libeskind, Morphosis, and Stanley Tigerman.

Many of the participants were involved in "Deconstructivist Architecture," and a few of those who were not used the opportunity to critique the (as yet unseen) MOMA exhibition. Wines, for instance, made a case as to why the work of Matta-Clark should be included in the show. Several of the papers presented at the symposium addressed the successes and failures of postmodernism and its relationship to the developing interest in deconstruction and fragmentation. Cooke made a case for the influence of Russian Constructivism and Suprematism on contemporary architecture, citing the work of Hadid and Koolhaas.[9] While Derrida himself did not attend the symposium, he submitted a filmed interview with British theorist Christopher Norris in which he described his engagement with architecture. As Lodge explained in his review of the proceedings:

> Derrida...admitted that he had himself once been doubtful about the application of Deconstruction to architecture, but the persistence of architectural metaphors in philosophical and theoretical discourse ("foundation," "superstructure," "*architectonice*," etc.) had encouraged him to investigate further. Architects, he suggested, used Deconstruction to challenge the hegemony of architectural principles such as "function" and "beauty," reinscribing this challenge in their work.[10]

Wigley found himself in the position of defending the thesis and choice of participants for the MOMA exhibition, which, though it had not opened yet, was already the subject of much conjecture. In defense of the exhibition, Wigley expressed concern with the perception that it merely highlighted a banal sense of fragmentation, stating, "I believe the projects in the Deconstructivist Architecture exhibition at MOMA mark a different sensibility, one in which the dream of pure form has been disturbed."[11] If, as Wigley later described in his catalogue essay, the works in the MOMA exhibition "irritate modernism from within, distorting it with its own geneology,"[12] it is necessary to examine what kinds of forms were being distorted and what factors coalesced to impact both the built form and critical discussion that led to "Deconstructivist Architecture."

9 Catherine Cooke mentioned in her paper "Russian Precursors" that Rem Koolhaas made a special trip in the 1970s to Russia to look at Ivan Leonidov's drawn and painted projects firsthand.

10 David Lodge, "Deconstruction: A Review of the Tate Gallery Symposium," in *Deconstruction: Omnibus Volume*, eds. Andreas Papadakis, Catherine Cooke, and Andrew Benjamin (New York, Rizzoli, 1989), 88.

11 Wigley, "Deconstructivist Architecture," in *Deconstruction*, 132.

12 Wigley, "Deconstructivist Architecture," in *Deconstructivist Architecture*, 16.

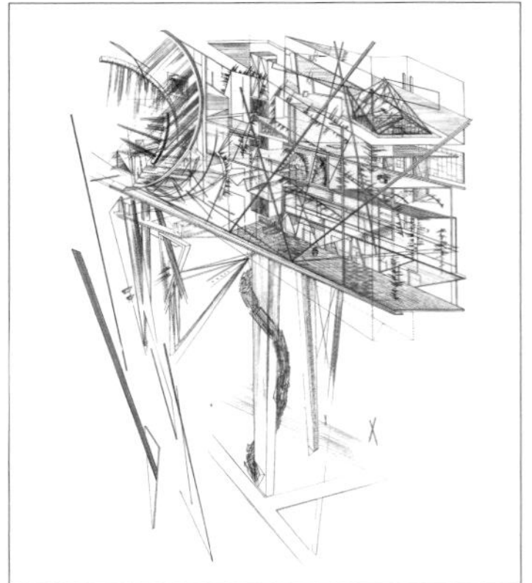

40–41
DANIEL LIBESKIND
City Edge (unbuilt), Berlin, 1987, sections and exploded axonometric projection (left) and site model (right)

Modernism in architecture—very simplistically characterized as pure geometric forms stripped of ornament and based on rationalist thinking about the relationship between form and function—was founded on aesthetic as well as social concerns (such as public housing and industrialization) and influenced by utopian thinking. When modernism traveled from Europe to America via MOMA's "Modern Architecture" exhibition, it was relieved of these social concerns, largely because the curators foregrounded modernism as a style and all but ignored its political and social content.[13] From sleek curtain-wall skyscrapers like Ludwig Mies Van der Rohe's Seagram Building (1954–58) in New York to the International Style houses of Le Corbusier, Walter Gropius, and Richard Neutra, the severely rectilinear forms of modernism were considered to be radically new—clean, spare, and straightforward, expressive of technology and function. Louis Sullivan's edict "form follows function" and Mies van der Rohe's dictum "less is more" were adopted wholeheartedly by architects, developers, and builders as aesthetic directives.

However, like many major architectural developments, the initially strict application of principles and the physical representation of ideology soon devolved into a set of superficial stylistic concerns; late modernist buildings lacked the purity of form and thought that characterized the original masterpieces. By the 1970s, it seemed as if every city had glass-box skyscrapers—most of them mediocre pastiches—and every suburb had tract homes based on the modernist box. Tom Wolfe's 1981 book *From Bauhaus to Our House* underscored the situation by opening with a biting, yet humorous, critique of the ubiquity and banality of so-called modern architecture:

> O Beautiful, for spacious skies, for amber waves of grain, has there ever been another place on earth where so many people of wealth and power have paid for and put up with so much architecture they detested as within thy blessed borders today?[14]

Two new strains of architectural discourse (and aesthetics) emerged during the 1970s: postmodernism and post-functionalism. The latter largely resulted in writing and analysis and the former in actual buildings. Both represented attempts to shake off the malaise of modernism. The promise of postmodernism was to remedy its problems by referencing other moments—not just from architecture's past but from political, social, and cultural history as well—whereas post-functionalism sought to free architecture from cultural associations of any kind.

For many architects who had committed themselves to developing contemporary architectural forms that would serve as alternatives to modernism, the writings of Robert Venturi and Denise Scott Brown—including *Learning from Las Vegas* (1972) and "Learning from Pop" (1971), which advocated a closer examination of vernacular and commercial buildings and artifacts—were influential. In addition, MOMA's 1975 exhibition "The Architecture of the École des Beaux-Arts" encouraged architects to re-examine forms and motifs from the classical past. Incidentally, the beauty and sheer technical prowess of the drawings on view signaled the return of drawing to a position of importance.

Architect Robert A. M. Stern enumerated a number of strategies that he believed characterized postmodern architecture. These included the "use of ornament," the introduction of "explicit historical reference," the "conscious and eclectic utilization of the formal strategies of orthodox modernism together with strategies of the pre-Modern period," the "preference for incomplete or compromised geometries," the "use of rich colors and various materials," the "emphasis on intermediate spaces" (such as circulation), and the "configuration of spaces in terms of light and view as well as of use."[15]

Probably the most iconic of postmodern buildings is Johnson's AT&T (now Sony) Building in New York City, which was completed in 1984. The building's most recognizable feature is its split-pediment crown. The thirty-four-story skyscraper, clad in pink granite, evokes the grand tradition of New York skyscrapers such as the Chrysler Building, itself a simple shaft capped by an articulated crown. While the AT&T Building's thirty-foot-high crown evokes a classical pediment, it is also thought to resemble the top of a Chippendale highboy dresser. The AT&T Building was instantly recognizable in the New York skyline and brought Johnson a great deal of attention: he was photographed for the cover of *Time* magazine holding a model of the building.

While the press and the public embraced postmodern architecture with enthusiasm, it inspired scathing criticism from many in the architecture profession. Detractors thought that such historical references were applied superficially, with no impact on a building's form. Postmodern architecture remained rather conventional; stylistically, it was thought to be frivolous, a pastiche—even kitschy.

Post-functionalism arose through the study, analysis, and critique of architecture by many who made their living

13 For a full discussion of the curatorial process and thinking that led to "Modern Architecture: International Exhibition," see Terence Riley, *The International Style: Exhibition 15 and The Museum of Modern Art* (New York: Rizzoli and Columbia Books of Architecture, 1992), 25. Riley stated "the basis of Hitchcock and Johnson's aesthetic position is artifact-oriented connoisseurship."

14 Tom Wolfe, *From Bauhaus to Our House* (New York: Farrar Straus Giroux, 1981), 3.

15 For an elaboration of these strategies, see the reconstructed and translated text of Robert A. M. Stern, "Gray Architecture as Post-Modernism, or, Up and Down from Orthodoxy," in K. Michael Hays, ed., *Architecture Theory Since 1968* (Cambridge, Massachusetts: The MIT Press, 1998), 242–45.

42
JOHNSON & BURGEE ARCHITECTS
AT&T Building (now **Sony Building**), New York, 1980–84

largely as academics. These architects did not focus on building per se, but instead spent a great deal of time thinking about architecture—its origins, formal vocabulary, and meaning. They related architecture to other types of cultural and intellectual production, often looking to the methods and constructs of philosophy, structuralism, semiotics, and phenomenology in order to open up new ways of thinking. Architecture theory as it exists today is generally considered to have taken root during the 1960s and to have become a prevailing force in architectural education and discourse after 1968.[16]

At the same time, architects were seeking new ways to represent their designs. The traditional set of architectural drawings—plan, section, elevation—used to communicate the physical properties of a design to both clients and builders was no longer adequate to represent more complex projects that had many layers of information and were often quite abstract. Soon, drawing became a project in itself as architects experimented with collage, silkscreen, painting, and other artistic techniques. Architects began to layer text with image, incorporate color, and merge models and drawings into hybrid three-dimensional forms. Often, the projects for which these drawings were made were not intended to be built, but were created for competitions or as purely artistic or intellectual exercises. "Paper" architecture, as it came to be called, was a hallmark of the late 1970s and much of the 80s when architects, largely for economic reasons, had less opportunity to translate their ideas into built form. Both theory and paper architecture served as platforms for exploration as architects sought new and creative ways to think, write about, and represent their work.

Postmodernism and post-functionalism represented a fracture within the architecture world, and neither had the strength, vision, or public acceptance to overtake modernism in any significant way. However, they were among the factors responsible for the energetic dialogue that took place in the 1980s, which ultimately helped to redefine architectural practice and pedagogy. In the early to mid-1980s, fragmented forms began to appear in projects for competition entries, in student work, and in drawings. This was ascribed to, among other causes, a preoccupation with the increasingly fragmented and unstable societies developing as a result of globalization and the breaking down of boundaries through travel and commerce, increased electronic communication, and the development of new technologies, including a more widespread adoption of the computer.[17] It is also likely that this new approach to form developed from explorations related to drawing as well as the emergence of new architecture theories linked to philosophical movements such as post-structuralism and deconstruction:

> A new architectural tendency, associated both with poststructuralist theory and constructivist forms...is in part a vehement reaction against postmodernism and what are perceived as its conservative dimensions: its historicist imagery, its complacent contextualism, its conciliatory and affirmative properties, its humanism, its rejection of technological imagery, and its repression of the new.[18]

If there was any single event where these ideas began to coalesce and manifest themselves in an architectural project, it may have been in 1982, when Tschumi was commissioned to design an "Urban Park for the Twenty-First Century" at La Villette, in the northeast corner of metropolitan Paris. Tschumi, a French-Swiss architect, won the international competition to design the 125-acre park on the former site of a complex of slaughterhouses as part of President François Mitterrand's ambitious Grands Projets. An elite urban renewal scheme that would put Paris's largest park in the heart of a working-class neighborhood with a significant immigrant population, the project came with both a large budget and a great deal of controversy.

Tschumi's Parc de la Villette, which was not completed until 1998, consists of a series of freestanding pavilions, or "follies," scattered throughout the site and linked by a series of gardens and walkways. The follies could, in principle, be functional, but the architect avoided specifying particular uses for them, instead tying them to the overall program of the mixed-use urban park, which contains a museum of science and industry, recreational areas, and amenities such as a café, cinema, video studios, and post office. Tschumi designed the individual follies (thirty-five were planned, but only twenty-six were realized)—a key element of the overall plan, and the master plan of the park itself. Each folly began as a ten-meter partially enclosed cube of painted red steel that was fragmented, deformed, and manipulated so that the initial form is often indiscernible and no two are alike. Comparisons have often been made between the follies and the fragmented red forms that appear in the Russian Constructivist drawings of El Lissitzky and Kasimir Malevich, among others.

Tschumi's master plan took the form of an architectural collage in which three ordering systems were superimposed:

16 For a thorough discussion of the emergence of architecture theory and its impact on and transformation of architectural discourse and the profession, see introduction to *Architecture Theory Since 1968*, x–xv.

17 It wasn't until 1994 that Columbia University's Architecture School introduced the first "paperless" studio where design would be generated digitally using specialized computer software rather than by hand. See Joseph Rosa, *Folds, Blobs, and Boxes: Architecture in the Digital Era* (Pittsburgh: Heinz Architectural Center Books, 2001), 15.

18 Mary McLeod, "Architecture and Politics in the Reagan Era: From Postmodernism to Deconstructivism," *Assemblage* 8 (February 1989), reprinted in K. Michael Hays, *Architecture Theory Since 1968*, 690.

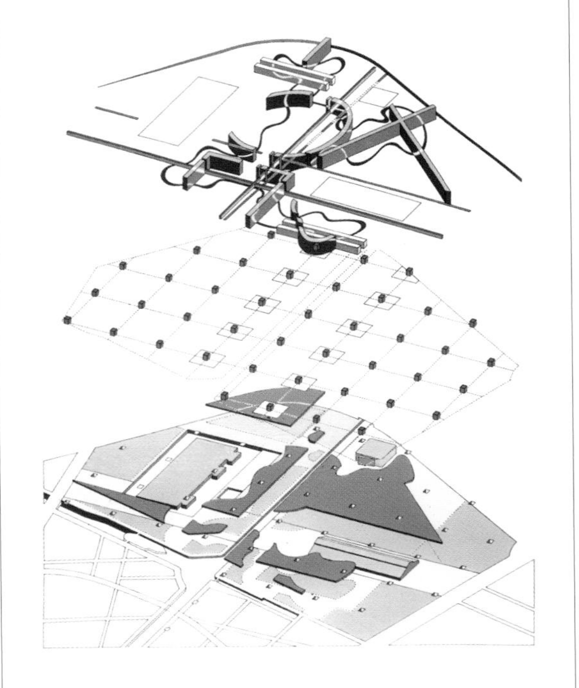

43–44
BERNARD TSCHUMI ARCHITECTS
Parc de la Villette, Paris, 1982–98, exploded axonometric projection showing project layers and site (below) and view of follies (opposite)

the placement of the follies, the lines of the paths, and the plans of the recreation areas. He wanted to create an architecture of disjunction where, through layering, the systems of the park would mutually distort and clash with one another. As Tschumi wrote:

> The Parc de la Villette project had a specific aim: to prove that it was possible to construct a complex architectural organisation without resorting to traditional rules of composition, hierarchy, and order.... if historically architecture has always been defined as the "harmonious synthesis" of cost, structure, use and formal constraints ("*venustas, firmitas, utilitas*"), the Park became architecture against itself.[19]

He encouraged the functional requirements of the follies to collide with their conceptual foundations in a way that created instability rather than synthesis, or even coherence. Tschumi had already begun to develop his ideas about the disjunction of use, form, and social values during the 1970s in various writings and projects, including *The Manhattan Transcripts* (1976–81), but La Villette was the first large-scale built realization of the architect's critical thinking. Significantly, the project also introduced the work of Derrida to a much larger audience when, in 1983, Tschumi invited Derrida to collaborate with Eisenman on the design of one of the individual gardens at La Villette.

Eisenman knew Derrida's work but had not previously met or corresponded with him. Eisenman, whose (largely theoretical) work had for some time demonstrated an interest in uncovering the hidden meanings of a particular site, often based on its history, found Derrida's work to be extremely sympathetic to his own. Eisenman saw the potential for Derrida's analytic strategies to be brought to bear on architecture. His approach to making an architecture that was a "critique of architecture"[20] is embodied in projects such as Cannaregio Town Square, Venice, Italy (1978); the Wexner Center for the Visual Arts and Fine Arts Library, Columbus, Ohio (1983–89); "Moving Arrows, Eros, and Other Errors," Verona, Italy (otherwise known as the Romeo and Juliet project), for the Third International Exhibition of Architecture, Venice Biennale (1985); and the University Art Museum of California State University at Long Beach (1986).

Indeed, the open-endedness and transferability of Derrida's ideas is what allowed them to be appropriated by architecture. Since it does not mandate a rigidly prescribed system of application but advocates multiple meanings and interpretations, deconstruction is quite adaptable

19 Bernard Tschumi, "Parc de la Villette, Paris," in *Deconstruction*, 177–80. The article originally appeared as "Deconstruction" in *Architectural Design* 58, nos. 3–4 (1988): 32–39.

20 Peter Eisenman, cited in David Lodge, "Deconstruction: A Review of the Tate Gallery Symposium," in *Deconstruction*, 90.

21 *Point de folie—maintenant l'architecture* can ne translated as "the point [as in Tschumi's point grid] of the folly—now the architecture" or more loosely, "what is the point of the folly—maintaining architecture."

22 One written document of their friendship exists in Derrida's essay "Why Peter Eisenman Writes Such Good Books," *Threshold* (spring 1988): 99–105.

in terms of its application to buildings. The notion within deconstruction of "the play of difference" was seen as a way to dismantle the ongoing dominance of modernism, yielding something that could break with or challenge established ideas about form, value, and aesthetic representation.

Tschumi's proposed collaboration between Eisenman and Derrida on La Villette marks the beginning of the architecture profession's public engagement with Derrida and the concept of deconstruction. While Eisenman and Derrida's garden for La Villette, titled Chora L Works: Project for a Garden (1985–86), was never built, drawings and writings for the project were ultimately published in book form under the same name in 1997. In addition, Derrida wrote a text on Parc de la Villette called "Point de folie—Maintenant l'architecture," which was published in *La Case Vide*, Tschumi's 1986 collection of drawings and texts related to La Villette. The titles "Chora L Works" and "Point de folie" each constitute a play on words that yields several different interpretations. Both Derrida and Eisenman favored the strategy of wordplay as a way to open up possibilities for meaning.[21]

Whether Derrida's work directly inspired or influenced Eisenman's designs is questionable, but it is clear that their intellectual exchange informed Eisenman's process of drawing out and developing abstract systems and narrative structures that were then overlaid onto a specific project and site. The Eisenman/Derrida dialogue continued for many years, manifesting itself largely through informal exchanges and communications.[22] However, the impact of their relationship was never as great as it was in the early to mid-1980s, when the lively debate and exchange of ideas around deconstruction and architecture was at its most vigorous. The debate moved from practice into schools and vice-versa, creating a sense of excitement because of its promise of a new formal vocabulary for architecture. The interest in fragmented forms that was predominant at the time had a natural place within this dialogue, but it was not until the MOMA exhibition in 1988 that the label "deconstructivist" was applied.

Parallel to Eisenman and Tschumi's involvement with Derrida and deconstruction, another related story was unfolding that would directly affect the way deconstruction was disseminated in North America. As early as 1984, the tendency toward fragmented and unstable forms was readily apparent in architectural discourse, drawing, and pedagogy. That year, Paul Florian and Stephen Wierzbowski, two young architects in charge of the exhibition program for the architecture school

at the University of Illinois at Chicago, proposed "Violated Perfection: The Meaning of the Architectural Fragment" to investigate this emerging paradigm. Though they failed to obtain funding from the National Endowment for the Arts, they did manage to establish a roster of architects for the exhibition. Aaron Betsky (then working for Gehry) offered to help find a West Coast venue for the exhibition. Independent of his efforts, Betsky proposed a similarly titled book to Rizzoli, the preeminent publisher of architectural monographs, at which time Johnson was apprised of the project and developed his own proposal for "Deconstructivist Architecture," which was rushed onto MOMA's exhibition schedule with an opening slated for June 1988.[23] Incidentally, architecture critic Joseph Giovannini had also spoken with Johnson about a book he planned to write called *The Deconstructivists*, which was never published.

Almost twenty years later, the curators' choice to contextualize the projects in the "Deconstructivist Architecture" exhibition solely through Russian Constructivism remains puzzling, especially given Wigley's expertise in the area of deconstruction and Derridean theory along with the participation (and, presumably, consultation) of Eisenman, whose commitment to deconstruction was well established. Visitors to "Deconstructivist Architecture" entered the exhibition through a red gallery filled with Russian Constructivist drawings, paintings, and sculptures from the museum's collection. By introducing visitors to the architecture projects by way of art, the curators also contextualized the architecture as artistic production, since many of the models looked more like abstract sculpture than actual buildings, and the two-dimensional works were more evocative and "artistic" than conventional sets of technical drawings. In this way, they inadvertently undermined their claim that many of the projects on view could or would be built.

Borrowing a phrase Eisenman made famous, we can speculate about the "presence of the absence" of Derrida and his thinking, but it is likely that what seems in retrospect a glaring absence was essentially a case of trying to make the difficult and complex thinking underlying many of the architectural projects more palatable and accessible to both the museum administration and the museum-going public. It is important to note that while Derrida's work on deconstruction was not the direct source of the projects on view, it certainly had a pervasive influence in architectural education and thinking in the United States and abroad at the time of the exhibition. Russian Constructivism, however, had a place both in MOMA's collections and in the public consciousness due to a number of large-scale exhibitions of Russian avant-garde art (such as the one that had been mounted in 1981 at New York's Solomon R. Guggenheim Museum featuring drawings from the collection of George Costakis). By using the framework of Russian Constructivism for the exhibition, the curators misrepresented the works on view by suggesting that they sprang from a single source:

> Other important formal influences on these designers include Russian constructivism of the mid and late 1920s (Koolhaas, Tschumi), German expressionism (Coop Himmelblau), the architecture of the 1950s (Hadid, Koolhaas), and contemporary sculpture (Gehry). Of the MOMA participants, only Coop Himmelblau, Hadid, and Libeskind are involved with the extreme fragmentation of diagonal forms—the dismantling of constructivist imagery—that curator Mark Wigley claims as a basic attribute of deconstructivism.[24]

CONCLUSION

Despite the fact that the theoretical underpinnings of "Deconstructivist Architecture" were significantly diluted by the curatorial connection to Russian Constructivism, the exhibition was a milestone both for the architects whose work was presented and for the younger generations of students and architects who went to see it. Perhaps naively, one might speculate that it enabled the public to envision the potential of architecture beyond modernism. The role of MOMA—and that of Johnson in particular—in shaping and defining architectural history through significant exhibitions cannot be underestimated. From the 1932 International Style exhibition, which imported modern architecture to America, to groundbreaking monographic exhibitions on individual architects such as Koolhaas, Neutra, and Mies van der Rohe, to the 1975 "Beaux-Arts" exhibition, MOMA has consistently given architecture an important role in the museum, thereby acknowledging its significance in the public realm. By choosing to present particular works to the public, exhibitions often serve to canonize a movement or legitimize the work of a practitioner. A museum's seal of approval elevates the work to an influential status—something to take special note of, something to discuss, an augur of things to come.

"Deconstructivist Architecture," unlike the 1932 exhibition, did not import a new architectural aesthetic to America, but it did open minds to a new way of thinking about architecture. The architectural projects included in the exhibition

23 For a full discussion of the story of how Johnson came to be the curator of the deconstructivist exhibition, see Michael Sorkin, "Canon Fodder," originally published in *The Village Voice* (1 December 1987) and reprinted in Sorkin's anthology *Exquisite Corpse: Writing on Buildings* (New York: Verso, 1991), 254–59. See also Aaron Betsky's *Violated Perfection: Architecture and the Fragmentation of the Modern* (New York: Rizzoli, 1990), which includes a wider range of projects than were featured in MOMA's deconstructivist architecture exhibition.

24 McLeod, "Architecture and Politics of the Reagan Era," 691.

were, for the most part, successful in illustrating Wigley's thesis that pure form was being disturbed. Many of the projects were unfamiliar, even unsettling, in the sense that they didn't conform to any kind of normative formal architectural vocabulary. They challenged thinking about familiar typologies such as housing, institutions, and parks. And, in many cases, the buildings themselves seemed disrupted, deranged, or put together in unusual ways. All of these qualities made the projects on view radically different from anything modern or postmodern.

The paradigm shift in architecture—caused by deconstruction and, most visibly, by the "Deconstructivist Architecture" exhibition—gave way to an unprecendented plurality in architecture, making room for multiple approaches, aesthetics, and ideologies. Since 1988, there has been no one dominant style or architectural movement. The MOMA exhibition—and, moreover, the theoretical discourse that informed and surrounded it—suggested that multiplicity and fragmentation can coexist, opening up new ways of thinking about and building the architecture the future.

45
"Deconstructivist Architecture," installation at The Museum of Modern Art, New York, 1988

PARALLEL PRACTICES: ARCHITECTS and DESIGNERS in the EXHIBITION

AZZEDINE **ALAÏA** Paris

b. 1939, Tunis, Tunisia

Azzedine Alaïa rose to prominence in the 1980s with the creation of precisely constructed, highly body-conscious women's wear that prompted architect Jean Nouvel's observation: "If there is one artist who is extremely interested in the architecture of the female form and who knows how to display it, it is Azzedine Alaïa."[1] Alaïa pioneered the use of stretchy fabrics such as Lycra—previously reserved for swimwear, sportswear, and underwear—for dresses and eveningwear. His Bandage Dresses each function like a second skin, wrapping the body closely both to define and support its shape. First conceived for stretch and knit fabrics, the dresses were later constructed in a combination of fabric and leather sewn together in an intricate web to create a sculptural feminine silhouette.

Alaïa refines the cut, drape, and construction of his garments directly on the body rather than on a dress form. While his designs may appear simple, their manufacture is complex; he manipulates the tensile properties of fabric to create shape, and a single garment may comprise as many as forty pieces of cloth sewn together to form a meshlike support for the body. Adopting the stitching and seaming used in corsetry, he applies the delicate techniques of lingerie-sewing to his garments to create structure. Refusing to follow the vagaries of the fashion world, Alaïa shows his work when he chooses and, instead of producing a new collection each season, prefers to refine existing designs.

1 Jean Nouvel, in Pamela Golbin, *Fashion Designers* (New York: Watson-Guptill, 1999), 21.

opposite: DRESS FROM **VÊTEMENTS ÉPINGLÉS** COLLECTION, SPRING/SUMMER 1987

DRESS FROM **ZIPPER KNITS** COLLECTION, SPRING/SUMMER 1997

WEDDING DRESSES FROM COLLECTION, SPRING/SUMMER 1988

BANDAGE DRESS FROM COLLECTION, SPRING/SUMMER 1988

CURTAIN WALL HOUSE, TOKYO, 1993–95

SHIGERU **BAN** ARCHITECTS Tokyo and Paris

Shigeru Ban, b. 1957, Tokyo

Shigeru Ban's architecture demonstrates his ongoing exploration of the structural properties of simple yet unusual building materials and his commitment to humanitarian and ecological issues. Ban began using paper tubes in 1986 as a structural material in an exhibition installation design. Inexpensive, easily replaceable, and low-tech, paper tubes can be made to any length and are also recyclable, with little waste produced during their manufacture. Ban explored their potential in the range of temporary shelters that he designed for earthquake victims in Japan, Turkey, and India and for more than two million Rwandan refugees. Each of the Rwandan paper-tube structures (1995–99) ingeniously uses the standard plastic sheet issued to refugees by the United Nations to form its walls and roof. Ban worked together with a paper manufacturer to devise ways to produce the tubes on site, thereby expediting the process of providing shelter and eliminating the need to transport materials from afar—in addition to addressing local deforestation issues by requiring no timber.

Playing on the idea of a glass curtain-wall structural system, Ban used the unexpected material of fabric for his Curtain Wall House (Tokyo, 1993–95), transforming conventional domestic drapery into the exterior of the building. An immense two-story fabric curtain—working in tandem with an inner series of sliding glass doors—wraps two sides of the house and, when drawn shut, provides protection from the elements and a cocoonlike sense of privacy. For Naked House (Saitama, Japan, 1999–2000), Ban created a translucent skin of corrugated–fiberglass-reinforced plastic for the warehouselike structure, echoing the greenhouses of the surrounding agricultural region. The interior of the house is an open plan that fosters a communal atmosphere for its inhabitants: three generations of the client's family.

Ban's exploration of unusual materials can also be seen in his institutional architecture. Responding to the Expo 2000's theme of sustainable development, Ban designed a recycled-paper–tube framework, covered with a skin of fiberglass-reinforced paper, for the Japan Pavilion (Hannover, Germany, 1997–2000). For the Centre Pompidou's satellite facility in Metz, France (2003–projected 2008), the architect designed an intricate woven roof structure of hexagonal wood units (made waterproof with fiberglass and Teflon) that appears to float above the exhibition spaces. Ban is working on the project in an arched-roof temporary paper-tube office (covered in the same waterproof membrane) constructed on an exterior terrace at the Centre Pompidou in Paris.

CURTAIN WALL HOUSE, TOKYO, 1993–95

PAPER EMERGENCY SHELTERS FOR THE UNITED NATIONS HIGH COMMISSIONER FOR REFUGEES, BYUMBA REFUGEE CAMP, RWANDA, 1995–99

CENTRE POMPIDOU, METZ, FRANCE, 2003–PROJECTED 2008
DIGITAL RENDERINGS OF BUILDING EXTERIOR AND FOYER INTERIOR

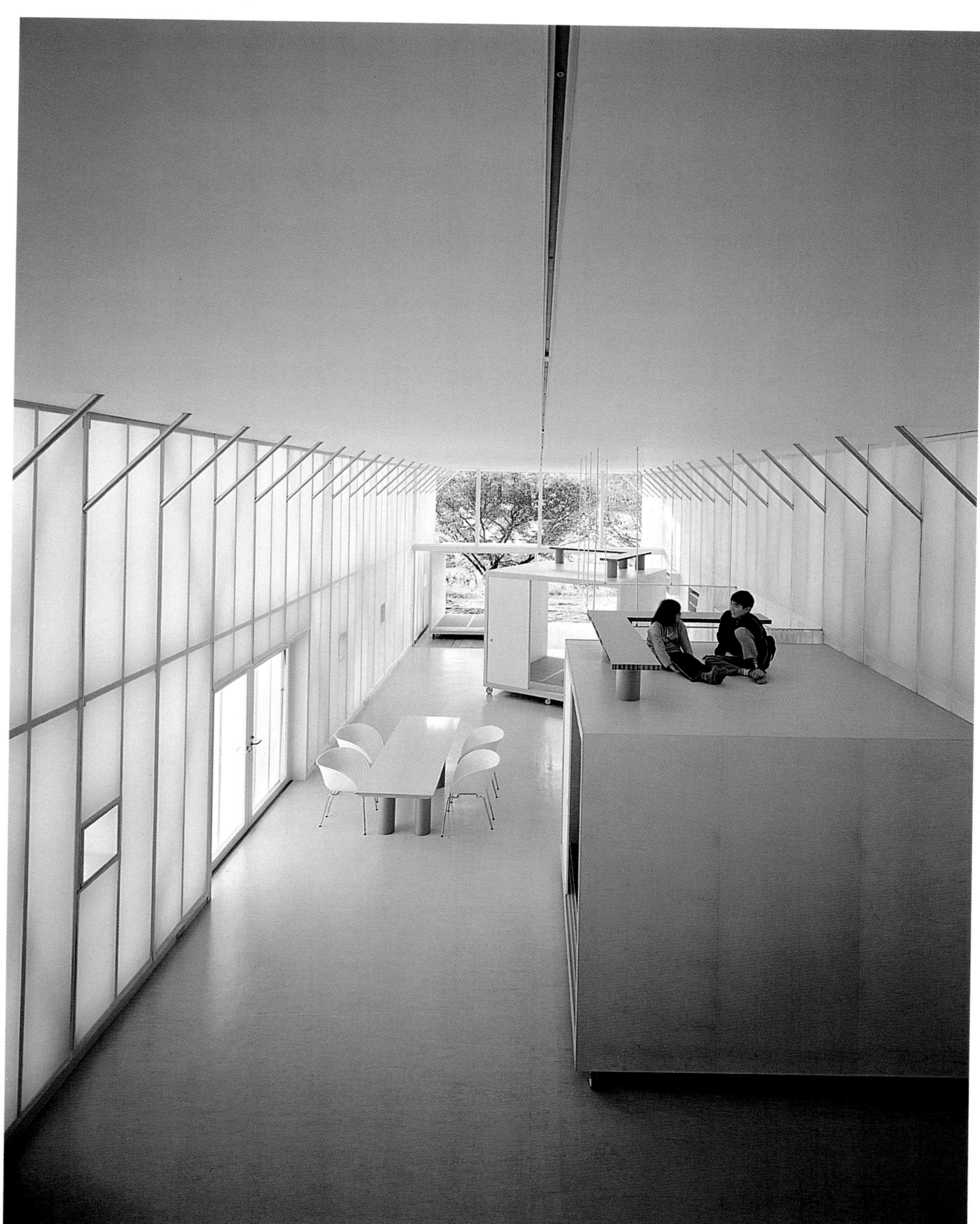

NAKED HOUSE, SAITAMA, JAPAN, 1999–2000

HUSSEIN **CHALAYAN** London

b. 1970, Nicosia, Cyprus

Hussein Chalayan is known for cerebral collections that, especially in the context of the performances he stages to present his work, are more connected to the art world than to commercial fashion. Inspired by nature, culture, and technology, his designs reveal an ongoing preoccupation with issues related to his experiences as a Turkish Cypriot living abroad and to the wider realms of religion, cultural identity, and migration. For Between (spring/summer 1998), Chalayan dressed a group of models in chadors, varying the length of each to progressively reveal their bodies until only a face was left veiled. Afterwords (autumn/winter 2000–01) explored the idea of having to flee home in times of strife. The collection was presented in a domestic tableau that included chairs and a coffee table; models entered the setting and converted the furnishings into garments for themselves—the chairs were transformed into suitcases and their slipcovers worn as dresses, and the coffee table became a dramatic telescoping skirt. Chalayan experiments with unusual materials such as Tyvek and fiberglass to create protective enclosures for the female body that are sometimes functional (as in the Aeroplane [autumn/winter 1999–2000] and Mechanical [spring/summer 2000] Dresses) and sometimes decorative (as in his shaved tulle dresses).

CONVERTIBLE SKIRT/TABLE FROM **AFTERWORDS** COLLECTION, AUTUMN/WINTER 2000–01

SHAVED TULLE DRESS FROM **BEFORE MINUS NOW** COLLECTION, SPRING/SUMMER 2000

opposite, top row and bottom right: **MECHANICAL DRESS** FROM **BEFORE MINUS NOW** COLLECTION, SPRING/SUMMER 2000
opposite, bottom left: **AEROPLANE DRESS** FROM **ECHOFORM** COLLECTION, AUTUMN/WINTER 1999–2000
following spread: GARMENTS FROM **BETWEEN** COLLECTION, SPRING/SUMMER 1998

PRESTON SCOTT **COHEN** Cambridge, Massachusetts

b. 1961, Asheville, North Carolina

Complex geometry is at the core of Preston Scott Cohen's architecture. Cohen's work with difficult sites, programmatic constraints, and spatial configurations has resulted in a formal virtuosity that is evident in projects such as the Cornered House (unbuilt, 1991), Torus House (unbuilt, 1998–2000), and Tel Aviv Museum of Art (2003–projected 2008). Each new project develops out of an elaborate ongoing investigation into geometry's potential to reshape architectural language. His repertoire of three-dimensional architectural forms is based on familiar building types distorted by oblique projections.

Cohen's work has evolved from early projects in which intricate hand-drawn geometric projections remarkably foreshadow computer-generated forms to large-scale projects, in which the complex layers of the design demand new approaches to engineering and construction. For Cornered House in Longboat Key, Florida, Cohen employed projective geometry in rethinking the iconic American suburban dwelling; various elements, such as the pediment and hipped roofline, overlap or mutate to produce folded surfaces that wrap the volume of the house, appearing to flatten and elongate it. In Torus House, designed for a landscape painter on a site in Old Chatham, New York, the orthogonal features of the building—floor, walls, and ceiling—are connected to each other by a curvilinear form that alludes to the torus, a doughnut shape generated by revolving a circle along a coplanar axis. Thus, the orthogonal features seem part of a single undulating surface, and the interior of the house effects continuity with the surrounding hills.[1]

In 2003, as the result of an international competition, Cohen received the commission to design a new building for the Tel Aviv Museum of Art. The 180,000-square-foot structure is organized around a synthesis of oblique lines and hyperbolic parabolas. Twisting façades define a perambulatory sequence around and into the museum, while inside an extraordinary spiraling atrium pulls light into gallery spaces three stories below the ground. The building's discontinuous planes, which are actually aligned according to independent axes, resolve the difference between the idiosyncratic triangular site and the flexible rectangular galleries within. In essence, Cohen's work is a fusion of Baroque and modern conceptions of architectural space that produces uniquely contemporary buildings.

1 Preston Scott Cohen, *Contested Symmetries and Other Predicaments in Architecture* (New York: Princeton Architectural Press, 2001), 138.

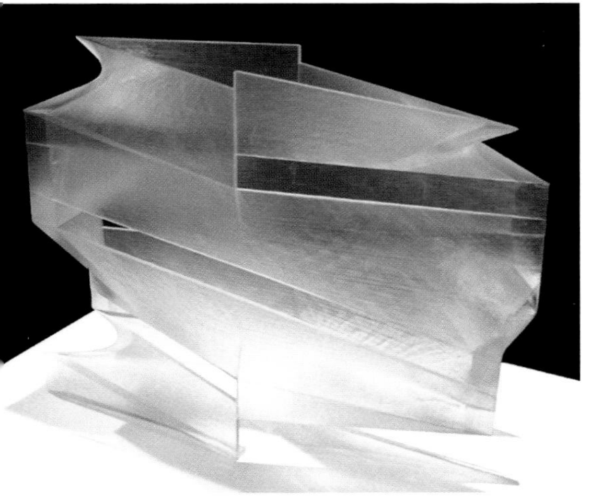

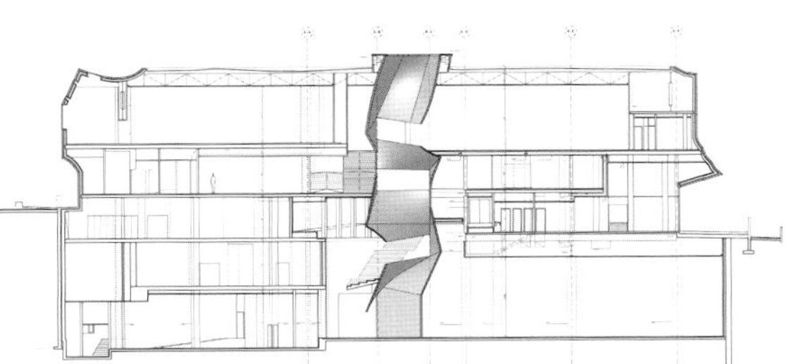

TEL AVIV MUSEUM OF ART, TEL AVIV, 2003–PROJECTED 2008

opposite and top left: DIGITAL RENDERINGS OF ATRIUM;
top right, center row, and bottom right: MODELS; bottom left: SECTION

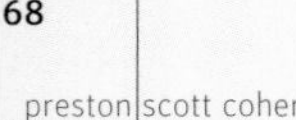

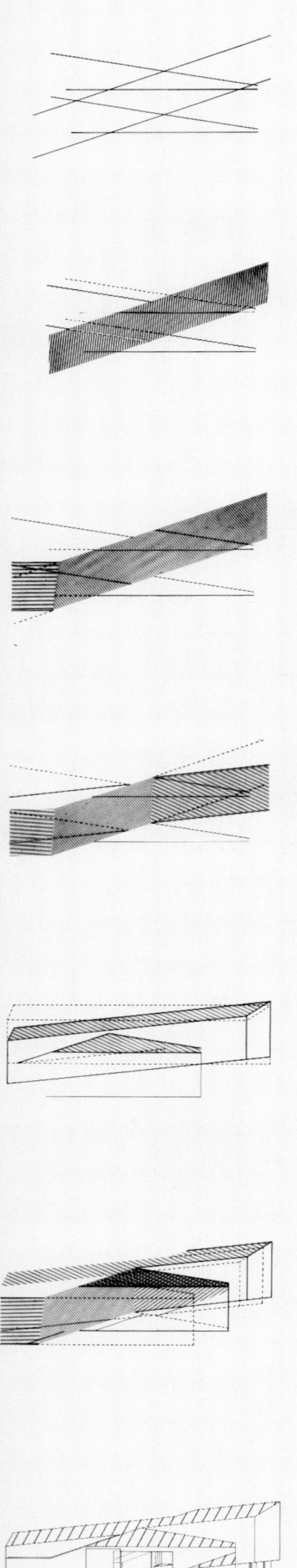

above and opposite: **TORUS HOUSE** (UNBUILT), OLD CHATHAM, NEW YORK, 1998–2000
DIGITAL RENDERINGS OF INTERIOR AND SECTIONAL MODEL

CORNERED HOUSE (UNBUILT), LONGBOAT KEY, FLORIDA, 1991, DIAGRAMS AND MODEL

COMME DES GARÇONS Tokyo

Rei Kawakubo, b. 1942, Tokyo

Since establishing Comme des Garçons in 1969, visionary designer Rei Kawakubo has consistently turned conventional notions of gender, beauty, and clothes-making upside down. Comme des Garçons' first Paris presentation in 1981 was a collection comprising mostly shapeless, tattered black garments—a dramatic counterpoint to the conventionally tailored designs seen on 1980s runways. Kawakubo has continued to create iconoclastic pieces characterized by asymmetry, sculptural forms, and clever combinations of fabric layered, wrapped, or draped in unusual ways. While taking inspiration from a range of disparate and unconventional sources such as a frog, a starkly graphic drawing of a crow, and a crumpled pillow, her designs manage to retain elements of classical form, such as the shape of a bodice or the cut of a jacket. For Body Meets Dress, Dress Meets Body (spring/summer 1997), Kawakubo distorted and deformed the silhouette of the female body by padding garments in unexpected places to create soft protuberances and bumps. The Adult Punk (Demolition and Reconstruction) collection (autumn/winter 1997–98) features conventional shapes taken apart and reconstructed with sheer or patterned-fabric insets. For Clustering Beauty (spring/summer 1998), the designer explored techniques of folding, pleating, draping, and ruching in neutral muslins to create sculptural forms. In both Fusion (autumn/winter 1998–99) and New Essential (spring/summer 1999), Kawakubo tweaked and disrupted simple silhouettes such as a skirt, by removing half, or a jacket, by making it appear half-finished—one side fully constructed, the other just a sleeveless lining. For Excellent Abstract (spring/summer 2004), Kawakubo chose to focus on skirts, creating startling shapes cut in circles or trefoils with inset strips to give the skirts structure and cause them to cantilever away from the body, underlining her guiding principle that a garment, like a building, is essentially a spatial construction.

GARMENTS FROM **CLUSTERING BEAUTY** COLLECTION, SPRING/SUMMER 1998

GARMENTS FROM **FUSION** COLLECTION, AUTUMN/WINTER 1998–99

GARMENTS FROM **NEW ESSENTIAL** COLLECTION, SPRING/SUMMER 1999

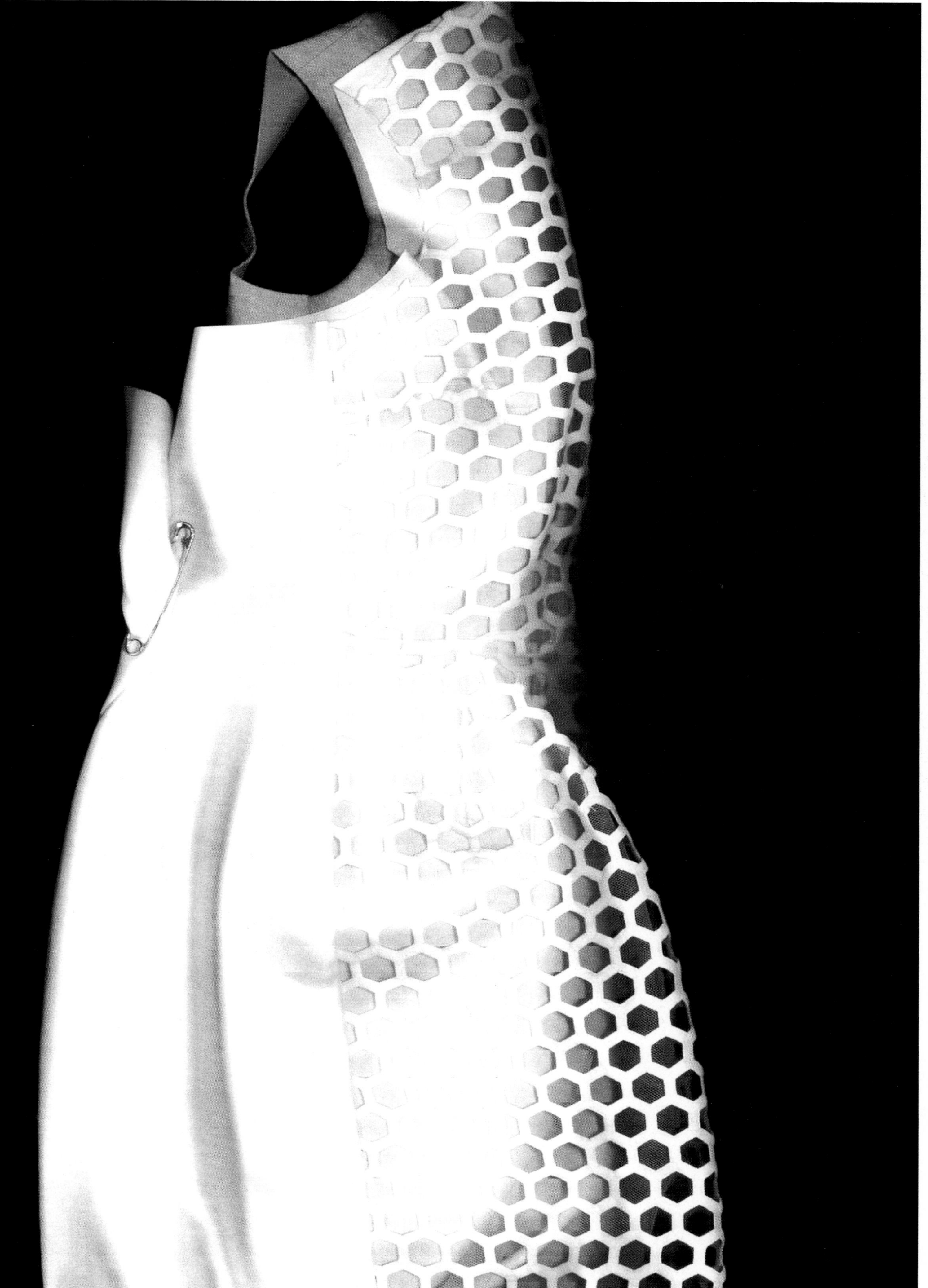

opposite: GARMENTS FROM **BEYOND TABOO** COLLECTION, AUTUMN/WINTER 2001–02
above: GARMENTS FROM **HARD AND FORCEFUL** COLLECTION, AUTUMN/WINTER 2000–01
below: GARMENTS FROM **ENFORCEMENT** COLLECTION, SPRING/SUMMER 2000

following spread: GARMENTS FROM **BODY MEETS DRESS, DRESS MEETS BODY** COLLECTION, SPRING/SUMMER 1997

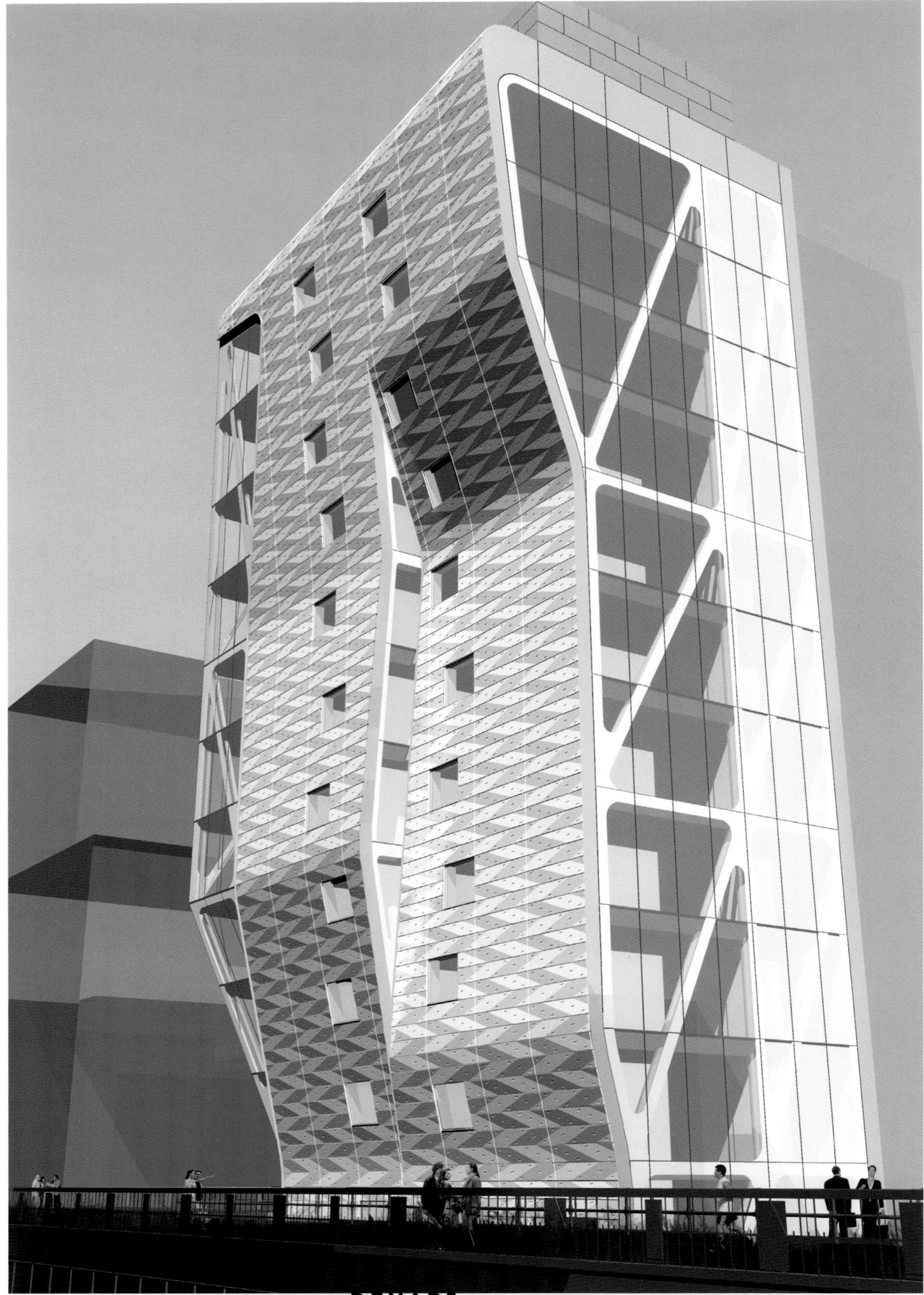

NEIL M. **DENARI** ARCHITECTS Los Angeles

Neil M. Denari, b. 1957, Fort Worth, Texas

Since its founding in 1988, Neil M. Denari Architects (NMDA) has been recognized as a leader in the use of computer-aided architectural design. A deep interest in new technology has consistently characterized the work of the studio, from Neil M. Denari's early independent projects that translated machinelike forms into buildings to the firm's more recent work, which strives for a "cultural ergonomics" ("those forms that 'fit' our contemporary life"[1]) to generate expressive, fluid architecture. NMDA's interest in incorporating a sense of movement into each building is seen in dynamic interior spaces and sensual exterior surfaces that shift, curve, bend, fold, and unfold, challenging the conventional idea that architecture is a contained orthogonal form or box.

High Line 23 Condominium Tower (2005–projected 2007) is a thirteen-story mixed-use building located on a narrow site adjacent to Manhattan's High Line, a twenty-two-block–long disused elevated railway bed that is being transformed into an urban park. The mass of NMDA's slim building, which will house ground-floor gallery spaces and twelve condominium loft apartments (one per floor), was determined by both its proximity to the High Line and New York City's zoning laws and setback requirements. The exterior skin of High Line 23 gives the building the appearance of being partially dressed. On the east façade, which faces the High Line, an opaque skin of stainless-steel panels with a repeated pattern of elongated diamond shapes conforms to the undulating folds of the building's cantilevered skeleton and is punctuated by small windows, allowing for privacy and framed views of the city. The entire south façade is left exposed, an expanse of clear glass that provides light and views for the main living areas of each loft unit. By covering and uncovering certain parts of the building, High Line 23's stylish skin functions like a piece of clothing to conceal or shelter its inhabitants while also partially revealing what is underneath.

1 Neil M. Denari Architects, firm profile, http://www.nmda-inc.com.

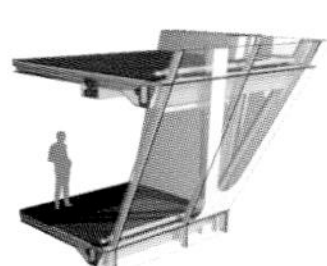
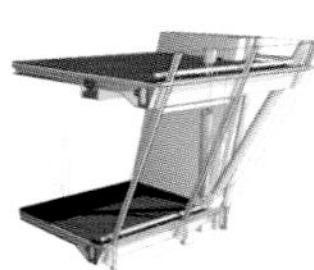

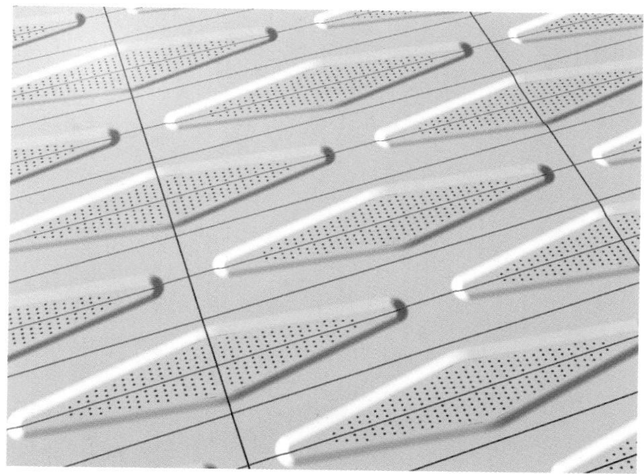

HIGH LINE 23 CONDOMINIUM TOWER, NEW YORK, 2005–PROJECTED 2007

DIGITAL RENDERINGS

opposite: EAST AND NORTH FAÇADES

left column: PROJECTIONS SHOWING RELATIONSHIP OF SKIN TO INTERIOR

right column: ELEVATION AND DETAIL OF SKIN

bottom row: SECTIONS AND ELEVATION

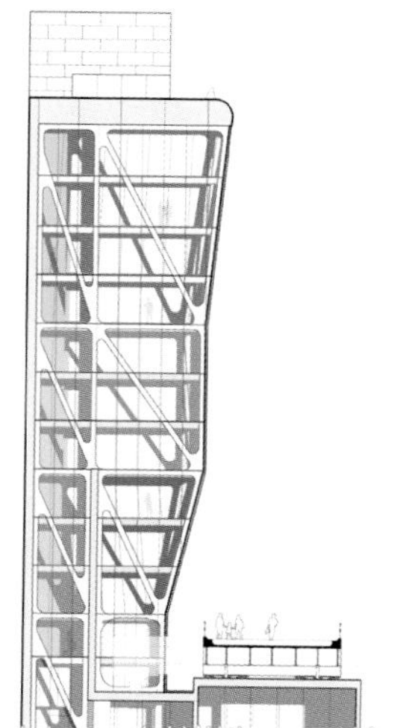
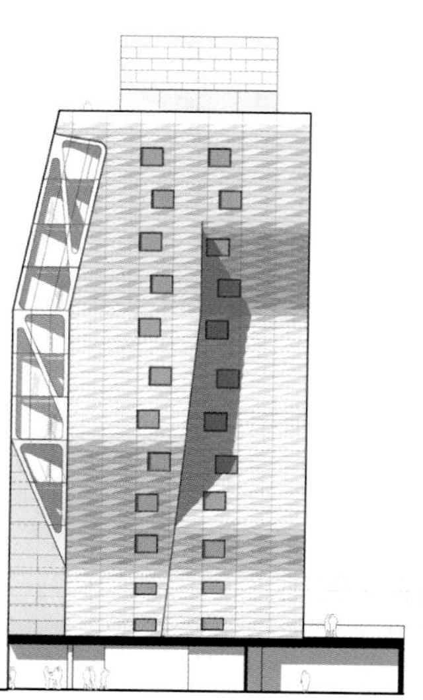
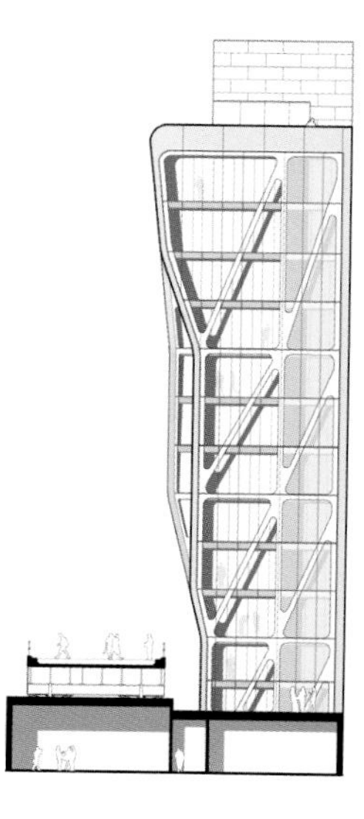

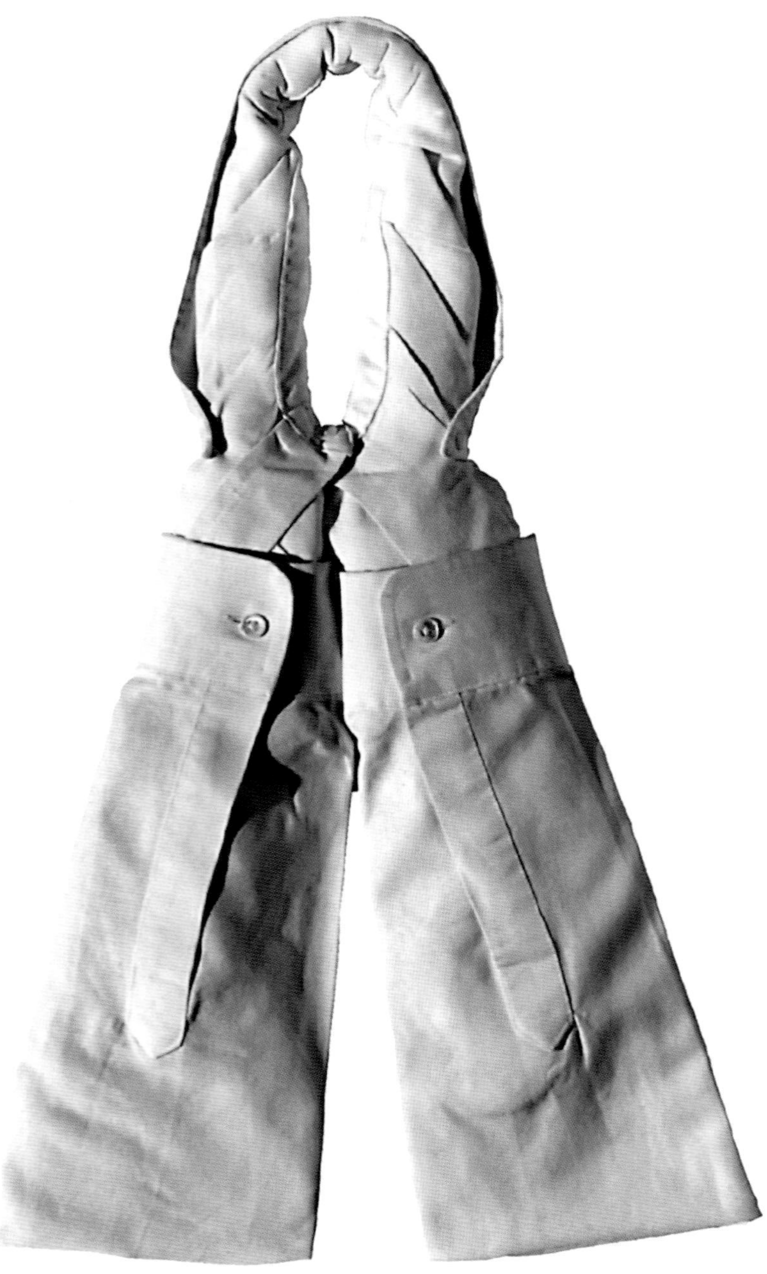

DILLER SCOFIDIO + RENFRO New York

Elizabeth Diller, b. 1954, Lodz, Poland Ricardo Scofidio, b. 1935, New York Charles Renfro, b. 1964, Houston

The work of Diller Scofidio + Renfro operates between architectural design, performance, and conceptual art. Since the founding of their joint practice in 1979, Elizabeth Diller and Ricardo Scofidio have worked with new materials and construction processes to create intellectually grounded pieces that challenge notions of functionality in architecture. Charles Renfro, who has been with the firm since 1997, became a partner in 2004.

Bad Press: Dissident Housework Series (1993–98), an installation project initially created for a 1993 exhibition at Richard Anderson Gallery, New York, exemplifies their conceptual work: eighteen men's white dress shirts were deformed into various configurations of origami-like folds through a process of "mis-ironing," thereby disrupting the idea of domestic maintenance and freeing the task of ironing from the aesthetics of order.

The firm's architectural work frequently addresses issues of enclosure. For the Institute of Contemporary Art on Boston's Fan Pier (2002–06), vertical sheets of transparent glass, translucent glass, and opaque metal form a continuous external skin that blurs the distinction between walls, windows, and doors. Similarly, for the Alice Tully Hall Renovation, New York (2005–projected 2008), the auditorium walls house an innovative house lighting system, with illumination emerging from the seamless surface of translucent, custom-molded resin panels sheathed in a blood-red wood veneer.

The Blur Building, built for Swiss Expo 2002, confounds traditional notions of what constitutes enclosure. The building was essentially a "tensegrity" structural system that rests on piles on Lake Neuchâtel in Yverdon-les-Bains. 31,500 nozzles placed throughout the framework sprayed a fine mist of water pumped from the lake, creating an enormous cloud that both "enclosed" and was the building. Through a computer that monitored the weather, the Blur Building continuously changed form in response to climatic variations. The architects originally envisioned that visitors would wear Brain-Coats, or "smart" raincoats that would be programmed with each wearer's personality profile. A central computer would then compare profiles, changing coat colors to indicate potential affinity or antipathy as visitors encountered one another, thereby fostering impromptu meetings and connections in the building's foggy environment.

BAD PRESS: DISSIDENT HOUSEWORK SERIES, 1993–98

DETAILS OF CUSTOM-IRONED SHIRTS AND VIEW OF INSTALLATION AT THE WHITNEY MUSEUM OF AMERICAN ART, NEW YORK, 2003

following spread: **ALICE TULLY HALL RENOVATION**, LINCOLN CENTER, NEW YORK, 2005–PROJECTED 2008

DIGITAL RENDERINGS OF INTERIOR VIEWS AND DETAILS

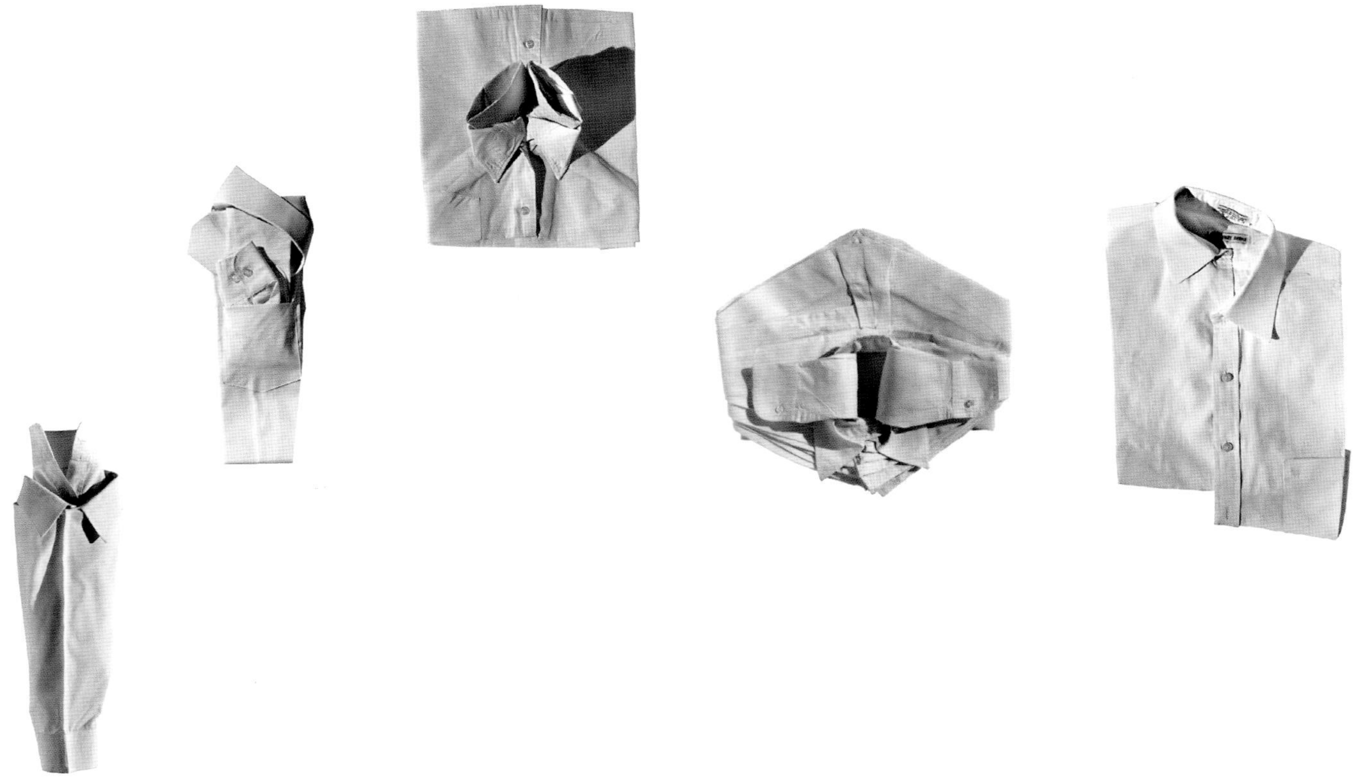

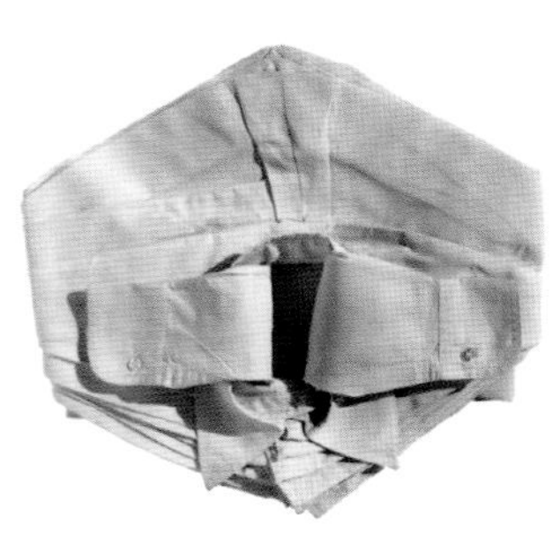

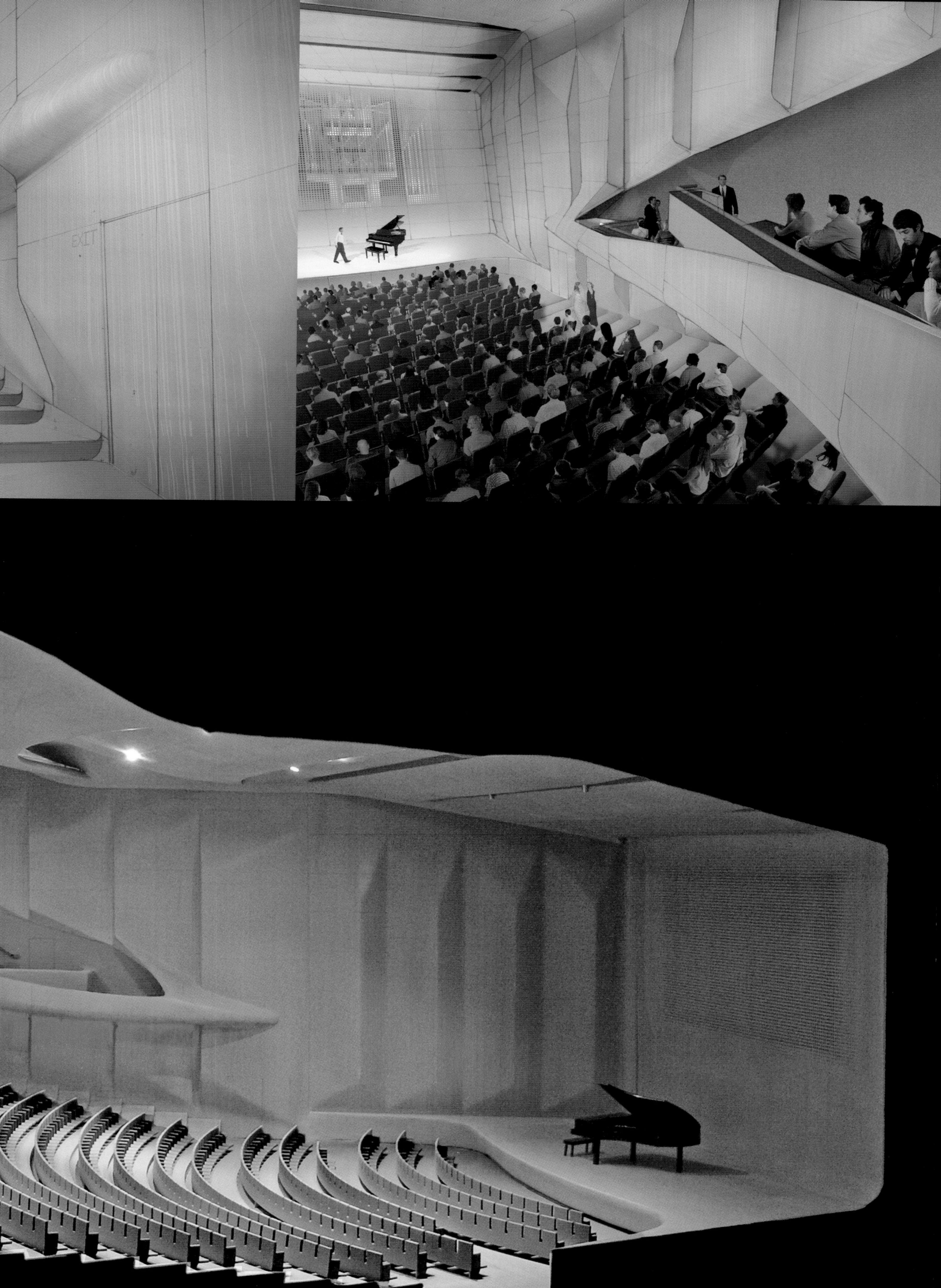

INSTITUTE OF CONTEMPORARY ART, BOSTON, 2002–06; DIGITAL RENDERINGS OF INTERIOR AND EXTERIOR

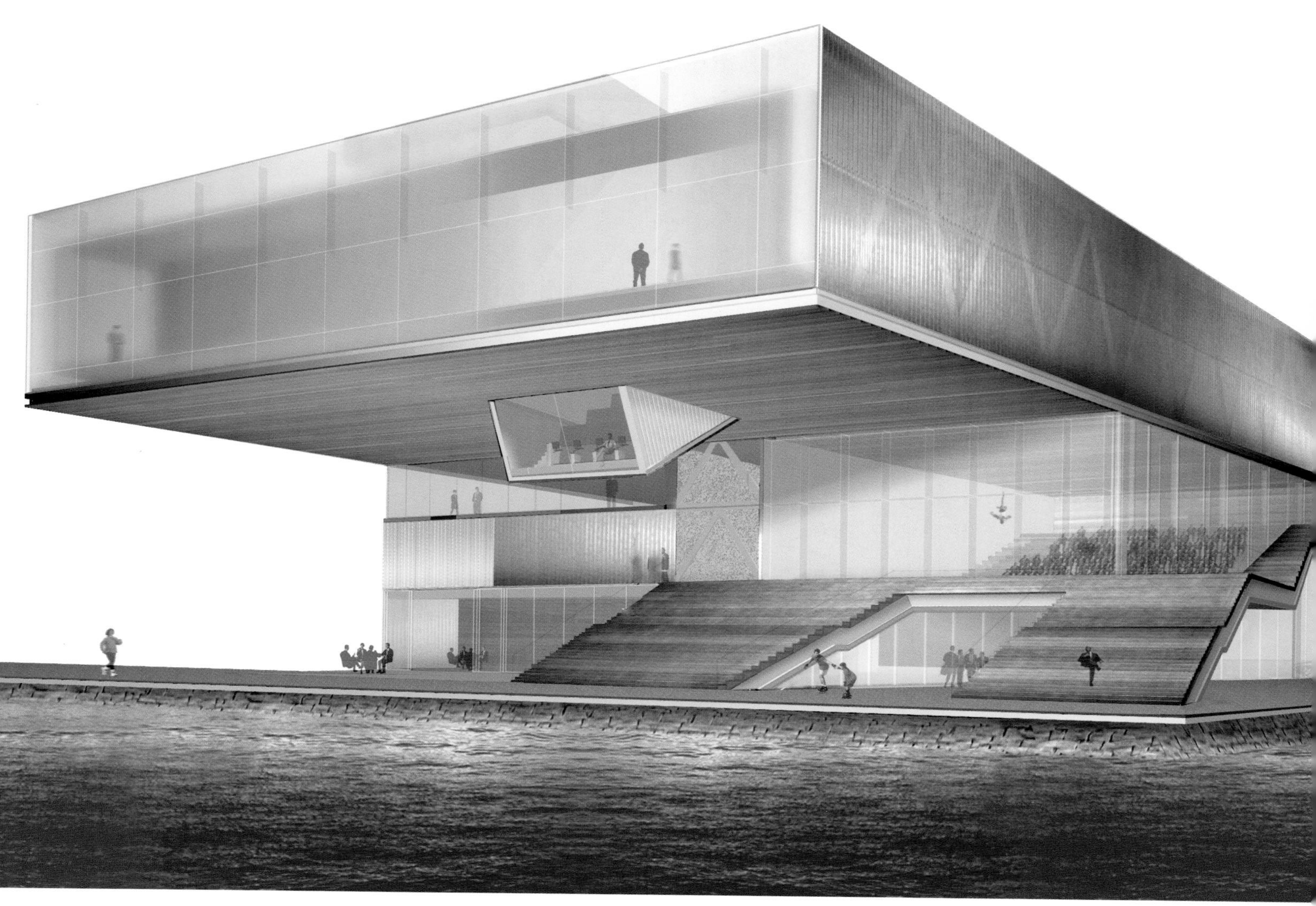

BLUR BUILDING, SWISS EXPO 2002, YVERDON-LES-BAINS, SWITZERLAND, 2002

WINKA DUBBELDAM/ARCHI-TECTONICS New York

Winka Dubbeldam, b. 1960, Strijen, The Netherlands

Winka Dubbeldam's Greenwich Street Project (2000–04), located at the edge of New York's SoHo district, is a renovation of a six-story brick warehouse with an addition of a four-story penthouse that extends next door, where it becomes part of a new eleven-story residential loft building. The hallmark of the project is the new building's dramatic crystalline façade of insulated glass panels, which form a horizontally pleated skin that subverts the traditional flat surface of the modernist glass curtain wall. A vertical crease in the façade creates a transitional zone between the steel-and-glass and brick structures. The crease is studded with cantilevered balconies, allowing the building to meet setback requirements mandated by the New York City building code while juxtaposing the new and the old, the urban and the private. Three-dimensional modeling software facilitated the complex design of the undulating façade. The blue-green glass panels—which actually bend where the façade "pleats"—were fabricated in Barcelona according to two-dimensional shop drawings that were derived directly from a three-dimensional computer model.

After completing her undergraduate studies at the Academy of Architecture in Rotterdam, The Netherlands, Dubbeldam relocated to New York City in 1991 to pursue a master's degree in advanced architectural design at Columbia University. As the principal of her New York–based firm Archi-Tectonics (founded in 1994), Dubbeldam is committed to integrating theoretical and functional aspects of architecture in her practice. Archi-Tectonics specializes in creating projects through a team-based laboratory approach that converts high-tech research into innovative built work using cutting-edge software, hybrid materials, and "smart" building systems. The firm's Maashaven project in Rotterdam (unbuilt, 1999–2002), aspires to revitalize the city's harbor site through the ambitious conversion of a grain-silo into office and living spaces and the construction of three apartment towers with folded-glass skins that are cantilevered from the pier's edge.

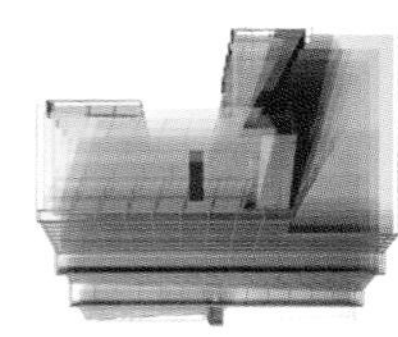

GREENWICH STREET PROJECT, NEW YORK, 2000–04

opposite: EXTERIOR; top: EXPLODED SECTIONAL DIAGRAM SHOWING BUILDING ELEMENTS; bottom: TRANSVERSE SECTION
right column: CUTAWAY DIAGRAMS SHOWING RELATIONSHIP OF INTERIOR TO SKIN

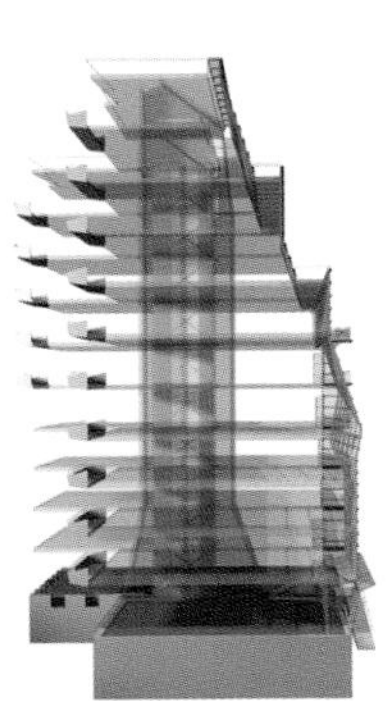

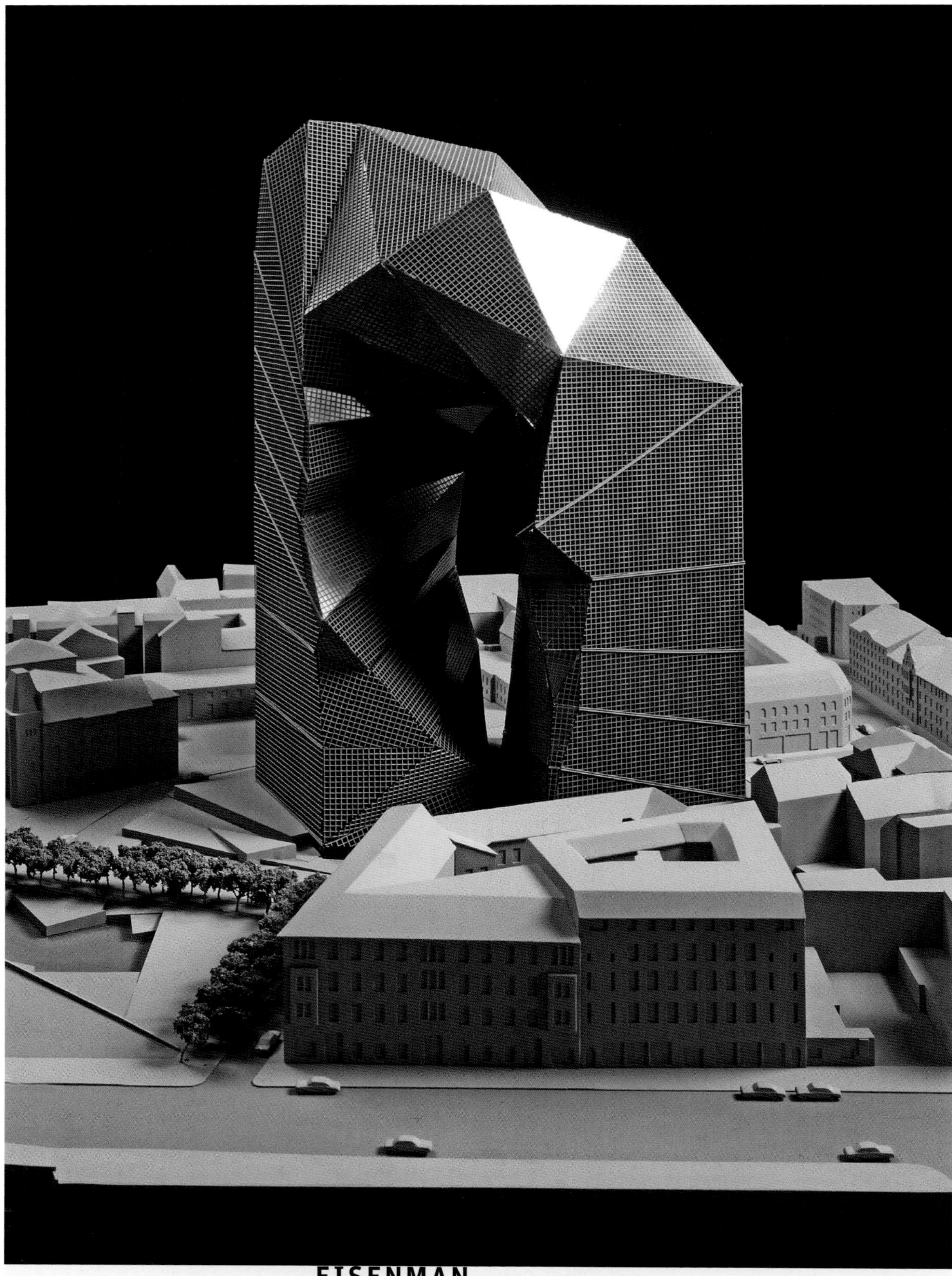

EISENMAN ARCHITECTS New York

Peter Eisenman, b. 1932, Newark

Over the course of a career spanning thirty years as a teacher, writer, theorist, and architect, Peter Eisenman has approached design by considering the physical and cultural layers of each project's site. For Chora L Works: Project for a Garden (unbuilt, 1985–86), Eisenman collaborated with Jacques Derrida on a garden design for Bernard Tschumi's Parc de la Villette in Paris (1982–98). Eisenman devised a system of superpositions by overlaying the grids of four projects—his own earlier but parallel redevelopment proposal for the Cannaregio section of Venice, Italy (unbuilt, 1978); Tschumi's La Villette; and each of the slaughterhouses that historically occupied the Cannaregio and La Villette sites—to reveal "reverberations…not only in scale but time."[1] Inspired by Plato's description of *chora*, Derrida proposed "a gilded object that would resemble at once a web, a sieve, or a grille [grid], and a stringed musical instrument," which was architecturally translated as "an inclined and striated object reflecting, at a smaller scale, the outline of the site."[2]

Eisenman's master plan for a large-scale residential/commercial development in Frankfurt's Rebstockpark (unbuilt, 1990–91) uses the idea of the "fold" as set forth by chaos-theorist René Thom and philosopher Gilles Deleuze's examination of Gottfried Leibniz's monad. Using a series of grids to generate form on the scale of both individual buildings and the overall site, Eisenman sought to project "new social organizations into an existing urban environment."[3] For Max Reinhardt Haus (unbuilt, 1992–93), a thirty-four–story mixed-use tower proposed for Berlin, Eisenman explored the idea of folding in a vertical orientation. Starting with the form of a Möbius strip, which can be seen as symbolizing the then newly reunified city, he transformed the shape through a series of iterative operations to create the complex prismatic form of two faceted towers joined by a twisting arch.

1 Peter Eisenman, in Jean-François Bédard, ed., *Cities of Artificial Excavation: The Work of Peter Eisenman, 1978–1988*, exh. cat. (Montréal: Centre Canadien d'Architecture; and New York: Rizzoli, 1994), 187.

2 Bédard, in ibid., 194.

3 Eisenman, "Unfolding Events: Frankfurt Rebstock and the Possibility of a New Urbanism," in *Unfolding Frankfurt*, exh. cat. (Berlin: Ernst & Sohn, 1991), 17.

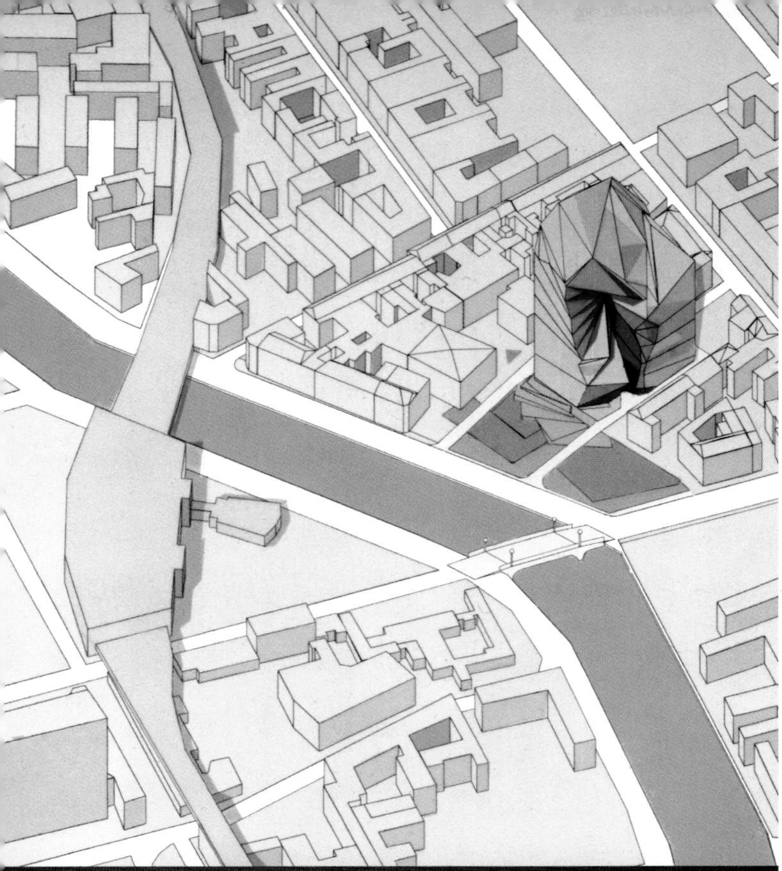

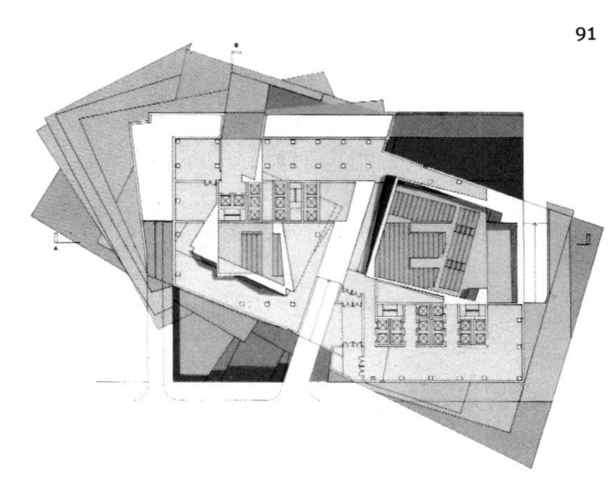

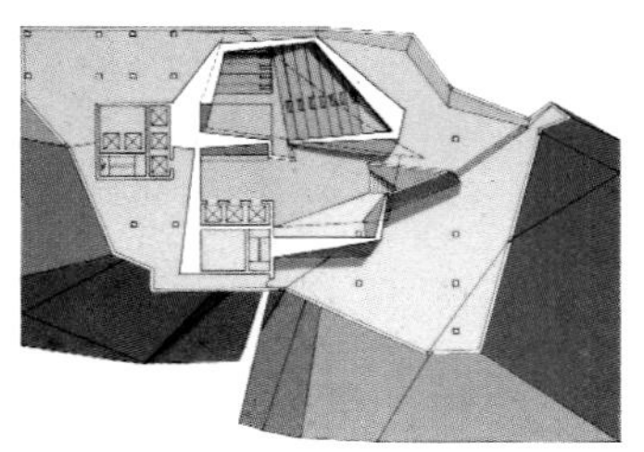

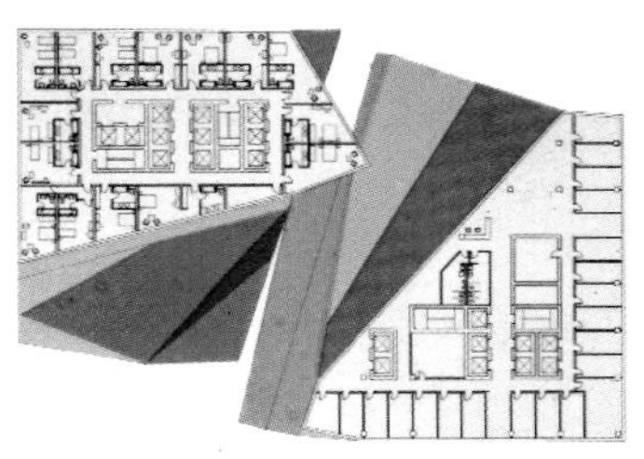

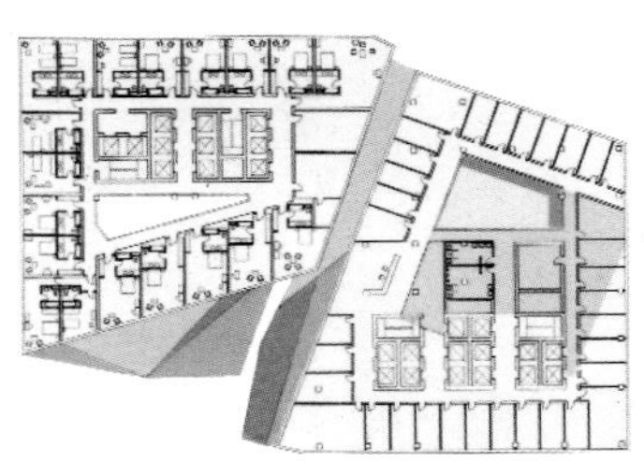

MAX REINHARDT HAUS (UNBUILT), BERLIN, 1992–93

opposite: MODEL; top left: AXONOMETRIC SITE PLAN; above left: MODEL; right column and below: PLANS AND SECTIONS

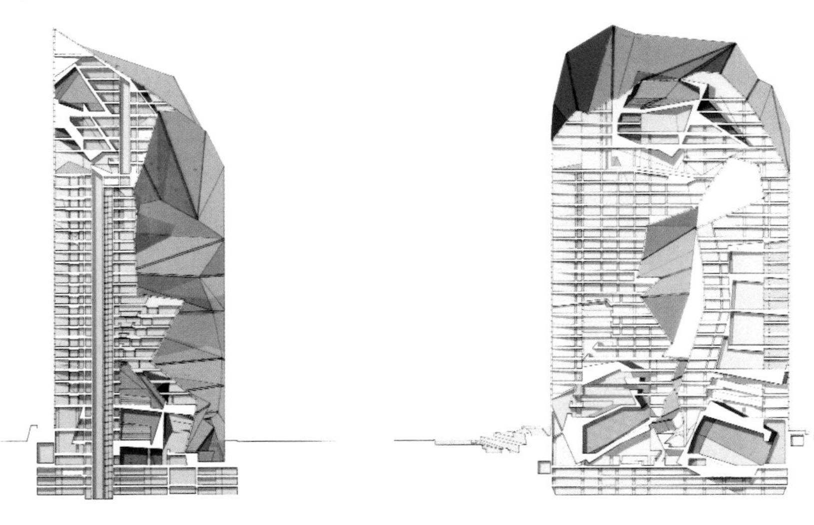

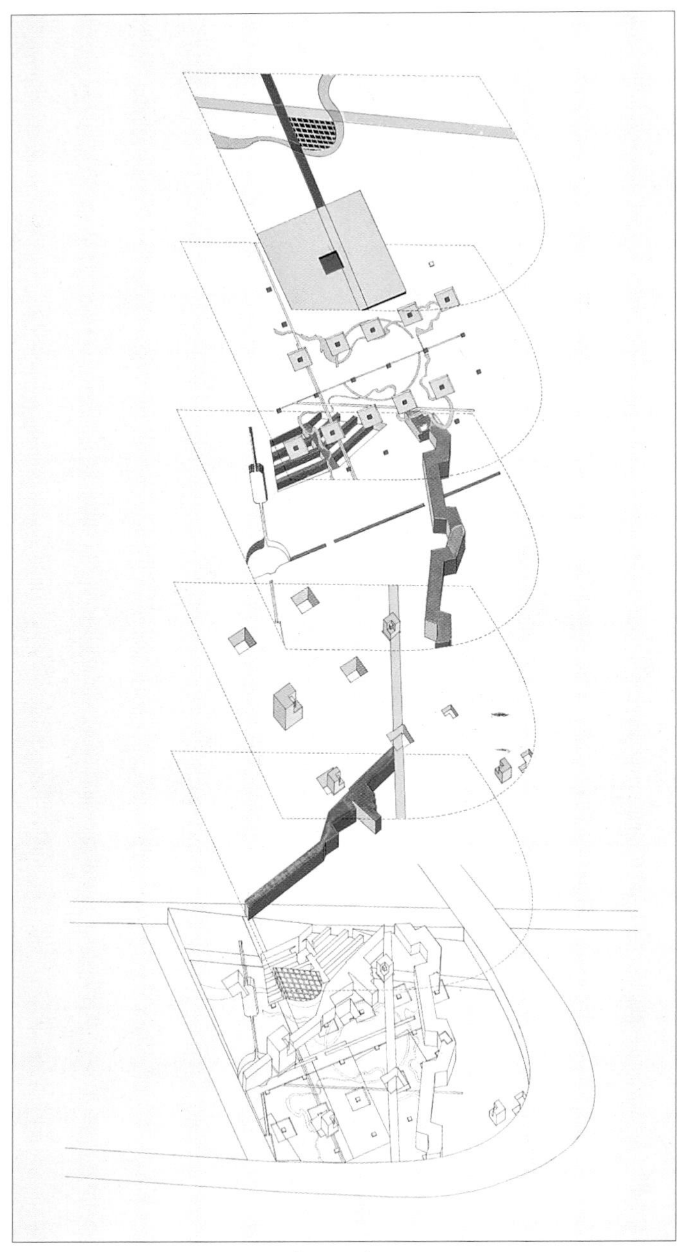

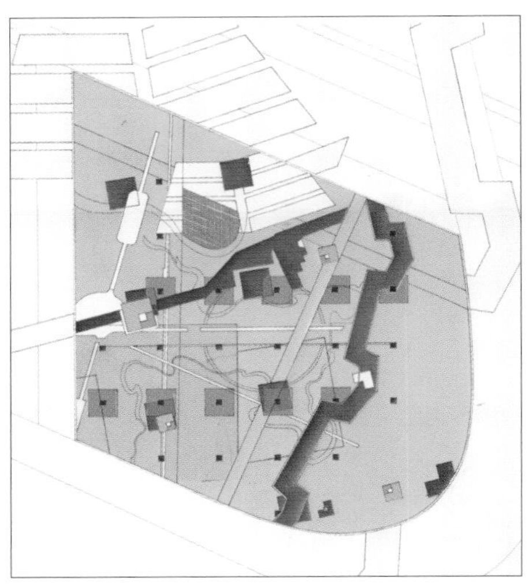

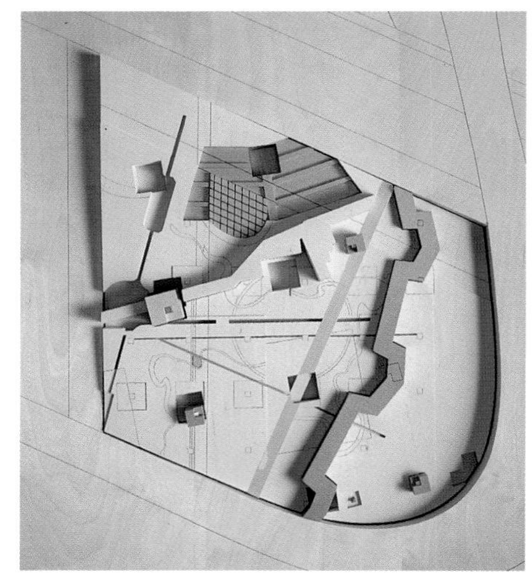

CHORA L WORKS: PROJECT FOR A GARDEN (UNBUILT), PARC DE LA VILLETTE, PARIS, 1985–86

above: EXPLODED AXONOMETRIC PROJECTION

right column, top to bottom: SITE PLAN, MODEL OF FIRST SCHEME, AND MODEL OF SECOND SCHEME

REBSTOCKPARK (UNBUILT), FRANKFURT, GERMANY, 1990–91

above: PERSPECTIVE VIEW OF OFFICE BLOCK; below: MASTER PLAN AND CONCEPT DIAGRAMS

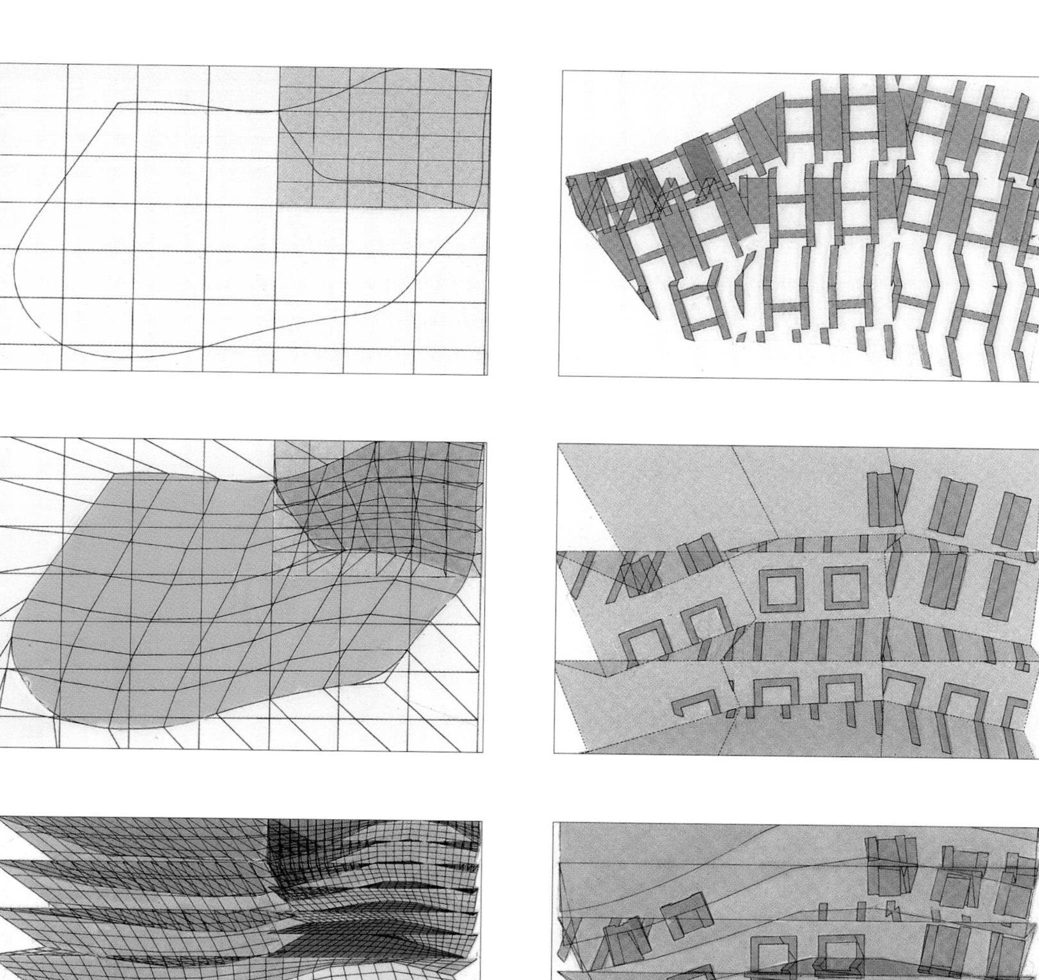

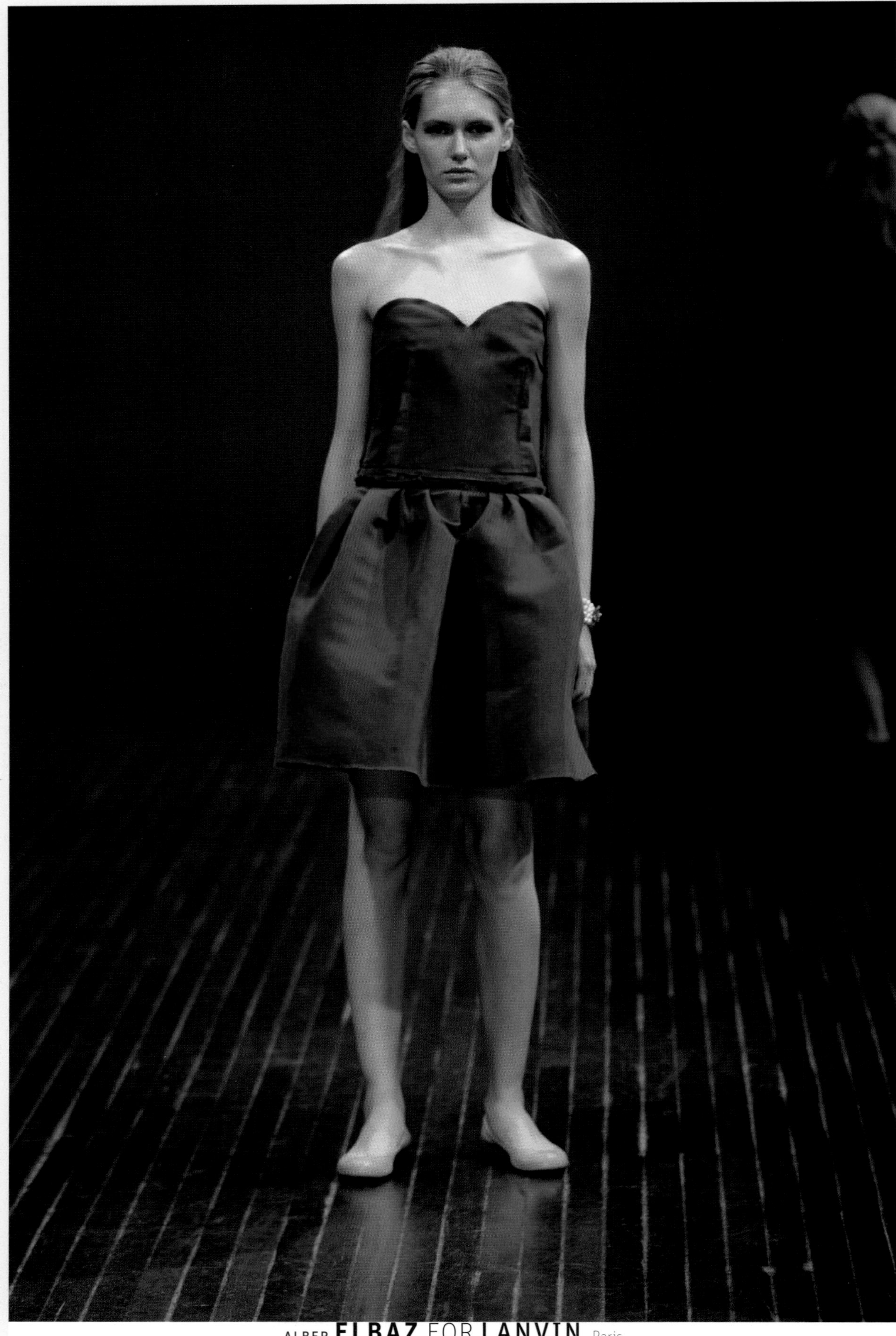

ALBER **ELBAZ** FOR **LANVIN** Paris

Alber Elbaz, b. 1961, Casablanca, Morocco

Alber Elbaz's garments are characterized by complexity, precision, and attention to detail. After working as head designer at Yves Saint Laurent, Elbaz was hired in 2001 as creative director of Lanvin, the French fashion house founded by Jeanne Lanvin just prior to the outbreak of World War I. Since then, Elbaz has modernized Lanvin's repertoire, designing garments in classic materials such as satin ribbon, Chantilly lace, and fine silk and taffeta and contemporizing them with raw edges, exposed zippers, and ribbed jersey trim. Elbaz is known for his mastery of complicated technical challenges such as fluting, pleating, and seamless draping—many of which he learned during the seven years he worked under designer Geoffrey Beene. (It has been said that his garments are so well constructed and finished they could be worn inside out.)

Elbaz once explained: "perfection is never interesting to me, but the search for perfection...is interesting."[1] Rather than pursue perfection for its own sake, he combines a highly refined technical ability with certain self-consciously unrefined details—like the raw edges—that add unexpected visual interest and a sense of open-endedness to the garments. Classical forms and opulent materials are often combined with industrial fasteners. For his autumn/winter 2006–07 collection, the designer focused on shape and proportion, presenting tent dresses, swing-back coats, pantsuits, and skirts with padding at the hip that reference the work of twentieth-century fashion-design icons Cristobal Balenciaga, Christian Dior, Yves Saint Laurent, and Elsa Schiaparelli.

1 Alber Elbaz, in Lynn Hirschberg, "The Classicist," *The New York Times Magazine* (25 September 2005): 35.

opposite: DRESS FROM COLLECTION, SPRING/SUMMER 2005

top left: DRESS FROM COLLECTION, AUTUMN/WINTER 2003–04

bottom left and center column: GARMENTS FROM COLLECTION, SPRING/SUMMER 2004, FRONT AND BACK VIEWS

right column: DRESS FROM COLLECTION, AUTUMN/WINTER 2006–07, FRONT AND BACK VIEWS

FOREIGN OFFICE ARCHITECTS London

Farshid Moussavi, b. 1965, Shiraz, Iran Alejandro Zaera-Polo, b. 1963, Madrid

Farshid Moussavi and Alejandro Zaera-Polo founded Foreign Office Architects (FOA) in 1992. In 1995, the husband-and-wife team won the international design competition for the Yokohama International Port Terminal (1995–2002) in Japan. A study of how circulation can shape space, the building challenges the traditional departure/arrival orientation of the cruise-ship terminal with its structure of interlaced, ribbon-like looping ramps that provide multiple paths for cars and pedestrians. The active roof surface of undulating "dunes" (made of wood planks) and green space echoes the origami-like folds of the interior, which is rather cave-like and features warped concave floor surfaces (also made of wood planks) and a crisply pleated ceiling.

FOA's theoretical project Virtual House (1997) was commissioned for a competition that asked architects "to explore the idea of the virtual through the unbounded program of a house."[1] Imagining an "artificial ground with indeterminate structural strength"[2] visually characterized by camouflage, the house is adaptable to any setting. The ribbonlike structural band can bend and change direction, shifting from a lining to a wrapping. Rooms are formed and separated by double-sided, double-use bands; each composite band can combine with others, creating a more complex organization of rooms unfolding three-dimensionally, theoretically ad infinitum.

In 2003, the architects won the competition to design the BBC Music Centre and Offices in London (2003–projected 2006) that will house two concert studios, rehearsal spaces, and production rooms. A continuous band snakes back and forth to create the main spaces of the building; the sections of the band that separate inside from outside feature exterior screens that relay the music performed inside through changing patterns of color and light. Windows bracket the sides of the structure formed by the band and allow the activities of the BBC Music Centre to be transparent and part of the public urban space.

1 ANY Magazine press release, "The Virtual House," available online at http://www.basilisk.com/ANY_virtual.html.
2 Foreign Office Architects (FOA), project description for Virtual House, in *Phylogenesis: FOA's Ark*, exh. cat. (Barcelona: Actar; and London: Institute of Contemporary Arts, 2004), 592.

YOKOHAMA INTERNATIONAL PORT TERMINAL, YOKOHAMA, JAPAN, 1995–2002

above: DETAIL OF ROOFTOP; below: PLAN

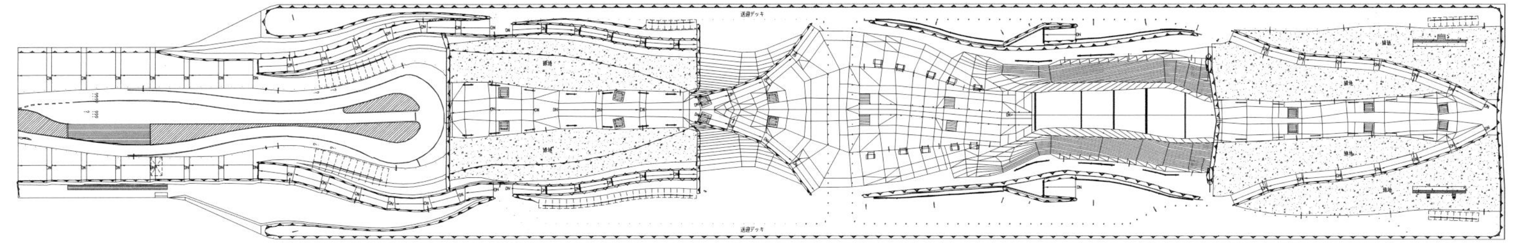

YOKOHAMA INTERNATIONAL PORT TERMINAL, YOKOHAMA, JAPAN, 1995–2002, EXTERIOR AND INTERIOR VIEWS

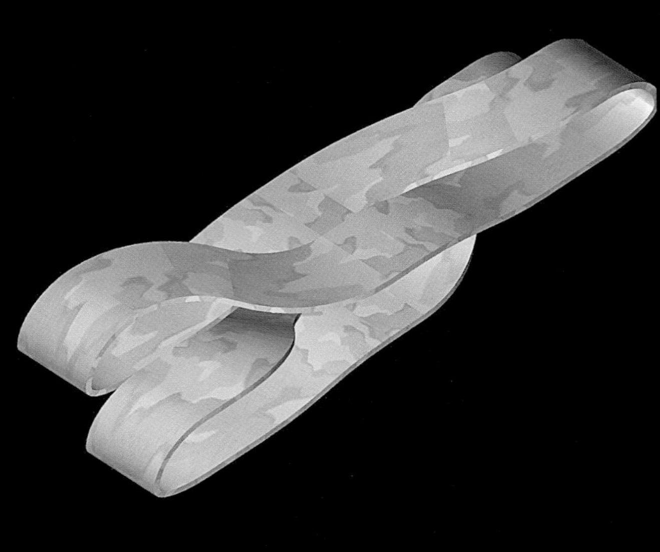

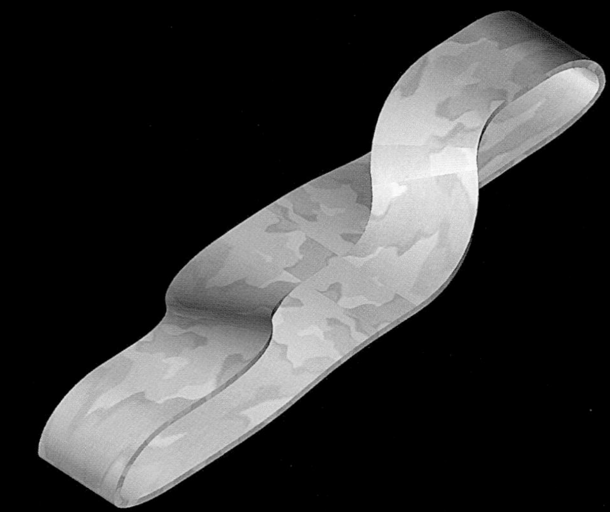

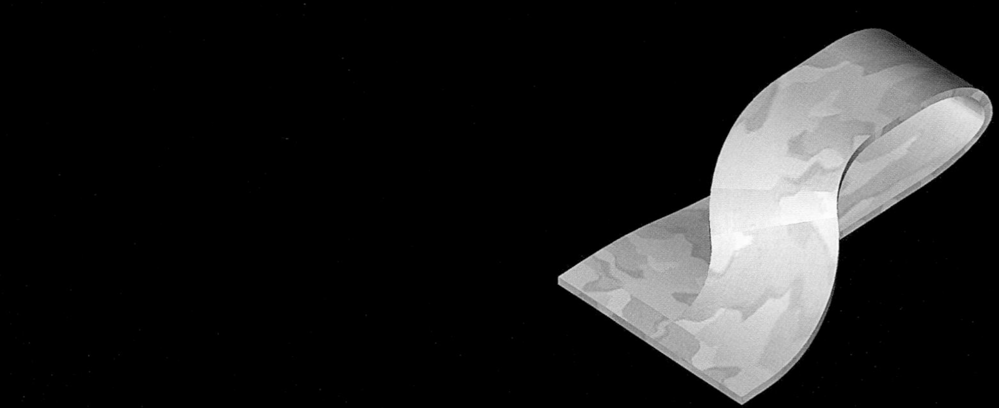

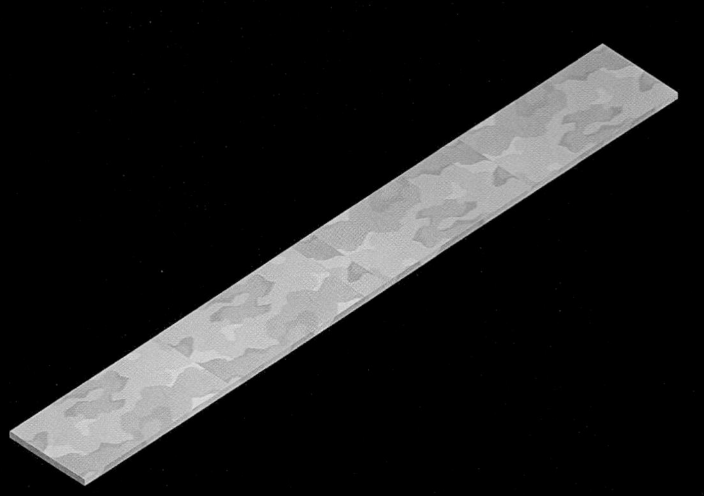

VIRTUAL HOUSE (UNBUILT), 1997

opposite: DIGITAL RENDERINGS OF FOLDED AND UNFOLDED STRUCTURE

above: DIGITAL RENDERING OF EXTERIOR; below: SECTION/PLAN DIAGRAM

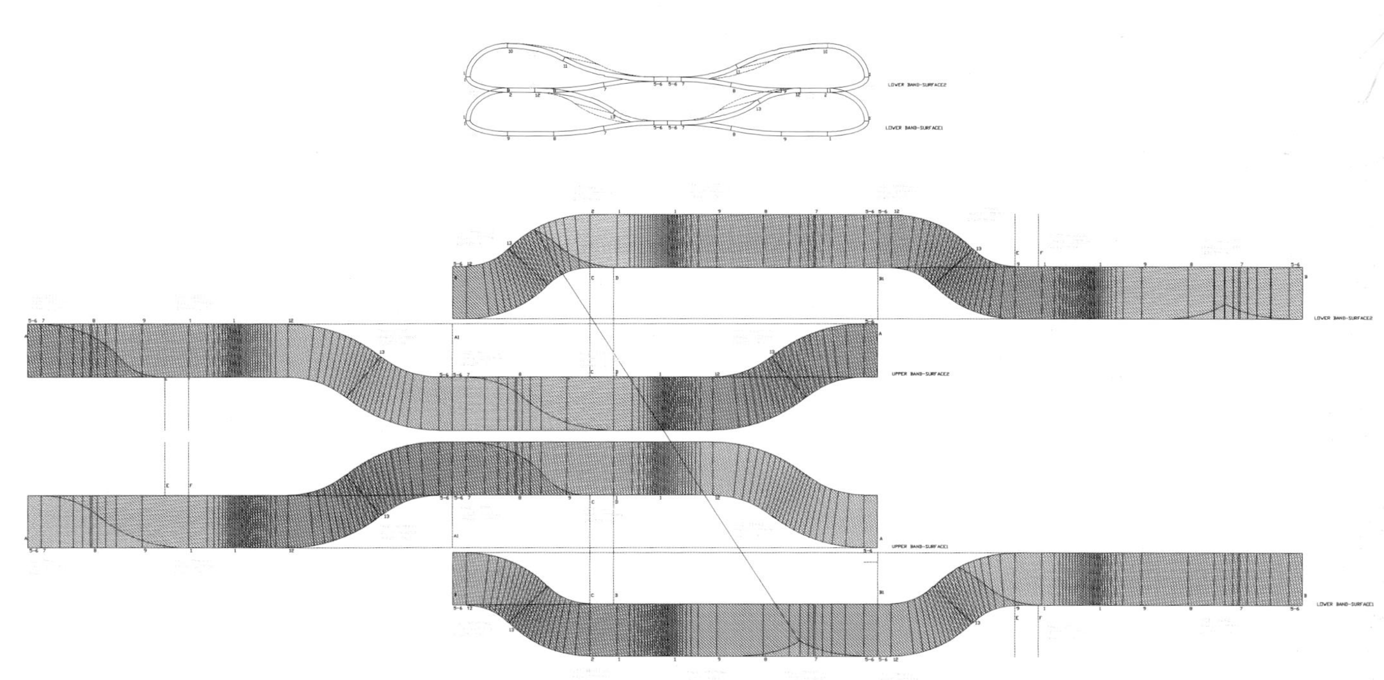

MULTIPLE SURFACE CODING : FACE – SPACE – GRAVITY

BBC MUSIC CENTRE AND OFFICES, WHITE CITY, LONDON, 2003–PROJECTED 2006
below: DIGITAL RENDERINGS OF EXTERIOR AND AUDITORIUM INTERIOR
opposite top: SECTIONS AND DIGITAL RENDERING OF GALLERY INTERIOR

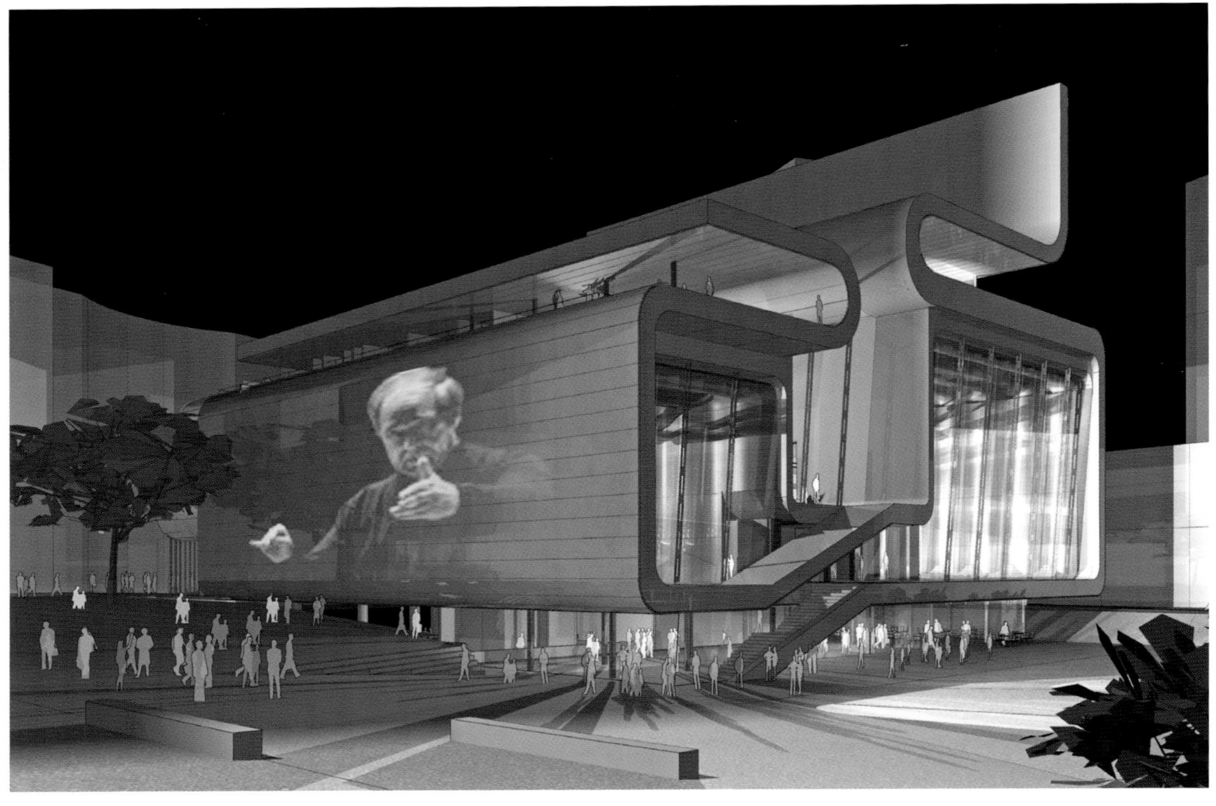

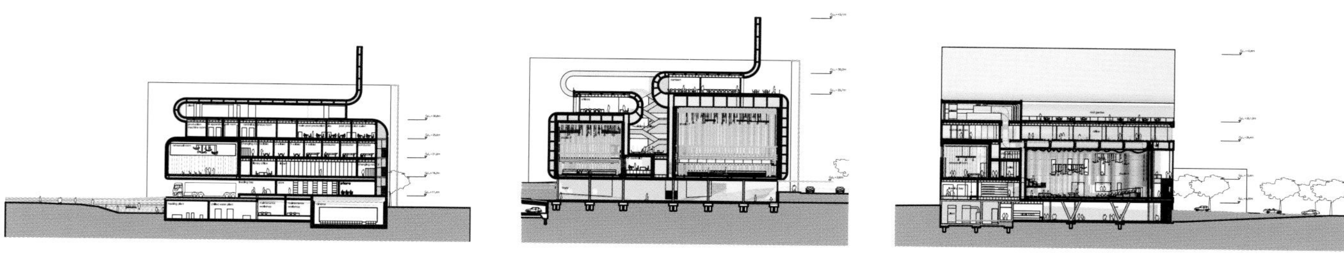

FUTURE SYSTEMS London

Jan Kaplicky, b. 1937, Prague Amanda Levete, b. 1955, Bridgend, England

Cofounded in 1979 by Jan Kaplicky, who was joined by partner Amanda Levete in 1989, Future Systems is known for its sleek and innovative projects. The firm's work consistently challenges preconceptions of architectural space, resulting in buildings and interior-renovation projects that feature smooth curvaceous forms with a distinctly futuristic sensibility. Future Systems' building for Selfridges Department Store (1999–2003) in Birmingham, England, takes the form of a four-story amorphous blob clad in a blue stucco skin studded with fifteen thousand shimmering anodized-aluminum disks. The shape and skin of the building are so unusual that it seems alien next to its neighbor, a nineteenth-century church. Kaplicky and Levete compare the undulating curves of the building to those of a waistline and the fluidity of its billowing shape to the drape of fabric. Citing snakeskin and the 1960s paillette dresses of Paco Rabanne as inspirations, the architects designed a cladding system that wraps all surfaces of the building, including the roof, in one continuous movement, confounding conventional notions of front, back, and side façades. The building has been a catalyst for the urban regeneration of this northern English city, while providing a fresh and contemporary identity for the Selfridges chain of department stores, which was founded in 1909.

SELFRIDGES DEPARTMENT STORE, BIRMINGHAM, ENGLAND, 1999–2003

opposite: DIGITAL RENDERINGS OF BRIDGE INTERIOR AND EXTERIOR; above: EXTERIOR VIEW

SELFRIDGES DEPARTMENT STORE, BIRMINGHAM, ENGLAND, 1999–2003

opposite: DETAIL OF SKIN; below, left column: SKETCHES AND SECTIONAL MODEL; below right: ATRIUM

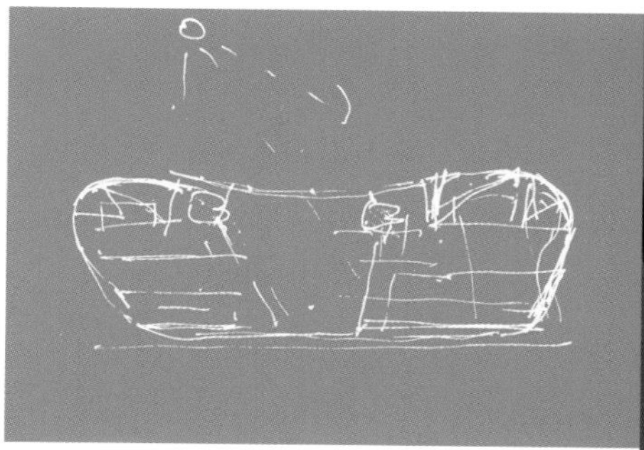

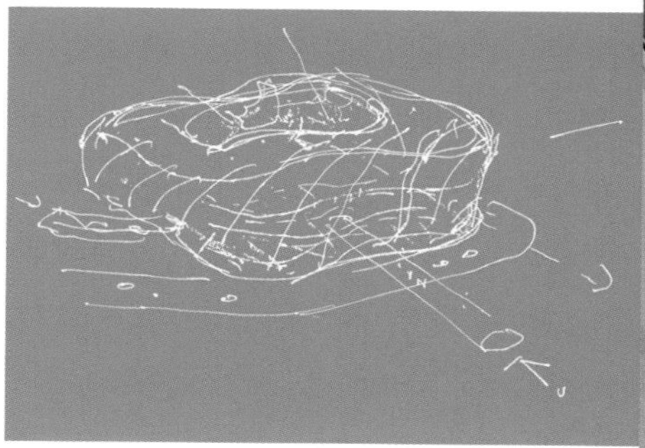

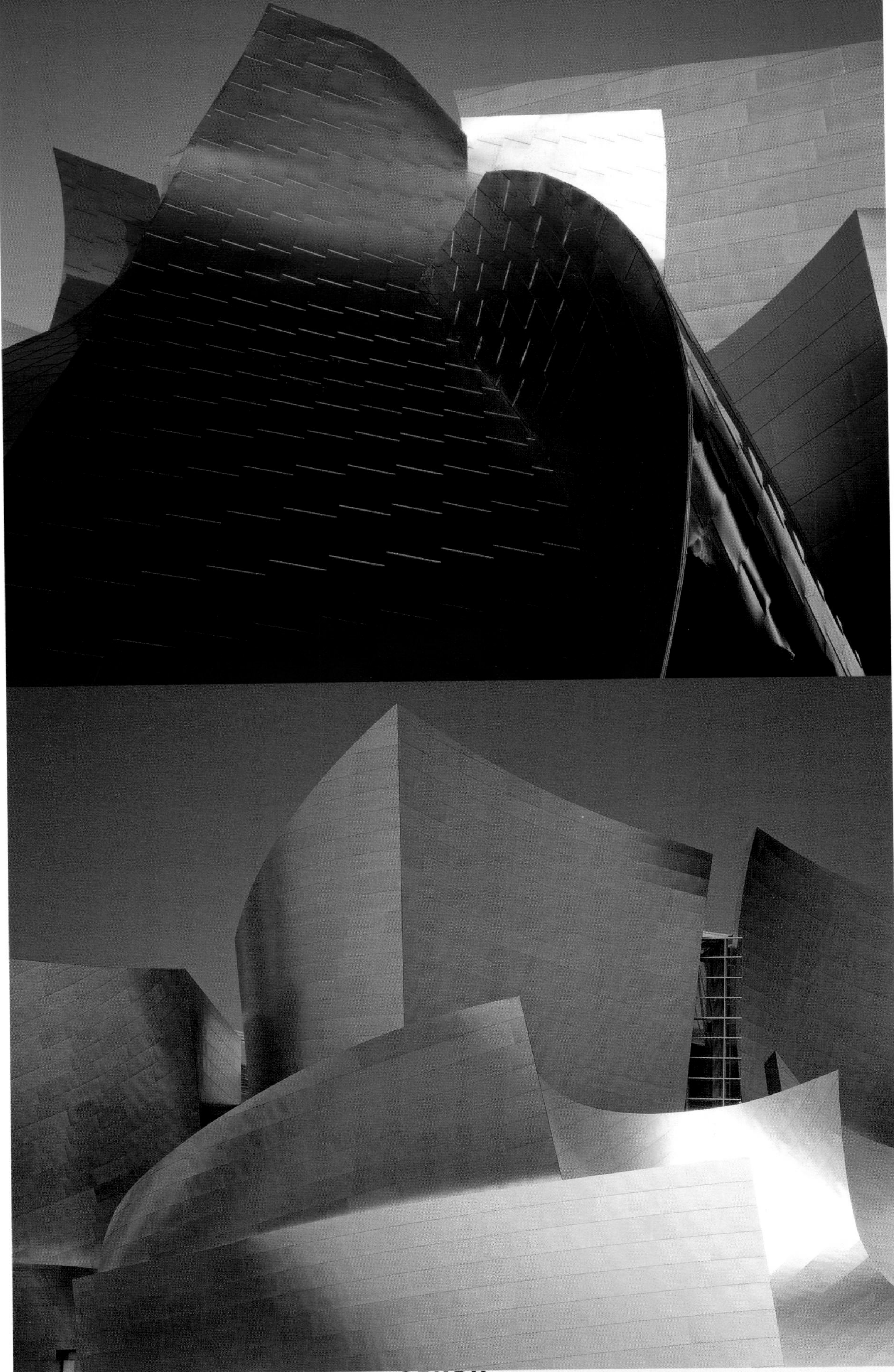

FRANK **GEHRY** Los Angeles

b. 1929, Toronto, Canada

Frank Gehry's buildings confound traditional notions of architectural space and form. His approach is rooted in a deep respect for art and art-making as well as a desire to explore the potential of new technology and materials. In 1977, Gehry began an ongoing renovation (1977–78/1991–94) of his family's 1920s two-story bungalow in Santa Monica, California. He appropriated off-the-shelf industrial materials such as chain-link fencing, corrugated metal, and plywood and used them to loosely wrap the north and east façades. The bold volumetric assemblage of the exterior was matched in the interior, where select walls and ceilings were stripped to reveal lathing and/or the house's wood-frame construction.

For the Walt Disney Concert Hall in Los Angeles (1987–2003), Gehry wrapped the complex billowing structure with stainless steel to create a shimmering curvaceous building reminiscent of a ship's sails or a flower's petals. The architect clad the floors, walls, and ceilings of the 2,265-seat auditorium with Douglas fir, creating the sense of being inside a basket or a musical instrument. Designed well before the opening of Gehry's groundbreaking building for the Guggenheim Museum in Bilbao, Spain (1991–97), Disney Hall marks his adoption of Computer-Aided Three-Dimensional Interactive Application (CATIA), a software program originally developed for the aerospace industry. By applying software like CATIA to architectural design, Gehry has been able to transform his fluid sketches and sculptural paper models into lyrical and complex built forms.

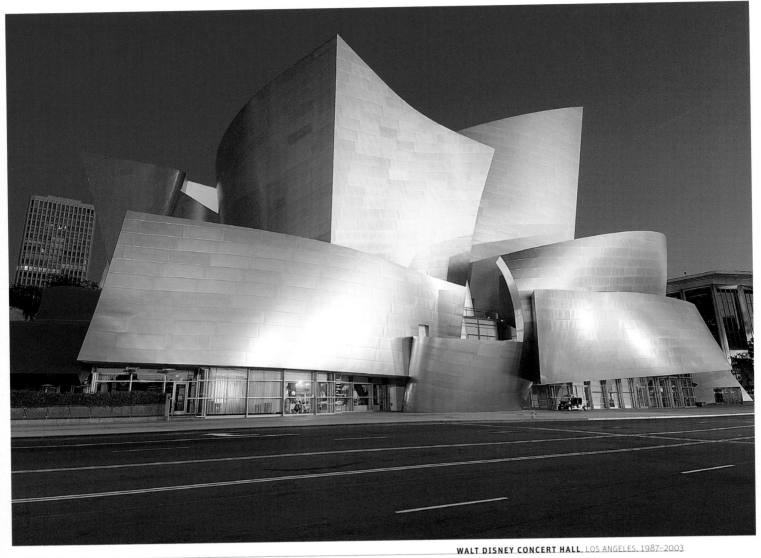

WALT DISNEY CONCERT HALL, LOS ANGELES, 1987–2003

pages 108–09 and above: EXTERIOR VIEWS; below left: AUDITORIUM; below right: SECTION THROUGH AUDITORIUM

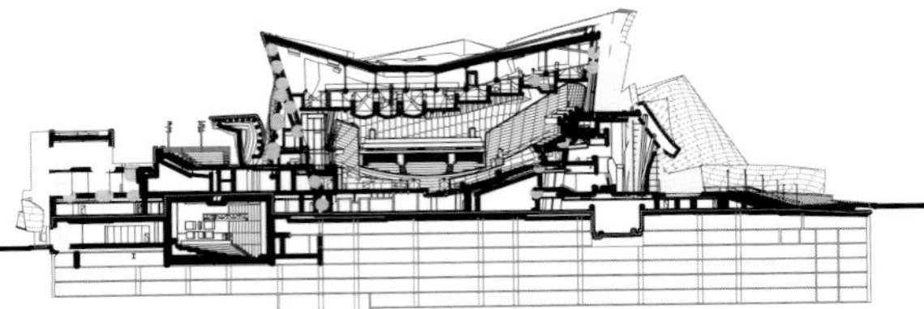

GEHRY RESIDENCE, SANTA MONICA, CALIFORNIA, 1977–78/1991–94, INTERIOR AND EXTERIOR VIEWS

TESS **GIBERSON** New York

b. 1971, Concord, New Hampshire

Intricately handcrafted details are critical elements in Tess Giberson's clothing designs. She hand-finishes every garment herself with crochet trim, knitted elements, smocking, ruching, overstitching, pintucking, or pleating, creating small seasonal collections of one-of-a-kind garments. Using conventional silhouettes and simple fabrics, she distorts and recomposes textiles, cutting, rearranging, then piecing them together in new ways to create a skirt or an abstracted ruffle on the front of a blouse.

Eschewing the traditional runway show, Giberson devises performance-like presentations to communicate the central ideas behind each collection. The show for her Structure 1 autumn/winter 2003–04 collection explored the roles of the individual and community. Ten models entered a room containing a circular wooden platform that featured inner and outer rings of erect poles. Each model wore a unique multi-layered outfit that combined various lengths, colors, and textures. During the course of the show, the models undressed down to identical white slips, transferring elements of their outfits to the wooden structure by hooking them from pole to pole or laying them across pole tops, gradually layering and overlapping pieces until they transformed the structure into an enclosed communal shelter. Giberson described its genesis as the "memory of making forts as a child. As a child there is a common need to build one's own environment pulling from whatever resources are around: blankets, pillows, sheets.... The need for humans to create shelters is instinctual and I began to study various types of structures made for shelter. I wanted to create a structure pulling from the very direct and honest methods a child might use."[1]

1 Tess Giberson, quoted in Diane Pernet, "Tess Giberson," *b-guided* (Barcelona) (autumn 2003): 99.

STRUCTURE 1 COLLECTION, AUTUMN/WINTER 2003–04, GARMENTS AND VIEWS OF SHELTER ASSEMBLY

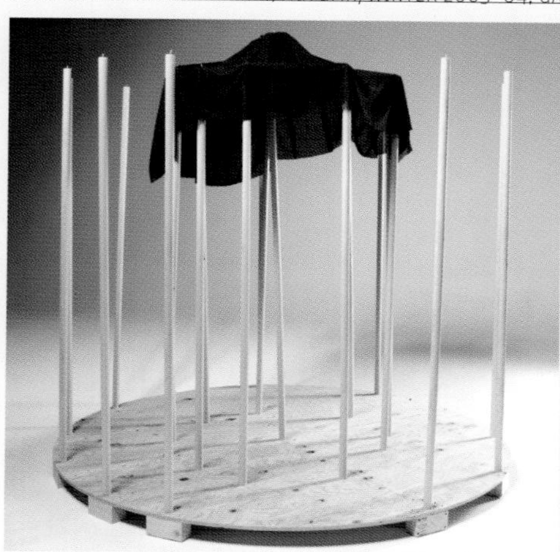

VITRA FIRE STATION, WEIL AM RHEIN, GERMANY, 1990–94

below: BIRD'S-EYE-VIEW PAINTING

opposite: EXTERIOR VIEW AND CORRIDOR PAINTING

ZAHA **HADID** ARCHITECTS London

Zaha Hadid, b. 1950, Baghdad

Zaha Hadid's provocative architectural vision began to take built form with the completion of her first freestanding building, a fire station (1990–94) for the Vitra furniture company's campus in Weil am Rhein, Germany. The two-story station is a long narrow building of concrete and glass featuring "a linear, layered series of walls" that "puncture, tilt, and break according to functional requirements."[1] From the front, the structure appears hermetic and enclosed; its interior spaces are only visible through windows on the sides and back. The building's dynamic cantilevered planes seem suspended in motion, evoking the tension of firemen constantly on alert.

Hadid's project for MAXXI National Center of Contemporary Arts in Rome (1997–projected 2007), designed in collaboration with Patrik Schumacher following an international competition, is a low-slung composition of interwoven tendrils. Like the fire station, MAXXI also embodies a sense of movement, albeit one that is sinuous and fluid rather than sharp and violent. Hadid likened MAXXI to an "urban graft" or a second skin that knits together the L-shaped site with its former army barracks, overlaps circulation patterns with those of the city, and aligns with the urban grid.[2] The building's organization and circulation follow the drift of its gently scrolling forms; it becomes a porous immersive field in which one moves experientially through the galleries rather than in the linear fashion common to museums. The immutable verticality of the museum wall becomes pliable, as it constantly changes in dimension and geometry: "walls become floors, or twist to become ceiling, or are voided to become large windows."[3]

1 Project description of Vitra Fire Station, in *Major and Recent Works*, vol. 4 of *Zaha Hadid* (New York: Rizzoli, 2004), 63.
2 Project description of MAXXI National Center of Contemporary Arts, ibid., 134.
3 Ibid.

VITRA FIRE STATION, WEIL AM RHEIN, GERMANY, 1990–94

left, above and below: EXTERIOR AND INTERIOR VIEWS

right, above and below: RELIEF MODEL AND SITE-PLAN PAINTING

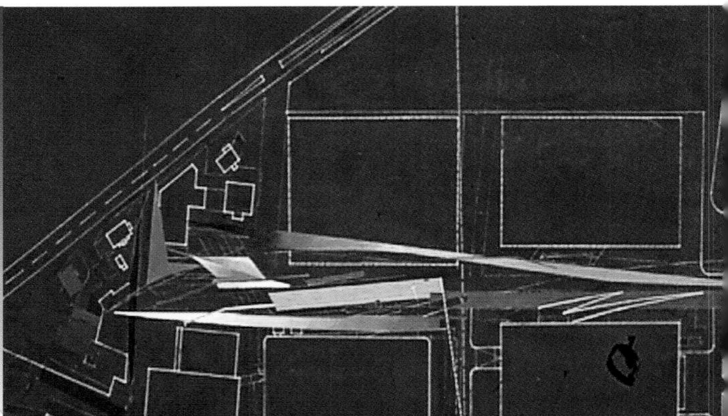

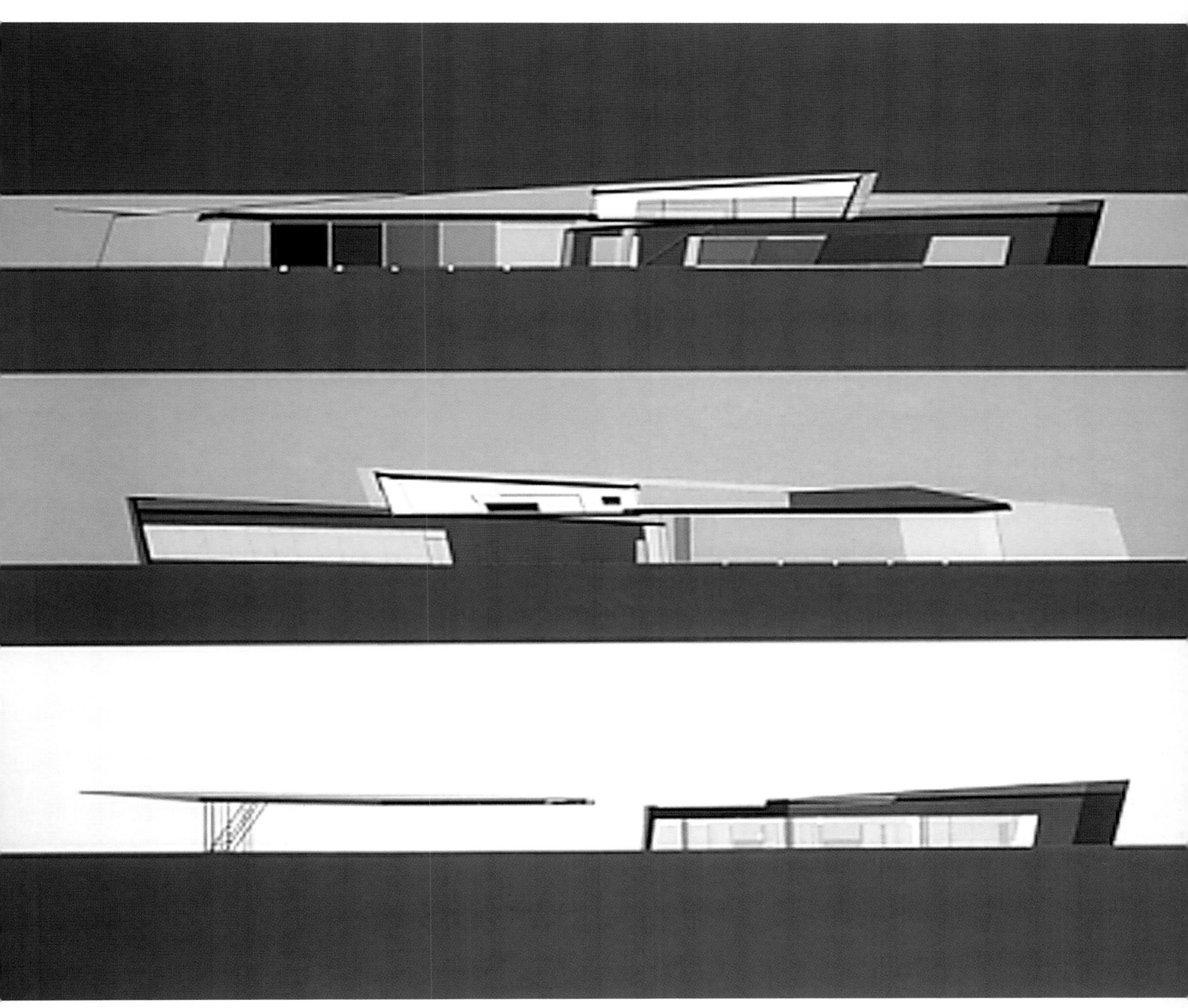

VITRA FIRE STATION, WEIL AM RHEIN, GERMANY, 1990–94, ELEVATION PAINTINGS

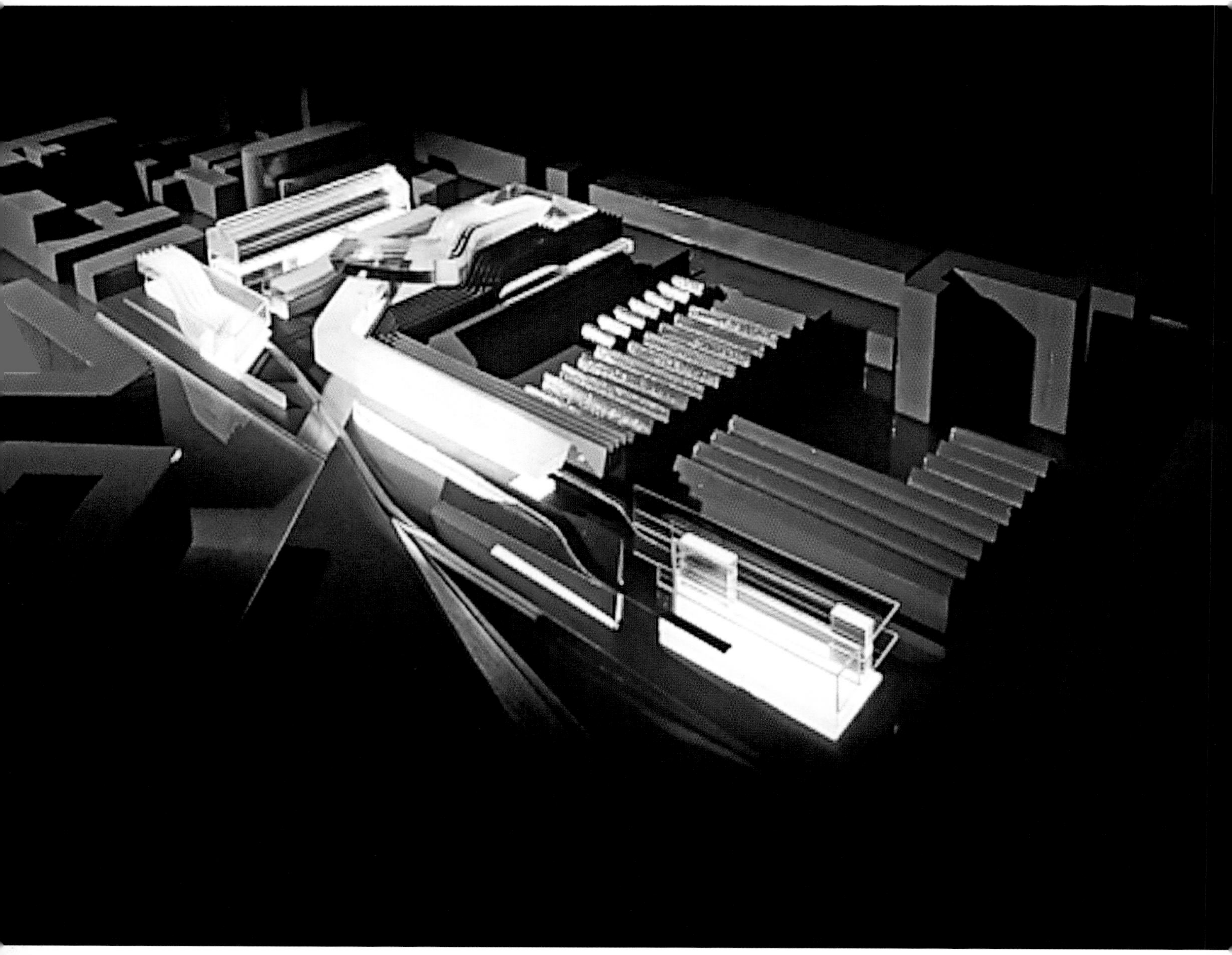

MAXXI NATIONAL CENTER OF CONTEMPORARY ARTS, ROME, 1997–PROJECTED 2007
above: SITE MODEL; below: FINAL DESIGN MODEL

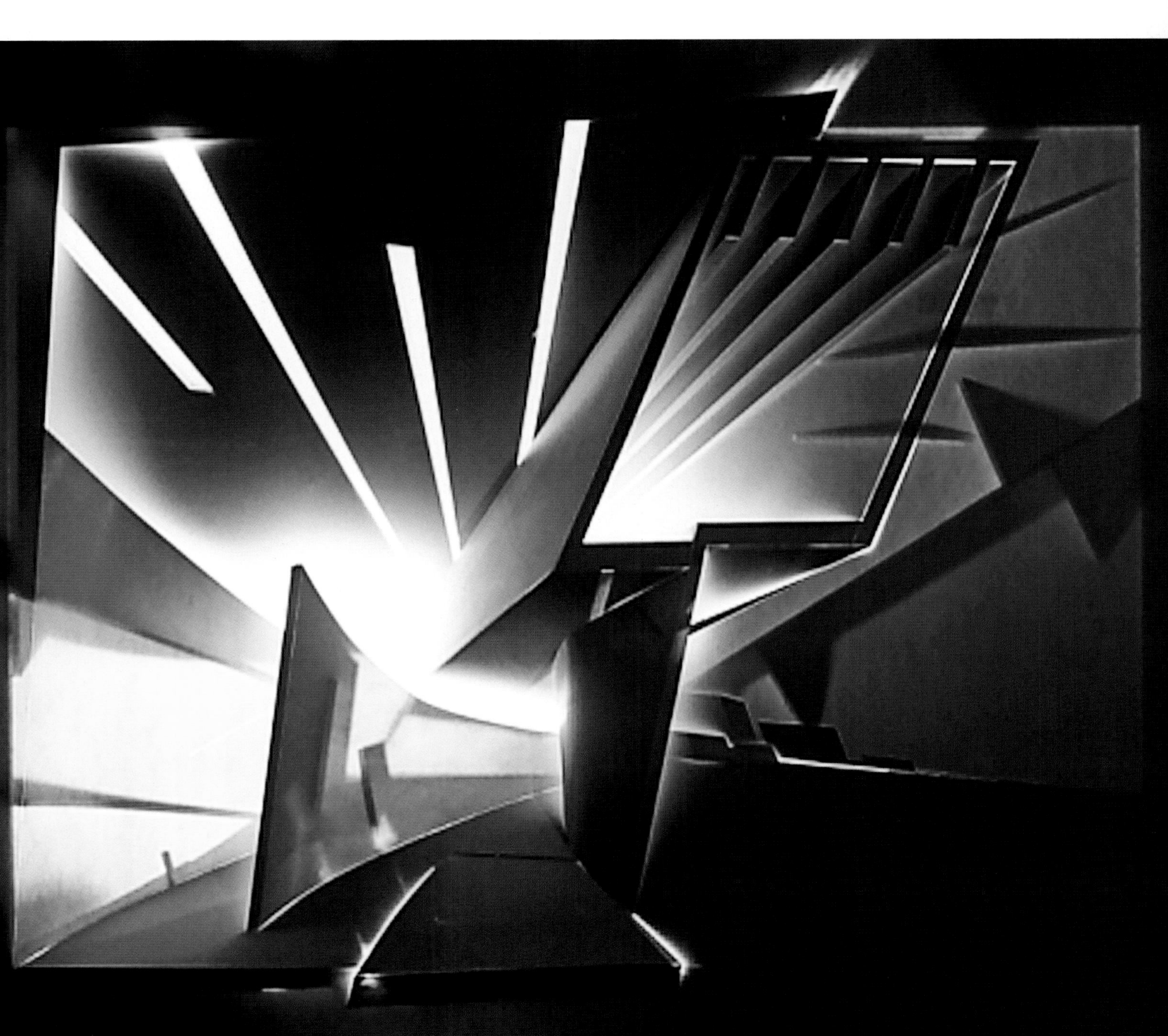

MAXXI NATIONAL CENTER OF CONTEMPORARY ARTS, ROME, 1997–PROJECTED 2007, DETAIL OF STUDY MODEL

DOMINUS WINERY, YOUNTVILLE, CALIFORNIA, 1995–98

HERZOG & DE MEURON Basel, Switzerland

Jacques Herzog, b. 1950, Basel Pierre de Meuron, b. 1950, Basel

Jacques Herzog and Pierre de Meuron are known for their innovative wrapping and cladding of buildings as well as their attention to material, pattern, and surface manipulation. Herzog's personal interest in fashion—in particular, the qualities of pattern and texture—derives in part from growing up surrounded by the textiles of his mother's tailoring business: "It is not the glamorous aspect of fashion which fascinates us.... we are more interested in what people are wearing, what they like to wrap around their bodies...We are interested in that aspect of artificial skin which becomes so much of an intimate part of people."[1] Herzog & de Meuron's engagement with architectural skins is evident in their design for Central Signal Box in Basel, Switzerland (1994–99), a box wrapped in thin copper strips that twist and bend like fine pleats, serving to "dematerialize" and soften the monolithic structure. For the Ricola-Europe SA Production and Storage Building in Mulhouse-Brunstatt, France (1992–93), and the Eberswalde Technical University Library in Eberswalde, Germany (1994–99), the architects printed the buildings' main façades with images related to their functions. At Dominus Winery in Yountville, California (1995–98), the building's mass and skin are one and the same, composed of stacked wire gabions filled with rocks gathered from the site.

While the firm's recent buildings incorporate more complex forms, their interest in developing unconventional cladding remains. Their six-level, five-sided flagship building for Prada in Tokyo (2000–03) resembles a gigantic crystal. The structure is covered with a complex faceted skin of diamond-shaped glass panes set in a steel frame. The panes alternate between flat, concave, and convex, encasing the structure like bubble wrap. The de Young Museum in San Francisco (1999–2005) features a skin of copper mesh that wraps around its twisted triangular tower. Herzog & de Meuron's National Stadium in Beijing (2002–projected 2007) features a colorful skin of woven steel that encloses the intricate latticed steel framework beneath: "The basket weave of steel that composes its façade is also its load-bearing structure. Its skin is made of bones."[2]

1 Jacques Herzog, in Jeffrey Kipnis, "A Conversation with Jacques Herzog," *El Croquis*, no. 84 (1997): 7.
2 Arthur Lubow, "The China Syndrome," *The New York Times Magazine* (22 May 2006): 71.

EBERSWALDE TECHNICAL UNIVERSITY LIBRARY, EBERSWALDE, GERMANY, 1994–99

top: FAÇADE DETAIL; bottom: THOMAS RUFF, **BIBLIOTHEK, EBERSWALDE**, 1999, CHROMOGENIC COLOR PRINT, 72⅞ X 90½ INCHES

RICOLA-EUROPE SA PRODUCTION AND STORAGE BUILDING, MULHOUSE-BRUNSTATT, FRANCE, 1992–93

NATIONAL STADIUM, THE MAIN STADIUM FOR THE 2008 OLYMPIC GAMES, BEIJING, 2002–PROJECTED 2007, DIGITAL RENDERINGS

PRADA AOYAMA TOKYO EPICENTER, TOKYO, 2000–03. above: MODEL STUDY; below: EXTERIOR VIEW

CENTRAL SIGNAL BOX, BASEL, SWITZERLAND, 1994–99
SIGNAL BOX AUF DEM WOLF, BASEL, SWITZERLAND, 1988–95

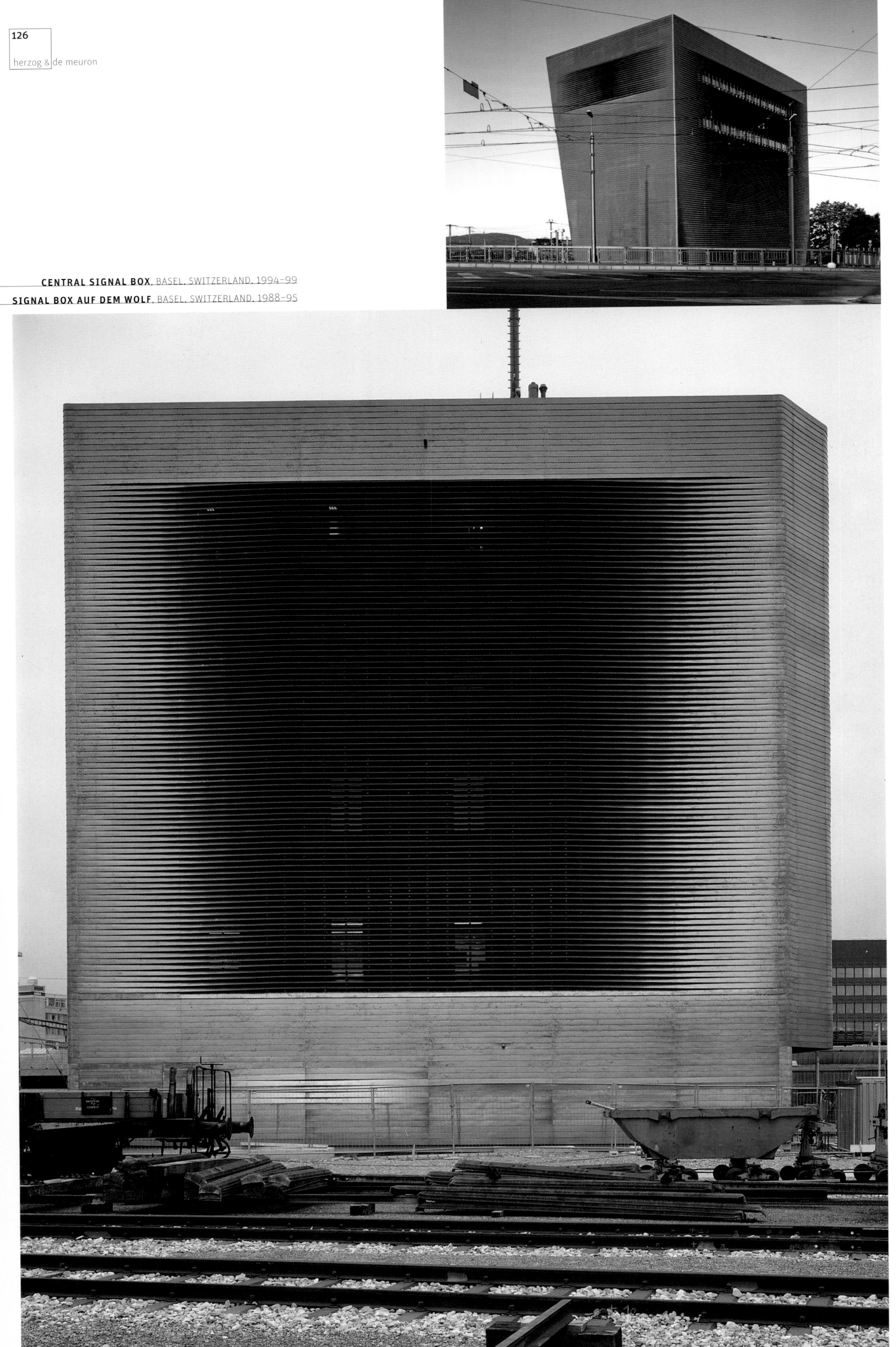

DE YOUNG MUSEUM, GOLDEN GATE PARK, SAN FRANCISCO, 1999–2005
left and bottom right: DETAILS OF SKIN; top right: EXTERIOR VIEW
center right: INTERIOR STAIRWAY

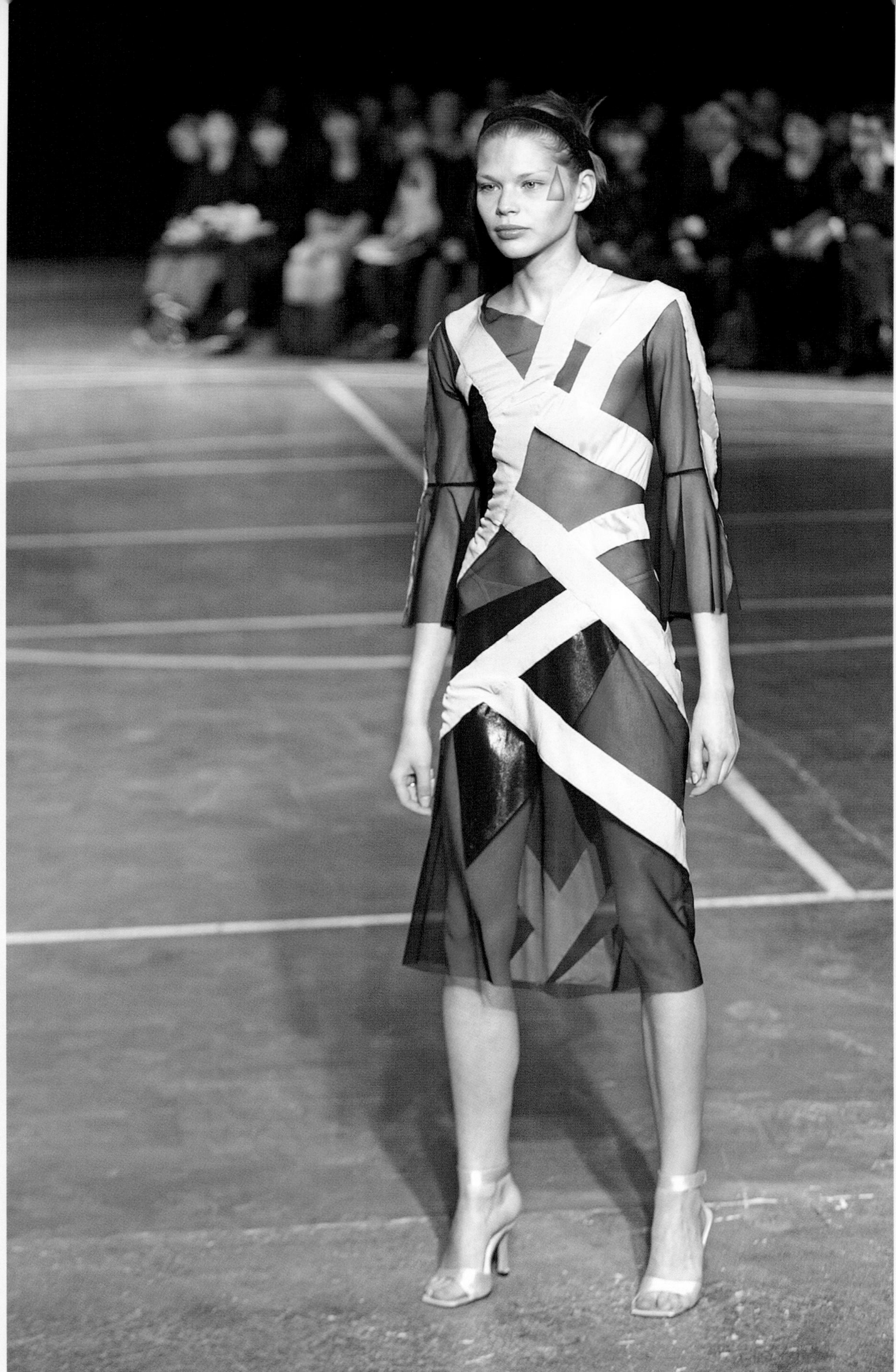

YOSHIKI **HISHINUMA** Tokyo

b. 1958, Sendai, Japan

Known for using innovative textiles and creating unusual shapes, Yoshiki Hishinuma launched his own label in 1996 with a presentation in Paris. Hishinuma, who worked briefly for Miyake Issey, combines new technology with traditional Japanese techniques such as *shibori* or tie-dying to develop textiles with effects like pleating, puckering, and crinkling that provide texture and volume. He most often works with synthetic fabrics such as polyester, Lycra, and synthetic leather, though he has recently started to develop fabrics that incorporate natural fibers.

Hishinuma's runway presentations are extravagant productions that feature a wide range of different looks and styles. Instead of presenting a tightly edited collection, the designer may show as many as one hundred different garments, rather like a series of collections within one presentation. The Inside-Out 2Way Dress (spring/summer 2004) is graphic and sheer, featuring seemingly random strips of opaque tape that both hold the dress together and strategically conceal parts of the body. Hishinuma's spring/summer 2000 Bellows Dress collection illustrates the designer's investigation of the properties of textiles to give volume and form to garments. He used fabric with origami-like folds to create a honeycomb effect that allows each dress to expand when occupied or manipulated by the wearer. The Cubism Dress collection of autumn/winter 2001–02, with its bright colors and fantastical shapes, shows the designer's theatrical side. While Hishinuma creates both women's and men's wear, he also does costume design for theater, dance, and film, most notably collaborating with the Netherlands Dance Theater and the Paris Opera.

opposite: **INSIDE-OUT 2WAY DRESS**
SPRING/SUMMER 2004

DRESSES FROM **BELLOWS DRESS** COLLECTION, SPRING/SUMMER 2000

following spread: DRESSES FROM **CUBISM DRESS** COLLECTION
AUTUMN/WINTER 2001–02

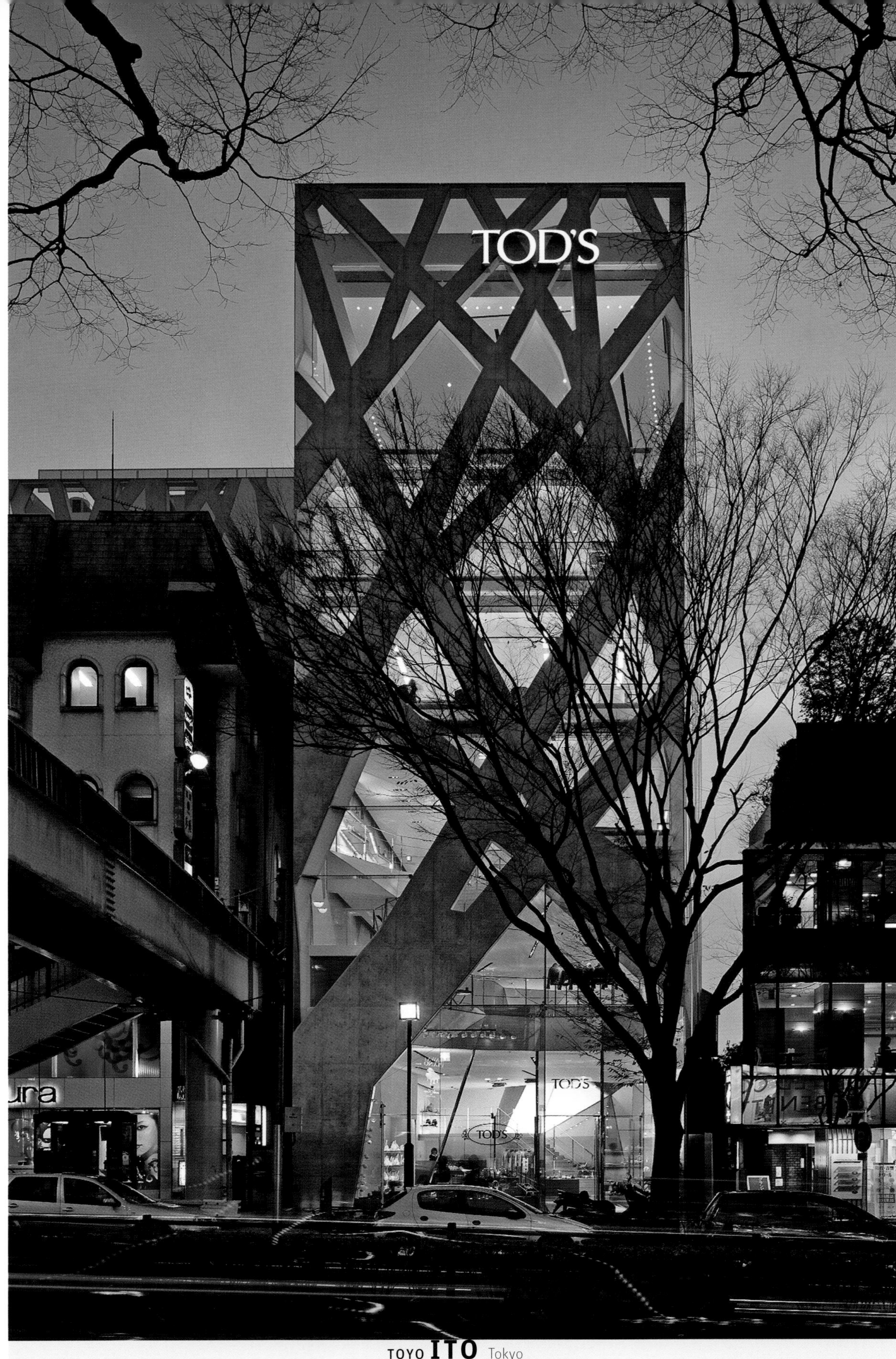

TOYO **ITO** Tokyo

b. 1941, Seoul

Japanese architect Toyo Ito combines an interest in structural systems with a desire to create architecture that appears light, transparent, and almost ephemeral. These two seemingly contradictory preoccupations have found highly refined resolution in projects such as Tod's Omotesando Building (2002–04), a seven-story retail space in Tokyo for the Italian luxury-goods company. Ito wrapped the building in a graphic pattern of glass and concrete that references the trees lining Omotesando Avenue. The pattern not only serves as an ornamental skin but provides structure, as the building surface supports the floor slabs, thereby eliminating the need for internal columns. Similarly, for Mikimoto Ginza 2 in Tokyo (2004–05), commissioned by a jewelry company famous for its pearls, Ito wrapped the nine-story building in thin pearlescent walls punctured by irregularly shaped windows, creating a decorative exterior that functions simultaneously as a structural system.

Ito's work is also distinguished by his incorporation of organic forms in all aspects of design. The architect's competition entry for the Forum for Music, Dance & Visual Culture in Ghent, Belgium (unbuilt, 2004), draws on the structures of the human mouth and ear, vehicles for sound emission and reception. Ito conceived the building as a continuous reinforced concrete shell enclosing a system of channels that move visitors through the space, branching from one another and leaving no formal distinction between floors, walls, and ceilings. Sendai Mediatheque (1995–2000), a seven-story multipurpose cultural center in Sendai, Japan, is also distinguished by the incorporation of elements that are analogous to body organs. The floor plates are punctured by thirteen steel tubes that run through the building's floors and serve as structural components in addition to containing circulation, communication, and mechanical systems. The double skin of the façade is both translucent and transparent, and, when not flooded by daylight, the structure glows artificially from within.

opposite: EXTERIOR; below, top to bottom: CONCEPTUAL MODEL, STUDY MODELS AND FINAL DESIGN MODEL, AND ELEVATIONS

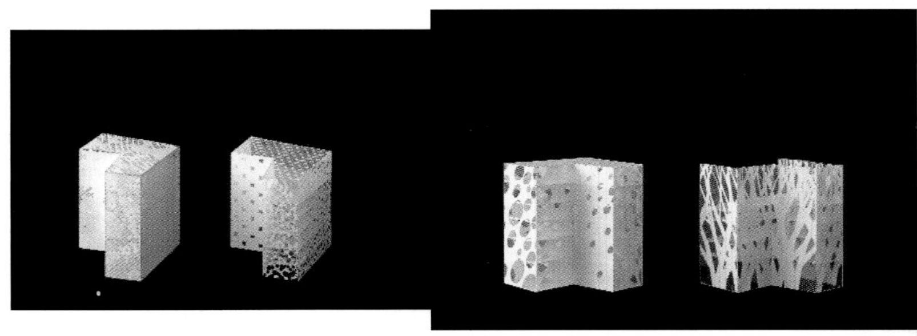

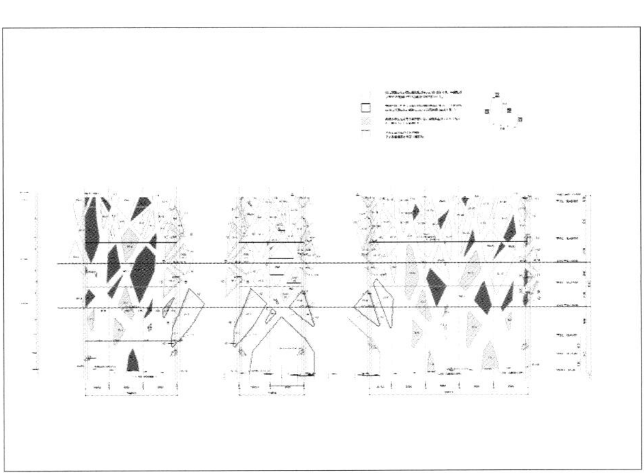

following spread: **MIKIMOTO GINZA 2**, TOKYO, 2004–05

DIGITAL RENDERINGS AND CONCEPTUAL MODELS EXPLORING VERSIONS OF SKIN

MIKIMOTO
MIKIMOTO
MIKIMOTO
MIKIMOTO

MIKIMOTO
MIKIMOTO

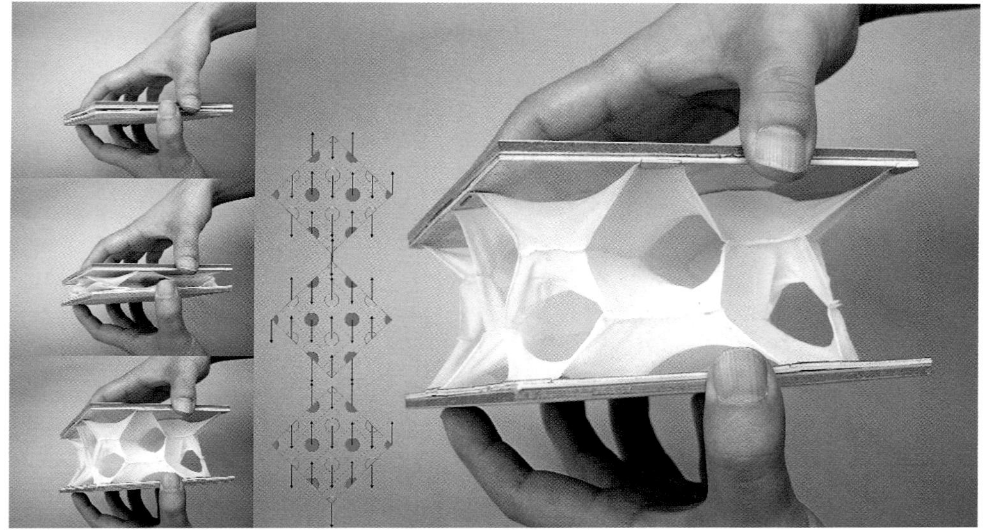

FORUM FOR MUSIC, DANCE & VISUAL CULTURE (UNBUILT), GHENT, BELGIUM, 2004
above: STUDY MODEL; below: MODEL AND GEOLOGY OF THE SOUND CAVE

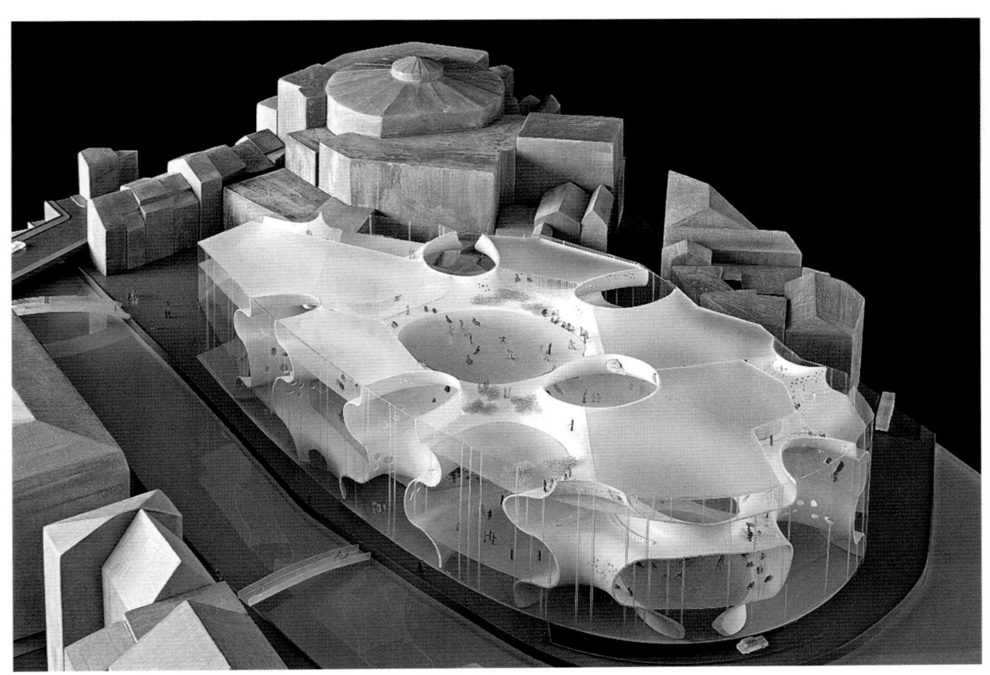

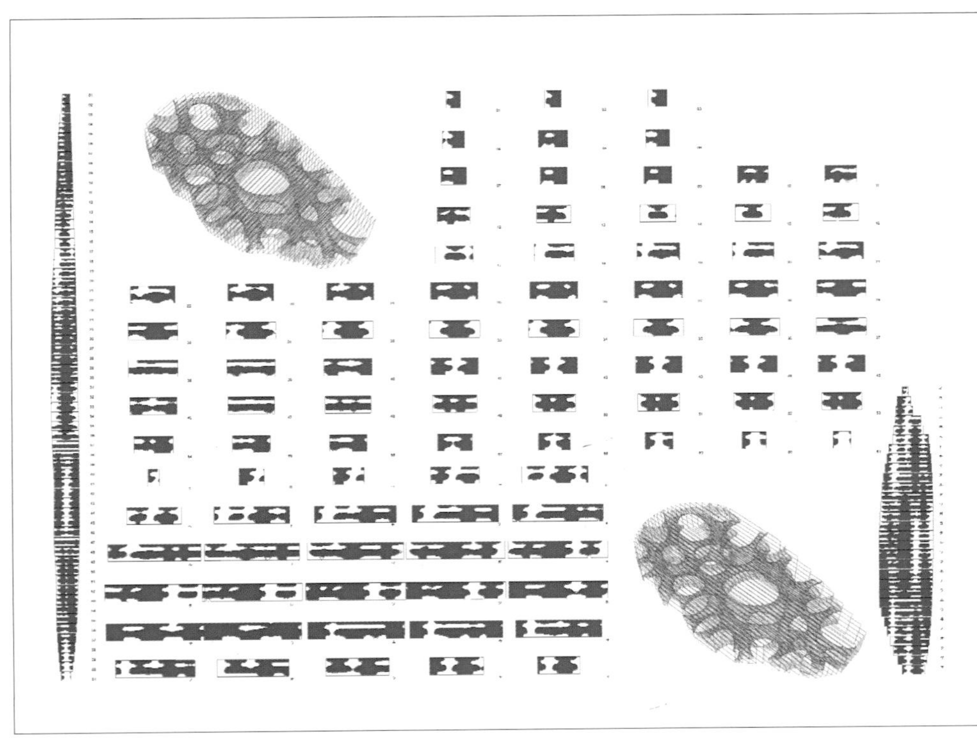

SENDAI MEDIATHEQUE, SENDAI, JAPAN, 1995–2000

above: EXTERIOR; below: AXONOMETRIC PROJECTION OF BUILDING STRUCTURE

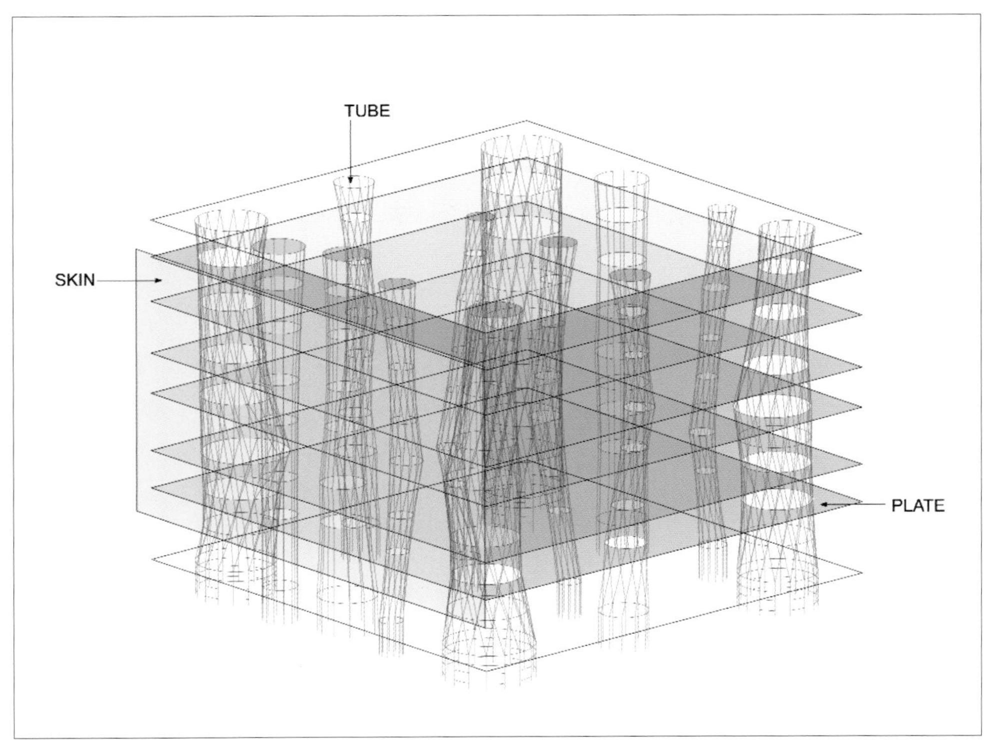

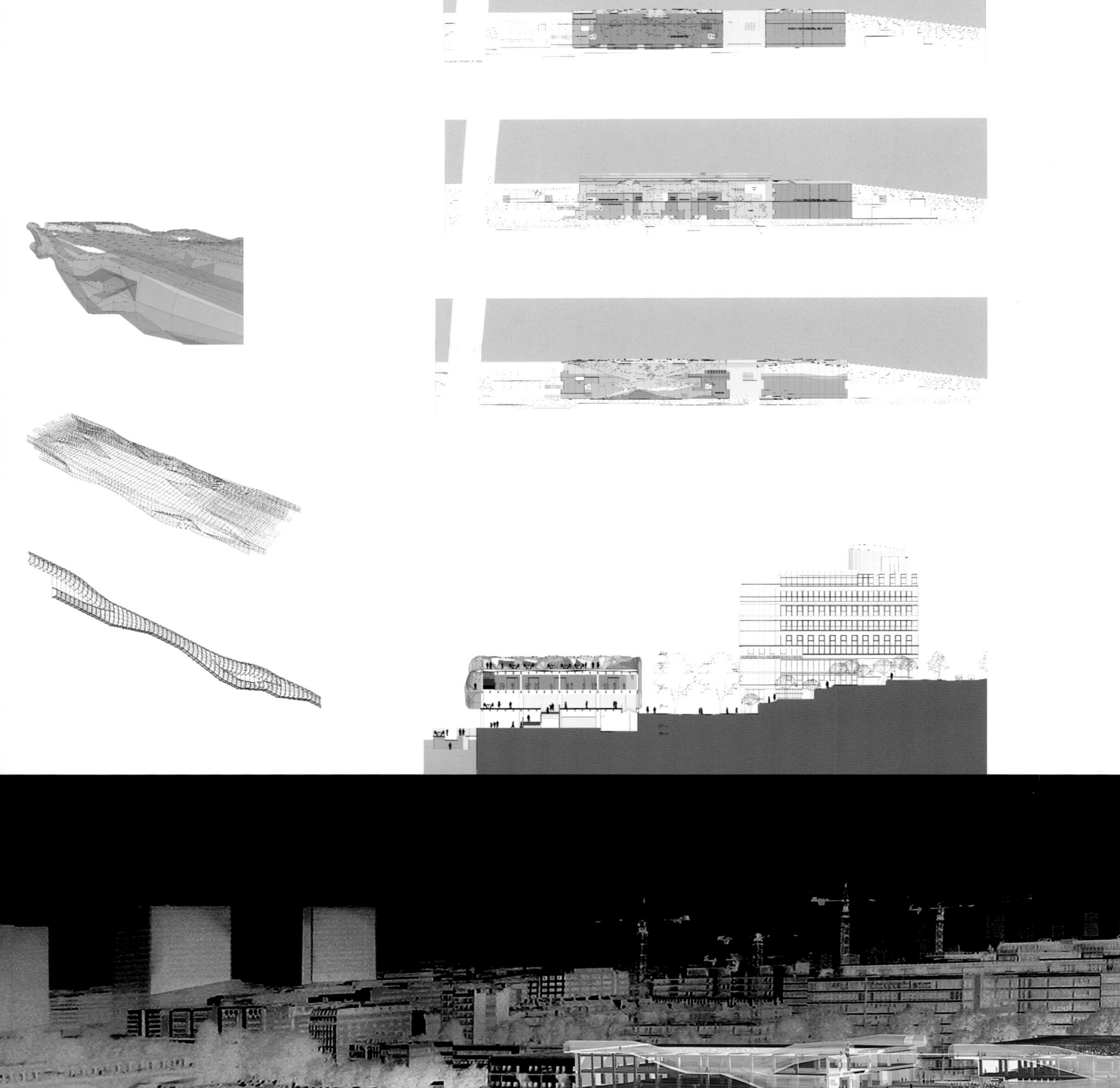

CITY OF FASHION & DESIGN, PARIS, 2005–PROJECTED 2008

top, left column: CONCEPTUAL STUDIES; top, right column: PLANS AND SECTION

opposite top: EXPLODED SECTIONAL DIAGRAMS SHOWING BUILDING ELEMENTS; bottom (pages 138–39): DIGITAL RENDERING

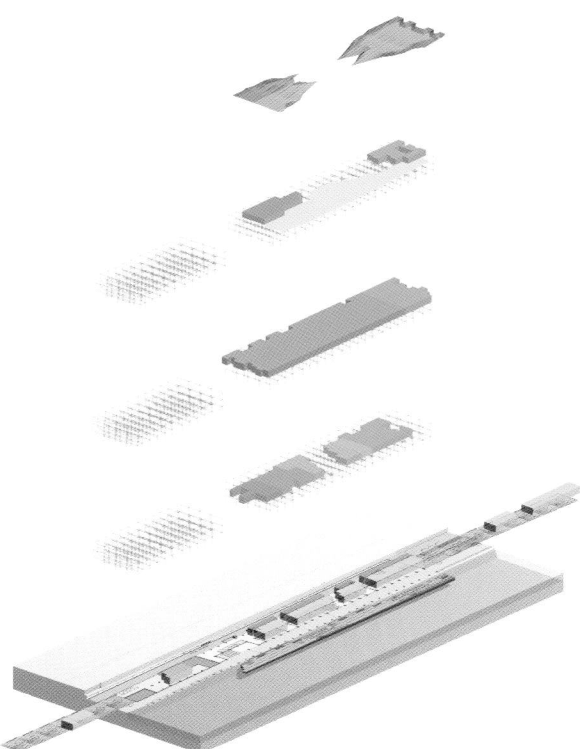

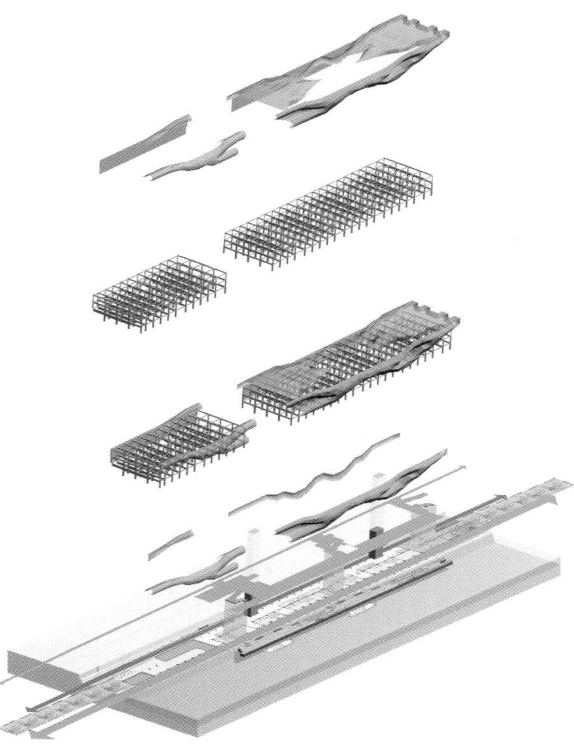

JAKOB + MACFARLANE Paris

Dominique Jakob, b. 1966, Paris Brendan MacFarlane, b. 1961, Christchurch, New Zealand

The husband-and-wife team of Brendan MacFarlane and Dominique Jakob established their practice in 1992, following several years of work at the architecture firm Morphosis. Jakob + MacFarlane's work is characterized by an ongoing exploration of the relationship of a building to its environment and of individual rooms to a building. A number of projects investigate the potential permutations of a building's exterior cladding. In Puzzle House (unbuilt, 1996), a competition design, the project's main elements—the house, a central courtyard, landscape, and access roads—interlock like pieces of a jigsaw puzzle. Rather than featuring private gardens, the architects envisioned a continuous landscape surface shared by neighboring houses. The landscape fabric folds over and encloses the exterior walls and roof of Puzzle House, situating the building nearly seamlessly within its environment. House H (2002), an unbuilt live/work project designed for clients in Corsica, France, consists of a series of triangulated translucent plastic panels that zip together to enclose the building's interior spaces and unzip to open rooms to the outdoors. The irregular faceted form of the building blurs conventional divisions between walls and ceilings as its synthetic-landscape roof blurs structure with surroundings.

Jakob + MacFarlane's competition-winning entry for City of Fashion & Design (2005–projected 2008)—a major cultural center for fashion and design located on Paris's Quai d'Austerlitz—retains the site's original long and thin concrete building running along the Seine River. Originally built in 1907 as a barge depot, the structure is wrapped in a new external skin of glass and steel that at once protects the existing building and forms a new architectural layer containing circulation spaces, a new top floor, and a roofscape.

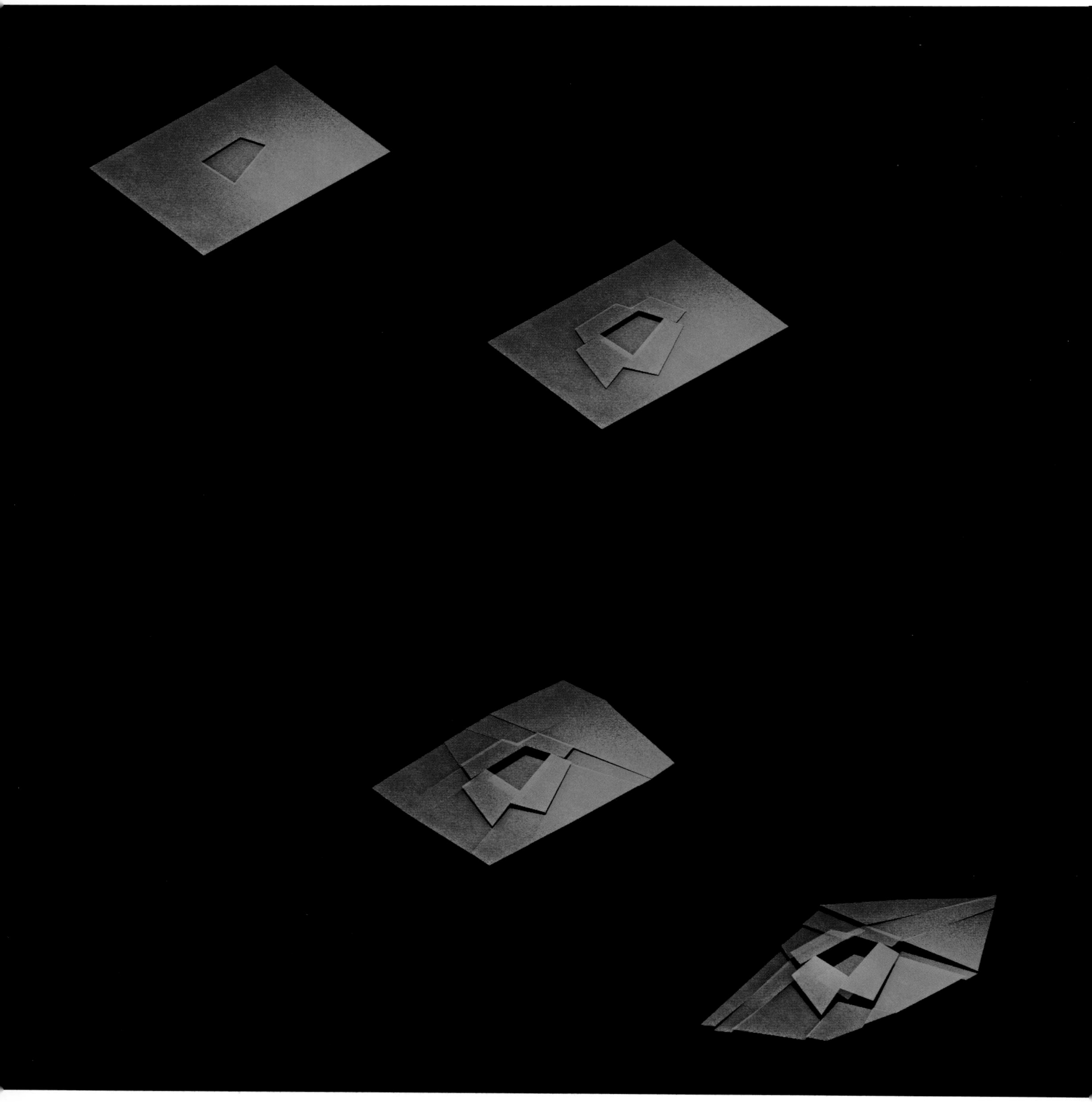

PUZZLE HOUSE (UNBUILT), 1996

above: DIGITAL MODELS; below: SITE PLAN

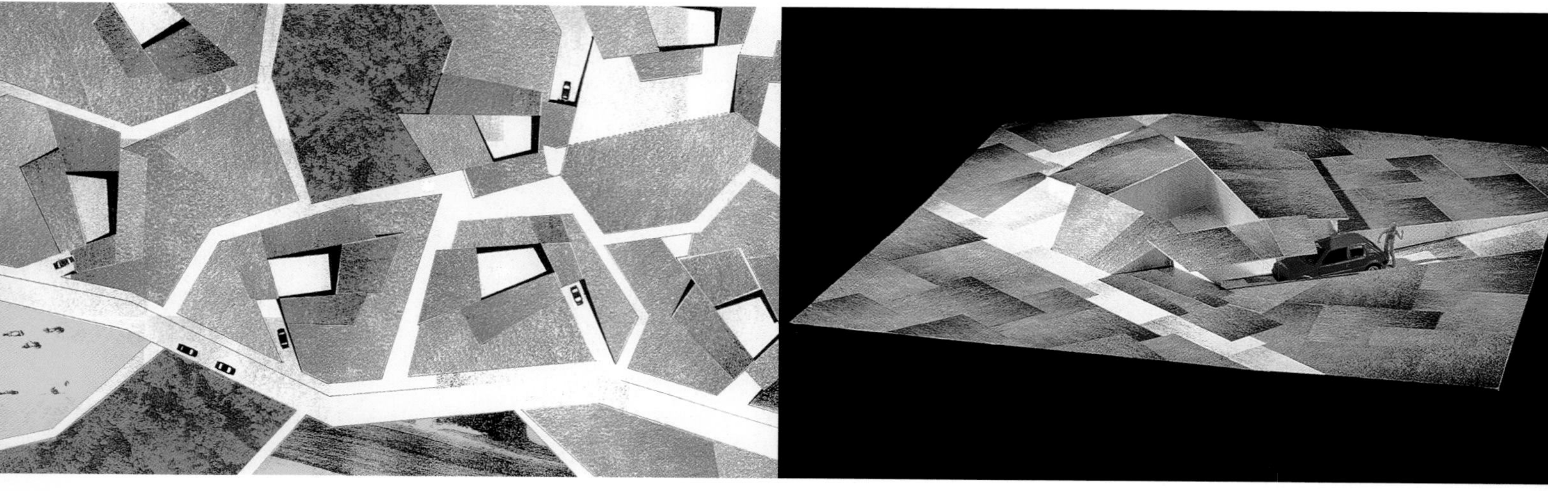

HOUSE H (UNBUILT), CORSICA, FRANCE, 2002

above: DIGITAL MODELS; below: DIGITAL RENDERINGS OF BUILDING AND SITE

SLAVIN HOUSE, VENICE, CALIFORNIA, 2004–PROJECTED 2008

above: ELEVATION; below: DIGITAL RENDERING OF INTERIOR "BUBBLE" WALL

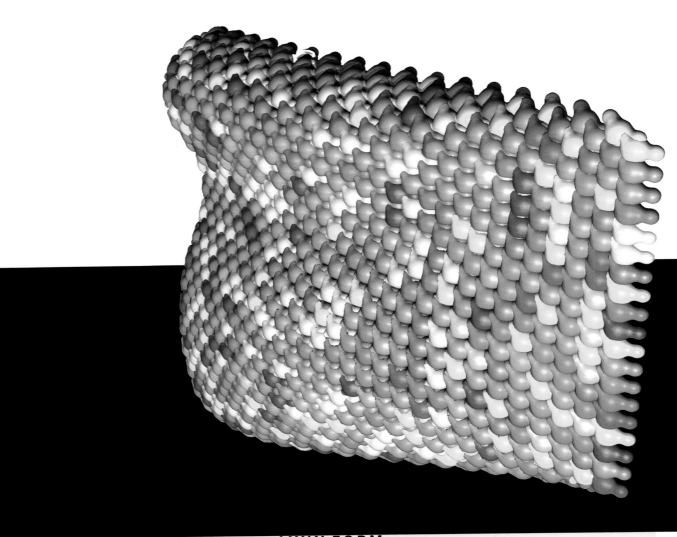

GREG LYNN FORM Venice, California

Greg Lynn, b. 1964, Vermillion, Ohio

Greg Lynn relocated his architecture practice from Hoboken, New Jersey, to Venice, California, in 1998 to take full advantage of technologies developed for Southern California's aeronautic, automotive, and industrial design industries. Lynn seeks out new design methods and manufacturing techniques in order to realize his complex architectural forms; in recent years, he has turned to product design in order to experiment with form and fabrication on a more manageable scale. His conversion of digital information into the coded paths that direct manufacturing tools to generate physical models and prototypes has resulted in complex built work characterized by intricate textures and voluptuous curves. Lynn uses materials and colors—including white corian, brightly colored plastic, transparent acrylic, and gold-toned metals—more common to product design. In fact, the Slavin House (Venice, California, 2004–projected 2008), his family residence, resembles a product blown up to the scale of architecture. Somewhat baroque in its incorporation of varied shapes and substances, the residence features two continuous rolled-steel trusses braided and looped through one another to function simultaneously as beams and pillars. A window/wall resembling a cluster of soap bubbles emerges from a corner of the house, and an interior wall comprising interlocking, multicolored plastic pegs recalls a 1960s Paco Rabanne dress.

For the Bloom House (Los Angeles, 2004–projected 2007), Lynn designed a box perforated with a series of eyelet-shaped windows trimmed in stainless steel. The curvilinear interior surfaces are unexpected and contradict the flatness of the exterior envelope. The architect applied smooth white corian to the interior, cutting, tucking, and seaming it to hug the gentle curves and bulges of surfaces. A luminous fiberglass lantern hanging from the ceiling spans the length of the open space containing living, dining, and kitchen areas.

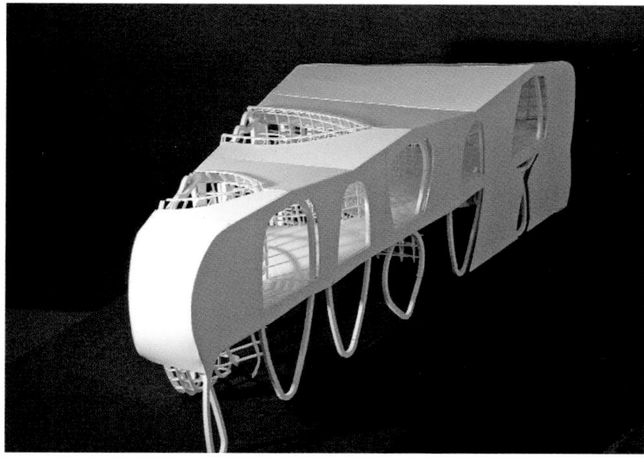

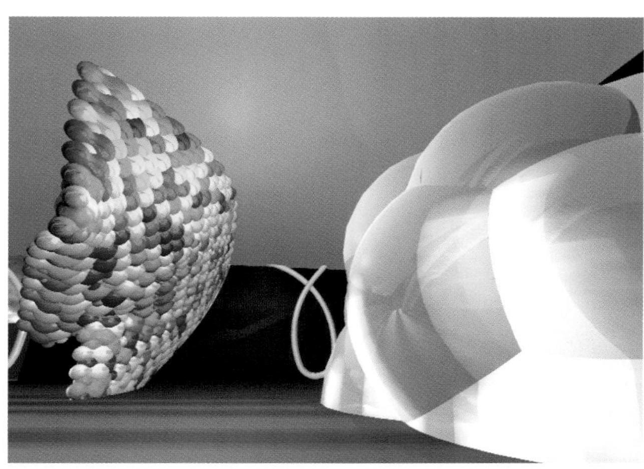

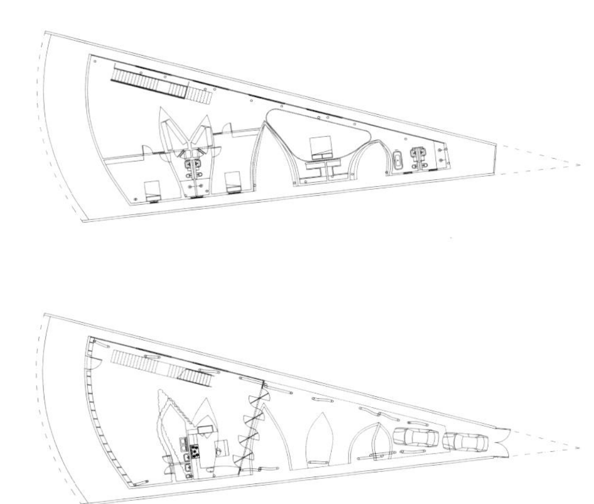

SLAVIN HOUSE, VENICE, CALIFORNIA, 2004–PROJECTED 2008

above, left column: DIGITAL RENDERINGS OF EXTERIOR AND INTERIOR; above, right column: MODEL AND PLANS; below: MODEL

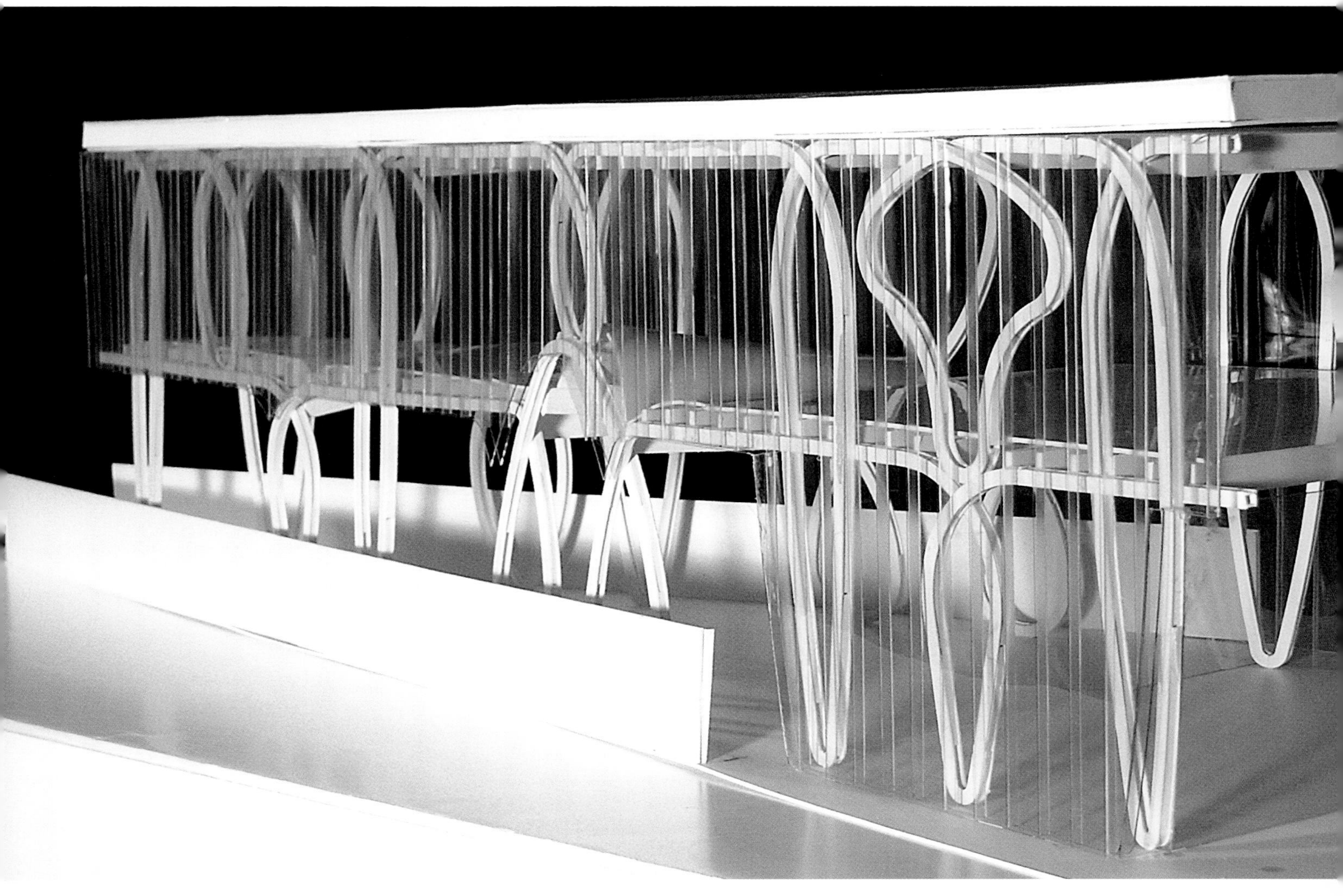

BLOOM HOUSE, LOS ANGELES, 2004–PROJECTED 2007, VIEWS OF MODEL AND SECTIONAL DIAGRAMS

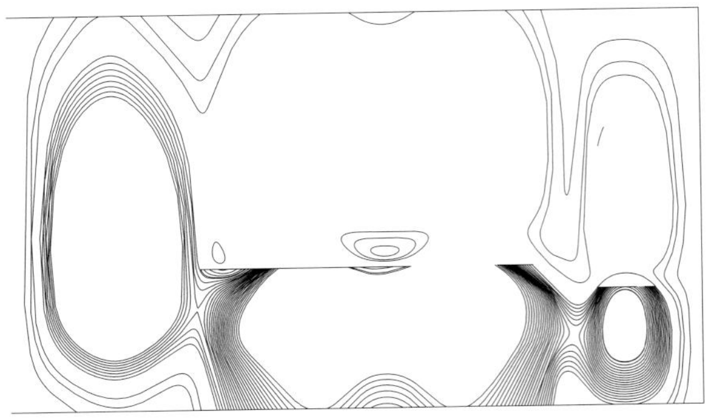

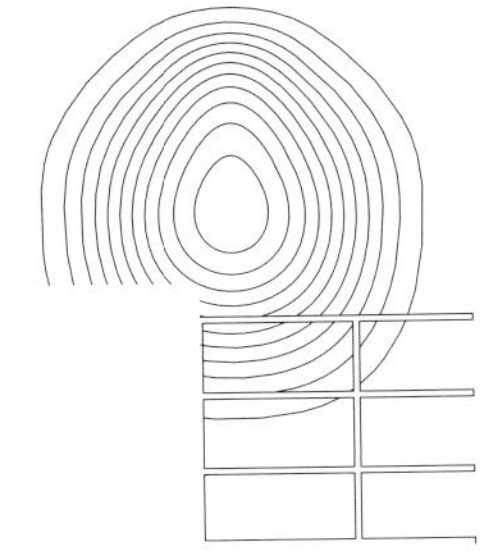

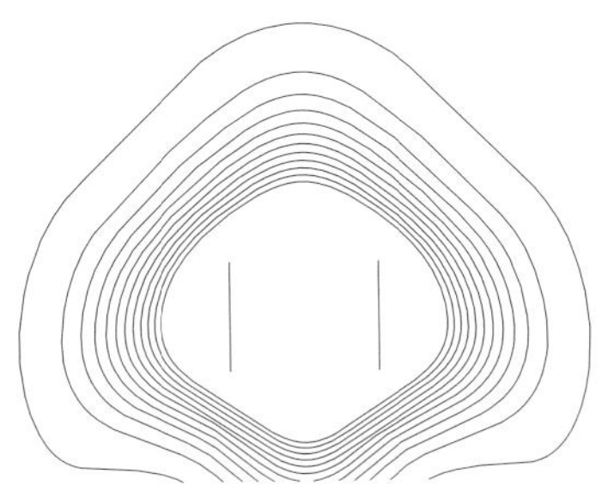

BLOOM HOUSE, LOS ANGELES, 2004–PROJECTED 2007; top: DIGITAL RENDERING OF INTERIOR; bottom: DETAIL OF MODEL

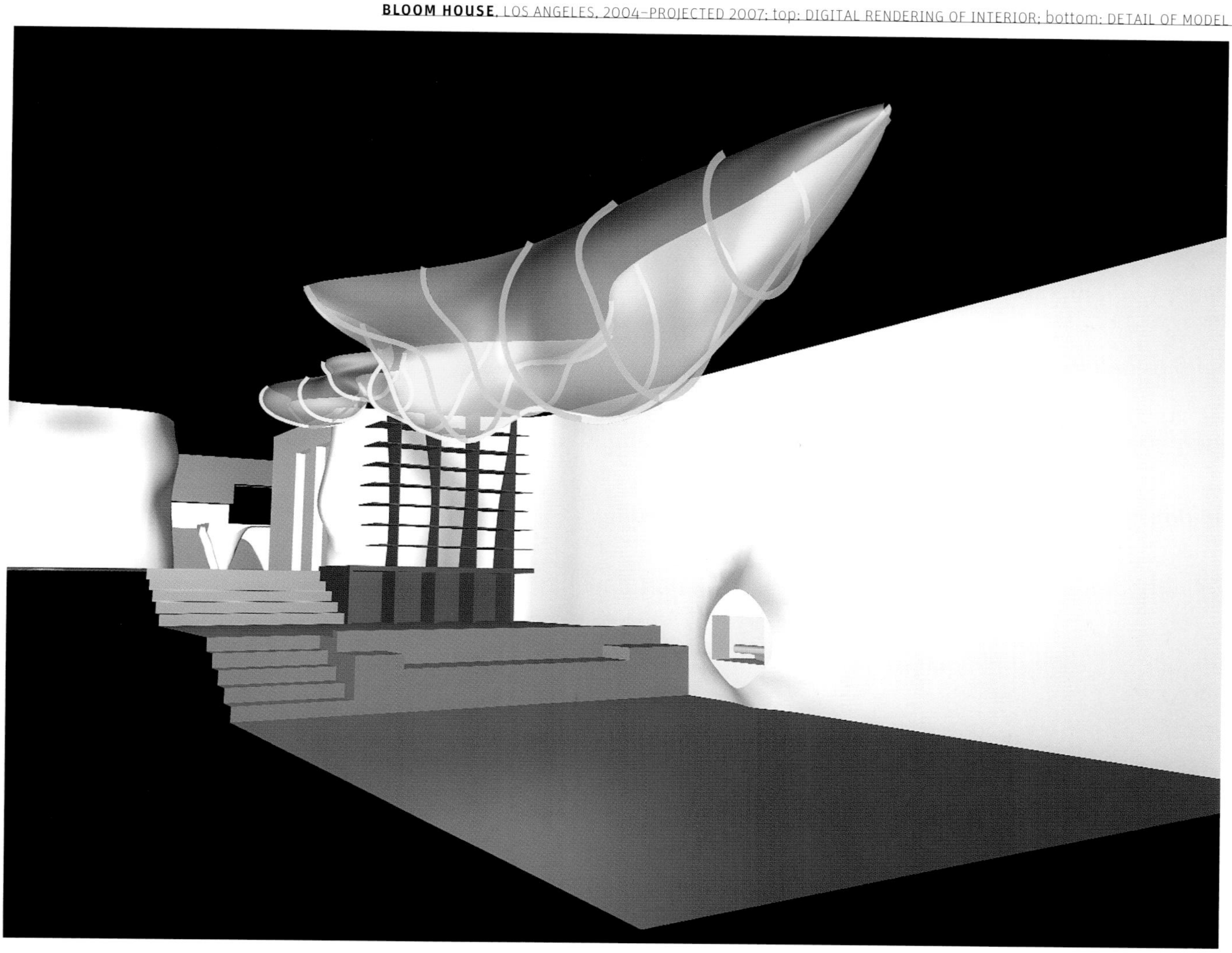

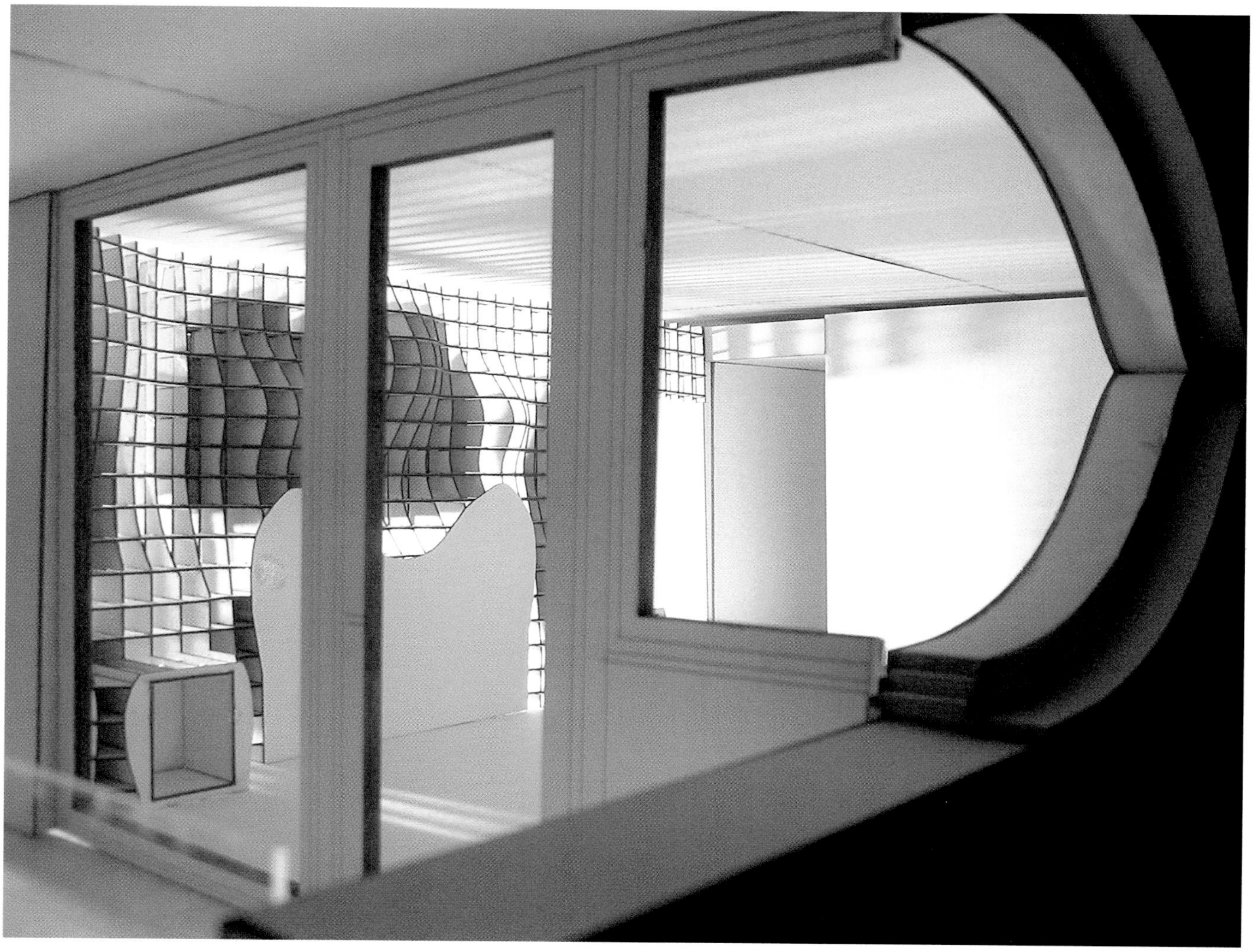

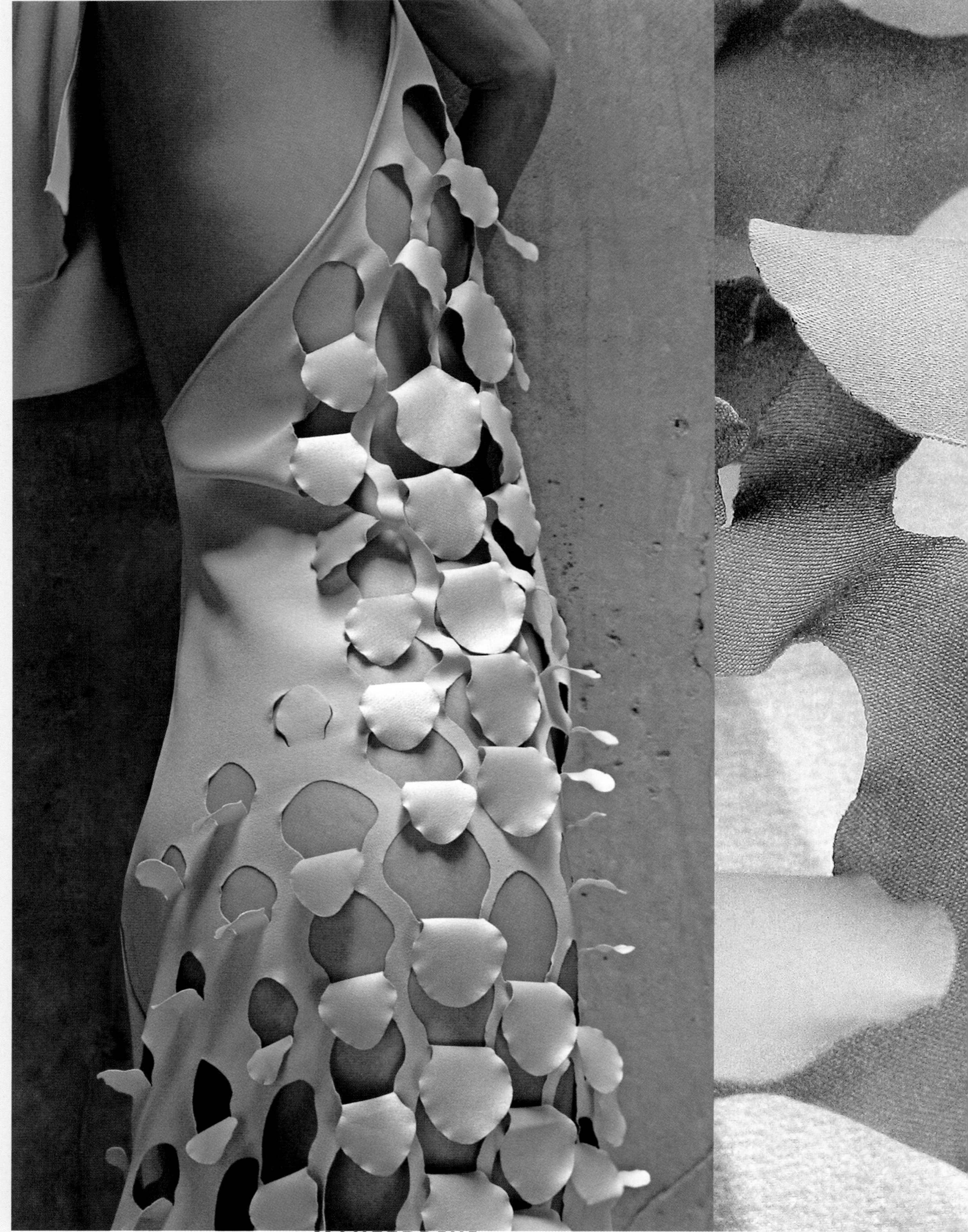

ELENA **MANFERDINI** Venice, California

b. 1974, Bologna, Italy

Elena Manferdini approaches the design of a garment as she would the skin of a building by using tools and techniques more commonly applied to architectural and aeronautical design. Trained as both a civil engineer and an architect, Manferdini has included fashion in her interdisciplinary practice since 2002. She creates garments using Maya three-dimensional modeling software, translating patterns through a machining computer application to laser-cut individual pieces of fabric and texturize them with slashes, cuts, or perforations. Manferdini experimented with numerous fabrics before settling on a cotton-polyester blend that can fluidly follow the curves of the body and yet does not burn or fray during the heat-intensive laser-cutting process.

Since 2004, inspired by geometry as a generator of form and interested in lush surface textures, Manferdini has created several solo collections of one-of-a-kind garments. Her first collection, Clad Cuts (spring/summer 2005), included designs that both reveal and conceal, cleave to and flow from, the body. Insects and butterflies inspired both their forms and surfaces, which feature patterns of laser-cut crescents, gills, waves, and petals. "It was trial and error at first...there are things you can't predict with the computer about how a fabric will fold.... The cuts are meant to create three-dimensionality on the curvature of the body. They move and stretch, they open and distort as you walk...The body shape is a perfect small-scale exercise in spatial design, a testing ground for ideas and techniques to apply to buildings. Openings, folds, panelizing, pattern-making—the concepts and problems are much the same, whether it's a sleeve or a curtain wall."[1]

1 Elena Manferdini, quoted in Eve M. Kahn, "Designer Labels," *I.D.* 52, no. 3 (May 2005): 55.

PETAL DRESS AND DETAILS FROM **CLAD CUTS** COLLECTION, SPRING/SUMMER 2005

opposite top and above left: **TENDONS JACKET** FROM **BONES** COLLECTION, AUTUMN/WINTER 2006–07, DETAIL, SIDE, AND FRONT VIEWS
above right, top row: **SCALES JACKET AND SKIRT** FROM **SCALES** COLLECTION, AUTUMN/WINTER 2005–06, BACK, SIDE, AND FRONT VIEWS
above right, bottom row: **SWARM JACKET** FROM **SWARM** COLLECTION, SPRING/SUMMER 2006, FRONT, SIDE, AND BACK VIEWS

opposite bottom and above: **SKIN JACKET** AND DETAIL FROM **BONES** COLLECTION, AUTUMN/WINTER 2006–07, DETAIL, FRONT, AND BACK VIEWS

MAISON MARTIN **MARGIELA** Paris

Martin Margiela, b. 1957, Louvain, Belgium

Since launching his own label in 1988, Martin Margiela has designed collections that address themes of age, decay, displacement, distortion, and transformation. The pieces in his Semi-Couture collection (spring/summer 1997) appear as if their manufacture is still in progress; raw linen garments have unfinished edges and pins left in place, and the fabric off of dressmaker's dummies is used to create tunics. While Margiela's designs are often described as "deconstructed," he employs extremely sophisticated construction techniques and consistently plays with conventions of tailoring and dressmaking. Details such as pockets, collars, and lapels are often unconventionally placed, and the designer may feature a fabric, such as acetate, not usually visible on the outside of a garment. In Margiela's autumn/winter 2000–01 collection, everything was made to the very large Italian clothing size 78, equivalent to the American size 44. Worn by an average-size woman, a sweater's extra long sleeves fall in multiple folds at the cuff; trousers, wrapped tight at the waist through a constructed folding system, have extremely roomy legs; and a vest made of stiffened acetate retains its bell shape, drawing attention to the space between it and the body.

Margiela's interest in textiles has led him to explore the effects of decay on fabric. Some garments are hand-silvered to create a patina of age, while others are treated to take on the appearance of a thick coat of dust. In recent collections, Margiela has looked at the construction of various forms of seating to inform his clothing designs. In autumn/winter 2004–05, the designer printed garments with images of tufted cushions and upholstery; for autumn/winter 2006–07, he repurposed upholstery fabrics, gathering, darting, and pleating the material to create garments that imitate the structure, volume, fabric, and finish of a chair.

opposite left: GARMENTS FROM COLLECTION, AUTUMN/WINTER 2000–01
opposite right: GARMENTS FROM **SEMI-COUTURE** COLLECTION, SPRING/SUMMER 1997
below: JACKET FROM COLLECTION, AUTUMN/WINTER 2004–05

overleaf: GARMENT FROM COLLECTION, SPRING/SUMMER 1990
page 153: GARMENTS FROM COLLECTION, AUTUMN/WINTER 1997–98

4 2
SEMI COUTURE

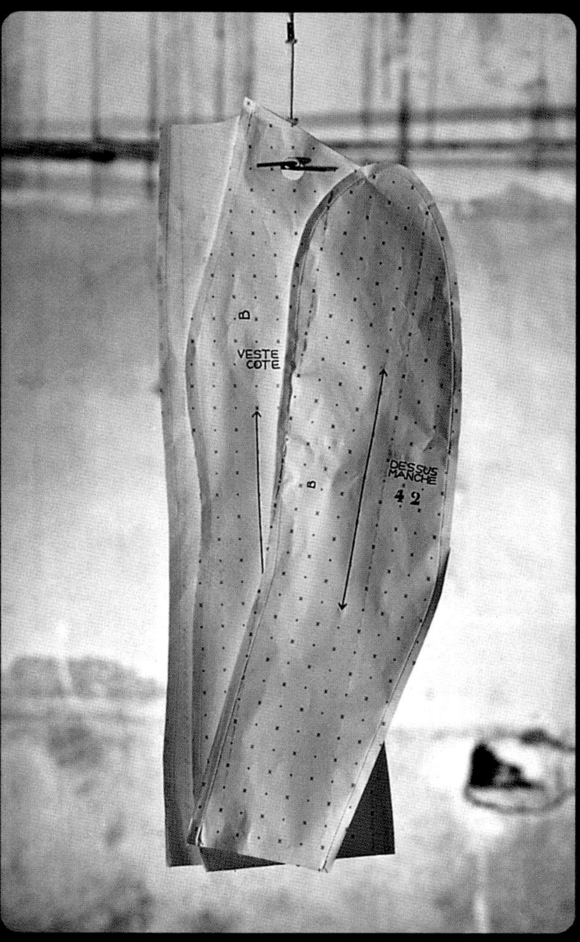
VESTE
COTE
DESSUS
MANCHE
42

ALEXANDER **MCQUEEN** London

b. 1969, London

Alexander McQueen is known for his clothing construction—in particular, the impeccable tailoring and precise execution of architectonic forms—as well as the elaborate sets he uses in his collection presentations. His Scanners collection (autumn/winter 2003–04), for instance, was shown on a set depicting a stark snowy landscape below a glass bridge that also served as a wind tunnel. Conjuring up visions of a nomadic traveler in a futuristic environment, the presentation featured McQueen's signature A-line skirts and fitted bodices in ornate or geometrically patterned fabrics, many of which were lavishly embroidered. An antique green dress from the collection featured rectangular panels of heavy brocade layered like shingles and a pinched waist belted with a padlock buckle. Though the effect was reminiscent of armor, the weight and embellishment of the fabric also evoked upholstery. McQueen's ability to combine contrasting qualities—such as hard and soft, rigid and fluid, violent and fragile—in the same garment is evident in the way the layers of a delicate fluted underskirt peek out from the stiff exterior cladding. This play of contradictions is also apparent in a one-piece molded dress from It's Only a Game (spring/summer 2005), which encloses the body like a carapace, as well as in more wearable garments employing similar shapes but executed in softer, more feminine fabrics.

The fantastical sets for McQueen's runway shows often serve as a foil for his clothing, echoing its architectonic construction. His autumn/winter 2006–07 Widows of Culloden collection includes garments that harken back to the slashed tartans of his notorious Highland Rape collection (autumn/winter 1995–96). The show was presented inside a simple wooden box containing a large pyramid of glass and steel that models walked around, inside of which appeared the ghostly hologram of a model wearing one of the collection's key pieces—a new Oyster Dress, which features hundreds of layers of frilled and fluted organza.

DRESSES FROM **IT'S ONLY A GAME** COLLECTION, SPRING/SUMMER 2005

opposite:
left column, top to bottom: GARMENTS FROM **WIDOWS OF CULLODEN** COLLECTION, AUTUMN/WINTER 2006–07, AND **ESHU** COLLECTION, AUTUMN/WINTER 2000–01
center column, top and bottom: GARMENTS FROM **WIDOWS OF CULLODEN** COLLECTION, AUTUMN/WINTER 2006–07; middle: GARMENTS FROM **EYE** COLLECTION, SPRING/SUMMER 2000
right column, top and bottom: GARMENTS FROM **ESHU** COLLECTION, AUTUMN/WINTER 2000–01; middle: GARMENTS FROM **WIDOWS OF CULLODEN** COLLECTION, AUTUMN/WINTER 2006–07

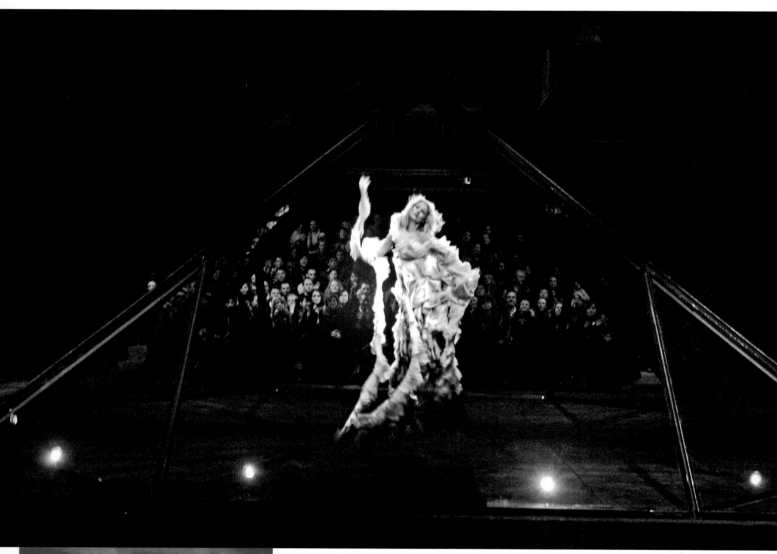

above: DRESS FROM **WIDOWS OF CULLODEN** COLLECTION, AUTUMN/WINTER 2006–07, VIEW OF PRESENTATION
left: **OYSTER DRESS** FROM **IRERE** COLLECTION, SPRING/SUMMER 2003

GARMENTS FROM **SCANNERS** COLLECTION, AUTUMN/WINTER 2003–04

ENRIC **MIRALLES** BENEDETTA **TAGLIABUE/EMBT** ARQUITECTES Barcelona

Enric Miralles, b. 1955, Barcelona; d. 2000, Barcelona Benedetta Tagliabue, b. 1963, Milan, Italy

The husband-and-wife team of Enric Miralles and Benedetta Tagliabue formed EMBT Arquitectes in 1993. For EMBT, the design process is of utmost importance; drawing, sketching, and collage-making are followed by extensive model-making to explore a range of variations until the final form is absolutely right. However, the underlying concept of a project remains constant and is usually arrived at early on in its development.

Inspired by organic forms such as leaves and plants, EMBT also uses the history of a site as a generator of architectural form. For the Santa Caterina Market (1997–2005), the architects renovated a dilapidated nineteenth-century market hall located in the Gothic Quarter of Barcelona, within walking distance of the Miralles/Tagliabue home and studio. Archeological remains of a Roman necropolis, discovered during excavations for the new building, led EMBT to recast its plans for the hall, which itself was built on the site of the medieval Convent of Santa Caterina. To reveal traces of the site's complex history, the architects kept three exterior masonry walls of the 1845 market structure and preserved the Roman ruins in the east corner of the market for public display. For EMBT, "construction/destruction" is "a mirror image of the same activity.... the pair should always act together."[1]

The primary feature of the building is the dramatic, brightly colored tiled surface that drapes in soft undulating folds over the fresh-food market's elaborate skeletal roof structure like an intricately printed skirt. Thousands of hexagonal ceramic tiles in sixty-seven colors create a pattern abstracted from images of a salad of vegetables and fruits. The tiles were made by the same artisans who are restoring the tiles of Antonio Gaudí's projects in Barcelona. The roof's folds were conceived to act "as if it were conducting flows and movement"[2] from the main street into the market at the heart of the neighborhood, and the market's colorful printed skin brings much needed vitality to the otherwise dark and cramped historic quarter.

1 Enric Miralles Benedetta Tagliabue (EMBT), "Construction/Destruction/Construction/Destruction," in *EMBT: Work in Progress* (Barcelona: Col-legi d'Arquitectes de Catalunya, 2004), 139.

2 EMBT, project notes in ibid., 145.

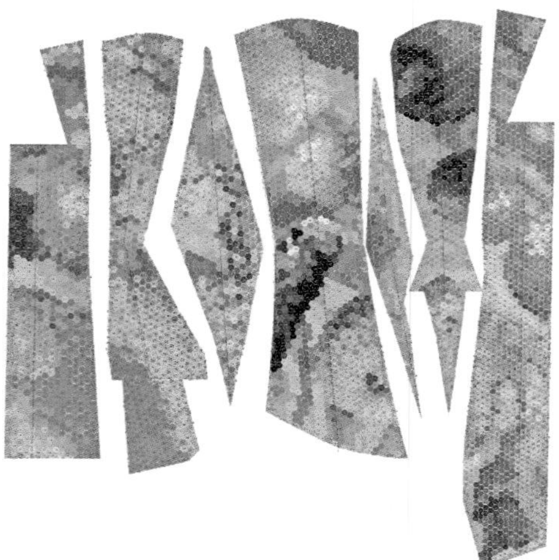

SANTA CATERINA MARKET, BARCELONA, 1997–2005. opposite: DETAIL OF FAÇADE; top: INTERIOR VIEW; bottom left: DIGITAL STUDY FOR ROOF TILES
bottom right: PHOTO-COLLAGE STUDY FOR ROOF TILES; following spread: BIRD'S-EYE VIEW

guapa

MIYAKE ISSEY Tokyo

b. 1938, Hiroshima, Japan

Miyake Issey[1] is renowned for innovation in both textile and clothing design. His technological explorations into clothes-making and the resulting organic sculptural creations have left an indelible mark on the design industry. Miyake pioneered a pleating process by which a piece of polyester is cut and sewn in the shape of a given garment, then sandwiched and pleated between layers of paper and fed into a heat-press machine. The "memory" of the fabric holds the pleats and, when the paper is cut open, the finished garment is revealed. This technology, called "Garment Pleating," is the foundation for the Pleats Please Issey Miyake line, and earlier and later variations on the process resulted in Rhythm Pleats and Minarets. Miyake's pleated garments take on architectonic shapes when worn, and the wearer's movement causes them to bounce, float, or jump like kinetic artworks that expand and contract.

Since 1997, Miyake has focused his attention on design research and technology. Together with Fujiwara Dai (b. 1967, Tokyo), his associate and design engineer, he pioneered the manufacturing method A-POC (A Piece of Cloth). A-POC is an industrial process by which fabric, texture, and a completed knit—the components of a fully finished woven garment—are made in a single process. The first iteration of A-POC comprised the production of continuous-knit tubes from which seamless garments can be extruded by cutting around lines of demarcation customized to the wearer's needs. Today's A-POC is applied to media other than clothing; for the recent A-POC 16, Miyake and Fujiwara not only created JUPITER, a distressed reversible denim jean, but also continued their investigation into furniture design. They presented two products at the 2006 Milan Furniture Fair in collaboration with designer Ron Arad—Trampoline, a knit, and Gemini, a woven—that work as both clothing and chair covers for Arad's Ripple Chair.

1 Though he has been known as Issey Miyake, the Western ordering of his name, the designer has recently recommitted himself to the Eastern convention, which places the family name first.

above: "ISSEY MIYAKE MAKING THINGS," INSTALLATION AT FONDATION CARTIER POUR L'ART CONTEMPORAIN, PARIS, 1998

following spread: **A-POC TRAMPOLINE©**, MIYAKE DESIGN STUDIO IN COLLABORATION WITH RIPPLE CHAIR BY RON ARAD FOR MOROSO, 2005

A-POC JUPITER©, 2006

MORPHOSIS Santa Monica, California

Thom Mayne, b. 1944, Waterbury, Connecticut

Morphosis's Sun Tower in Seoul (1994–97) is a ten-story multi-use building that includes five floors of retail space as well as corporate offices for an international clothing manufacturer. The building's most notable feature is a dramatic two-layer skin comprising an inner steel-and-glass building envelope and an outer perforated aluminum-mesh screen. The screen wraps and folds over the inner envelope like a garment, erupting into an abstract crown of sculptural forms on the roof. Morphosis, cofounded in 1972 by Thom Mayne, has since designed several buildings with two skins—such as Hypo Alpe-Adria Center in Klagenfurt, Austria (1996–2001), and CalTrans District 7 Headquarters in Los Angeles (2000–04)—but Sun Tower constituted the first opportunity to experiment with the concept on such a scale. The folds of the screen were inspired by origami as well as by the client's identity; there is a remarkable similarity between Morphosis's schematic diagrams for the folding skin and the patterns used to cut and assemble pieces of a garment. Shifting between translucent and opaque depending on the viewer's perspective or the time of day, the second skin serves both aesthetic and practical purposes, functioning simultaneously as a brise-soleil or sunscreen, an enclosure, and an oversized urban billboard.

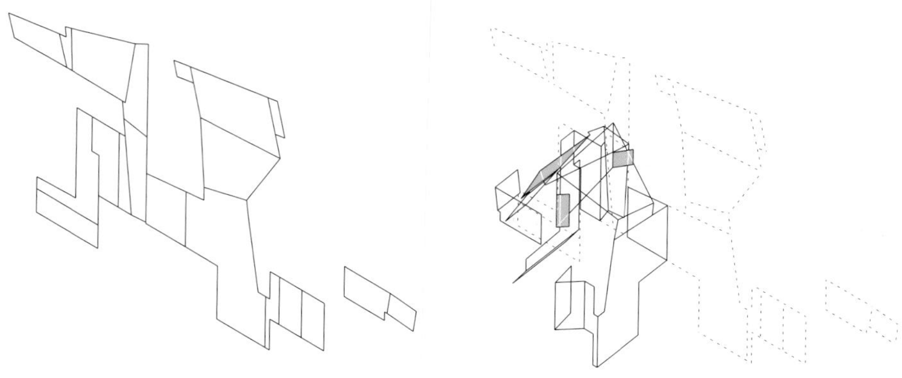

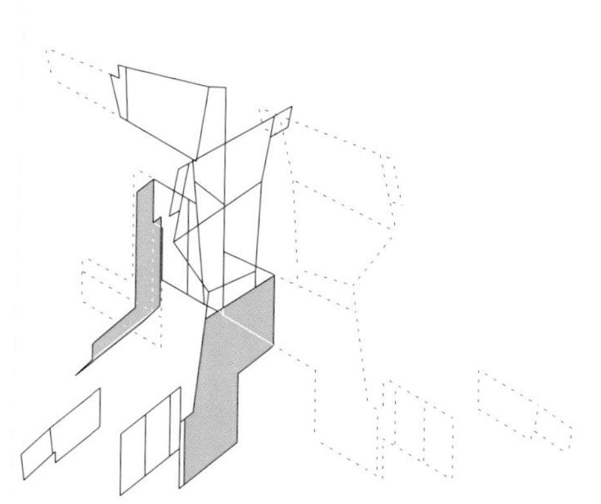

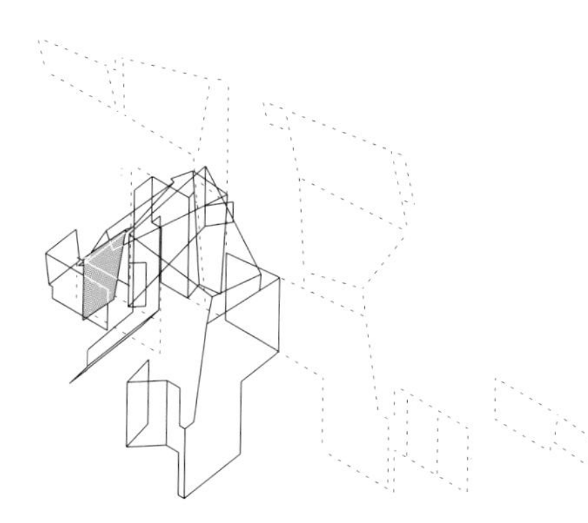

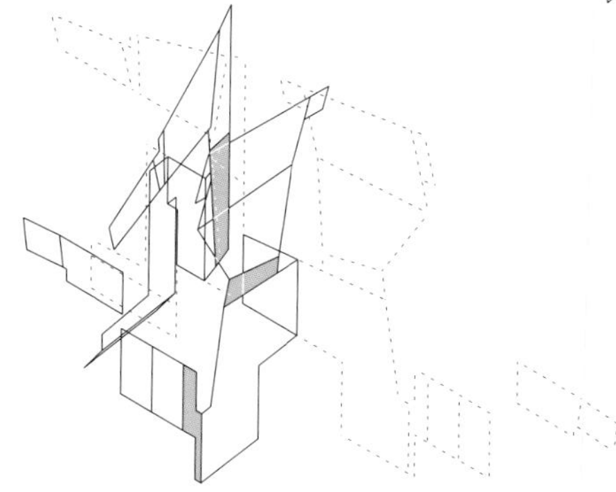

SUN TOWER, SEOUL, 1994–97

opposite: STREET VIEW

FOLDING DIAGRAMS AND DETAIL OF FOLDED MESH SKIN AT TOP OF TOWER

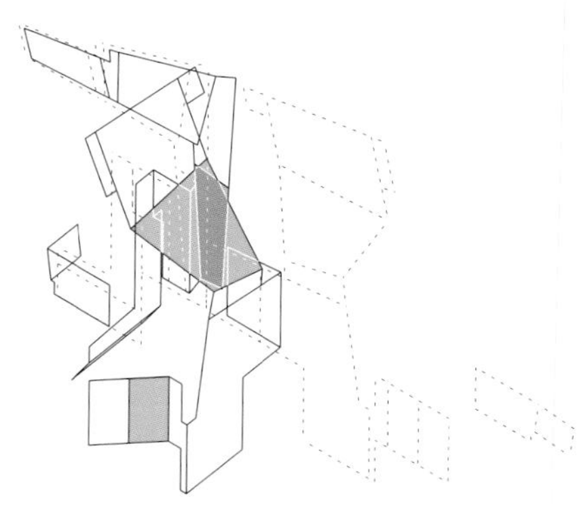

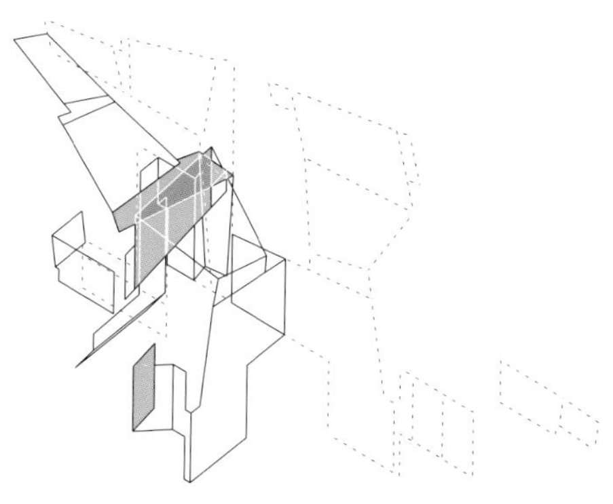

NEUTELINGS RIEDIJK ARCHITECTEN Rotterdam, The Netherlands

Willem Jan Neutelings, b. 1959, Bergan op Zoom, The Netherlands Michiel Riedijk, b. 1964, Geldrop, The Netherlands

Since becoming partners in 1992, architects Willem Jan Neutelings and Michiel Riedijk have completed a number of distinctively shaped and clad buildings. Their 1995–97 building for Veenman, a printing company in Ede, The Netherlands, is wrapped in a continuous skin of frosted glass panels mounted in a simple framework derived from greenhouse construction and backed by light-reflective insulation. Each panel was screen-printed with a letter from a poem by Dutch poet K. Schippers; the letters were designed and arranged by graphic designer Karel Martens. The printed skin reflects the identity of the client and the nature of their work.

For their entry to a 1998 competition for a new concert hall in Bruges, Belgium, Neutelings Riedijk designed a sculptural building that bridges two distinct sites: a park in the medieval city center and a thoroughfare leading down into an underground motorway. Above the building's base stands a tower, off of which a large music hall cantilevers over the roadway and a smaller hall juts over an area of the park. Two smaller elements—a balcony and a stage lift—project crosswise, so that the building "faces" all directions. To counteract the building's bulkiness, the architects wrapped around its exterior a delicate skin of sand-colored concrete punctured with a leaf-based pattern and backed with bronze paneling. The skin references the filigree work by stonemasons for neighboring medieval cathedrals and Bruges's history as an important center of lace-making.

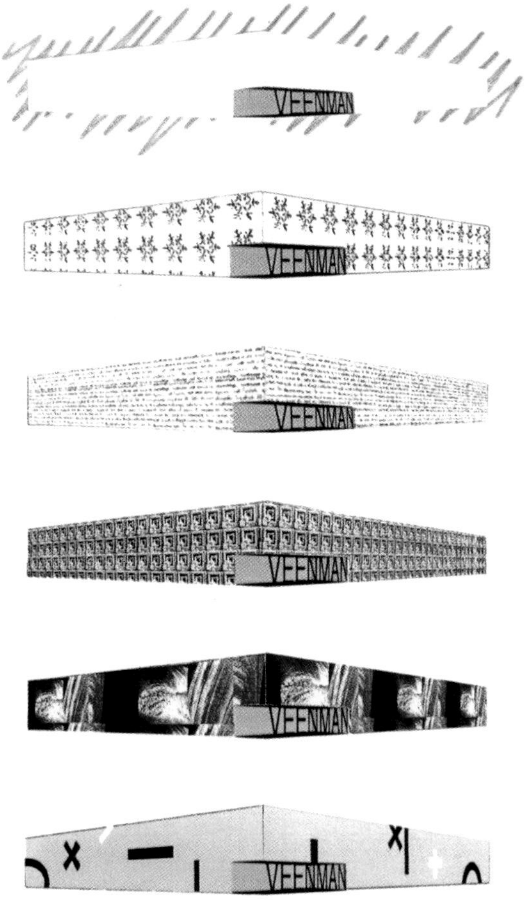

VEENMAN PRINTSHOP, EDE, THE NETHERLANDS, 1995–97

EXTERIOR VIEWS AND DIAGRAMS SHOWING FAÇADE-PATTERN STUDIES

following spread: **CONCERT HALL** (UNBUILT), BRUGES, BELGIUM, 1998

MODEL SHOWING EXTERIOR AND INTERIOR AND STUDY MODELS OF BUILDING VOLUMES

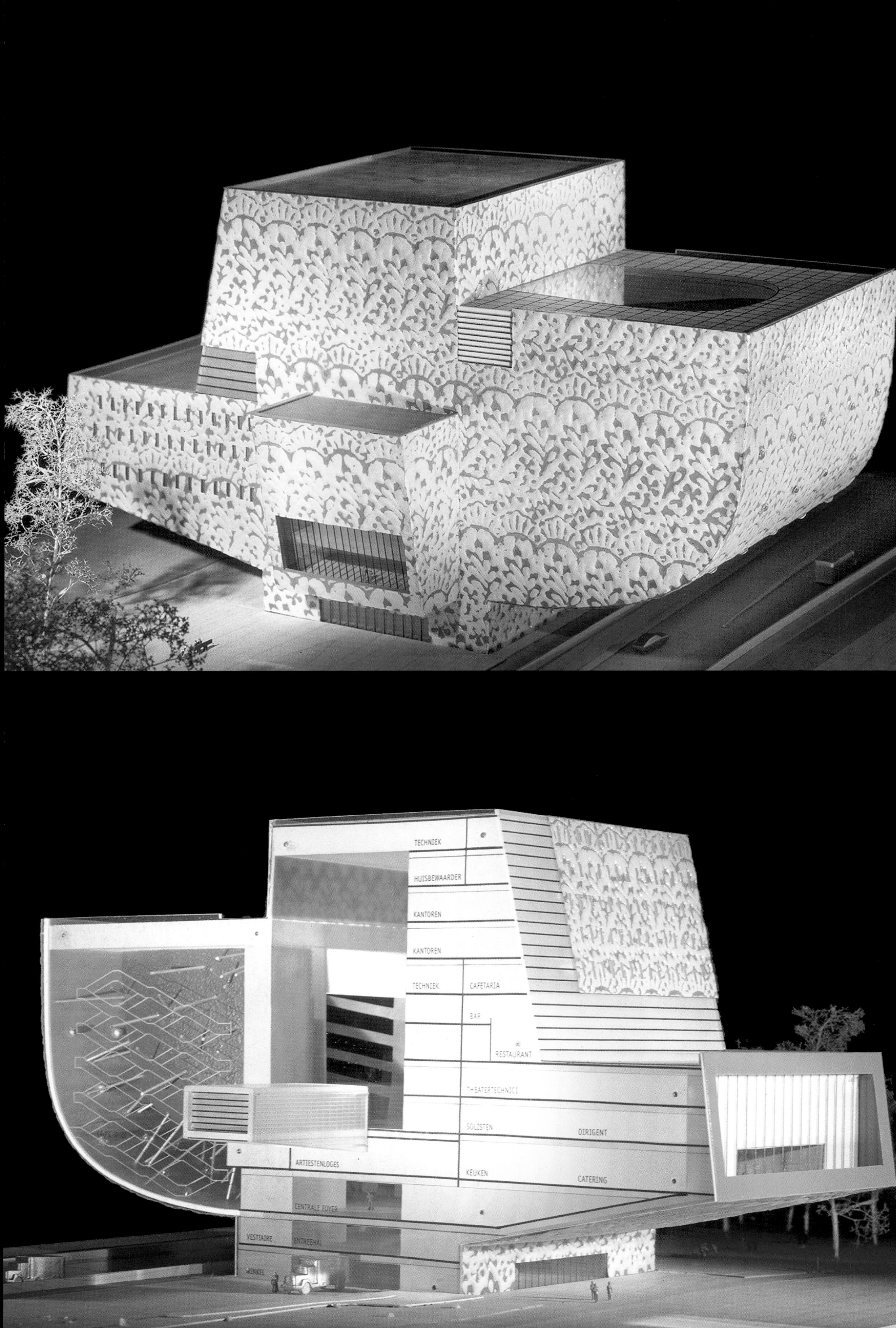
TECHNIEK
HUISBEWAARDER
KANTOREN
KANTOREN
TECHNIEK
CAFETARIA
BAR
RESTAURANT
THEATERTECHNICI
SOLISTEN
DIRIGENT
ARTIESTENLOGES
KEUKEN
CATERING
CENTRALE FOYER
VESTIAIRE
ENTREEHAL
WINKEL

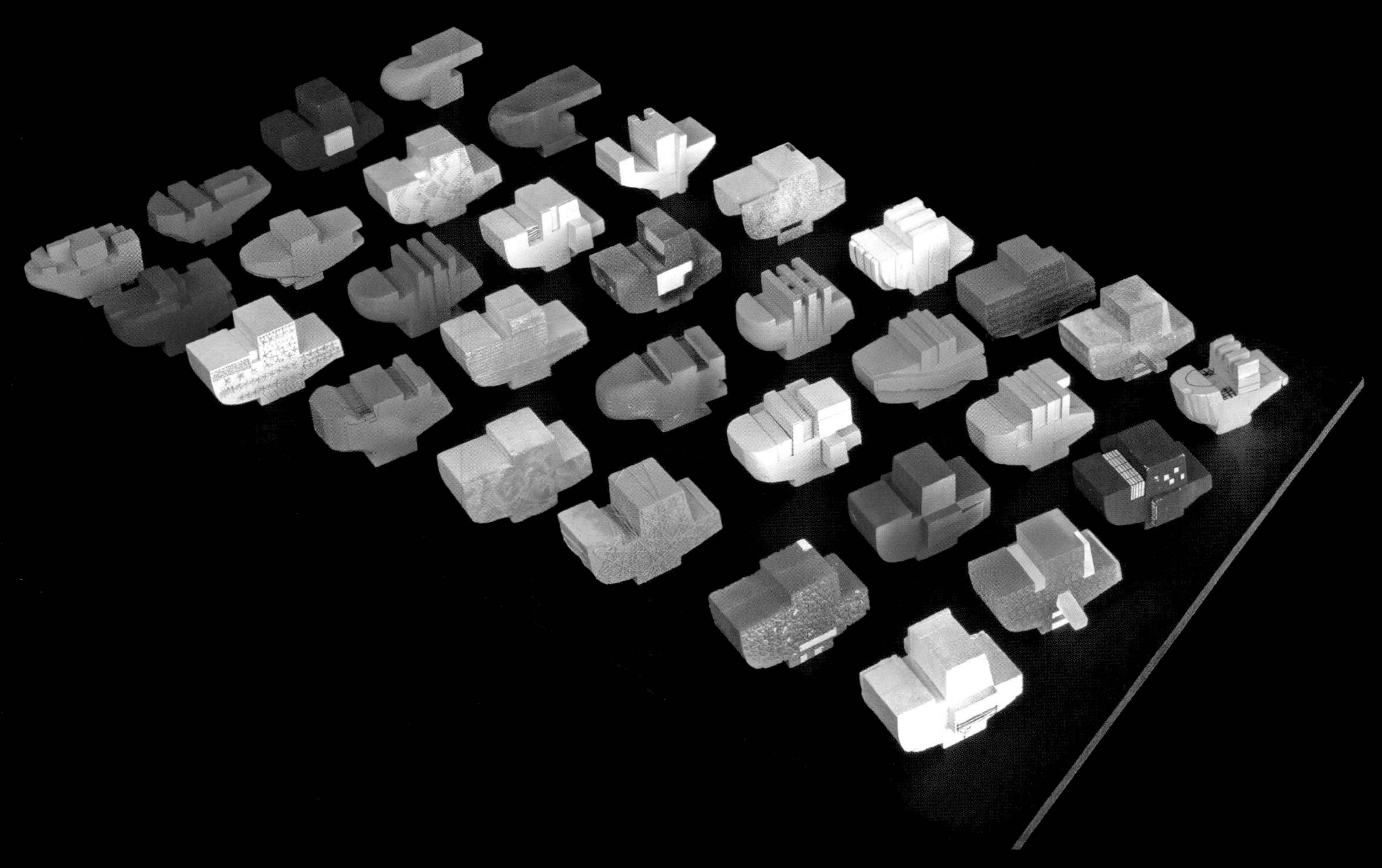

ATELIERS JEAN **NOUVEL** Paris

Jean Nouvel, b. 1945, Fumel, France

Jean Nouvel established his own practice in 1984, shortly after winning the competition to design the Arab World Institute in Paris (1981–87), one of French President François Mitterrand's Grand Projet initiatives of the 1980s. The institute, Nouvel's first major architectural project (executed in collaboration with Gilbert Lezenes, Pierre Soria, and Architecture Studio), was commissioned by representatives of nineteen Arab states to foster knowledge of Arab culture in the West. Nouvel described the building as "a hinge between two cultures and two histories."[1] Its patterned south façade is a contemporary expression of Arab culture and architecture, while the north façade is literally a mirror of Western culture—a glass curtain wall enameled with images of the Parisian cityscape. The south façade consists of variously sized metal diaphragms set behind a glass wall. The self-adjusting diaphragms or apertures operate like camera lenses; controlled by photoelectric cells, they open and close in response to changing exterior light conditions. The overall effect is that of a *moucharaby* (traditional Islamic latticework screen that adorns windows, loggias, and balconies whose original purpose was to shield women from view by outsiders), which permits one to observe from inside without being seen. During the day, the apertures are dramatically set off by incoming light, but from the exterior only a subtle and dense pattern is apparent; at night, this relationship reverses. The building, located in the center of Paris on the left bank of the Seine River, functions as a cultural center and includes a museum, library, auditorium, restaurant, and temporary exhibition spaces.

1 Jean Nouvel, project description for Arab World Institute, http://www.jeannouvel.com.

ARAB WORLD INSTITUTE, PARIS, 1981–87

opposite: INTERIOR VIEWS; above and below: EXTERIOR VIEWS

pages 178–81: **HOUSE IN NEW ENGLAND**, BOSTON, 2002–03

OFFICE dA Boston

Monica Ponce de Leon, b. 1965, Caracas Nader Tehrani, b. 1963, London

Monica Ponce de Leon and Nader Tehrani, who founded Office dA in 1991, conduct elaborate investigations into the properties of various materials in order to articulate a building's skin. Tectonic strategies such as weaving, folding, draping, or wrapping are executed using substances like rubber, brick, or wood, resulting in inventive fabrication techniques, the details of which are worked out in physical models and drawings and digital renderings. In Casa La Roca, Caracas (unbuilt, 1995), the house's brick façade resembles a woven curtain when the running bond pattern of the brick is stretched and folded at the point where the private areas of the house open up into outdoor areas. Another critical aspect of Office dA's work is the way a particular design strategy can seem to change the nature of a material. For Zahedi House (unbuilt, 1998), a renovation project for a home in Weston, Massachusetts, the architects proposed masking the existing structure by wrapping it in a skin of galvanized steel which they corrugated, thereby effecting "a 'domestic' transformation...onto a generally tough material."[1]

The spatial volume of House in New England (2002–03) features several distinct exterior skins. Two of its façades are clad in cedar siding, a material that relates to the vernacular architecture of the region, while another comprises a grid of windows that provides a view of the sylvan surroundings. A snug rubber skin, much like a wetsuit or a custom-fitted couture garment, wraps the roof, chimney, and remaining façade, where it features gill-like slits that expose the windows beneath.

1 Office dA, project description, http://www.officeda.com.

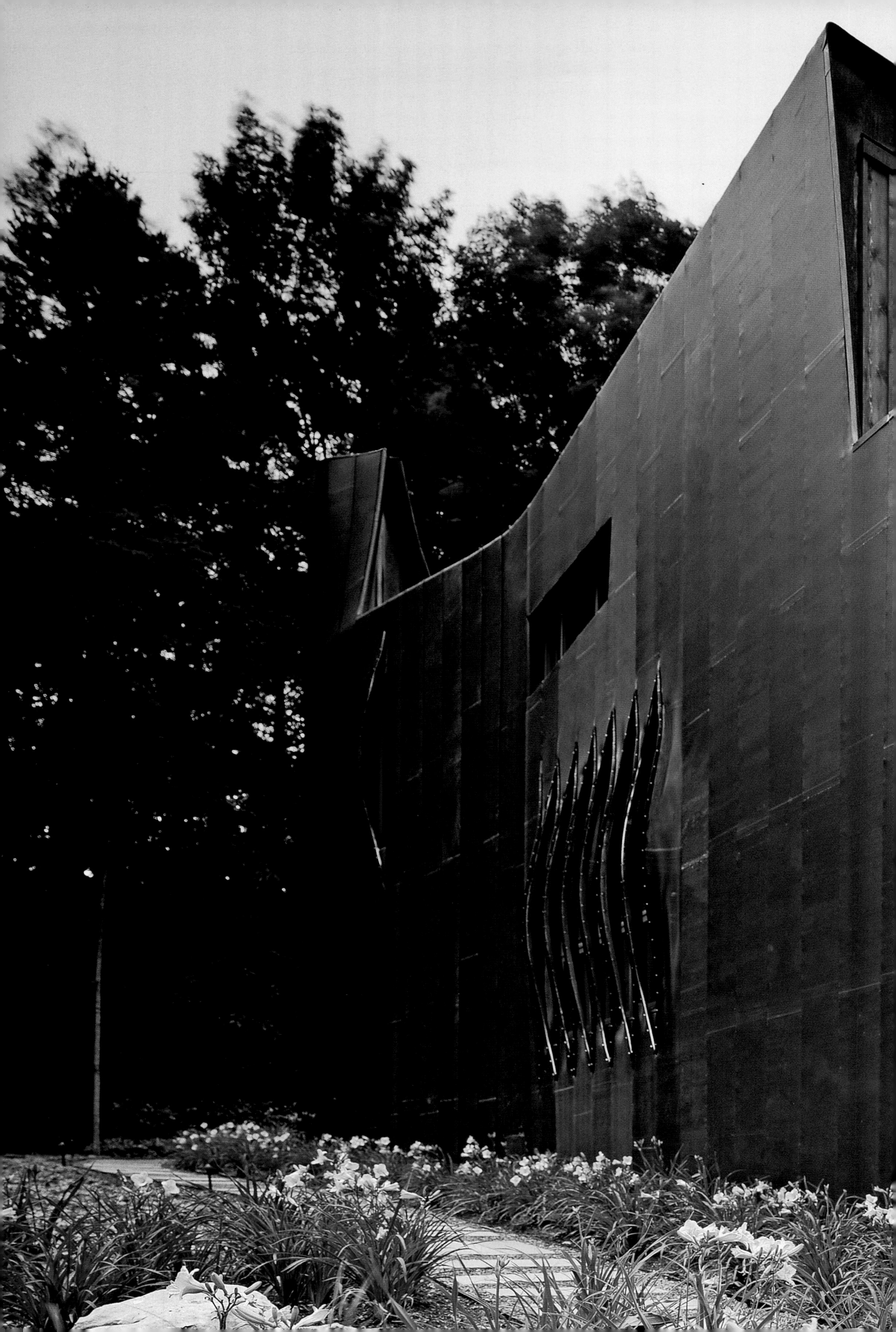

ZAHEDI HOUSE (UNBUILT), WESTON, MASSACHUSETTS, 1998, VIEWS OF MODEL

CASA LA ROCA (UNBUILT), CARACAS, 1995, VIEWS OF MODEL

OFFICE FOR METROPOLITAN ARCHITECTURE/REM KOOLHAAS

Rotterdam, The Netherlands; New York; and Beijing

Rem Koolhaas, b. 1944, Rotterdam Joshua Prince-Ramus, b. 1970, Seattle

Cofounded by Rem Koolhaas in 1975, Office for Metropolitan Architecture (OMA) researches architecture and urbanism, as well as engages in cultural analysis as part of their practice. For the Seattle Central Library (1999–2004), architects from OMA, cooperatively with their clients, visited libraries in Europe and the United States to research existing institutions and theorize about their future. Such extensive study and dialogue led the architects to conceive of flexible areas for the library—a reading room, "mixing chamber" (central reference area), "living room" (central meeting area), and centers for children and multilingual patrons—to set between five programmatic "boxes" established to serve the fixed needs of the project: administrative offices, book storage, meeting areas, staff areas, and a parking garage.

These programmatic spaces were reconceived as compartments in a vertical stack: the building's physical shape emerged from the pushing or pulling of forms in one direction or another. Such manipulation created four dramatically different façades, each undulating with recessions and cantilevered projections. The entire building is wrapped in a mesh skin of diamond-shaped panes of glass (much like a fishnet stocking) set into a matching steel grid that operates as both a transparent curtain wall and part of the structural system. As Herbert Muschamp described, "the interior's overhanging platforms have been draped with a metal and glass building skin, as if it were a piece of cloth. Hence the exterior folds. So what looks, from the outside, like a willful exercise in complex geometry is actually a simple envelope to enclose mass."[1]

The core of the building—a two-hundred-foot-square, forty-five-foot-high structure—is the Book Spiral, which houses the majority of the library's non-fiction collection. Instead of storing books on individual floors separated by stairs and elevators, a continuous ramp equipped with row upon row of bookshelves spirals upwards for four floors. This system of organization allows for easy accessibility and growth, as most of the collection is housed in a single space and is organized in numerical Dewey decimal order, rather than by subject.

1 Herbert Muschamp, "The Library That Puts on Fishnets and Hits the Disco," *The New York Times*, 16 May 2004, sec. 2.

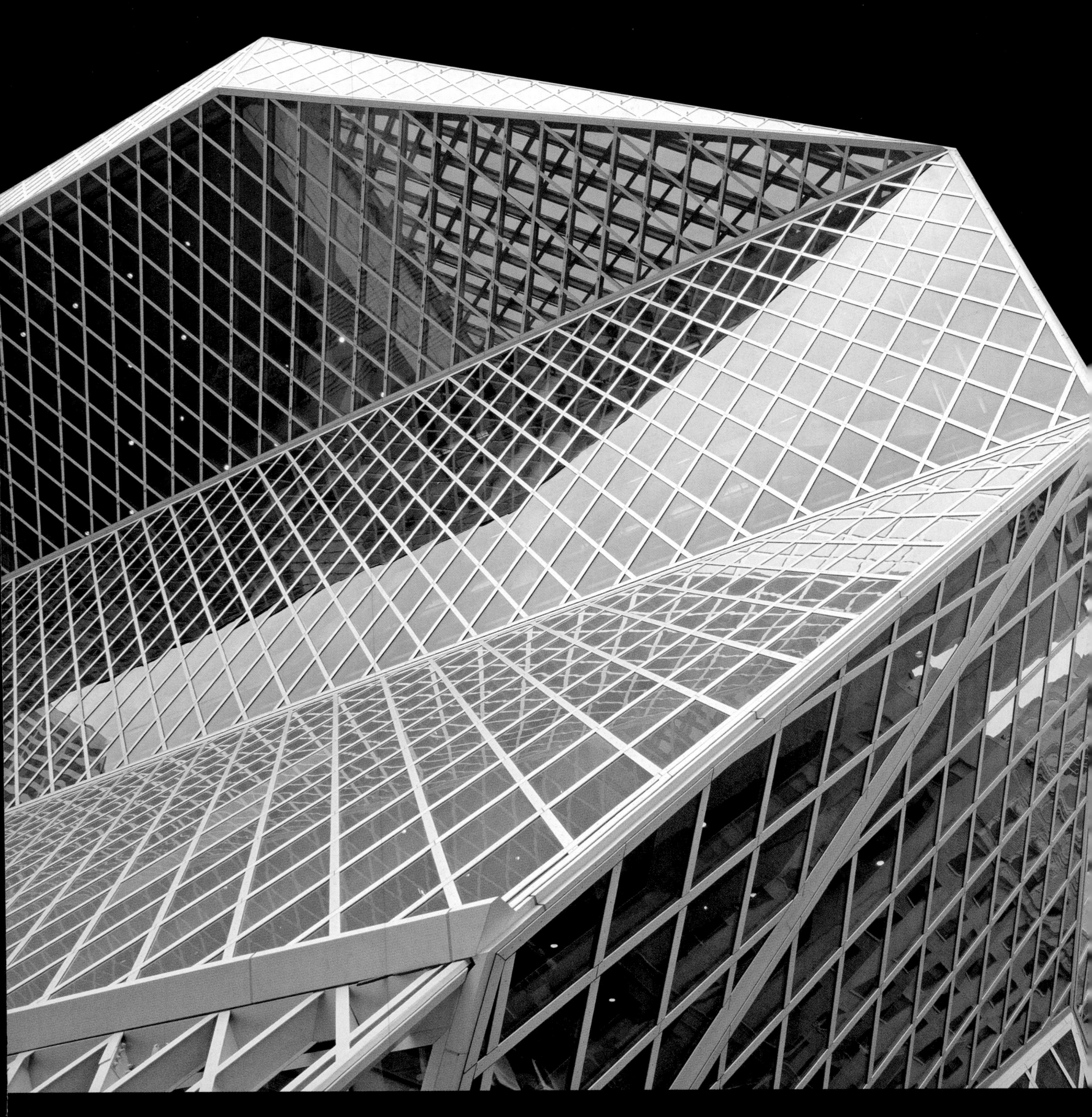

SEATTLE CENTRAL LIBRARY, SEATTLE, 1999–2004
pages 184–85: EXTERIOR VIEW AND DETAIL OF SKIN
above and opposite top: MODELS SHOWING BUILDING'S SKIN AND BONES
below: VIEW OF LIVING ROOM; opposite bottom: VIEW OF READING ROOM

NARCISO **RODRIGUEZ** New York

b. 1961, Newark, New Jersey

A love of modern architecture is at the core of Narciso Rodriguez's minimalist women's wear. The designer explained, "What I relate to is the creation of a form from structure and material. Although I don't use direct architectural references in my work, I approach designing a garment in much the same way an architect approaches designing a building with seaming for structure to create interesting fit lines and shape."[1] His approach to structure echoes the "form follows function" philosophy of the Bauhaus School and the "less is more" axiom of Ludwig Mies van der Rohe. Consistent with a key principle of architectural modernism, Rodriguez's creations possess no extraneous decoration. Their bold graphic sensibility is the result of allowing seams, darts, and fit lines themselves to serve as decoration and largely limiting his palette to white, black, and occasionally earth tones.

Every detail of Rodriguez's clothing is carefully composed; seams and fit lines follow curves of the body and show how a garment is put together. Unlike designers who create silhouettes based on independent volumes, Rodriguez typically restricts the amount of negative space between body and clothing and relies instead on structural elements such as a built-in bra or a corsetlike bodice to provide shape. As a result, the predominant silhouette of his early collections is narrow and close to the body. However, for his autumn/winter 2005 collection, Rodriguez introduced greater volume by pairing softly draping skirts with his trademark formfitting tops and bodices.

Rodriguez's design process is characterized by many hours spent draping and fitting garments on a live fit model rather than a dressmaker's form. He repeatedly marks, tapes, pins, and retapes fit lines to achieve precise proportions and balance. Wishing to emphasize certain parts of the body—such as the hips, waist, bust, shoulders, or back—the designer removes sections of fabric or inserts fabric panels. Rodriguez's garments are developed from an innate understanding and appreciation of structure, construction, and materiality.

1 Narciso Rodriguez, "His Vision," statement on the designer's website, http://www.narcisorodriguez.com/narciso.html#.

EARLY VERSIONS OF GARMENTS FROM COLLECTION, AUTUMN/WINTER 2005–06

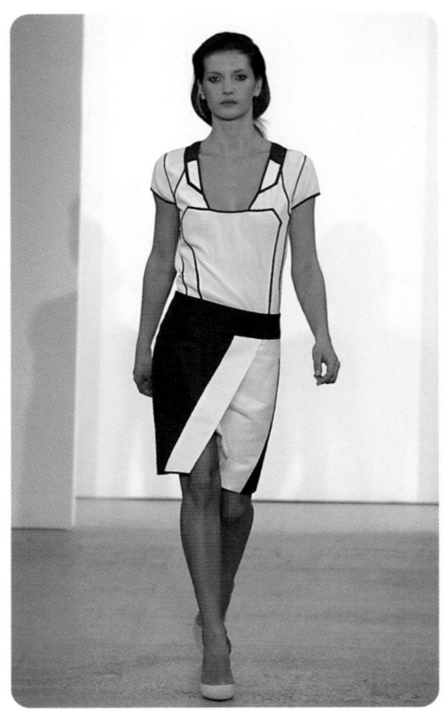

clockwise from above:

DRESS FROM COLLECTION, AUTUMN/WINTER 2004–05

DRESS FROM COLLECTION, AUTUMN/WINTER 2006–07

DRESSES FROM COLLECTION, AUTUMN/WINTER 2005–06

clockwise from right:

DRESS FROM COLLECTION, SPRING/SUMMER 2005

DRESS FROM COLLECTION, SPRING/SUMMER 2004

DRESS FROM COLLECTION, SPRING/SUMMER 2004

DRESS FROM COLLECTION, SPRING/SUMMER 2006

DRESS FROM COLLECTION, SPRING/SUMMER 2005

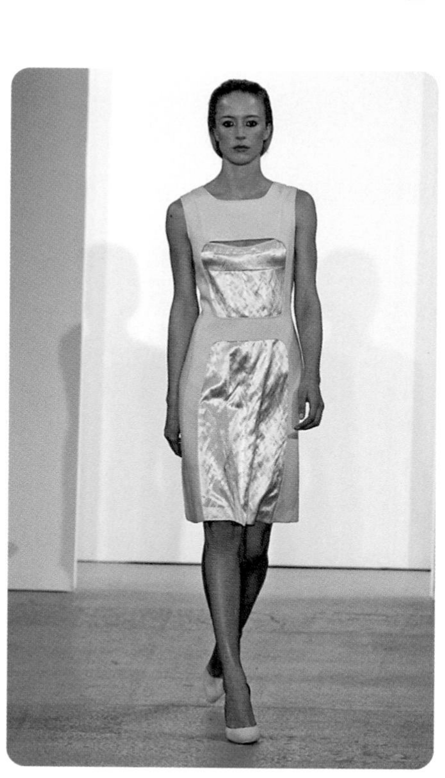

RALPH **RUCCI** New York

b. 1957, Philadelphia

Ralph Rucci's designs demonstrate refinement and impeccable craftsmanship. Since his debut collection in 1981, his one-of-a-kind haute couture garments feature fine handwork—including embroidery, knotting, stitching, and beading. These details are integral to the design, not applied as an afterthought. The Pauline Tunic (autumn/winter 2002–03), for example, features hand-looped ribbons loosely appliquéd to a long black gazar chemise that trails to the ground, creating an elaborate three-dimensional surface and a billowing silhouette. Rucci has been credited with resurrecting gazar, a heavy silk organza that was first developed by the Swiss textile firm Abraham for Cristobal Balenciaga in 1958. Rucci favors toothy fabrics—such as heavy silk jersey, double-faced wool, duchesse satin, faille, moiré, and silk gabardine, as well as double-, triple-, and quadruple-weight gazar—for their sculptural qualities; they allow for greater volume and hold their shape better than lighter, more fluid fabrics.

Such fabrics are the basis for Rucci's Infanta gowns. These reference Balenciaga's dresses of the same name that, in turn, were inspired by Diego Velázquez's painting *Las Meninas* (1656), which depicts the Spanish Infanta Margarita in a voluminous dress, and Second Empire fashions from the mid-nineteenth century. Rucci's Charcoal Infanta Dress (spring/summer 2003) features a system of interlocking circles and darts that provides volume and shape. Made of duchesse satin, the gown obscures the contours of the body in favor of creating a sculptural form. As with many of his designs, the most involved workmanship is virtually invisible from the deceptively simple exterior.

Another Rucci innovation is seen in his suspension garments, including the Ivory Suspension Suit (spring/summer 2005). Areas of the garment are broken up into fragments and reconnected through a system of hand-knotted threads so that they seem suspended and appear as forms in space, similar to those in Russian Constructivist paintings by Kasimir Malevich. Since 1994, Rucci has designed under the label Chado Ralph Rucci, named for a Japanese tea ceremony, emphasizing cut and construction while referencing the fashion, art, and culture of the past.

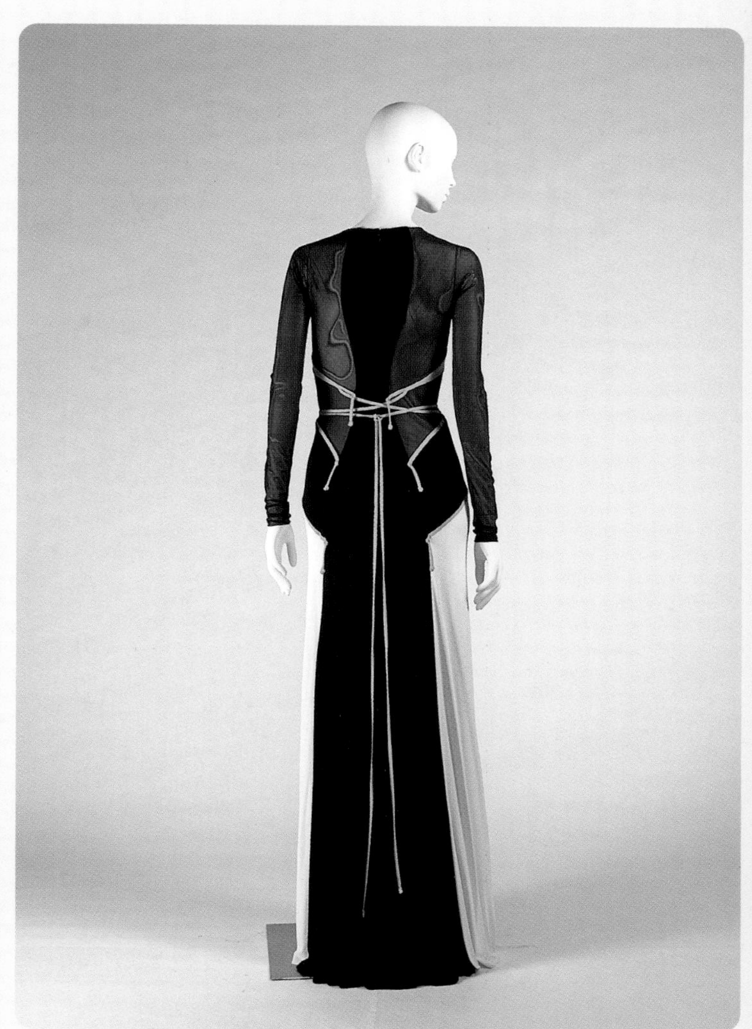

opposite: **PAULINE TUNIC** FROM HAUTE COUTURE COLLECTION, AUTUMN/WINTER 2002–03

above: **MONOLITHIC VERTEBRAE DRESS** FROM COLLECTION, SPRING/SUMMER 2005, FRONT AND BACK VIEWS

below: **INFANTA DRESS** FROM HAUTE COUTURE COLLECTION, AUTUMN/WINTER 2003–04, BACK AND SIDE VIEWS

top left: **PAGODA INFANTA DRESS** FROM HAUTE COUTURE COLLECTION, AUTUMN/WINTER 2003–04

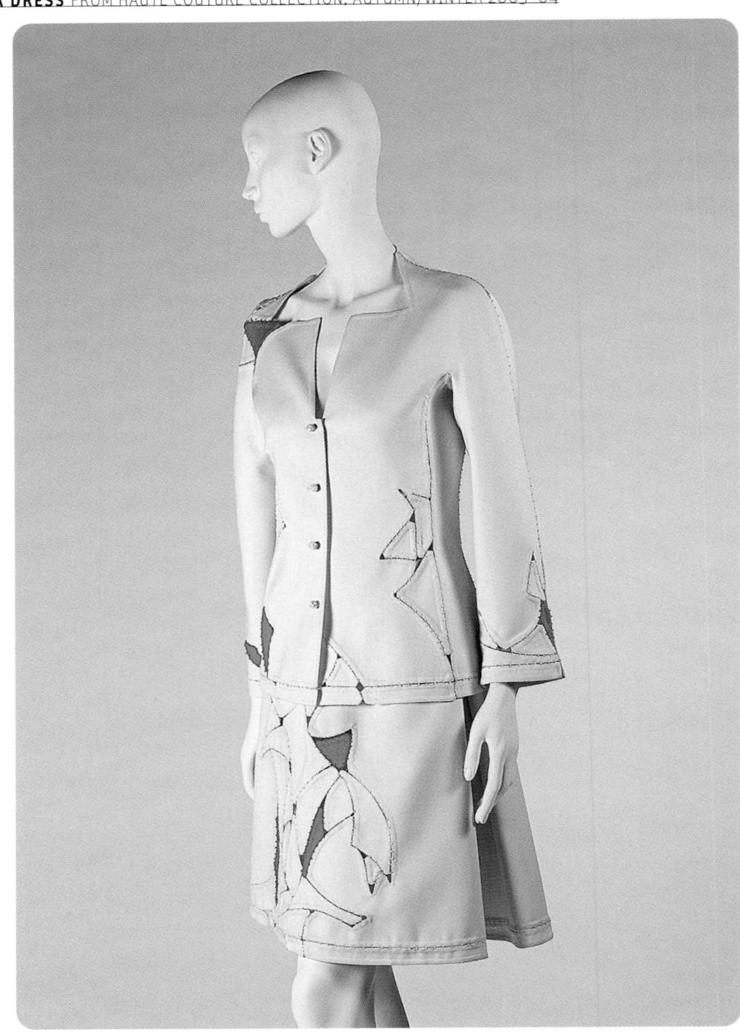

bottom left: **CHARCOAL INFANTA DRESS** FROM HAUTE COUTURE COLLECTION, SPRING/SUMMER 2003

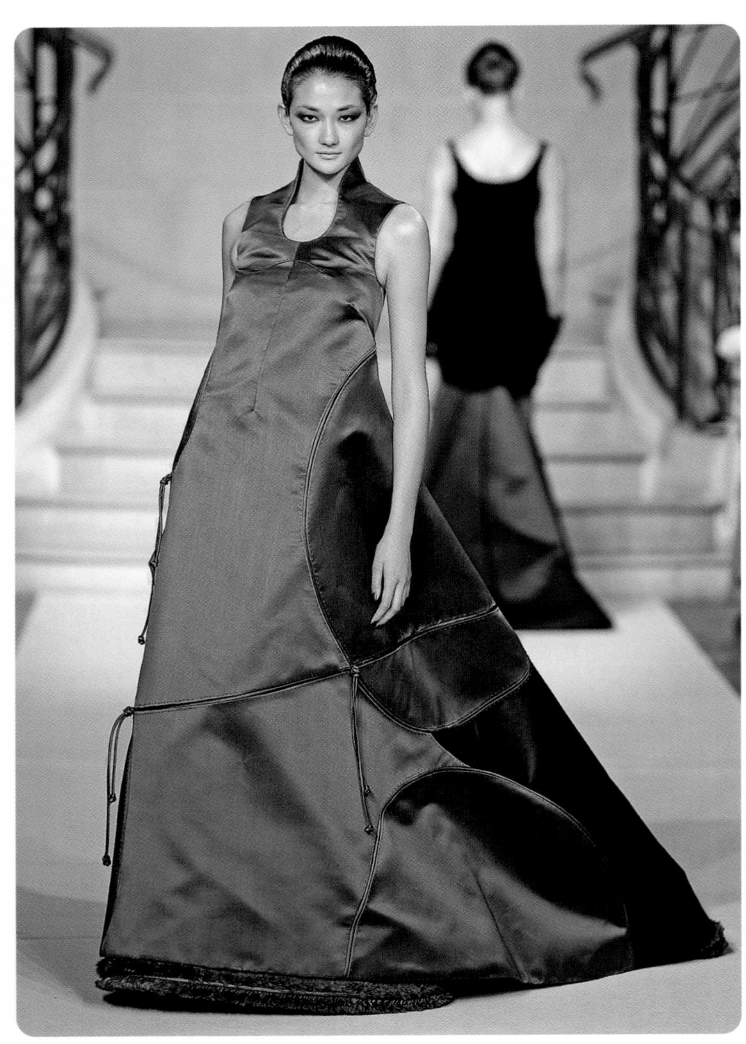

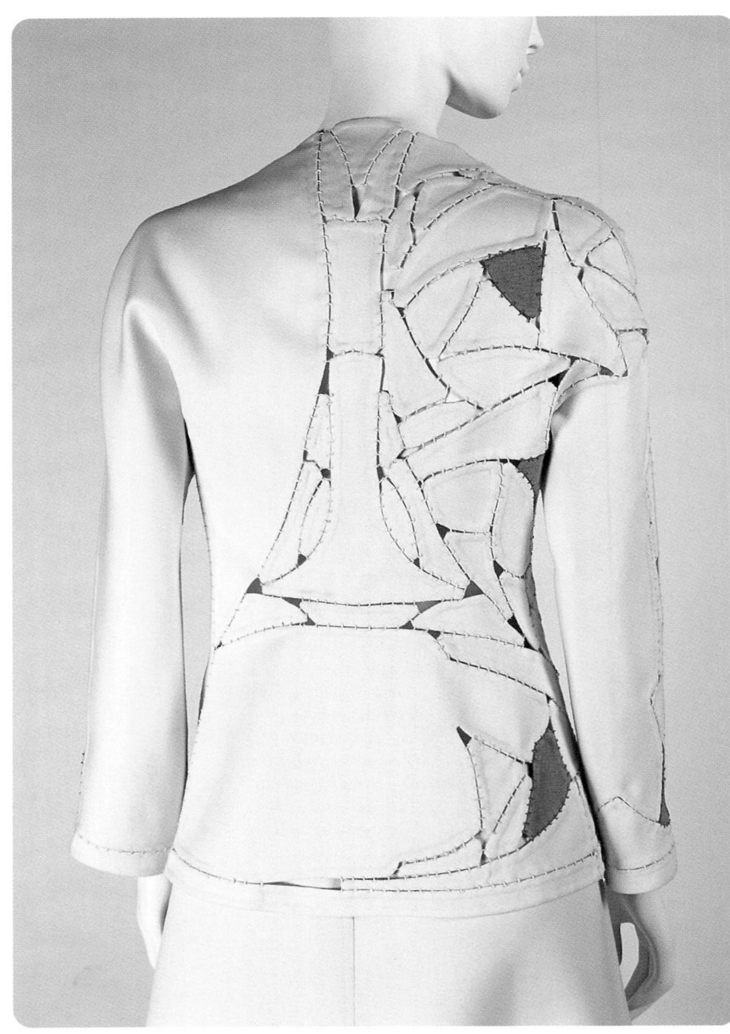

right column: **IVORY SUSPENSION SUIT** FROM HAUTE COUTURE COLLECTION, SPRING/SUMMER 2005, FRONT AND BACK VIEWS left column: DRESS FROM HAUTE COUTURE COLLECTION, SPRING/SUMMER 2003, FRONT AND BACK VIEWS

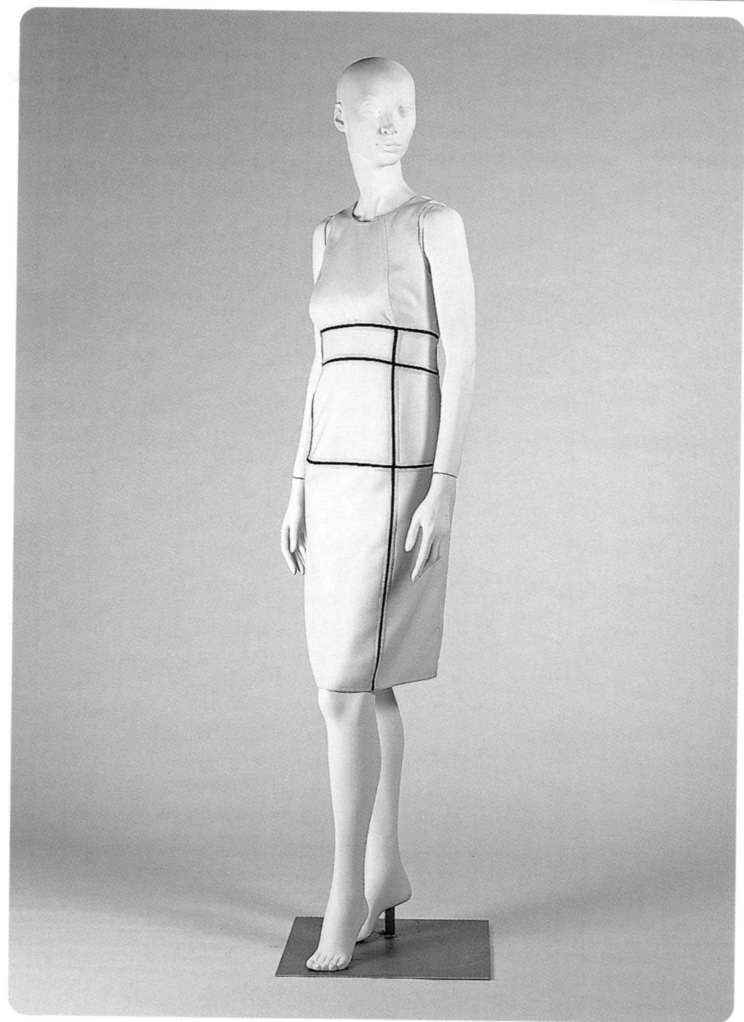

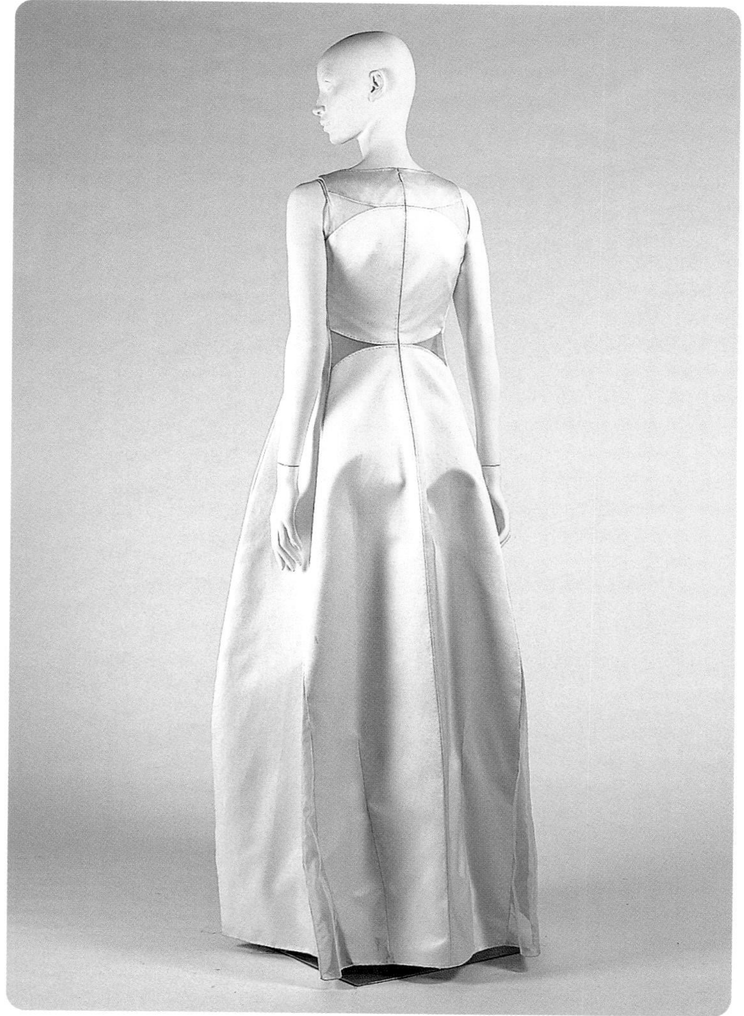

right column: DRESS AND COAT FROM HAUTE COUTURE COLLECTION, SPRING/SUMMER 2003, FRONT AND BACK VIEWS

KAZUYO **SEJIMA** + RYUE **NISHIZAWA**/SANAA Tokyo

Kazuyo Sejima, b. 1956, Ibaraki Prefecture, Japan Ryue Nishizawa, b. 1966, Kanagawa Prefecture, Japan

Luminosity, transparency, and a deceptively simple use of geometric forms to generate complex spatial compositions characterize the work of SANAA, which was founded in 1995 by Kazuyo Sejima and Ryue Nishizawa. SANAA's original use of continuous, often transparent or translucent exterior surfaces establishes subtle but provocative relationships between interior and exterior, individual and community, and public and private. The outer shell of the 21st Century Museum of Contemporary Art in Kanazawa, Japan (1999–2004), is a low-slung cylinder made of two layers of laminated glass. The building's circular plan eliminates the traditional hierarchy of façades and entrances (there are four entrances, one at each quarter-point of the circle) and encourages a multiplicity of approaches and directions. The museum contains a number of individual volumes—squares and circles of varying size—that house galleries, offices, courtyards, and other museum spaces. They are like boxes arranged inside a tray; their walls vary in height, many puncturing through the ceiling and roof of the single-story museum to reveal the interior division of space on the building's exterior.

SANAA's single-story Glass Pavilion for the Toledo Museum of Art in Ohio (2001–06), which also has a laminated glass exterior, is square in plan and houses discrete rounded spaces, like a clear container filled with variously shaped bubbles. Echoing the pavilion's function as an exhibition space for the museum's important glass collection and a facility for glass-making, most rooms are glass-walled. The space in between the individual rooms act as an insulation buffer and fosters a dynamic sense of separation and connection.

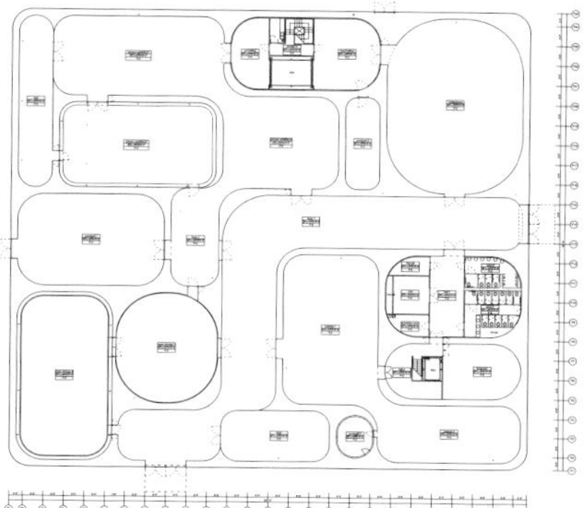

GLASS PAVILION, TOLEDO MUSEUM OF ART, TOLEDO, OHIO, 2001–06

opposite: DIGITAL RENDERING OF INTERIOR; top right: MOCK-UP; bottom right: PLAN

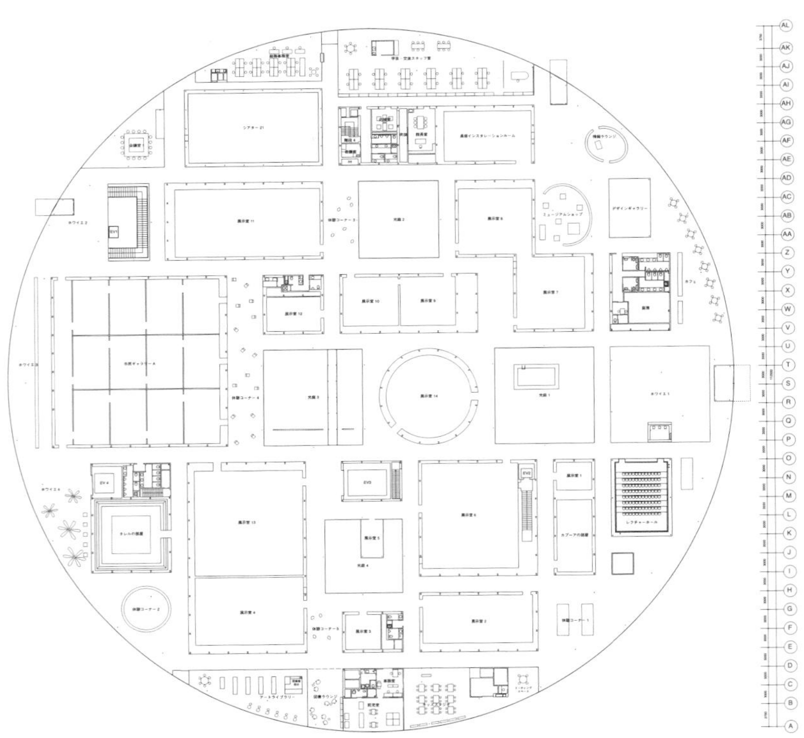

21ST CENTURY MUSEUM OF CONTEMPORARY ART, KANAZAWA, JAPAN, 1999–2004
opposite top: EXTERIOR; opposite bottom: PLAN; above: INTERIOR

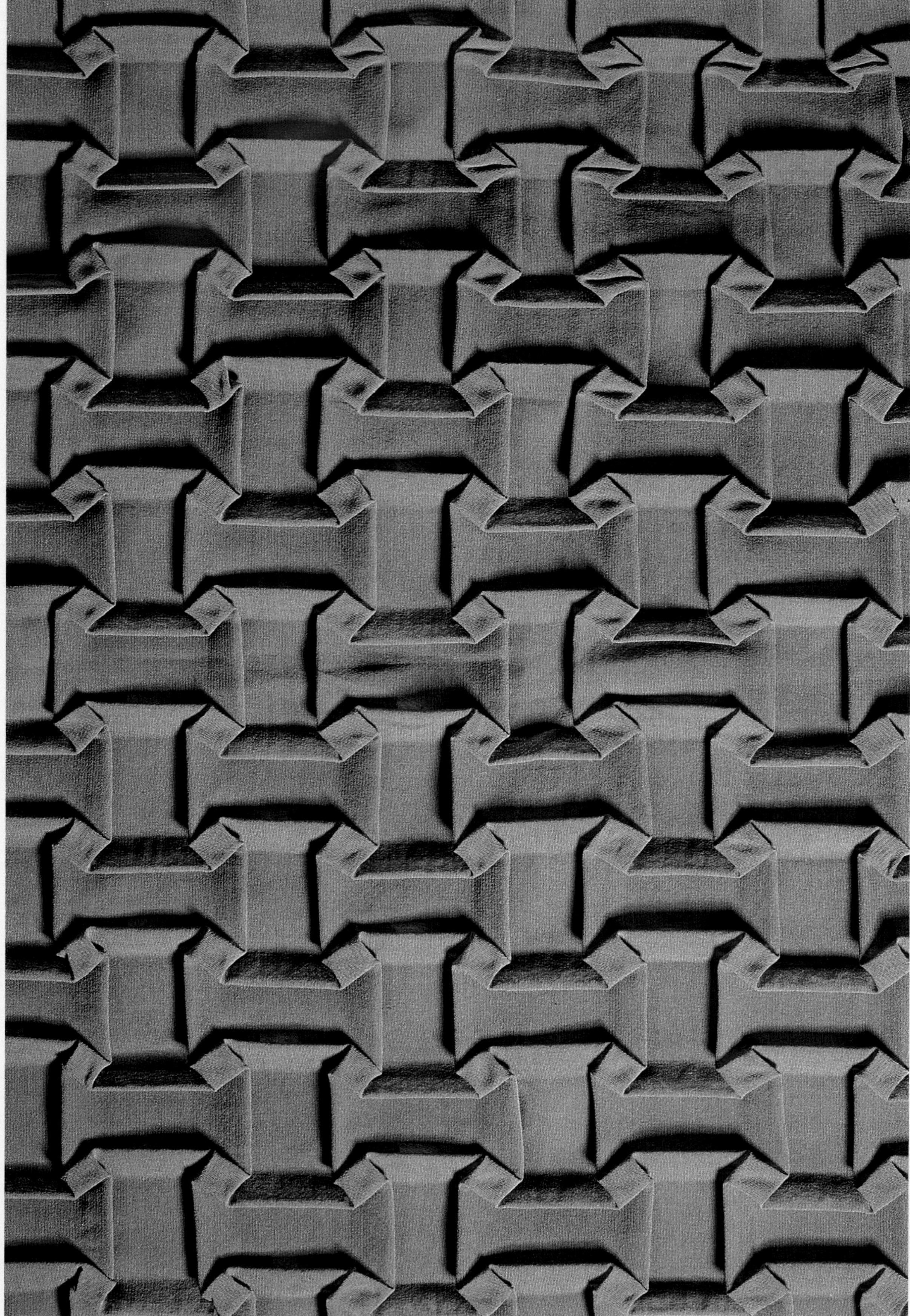

NANNI **STRADA** DESIGN STUDIO Milan, Italy

Nanni Strada, b. 1941, Milan

Over the course of her career, Nanni Strada has eschewed the seasonal dictates of fashion, focusing instead on innovation in both textile development and garment design. Strada's practice makes use of rational approaches, structural inventions, and technical processes more often associated with industrial design than with fashion. In 1972, inspired by research into traditional Asian dress, Strada created a simple, roomy geometric garment in a single size whose pattern maximizes the amount of fabric used by conforming to the planar nature of the cloth. The 1974 film *Il manto e la pelle* (The cloak and the skin) documents Strada's efforts to incorporate the technology used to generate tubular knits for hosiery into her own design methods. In 1979, the designer received the Compasso d'Oro award for industrial design in recognition of her creation of the world's first machine-knitted seamless dress.

The idea of creating clothes with "nomadic use" for the modern global traveler led her to investigate the compressibility of garments. For her 1986 Torchon line, Strada played with linen's natural tendency to crumple and crease by treating it industrially to create permanent wrinkles. In 1993, she introduced a line called Pli-Plà that uses innovative pleated and elasticized fabrics. A Pli-Plà dress is composed of sixteen identical panels that are assembled with visible seams. When the garment is folded, it lays flat, taking up very little space in a suitcase. In recent years Strada has focused on textile design, creating Matrix (1995), a fabric comprising a system of vertical and horizontal pleats. Her goal is "to liberate clothes from their sartorial origins, from the subordination that has always been inflicted on them by the body...To achieve a compromise between function and a poetic outlook, between anatomy and geometry, object and symbol."[1]

1 Ettore Bellotti, "Nanni Strada: L'abito flessibile," *Domus* 786 (October 1996): 64.

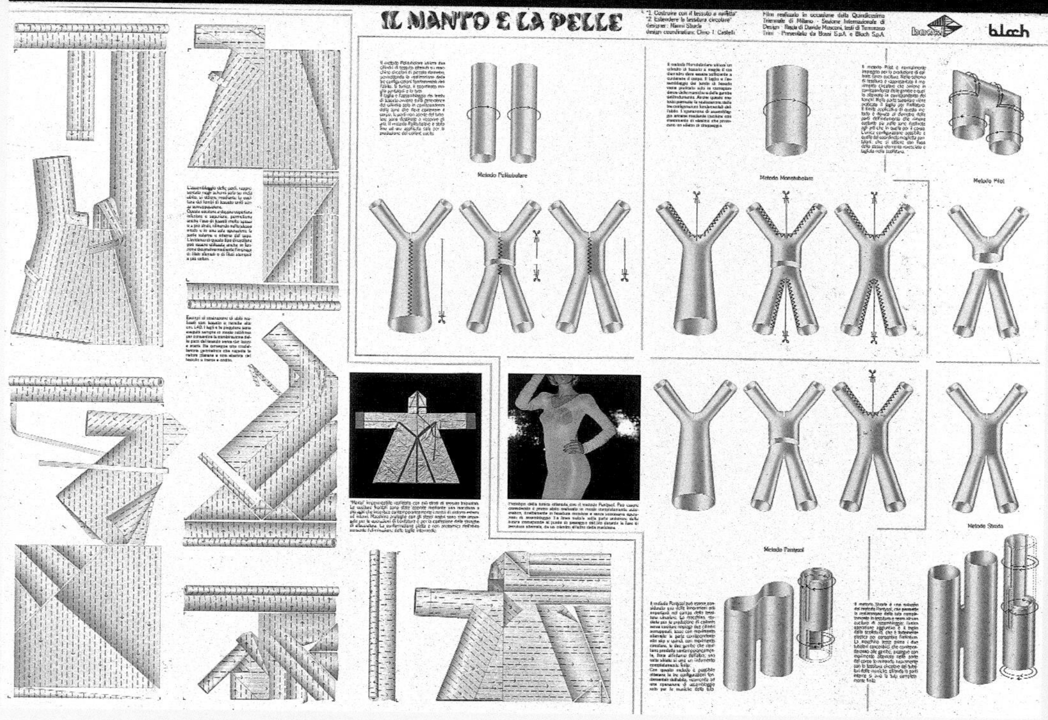

opposite: DETAIL OF **MATRIX** PLEATED FABRIC, 1995

above: CLOAK AND POSTER FOR **IL MANTO E LA PELLE**, 1974

below: COAT AND SKETCH FOR GEOMETRIC COAT FROM **SPORTMAX** COLLECTION, AUTUMN/WINTER 1971–72

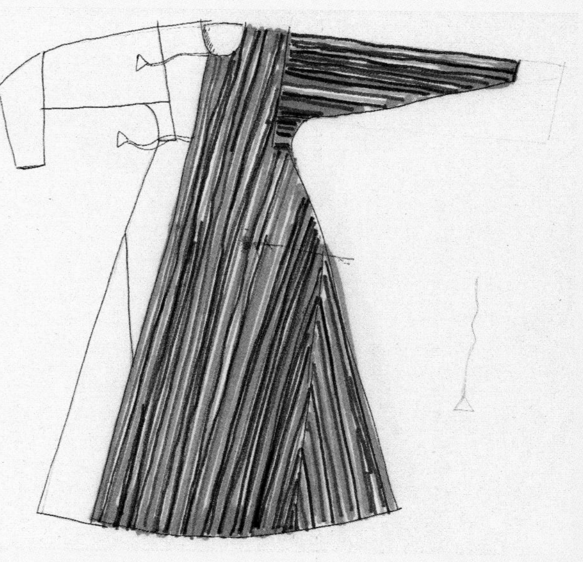

overleaf: GARMENTS FROM **PLI-PLÀ** LINE, 1993

page 203: T-SHIRTS, HEADWEAR, AND HOSE FROM **ETHNOLOGICAL** COLLECTION, AUTUMN/WINTER 1971–72

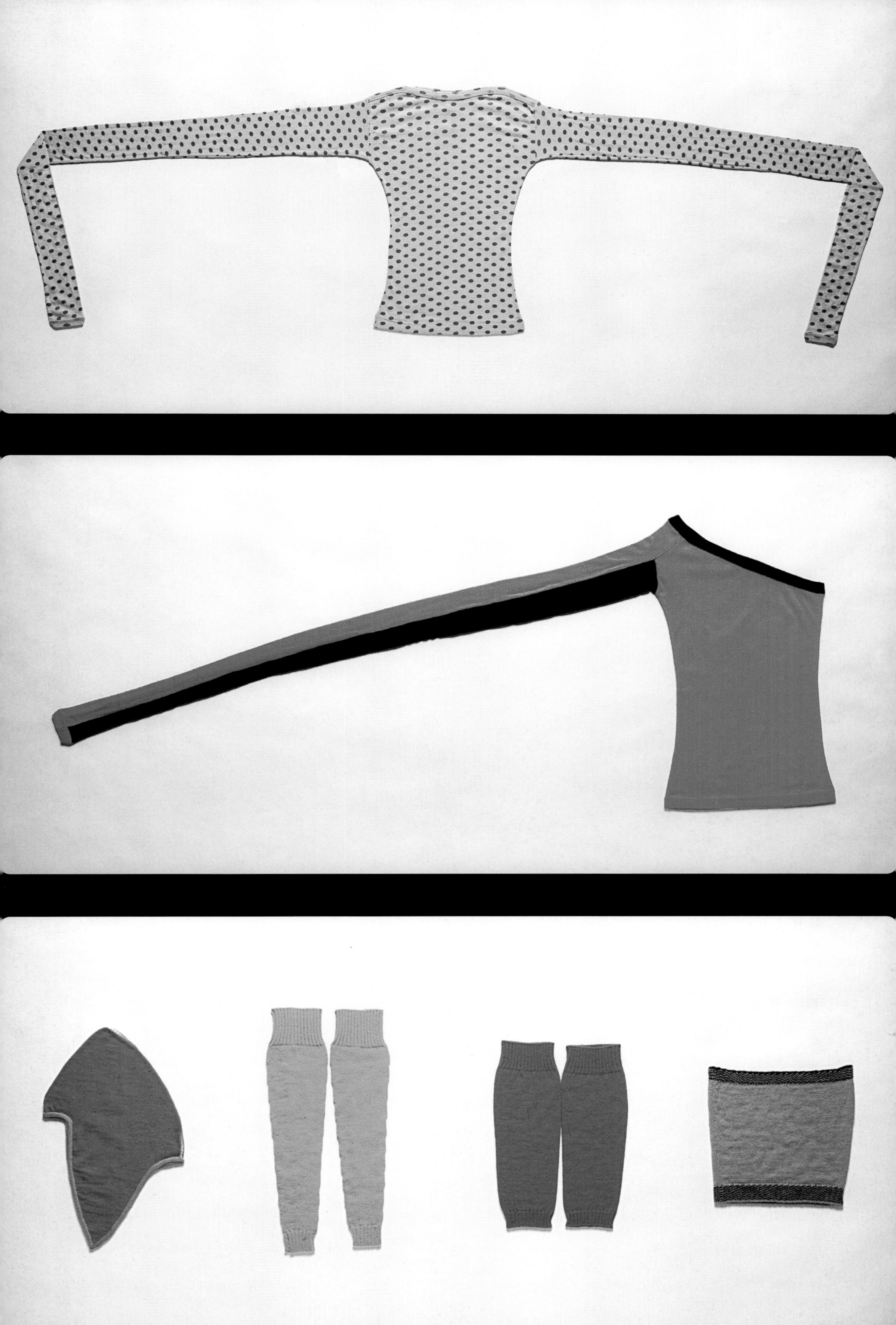

YEOHLEE **TENG** New York

b. 1955, George Town, Penang, Malaysia

For Yeohlee Teng, architecture is a significant source of inspiration; her study of building methods, tectonic properties, and various architectural concepts is evident in her collections for the label Yeohlee. This connection to architecture has been recognized in several exhibitions, including "Intimate Architecture: Contemporary Clothing Design" at the Massachusetts Institute of Technology, Cambridge, Massachusetts (1982), and "Energetics: Clothes and Enclosures" at Berlin's Aedes Gallery (1998), an exhibition that paired her designs with those of Malaysian architect Ken Yeang. Teng's spring/summer 2006 collection incorporates her study of suspension bridges and the work of Parisian architect Robert Mallet-Stevens, resulting in several Suspension Dresses whose skirts are hoisted with cables or straps to provide volume and surface articulation. Building on this research, in autumn/winter 2006–07 she developed a dress based on catenary curves.

The importance of geometry as a generative source for her work is evident in the starkly elegant, double-faced silk satin Shelley, Keats, and Byron Dresses (spring/summer 1992); in the black silk organza Infanta Skirt (autumn/winter 2005–06) composed of circles of fabric; and in the ink faille organdy Five-Square Skirt formed of layers of fabric cut in increasingly larger squares (autumn/winter 2005–06). When laid flat, the latter's hard-edged geometry is evident, but when worn, it falls in gentle folds. Ultimately, all of Teng's work is about function and economy of means. She designs for the "urban nomad," making garments that travel well and shelter the wearer. This pragmatic approach often results in complex designs for garments that appear simple and austere.

from left to right: **INFANTA SKIRT WITH BODYSUIT** FROM COLLECTION, AUTUMN/WINTER 2005–06, FRONT AND BACK VIEWS; **CATENARY HARNESS DRESS** FROM COLLECTION, AUTUMN/WINTER 2006–07

HOODED CAPE WITH DOESKIN PIPING FROM COLLECTION, AUTUMN/WINTER 1982–83

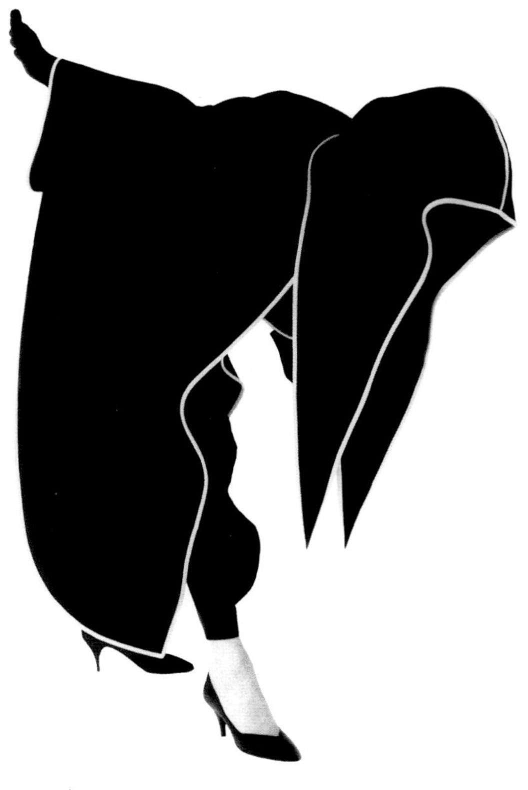

below, left to right: **BYRON, SHELLEY,** AND **KEATS DRESSES** FROM COLLECTION, SPRING/SUMMER 1992
opposite, top left: **COTTON HOIST DRESS** WITH CABLE-WRAP POUFFE FROM COLLECTION, SPRING/SUMMER 2006
top right: **MÖBIUS LOOP GOWN** FROM COLLECTION, AUTUMN/WINTER 2005–06
bottom: **ONE CIRCLE EMPIRE DRESS** WITH BOW FROM COLLECTION, AUTUMN/WINTER 2005–06

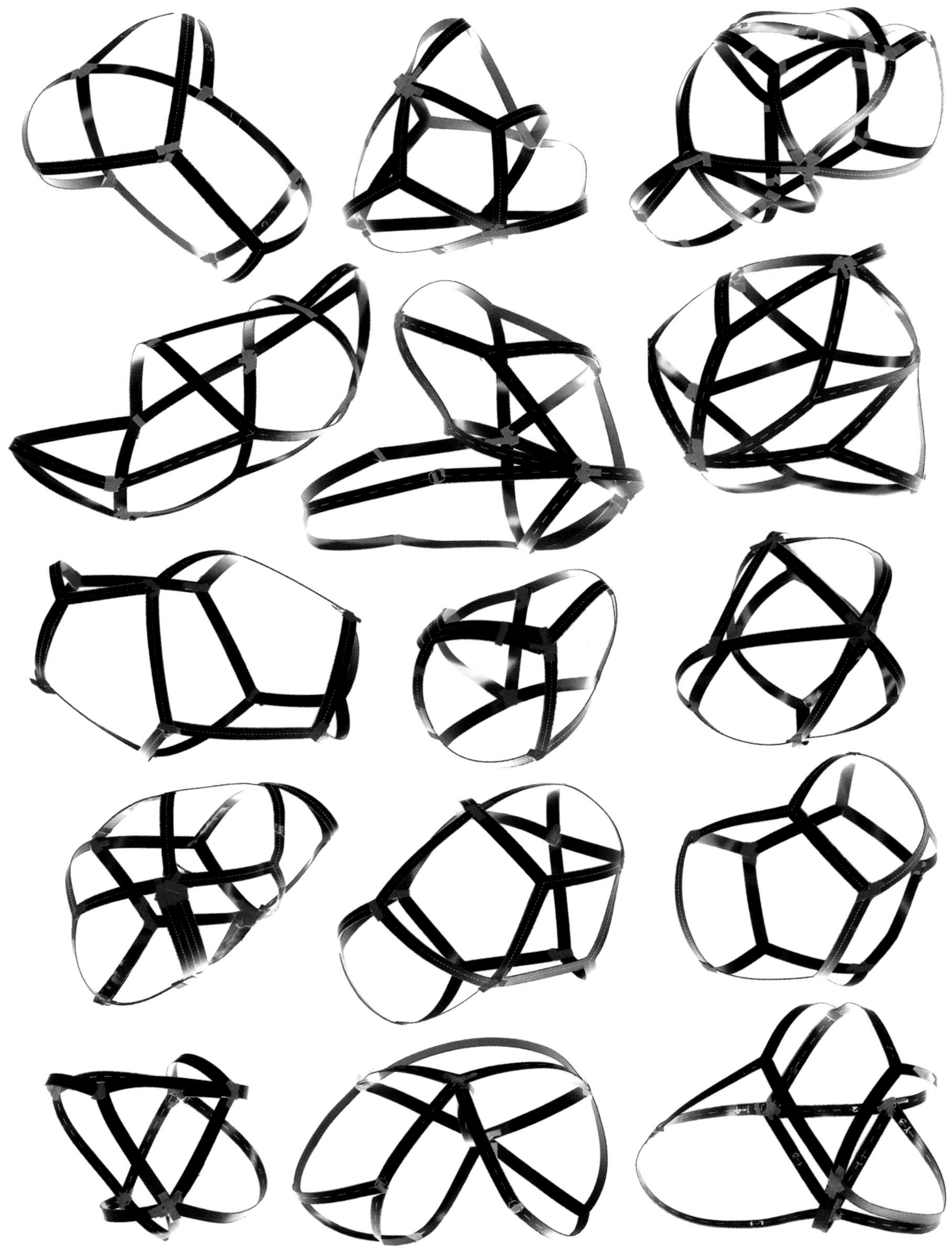

TESTA & WEISER Los Angeles

Peter Testa, b. 1952, Lisbon   Devyn Weiser, b. 1966, Los Angeles

Founded in 1997, Testa & Weiser's work represents a synergy or synthesis of ideas, materials, and tectonic strategies drawn from both fashion and architecture. The architects devote equal attention during the design process to material development, fabrication technology, and engineering issues. Carbon Tower (unbuilt, 2001–04) is a prototype for the first all-composite high-rise building and takes full advantage of the strength of carbon fiber. Conceived as a structural network of forty twisted strands of carbon fiber, the tower's skeleton would be significantly lighter and stronger than steel-frame construction. Made by purpose-built robotic pultrusion[1] and braiding machines that "knit" vertical and horizontal strands together to form an exterior helix, this skeleton allows for the elimination of the core and interior columns typical of conventional high-rises. Ultra-lightweight and breathable membranes replace the conventional curtain wall, ensuring a more efficient use of energy.

Carbon Beach House (unbuilt, 2006) represents a rethinking of residential construction in which all systems, surfaces, and structural components are integrated. The exterior shell and all interior floor plates and partitions are fabricated of carbon-fiber–faced cellular panels, which are assembled like a honeycomb and bound together by prepreg tape[2] that appears on the outside as if it was just a decorative element. Testa & Weiser have also developed innovative and environmentally sensitive building systems that have the potential to fundamentally change building construction methods: their Carbon Fiber Reinforced Timber (CFRT) (prototypes, 2005) uses bio- and nanotechnology to strengthen young growth timber from renewable forests, while M-BRANES (study models, 2006) uses the aerospace industry's rigidization process to transform architectural textiles into lightweight reinforced membranes.

1 Pultrusion is a method for producing continuous extrusions of composite materials.
2 Prepreg tape is carbon-fiber tape that is infused with soft resin.

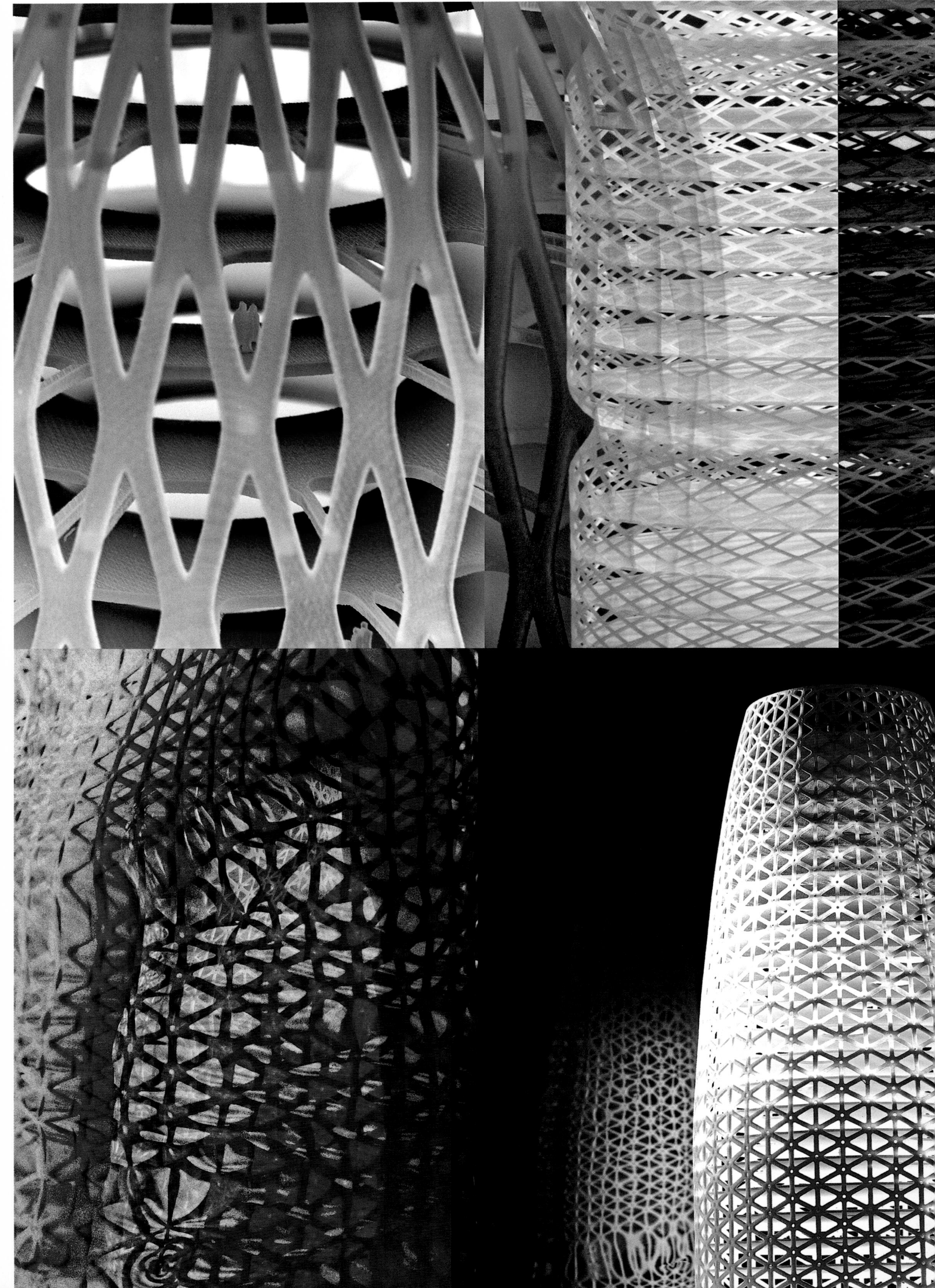

page 208: **M-BRANE** SERIES, 2006, STUDY MODELS

page 209: **CARBON BEACH HOUSE** (UNBUILT), 2006, MODELS

opposite and below: **CARBON FIBER REINFORCED TIMBER** (CFRT) PROTOTYPES, 2005, MODELS

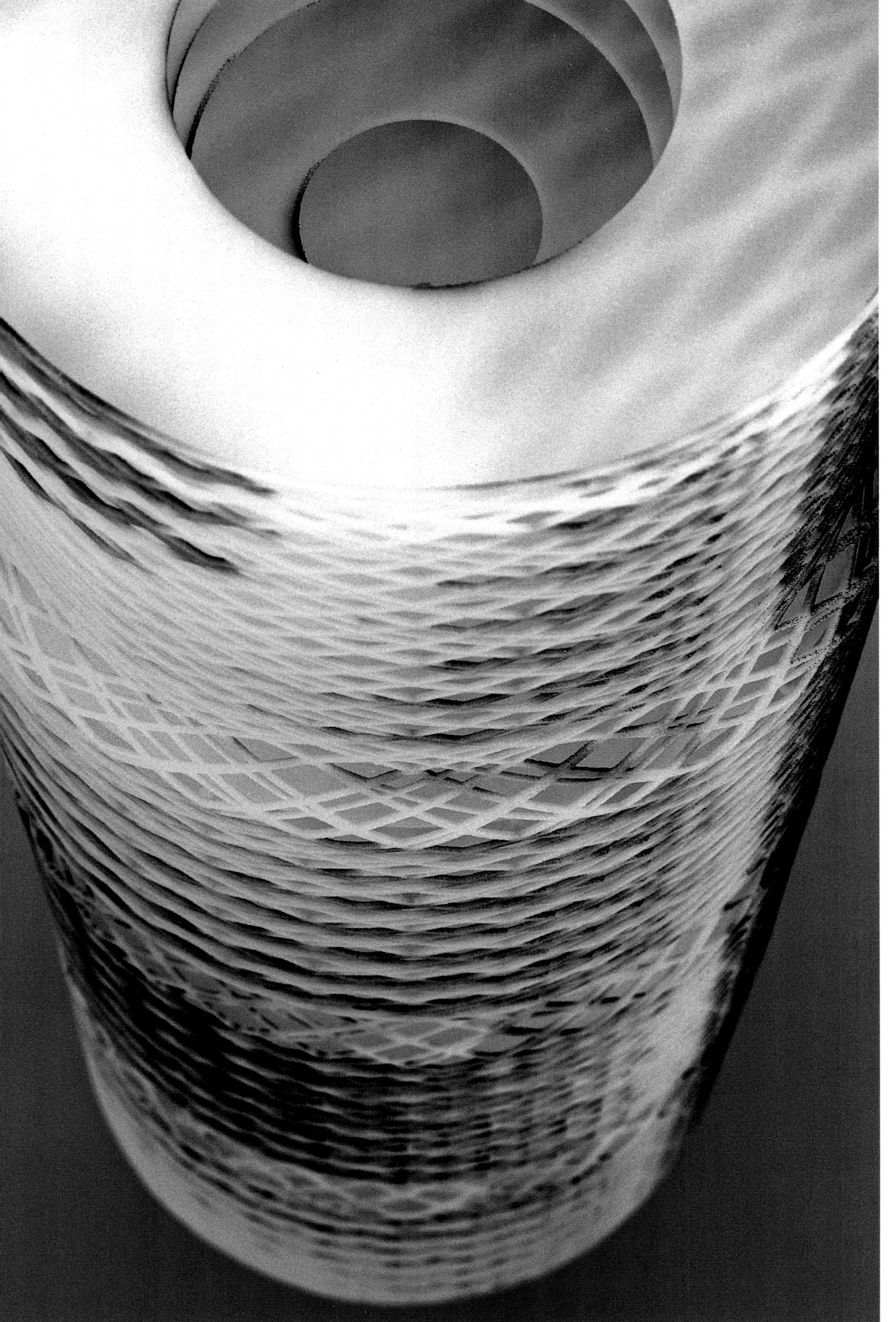

CARBON TOWER (UNBUILT), 2001–04, MODELS

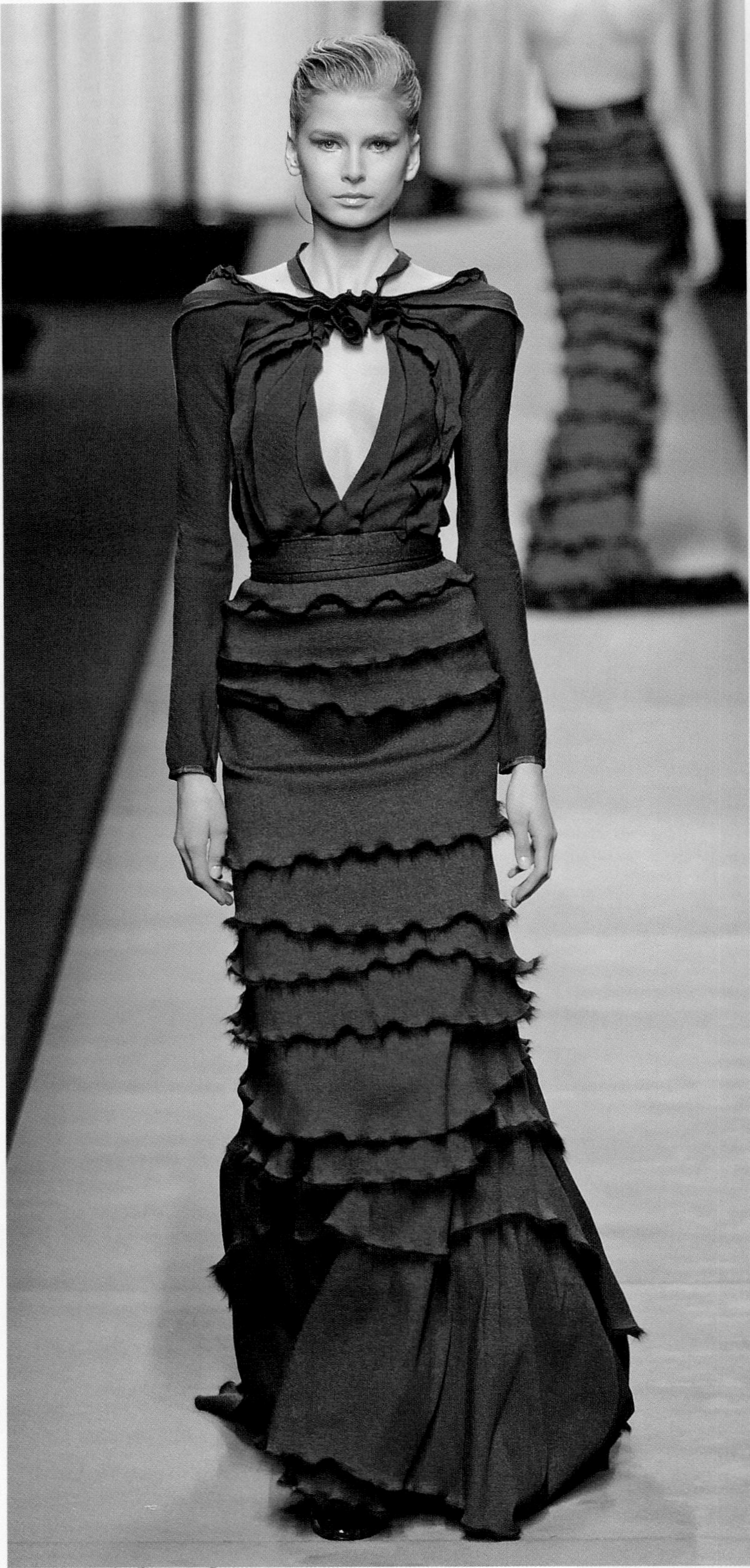

OLIVIER **THEYSKENS** FOR **ROCHAS** Paris

Olivier Theyskens, b. 1977, Brussels

Olivier Theyskens belongs to a second wave of fashion designers emerging from Belgium, following Martin Margiela, Dries Van Noten, Ann Demeulemeester, and others associated with the Antwerp Six. Upon leaving design school in 1997, Theyskens created ten collections under his own name before being appointed artistic director of the French couture house Rochas in 2003. Once renowned for its avant-garde designs, the house had shifted its focus from fashion to fragrance following the death of visionary founder Marcel Rochas in 1955. While Theyskens retained many of Rochas's signature references—including the emblematic rose, pinched waist, *guêpière* (corset), and Chantilly lace—he brought his own unique vision to the line. Determined to develop a resolutely modern, singular, and feminine style for Rochas, Theyskens designed garments that achieve a balance between structural rigor and languid delicacy. Favoring a long lean silhouette to compliment the shape of a woman's body, many of his gowns are fitted, with corseted tops and skirts that flare out beneath the curve of the hips. A black dress from his autumn/winter 2003–04 collection features sleeves that hug the shoulders, then billow out from the upper arm in a bell shape. The dress's dramatic two-tiered skirt resembles a hipped-roof construction, the shorter first tier flaring out from the body at the top of the thighs.

In this same collection, Theyskens referenced the voluminous silhouettes associated with the 1950s work of Cristobal Balenciaga. Using cantilevered construction to create an exaggerated empire waist that billows out like a parachute from just below the bustline, the designer made the look his own by dropping his signature bell-shaped sleeves below the shoulder and painting the backs of garments with an abstract floral pattern accented by the addition of the signature Rochas rose.

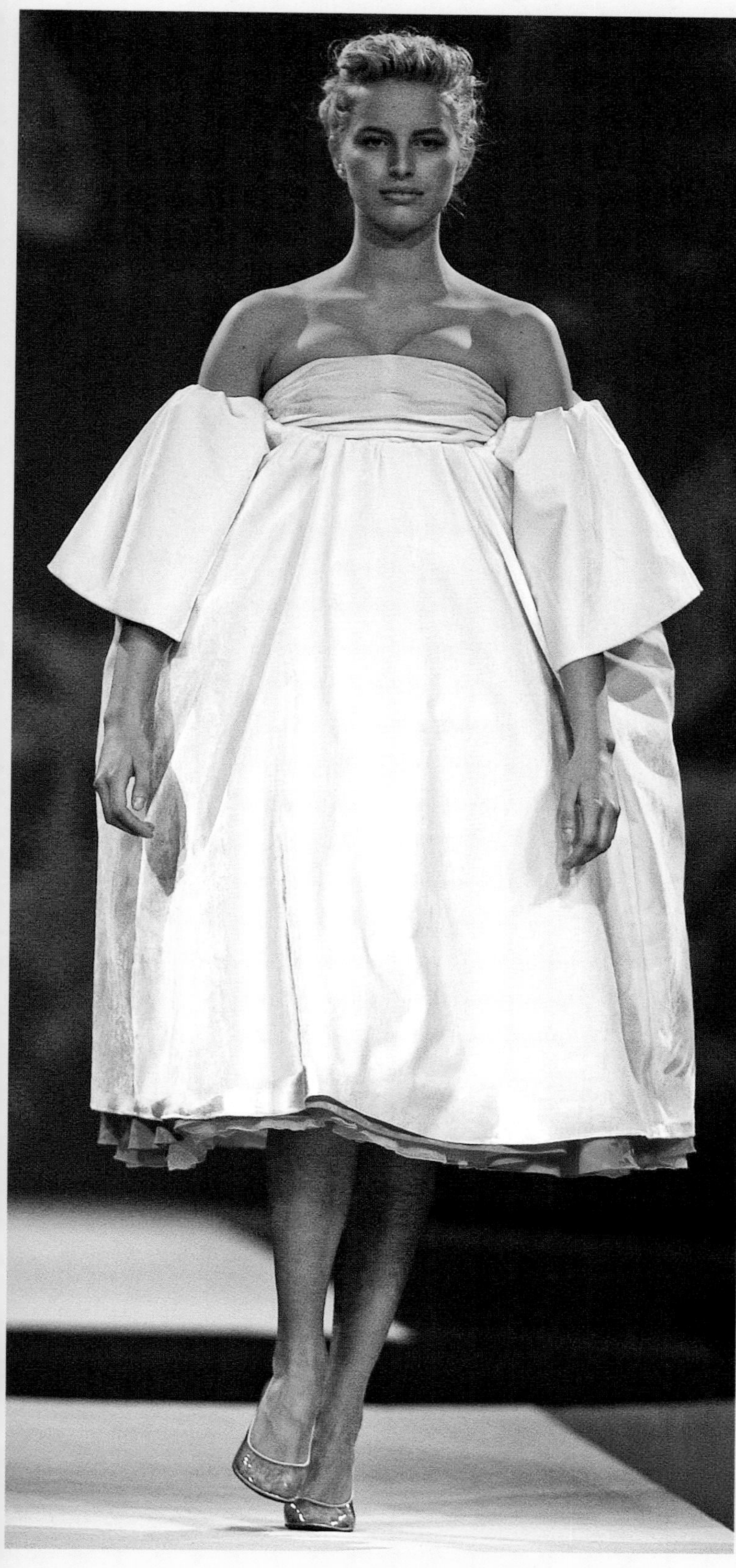

opposite: DRESSES FROM COLLECTION, AUTUMN/WINTER 2005–06
above: DRESS FROM COLLECTION, AUTUMN/WINTER 2003–04, FRONT AND BACK VIEWS

following spread, left to right:
top row: DRESS FROM COLLECTION, AUTUMN/WINTER 2003–04; DRESSES FROM COLLECTION, AUTUMN/WINTER 2004–05
bottom row: OLIVIER THEYSKENS, DRESSES FROM COLLECTION, SPRING/SUMMER 2002; DRESSES FROM SPRING/SUMMER 2005

TUBE JACKET FROM COLLECTION, SPRING/SUMMER 1995, BACK AND FRONT VIEWS

ISABEL **TOLEDO** New York

b. 1961, Havana, Cuba

Isabel Toledo approaches clothing design by focusing on function rather than choosing a concept or theme around which to develop a collection. Just as an architect might design a building based on the program of activities that it will house, Toledo looks at what a particular garment needs to do, how it will be used, and how it should work. As part of determining what a finished garment should look like, Toledo considers how it will respond to gravity; she incorporates precise engineering principles to ensure that a garment will fall, wrap, or enclose the body in a particular way. She also develops a structural framework—often as simple as a single seam—that will carry the weight of a dress. She investigates the properties of fabrics the same way an architect studies building materials, selecting the most appropriate fabric for each garment. She favors matte jersey for its fluidity and the way its weight allows it to cascade in gentle folds down the body.

Toledo's patterns are deceptively simple and belie the complex folding—where flat pieces of fabric form three-dimensional shapes to enclose the body—that is characteristic of much of her work. The Hermaphrodite Dress (spring/summer 1998) is constructed from a series of fabric rings that give it the appearance of a barrel when not worn. However, once hoisted by drawstrings around the shoulders and neck, it drapes the body in elegant folds. Toledo's Packing Dresses, made from two circles of fabric sewn together with holes cut for head, arms, and legs, collapse flat for easy travel and storage. Their voluminous form is a classic in her repertoire of shapes and structures, many of which she repeats from season to season in different fabrics.

PACKING DRESS FROM COLLECTION, SPRING/SUMMER 1988

VIEWS OF FRONT AND BACK AND LAID FLAT TO SHOW ITS GEOMETRY

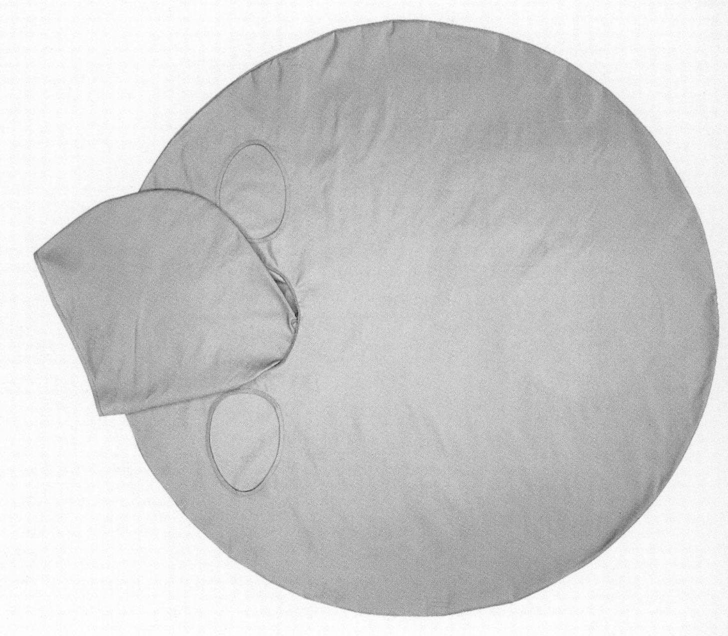

overleaf: **KIMONO SAILOR SUIT** FROM COLLECTION, AUTUMN/WINTER 2005–06

page 221: **MUSHROOM DRESS** FROM COLLECTION, AUTUMN/WINTER 2005–06

above: **ARMOR TRENCH COAT** FROM COLLECTION, SPRING/SUMMER 2004
left: **FELTED PIE COAT** FROM COLLECTION, SPRING/SUMMER 2004

DRAPED PATCHWORK DRESSES FROM COLLECTION, AUTUMN/WINTER 2005–06

opposite, left to right:
top row: **ENVELOPE DRESS** FROM COLLECTION, SPRING/SUMMER 1998, AND DESIGN SKETCH
center row: **HERMAPHRODITE DRESS** FROM COLLECTION, SPRING/SUMMER 1998; **ZIG ZAG TOP** FROM COLLECTION, AUTUMN/WINTER 1997–98, AND DESIGN SKETCH
bottom row: **CYLINDER DRESS** FROM COLLECTION, SPRING/SUMMER 1998, AND DESIGN SKETCH; **LIQUID POUCH DRESS** FROM COLLECTION, SPRING/SUMMER 1998

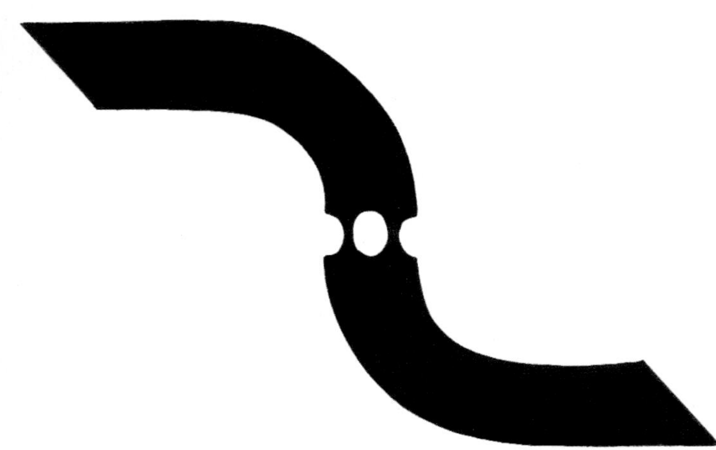

CATERPILLAR DRESS FROM COLLECTION, SPRING/SUMMER 1998, AND DESIGN SKETCH

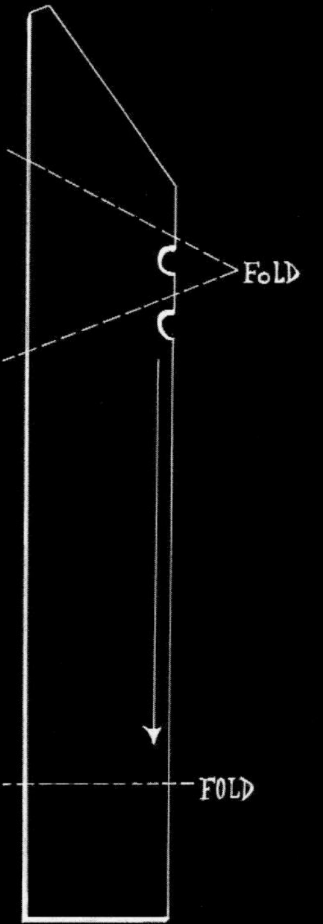
FoLD
FOLD

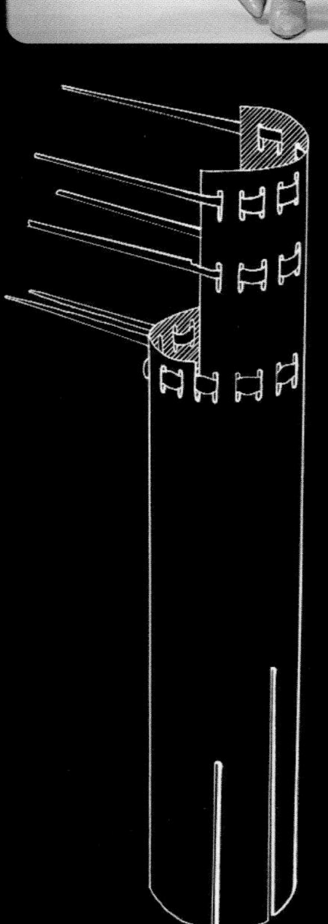

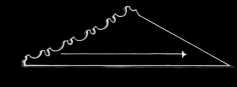

BERNARD **TSCHUMI** ARCHITECTS New York and Paris

Bernard Tschumi, b. 1941, Lausanne, Switzerland

Credited with introducing digital design as a critical element of architectural education, Bernard Tschumi had profound influence on a younger generation of architects, including Zaha Hadid and Rem Koolhaas, while teaching at London's Architectural Association in the early 1970s. In 1982, Tschumi won an international competition to design Parc de la Villette in Paris (completed 1998), an urban-renewal project for a vast site in the northeast corner of the city formerly occupied by slaughterhouses. Diverging from traditional notions of the park as an open green space, Tschumi scattered thirty-five freestanding pavilions (twenty-six were eventually built), or "follies," throughout the site and linked them by networks of gardens and walkways. Described as an "Urban Park for the 21st Century," the master plan is an architectural collage in which three ordering systems are superimposed: the discrete positions of the follies, the lines of the paths, and the configuration of the gardens. Tschumi aimed to create disjunction through layering so that the elements of the park mutually distort and clash; he encouraged the physical architecture and non-architecture to collide rather than synthesize into a single coherent outcome. Similarly disjunctive, each folly began as a ten-meter-square cube of red steel, which the architect then fragmented so that its initial form is often indiscernible and no two are alike. Some of the follies are functional, containing a café, cinema, video studios, or post office, while the uses of others were left undesignated. Tschumi invited French philosopher Jacques Derrida and American architect Peter Eisenman to collaborate on one of the smaller gardens within Parc de la Villette, bringing Derrida and in particular his work on deconstruction to the attention of a much larger audience. Their project, Chora L Works: Project for a Garden, is discussed elsewhere in this volume.

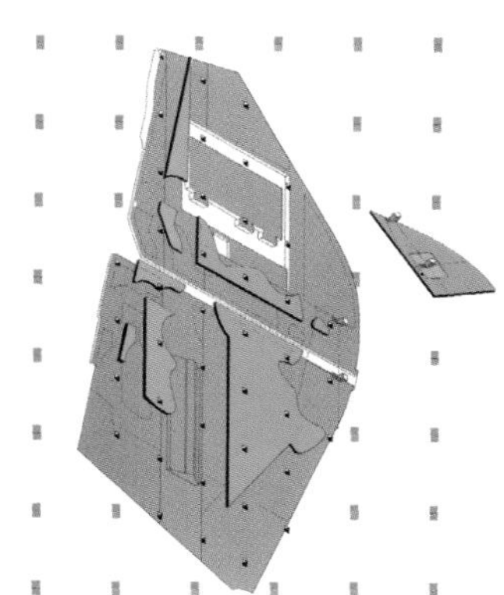

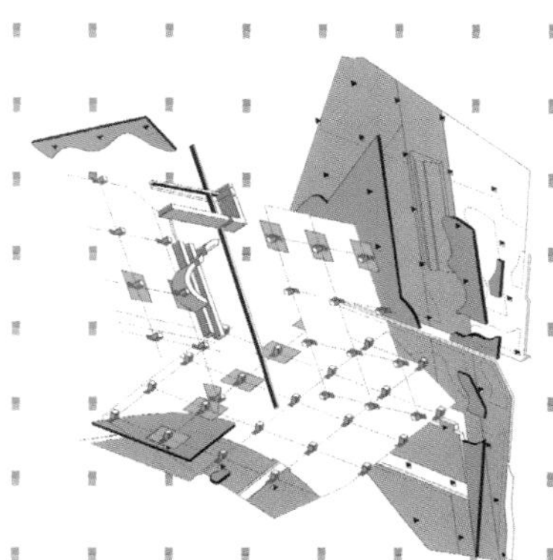

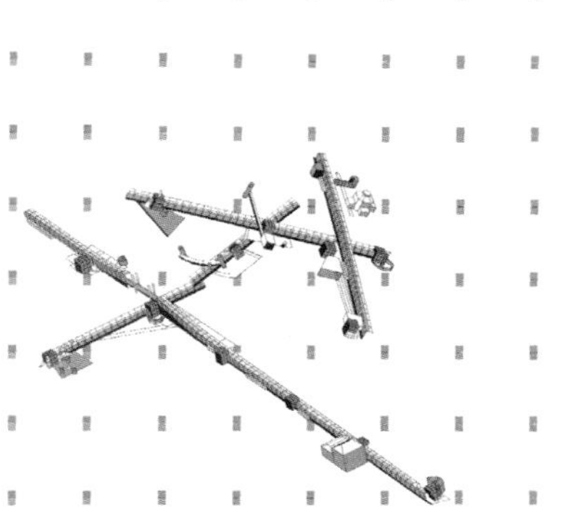

PARC DE LA VILLETTE, PARIS, 1982–98, VIEWS AND PLAN DIAGRAMS SHOWING OVERLAYS

DRIES **VAN NOTEN** Antwerp, Belgium; and Paris

b. 1958, Antwerp

Lush color, rich texture, and printed motifs and patterns are the hallmarks of Dries Van Noten's work. Van Noten, who comes from a family long involved in the garment industry, studied fashion design at Antwerp's Royal Academy. In 1986, he and five classmates gained international recognition as the Antwerp Six when each presented a small collection at London's British Designer Show.[1] For spring/summer 1994, Van Noten presented his first women's wear collection in Paris. The Indian-themed collection was built around a rose motif, a palette based on deep reds and golds, and a juxtaposition of textures such as "dry" chiffon and "liquid" silk. For his Turkish-inspired women's wear collection (autumn/winter 1996–97), he incorporated garments made of fabrics saturated with jewel-tone colors and shimmering with texture: silk lamé with a purple sheen and gold overprinting, a print based on a red cabbage leaf with purple lamé and fuchsia overprinting and a canary yellow dress printed with fuchsia and bright green roses. The presentation of his Moroccan-influenced spring/summer 1997 collection featured a tour through the color spectrum, beginning with outfits of blacks and dark browns and then progressing through cool blues and greens to warm oranges and reds.

While Van Noten retains certain shapes, such as voluminous skirts and wrapped blouses, his prints, textures, and colors evolve from season to season. His designs reference textile history, artisanal craft techniques, and the colors and patterns of fabric from India, Afghanistan, Morocco, Romania, Turkey, and Thailand. Van Noten often overprints graphic motifs onto patterned fabric. He uses unusual materials such as rubberized ink to screen-print a pattern onto metallic silk, or he layers beading, sequins, densely embroidered flowers, ornate prints of different scales and shades, or smocking on top of a printed ground. By keeping his focus on fabric, texture, and unusual color combinations, Van Noten has created a body of work with an exceptionally strong visual impact.

1 The group included Ann Demeulemeester, Dirk Van Saene, Marina Yee, Walter Van Beirendonck, and Dirk Bikkembergs, all of whom have since established successful careers.

following spread: COLLECTION, SPRING/SUMMER 1997, PRESENTATION FINALE

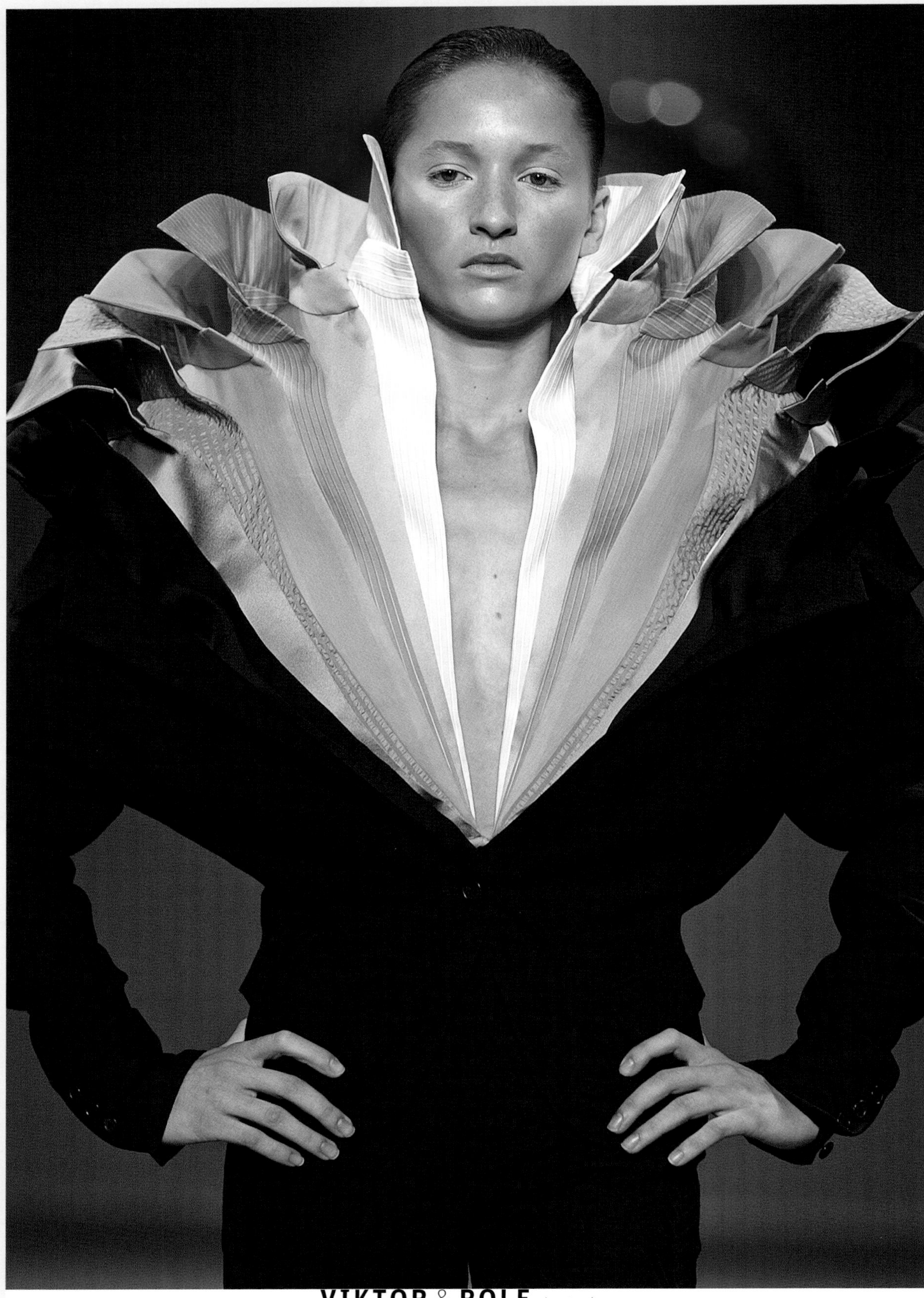

VIKTOR & ROLF Amsterdam

Viktor Horsting, b. 1969, Geldrop, The Netherlands Rolf Snoeren, b. 1969, Vongen, The Netherlands

Viktor Horsting and Rolf Snoeren began working together in 1993 after graduating from the Arnhem Academy of Art and Design in 1992. Their collections, based on ideas rather than current trends, are shown each season in Paris in extravagant unusual presentations that are more like performance art or theatrical spectacles. From 1997 through 2000, they focused their efforts on designing haute couture collections. For their autumn/winter 1999–2000 presentation, the designers explored concepts such as shelter and social class in Russian Doll, an haute couture collection that featured nine different garments reverently layered (by Horsting and Snoeren themselves) on a model standing on a slowly rotating platform. Beginning with a humble openwork jute dress, each garment was varyingly decorated with luxurious materials such as crystal beads, silk taffeta, and lace. By the show's end, the model was cloaked in a massive cape that both sheltered her and concealed the eight garments underneath.

In the presentation of the autumn/winter 2002–03 collection Long Live the Immaterial, also known as Bluescreen, the models on the catwalk became moving special-effects screens. An intense shade of cerulean blue that could be read as a bluescreen[1] was featured in the trim and patterns of some garments and was the sole color of others. On screens flanking the catwalk, live feed of the models was filtered so that the blue elements of their outfits were replaced with moving images of sea, sky, desert, cities, helicopters, and busy freeways. One Woman Show, Viktor & Rolf's tenth-anniversary (autumn/winter 2003–04) presentation, featured and was an homage to actress Tilda Swinton, the pair's muse. The collection included one-of-a-kind sculptural shirts and coats made of multiple tiers of collars and plackets that fanned from the models' necks to their shoulders, pushing ideas of layering and stacking to their limit to achieve extreme architectonic forms.

1 Bluescreen is the special-effect technique of shooting foreground action against a monochromatic background for the purpose of removing the background from the scene and replacing it with a different image.

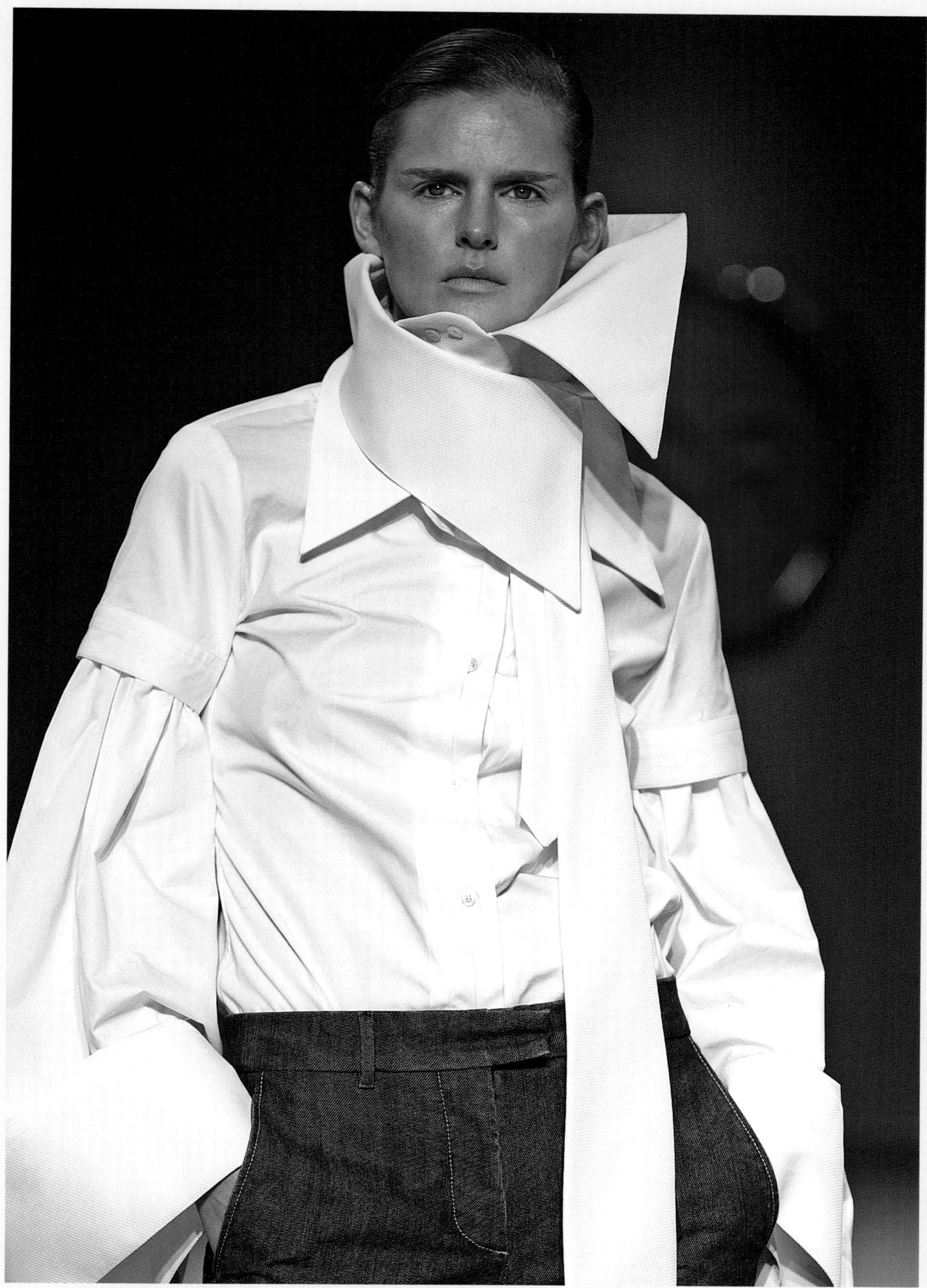

GARMENTS FROM **ONE WOMAN SHOW** COLLECTION, AUTUMN/WINTER 2003–04

following spread: GARMENTS FROM **LONG LIVE THE IMMATERIAL**, OR **BLUESCREEN** COLLECTION, AUTUMN/WINTER 2002–03

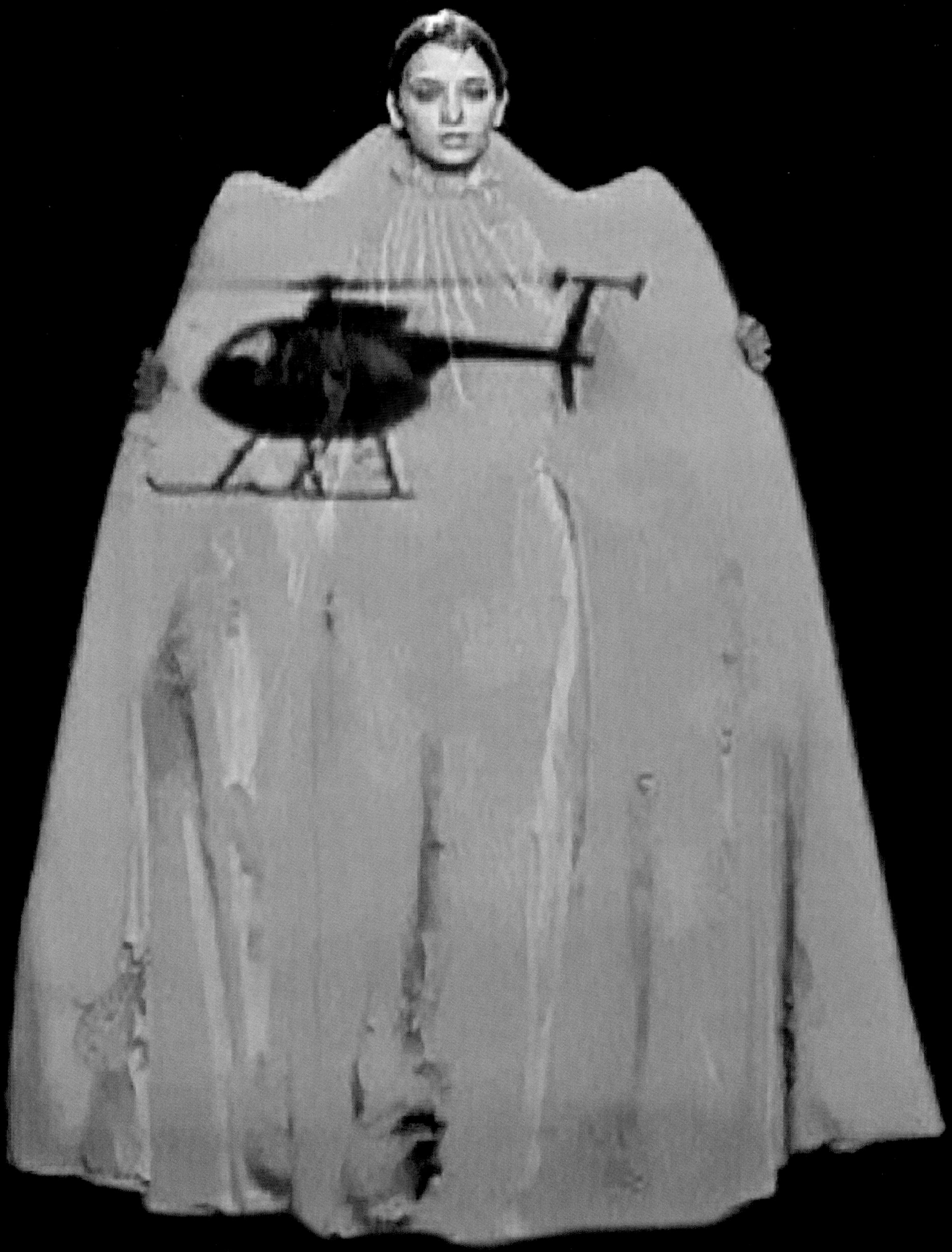

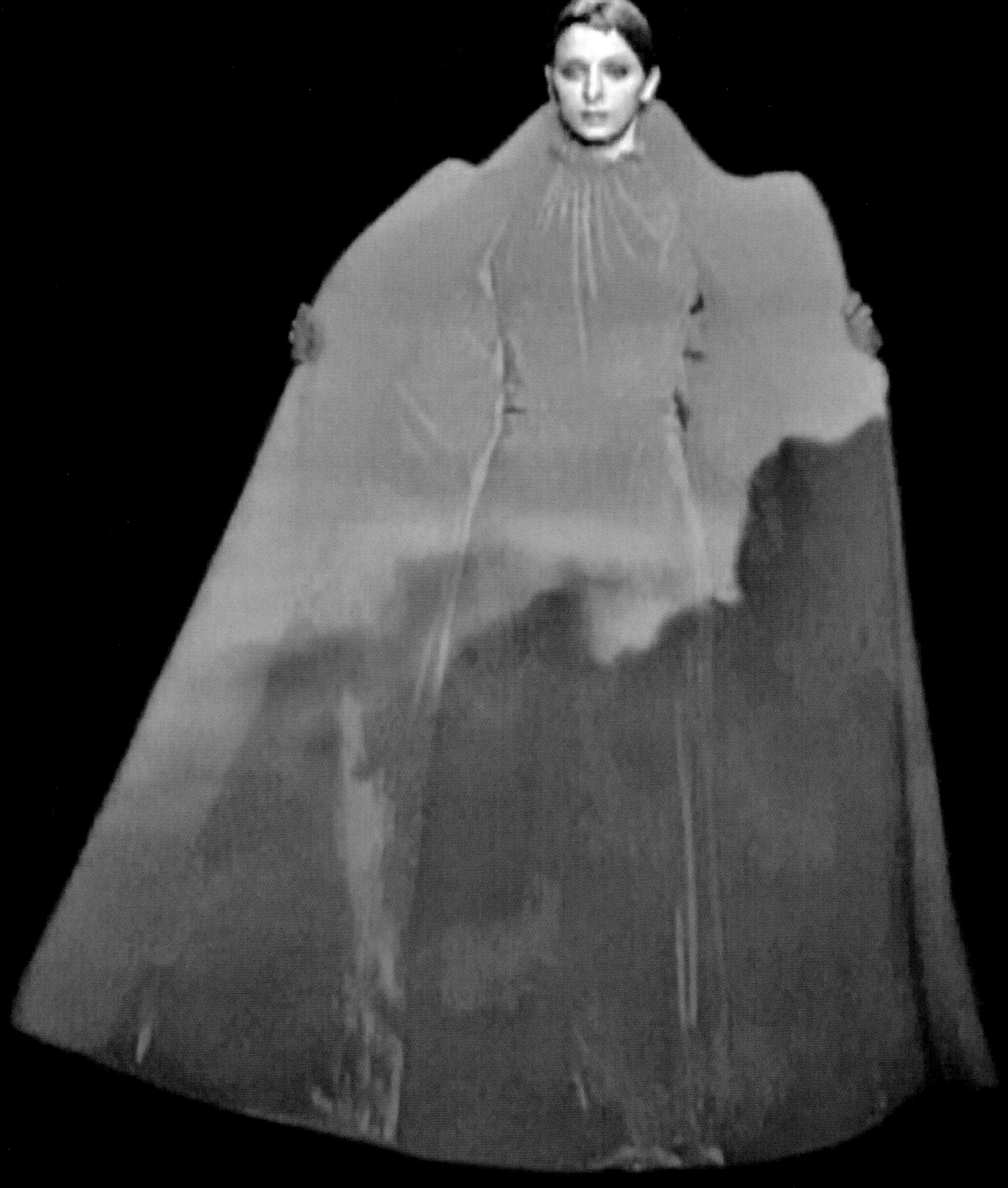

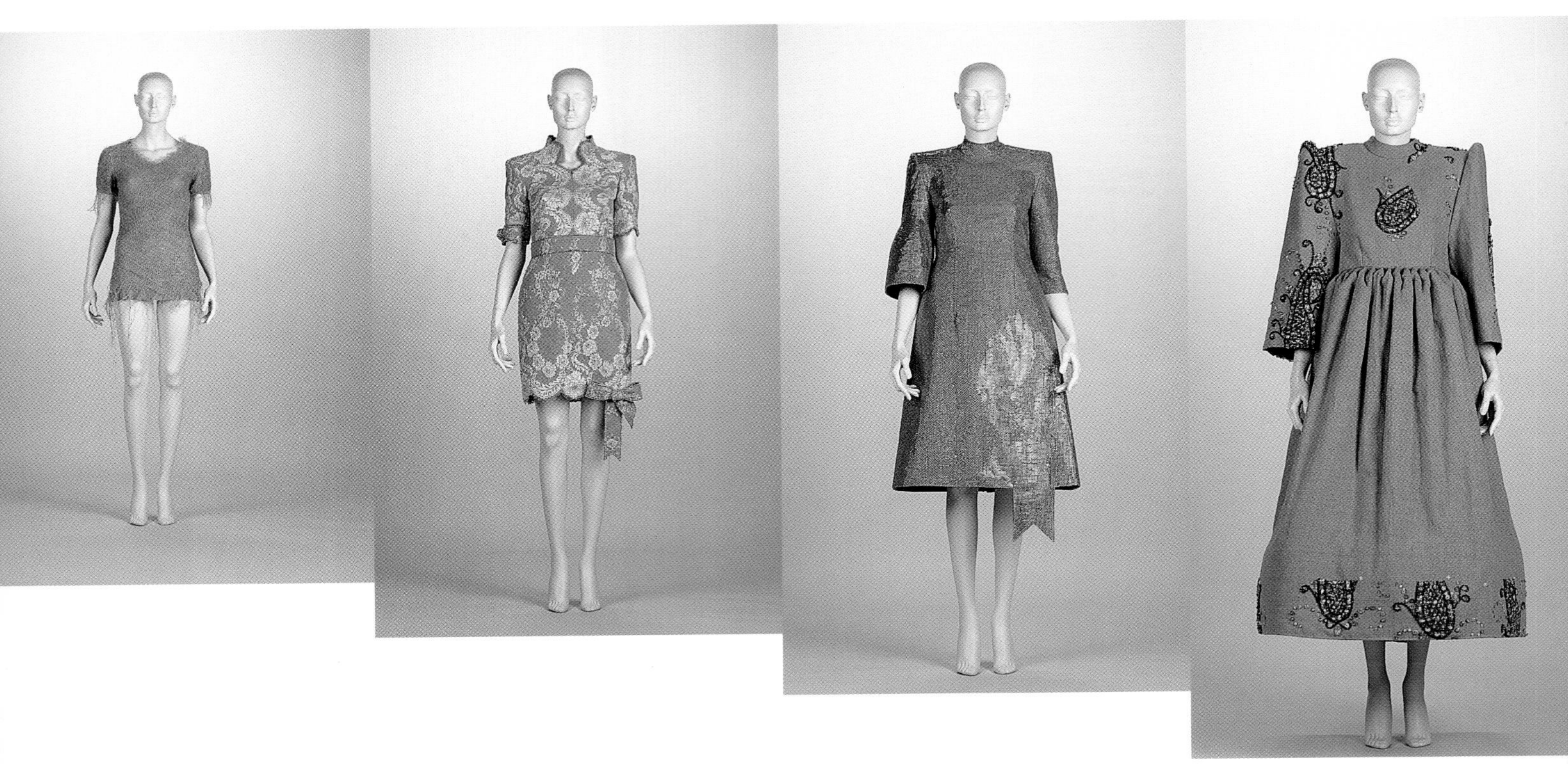

FIRST, SECOND, THIRD, FOURTH, FIFTH, AND SIXTH PREPARATION DRESSES FROM **RUSSIAN DOLL** HAUTE COUTURE COLLECTION, AUTUMN/WINTER 1999–2000

SEVENTH, EIGHTH, AND NINTH PREPARATION DRESSES FROM **RUSSIAN DOLL** HAUTE COUTURE COLLECTION, AUTUMN/WINTER 1999–2000

JUNYA **WATANABE** COMME DES GARÇONS Tokyo

Junya Watanabe, b. 1961, Fukushima, Japan

Originally hired as a pattern-cutter at Comme des Garçons by mentor Rei Kawakubo, Junya Watanabe was given his own label at Comme des Garçons in 1992, after several years designing their Tricot line. Watanabe's designs are often structurally ambitious—characterized by innovative cutting and draping techniques and ingenious sourcing of fabrics—and range from conceptually driven to easily wearable. His Soirée, or Techno Couture, collection (autumn/winter 2000–01) emphasizes the techniques and technologies used to make couture garments, featuring dresses made from hundreds of layers of ultra-lightweight polyester chintz, stitched, at times by hand, to form complex structures of honeycomb cells, concertina pleats, or frilly cocoons. The resulting intricate forms evoke underwater creatures such as coral, anemones, or oysters. For spring/summer 2001, Watanabe showed simple garments in solid colors and stripes overlaid with clusters of circles, squares, and rectangles cut from colored PVC plastic. For autumn/winter 2001–02, he presented plaid dresses with frayed cuffs and hems and inset with PVC panels, while his spring/summer 2002 collection featured dresses made from numerous pieces of recycled-looking denim stitched and draped to maximize fluidity and movement on the body. For spring/summer 2003, Watanabe wrapped elegant floral dresses reminiscent of paintings by Jean-Antoine Watteau and Jean-Honoré Fragonard with bondage-like straps that, when adjusted, alter both the shape and fit of the garments.

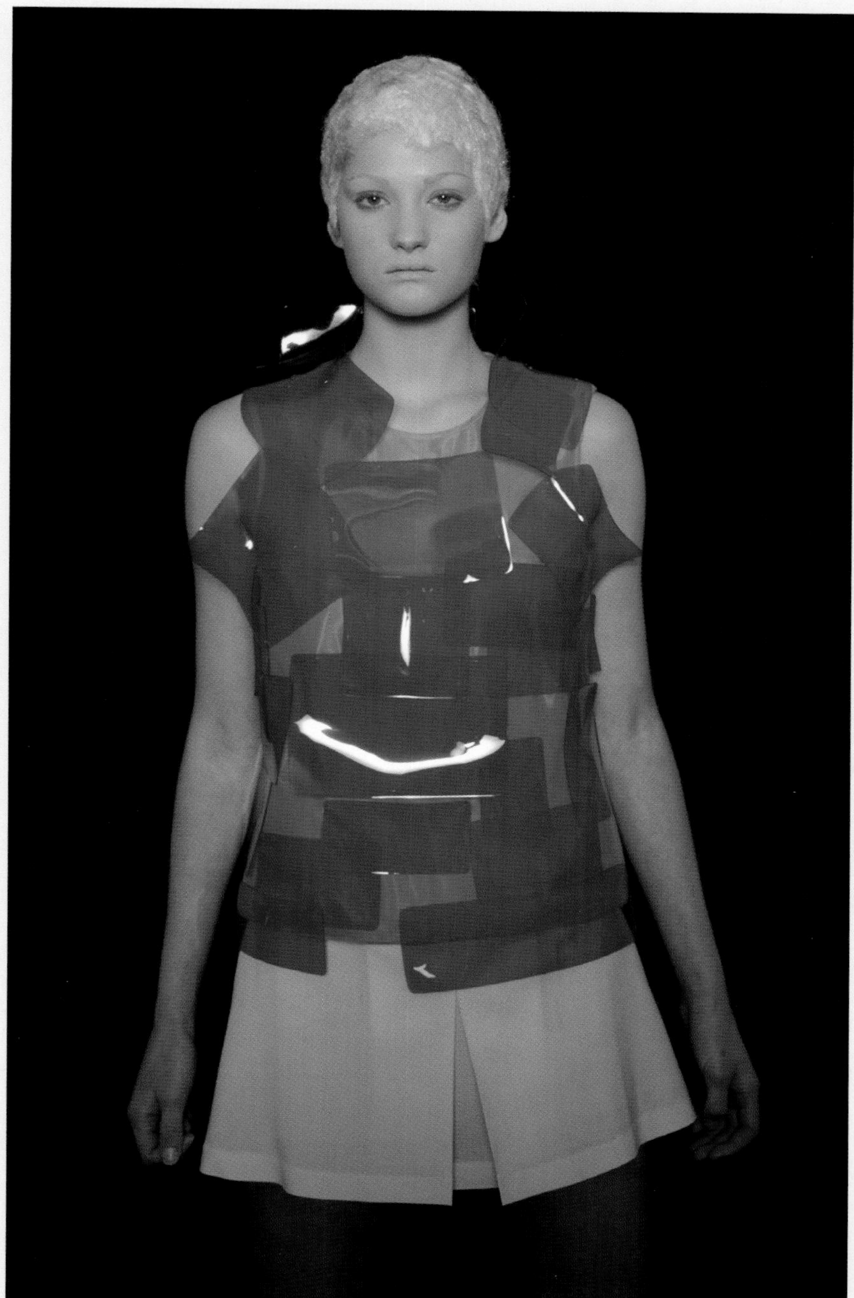

opposite: GARMENTS FROM COLLECTION, AUTUMN/WINTER 2001–02

top left: GARMENTS FROM COLLECTION, AUTUMN/WINTER 1998–99

top right: GARMENTS FROM **CLASSIC** COLLECTION, AUTUMN/WINTER 2004–05

bottom left: GARMENTS FROM COLLECTION, SPRING/SUMMER 2001

bottom right: GARMENTS FROM **OBJET** COLLECTION, SPRING/SUMMER 2003

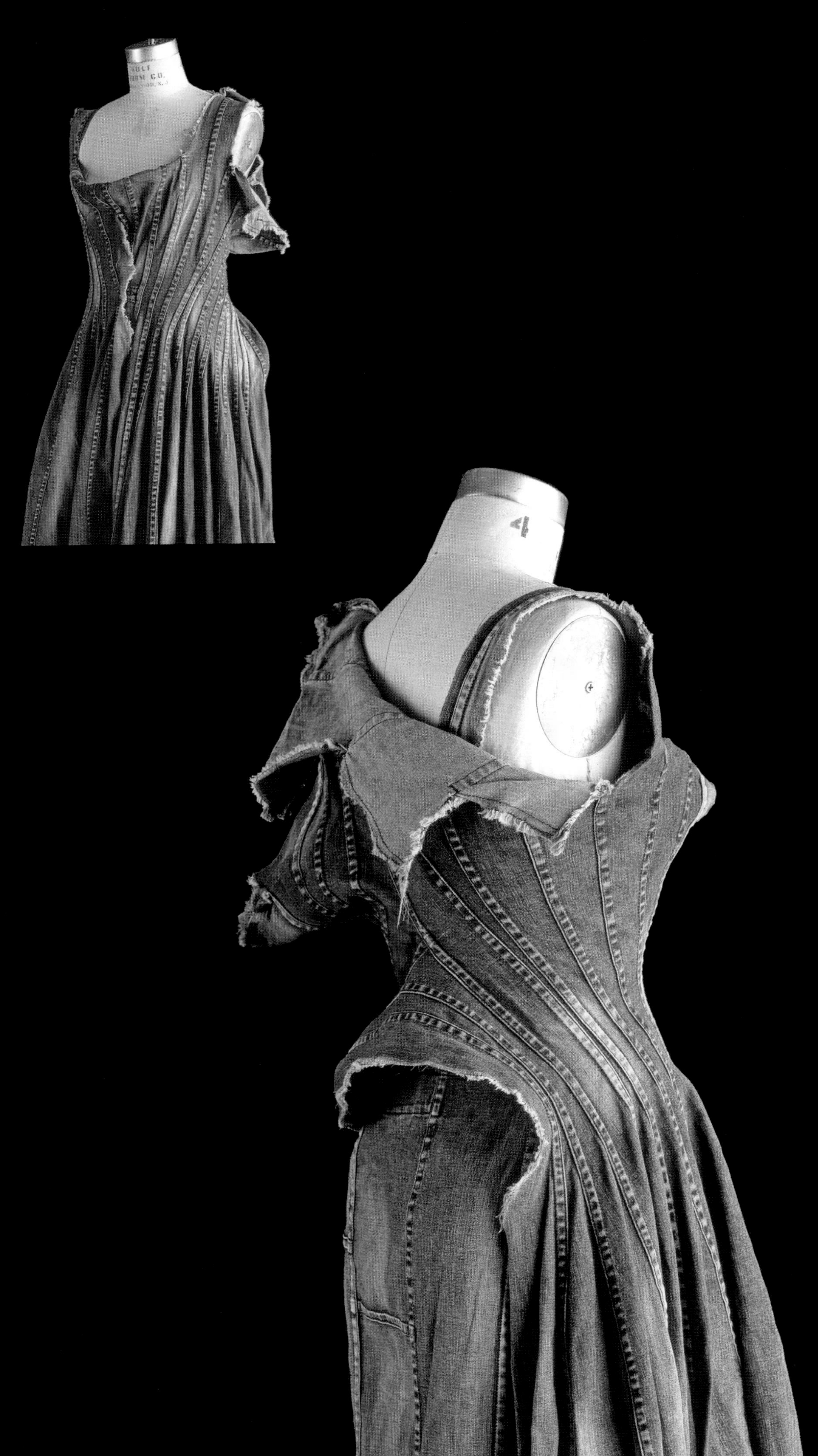

GARMENTS FROM **SOIRÉE**, OR **TECHNO COUTURE**, COLLECTION, AUTUMN/WINTER 2000–01

opposite: DRESS FROM COLLECTION, SPRING/SUMMER 2002, FRONT AND BACK VIEWS

VIVIENNE **WESTWOOD** London

b. 1941, Glossop, England

Since introducing the aggressive style of London's anarchic punks to high fashion in the late 1970s, Vivienne Westwood has remained at the forefront of avant-garde fashion. As engaged with street fashion as with the history of costume, her work often incorporates antiquated elements of dress such as the corset, which she is credited with reviving in the mid-1980s. Westwood is known for several design innovations that have had lasting influence in the fashion world, such as using undergarments as outerwear, incorporating bondage gear, and employing traditional British fabrics such as tartans and Harris Tweed in unorthodox ways. For her spring/summer 1985 Mini-Crini collection, Westwood contemporized crinolines and hoopskirts by shortening them and using fabrics in exaggerated prints of polka dots and stars and stripes. In the Harris Tweed collection (autumn/winter 1987–88), the designer featured tweed in corset tops, bubble skirts, and voluminous coats reminiscent of Cristobal Balenciaga's exaggerated styles of the 1950s.

Many of Westwood's garments—from the eccentric smocked plaids of Anglomania (autumn/winter 1993–94) to the sweeping ball gowns of Wild Beauty (autumn/winter 2001–02)—reveal a deep interest in proportion and silhouette. Designing garments that incorporate elements such as belts, straps, and corsets that constrict the body, Westwood draws attention to the figure by manipulating its form: "Historically, clothes have been about changing the shape of the body. Fashion has been about having a restriction, and about often radically changing the look of the body. Anything else I consider style."[1]

1 Vivienne Westwood, quoted in Claire Wilcox, *Vivienne Westwood*, exh. cat. (London: V & A Publications, 2004), 15.

opposite: SKIRT FROM **ANGLOMANIA** COLLECTION, AUTUMN/WINTER 1993–94
above: DRESS FROM **WILD BEAUTY** COLLECTION, AUTUMN/WINTER 2001–02

left: ANDREAS KRONTHALER FOR VIVIENNE WESTWOOD, **BOOZE JACKET** FROM **SUMMERTIME** COLLECTION, SPRING/SUMMER 2000
right: JACKET AND SKIRT FROM **STREET THEATER** COLLECTION, SPRING/SUMMER 2003

left: **POWER JACKET AND SKIRT** FROM **ON LIBERTY** COLLECTION, AUTUMN/WINTER 1994–95
right: **RED MINI-CRINI** FROM **HARRIS TWEED** COLLECTION, AUTUMN/WINTER 1987–88

WILKINSON EYRE ARCHITECTS London

Chris Wilkinson, b. 1945, Amersham, England James Eyre, b. 1959, Kingswood, England

Chris Wilkinson and James Eyre's partnership, founded in 1986, is based on a commitment to architectural design that makes creative use of technology. Wilkinson Eyre's Bridge of Aspiration (also known as Floral Street Bridge, 2001–03) spans thirty feet, four floors above Floral Street in London's Covent Garden neighborhood, to connect the Royal Ballet School and Royal Opera House. A link between studios and classrooms and the stage, the lightweight, semitransparent enclosed structure appears to stretch like an expanding accordion. Because the openings in each building are not directly aligned with each other in elevation or laterally, the architects offered a graceful solution: a sinuous aluminum spine supports the bridge's sleevelike enclosure, pleated with twenty-three square aluminum portals and glazed intervals. Each portal rotates four degrees from its neighboring one and shifts slightly to accommodate the skewed alignment. Achieving a quarter-rotation overall, the twisting concertina-like form appears frozen in motion and evokes the grace and fluidity of dance. In addition to the Bridge of Aspiration, Wilkinson Eyre has executed significant commissions, including Gateshead Millennium Bridge and Magna Science Adventure Center in Rotherham (both England, completed 2001).

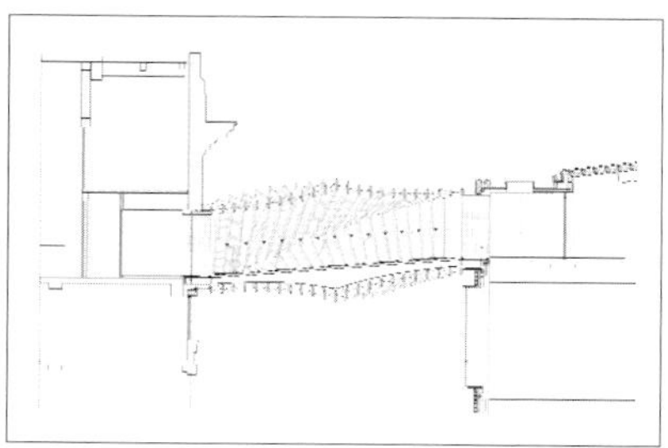

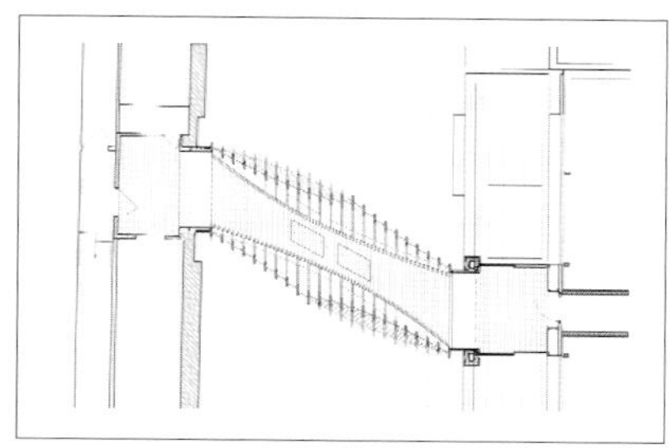

BRIDGE OF ASPIRATION, THE ROYAL BALLET SCHOOL, LONDON, 2001–03

above: VIEW FROM BELOW AND DRAWINGS OF PLAN AND LONGITUDINAL SECTION

below: INTERIOR VIEW AND CROSS SECTIONS SHOWING ROTATION OF BRIDGE PORTALS

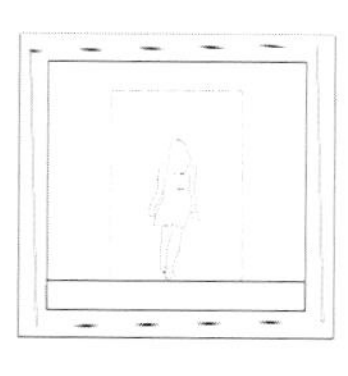

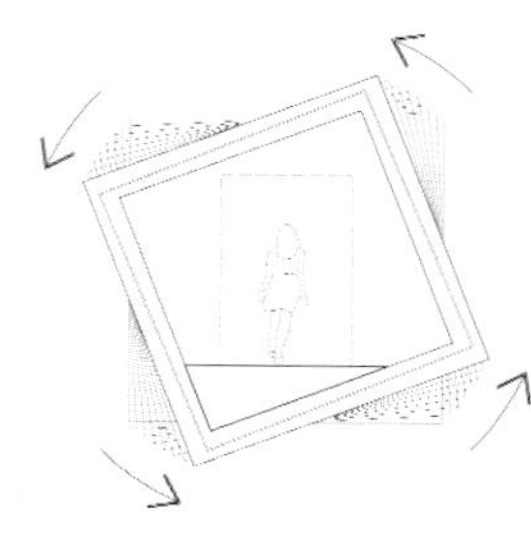

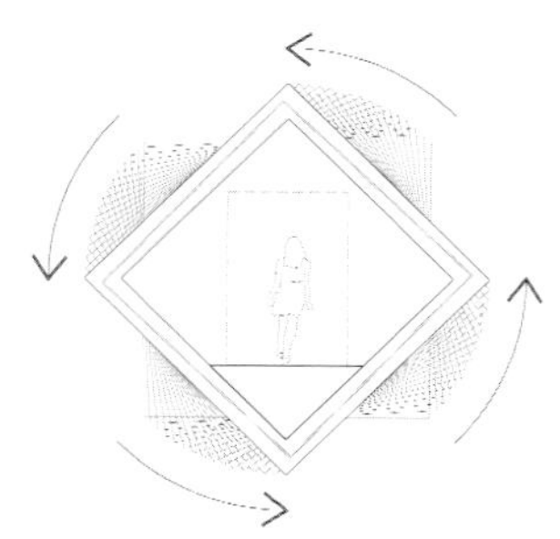

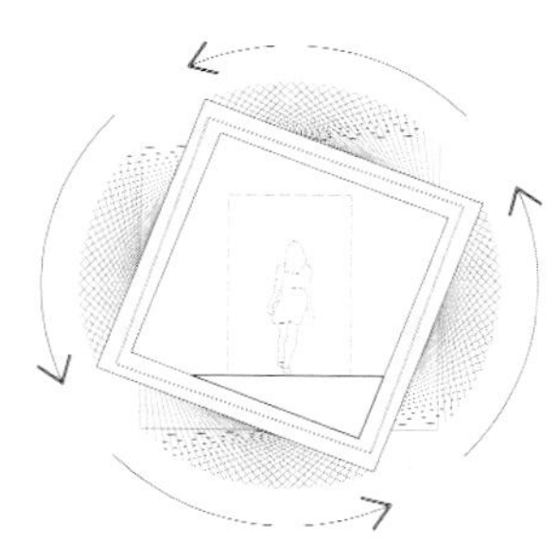

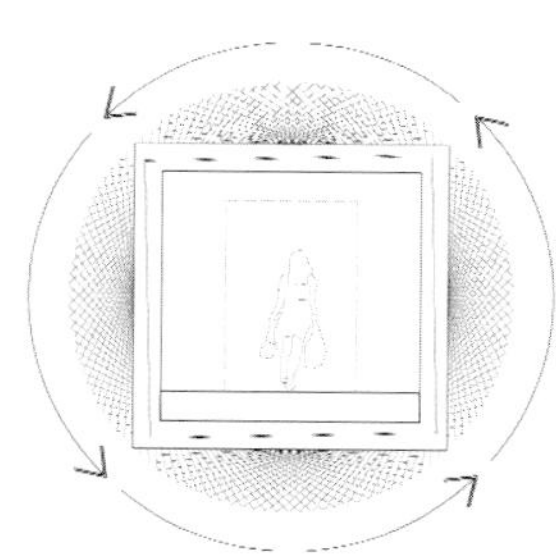

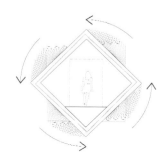

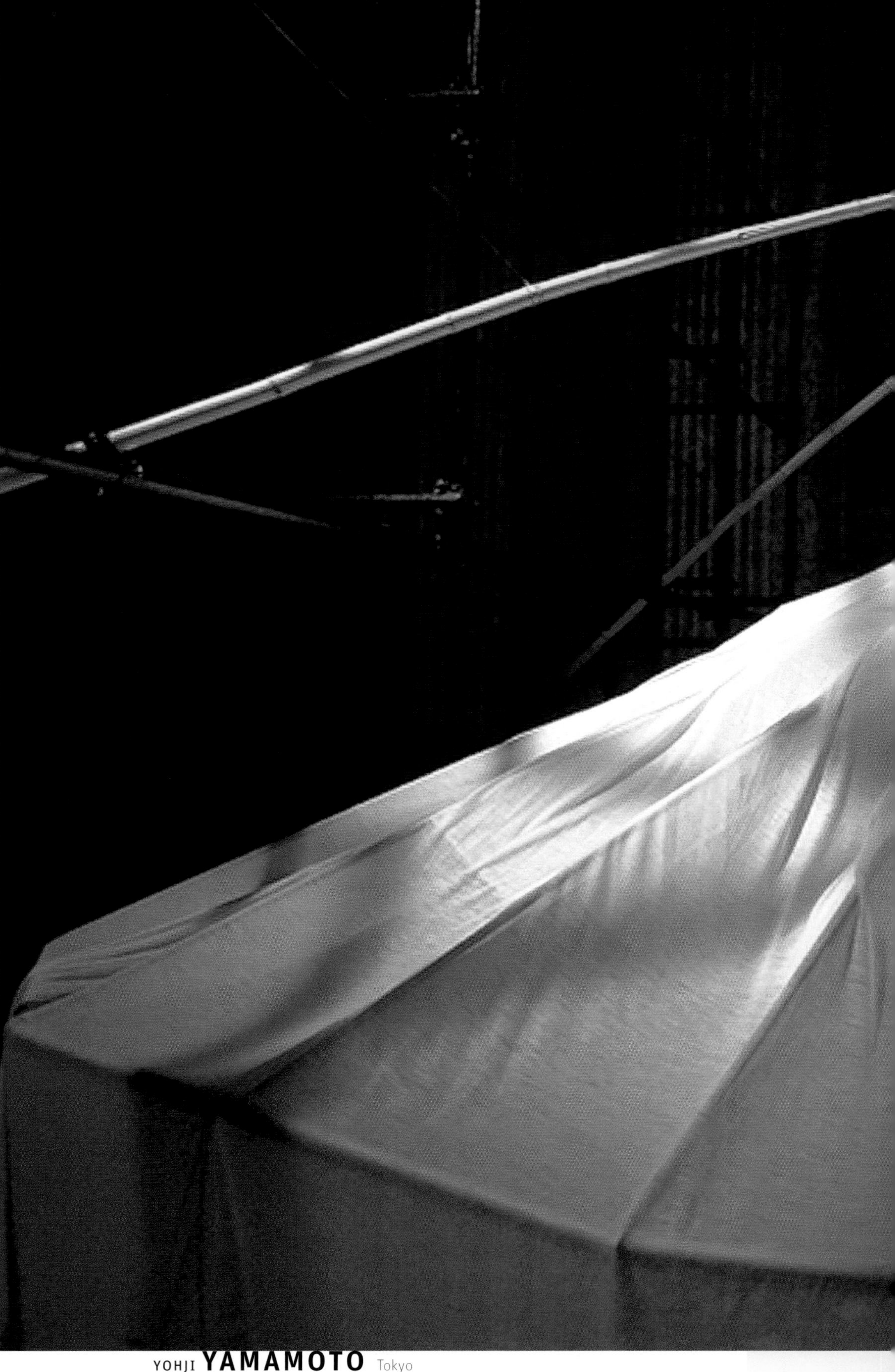

YOHJI **YAMAMOTO** Tokyo

b. 1943, Tokyo

Yohji Yamamoto established his design firm in 1972 but did not receive widespread recognition until 1981, when he showed a collection of so-called deconstructed clothes in Paris. These black, shapeless, tattered, and shredded garments challenged conventional fashion; by dismantling the prevailing body-conscious silhouettes, Yamamoto, along with Rei Kawakubo of Comme des Garçons, introduced new forms that proposed alternative modes of dress, especially for women. Rather than allowing the female form to dictate the shape of a garment, Yamamoto celebrates the space between body and fabric. His loose-fitting clothes emphasize the independent volume of the garment and its spatial, even architectural, character.

Yamamoto revels in imperfection: "I want to see scars, failures, disorder.... I think perfection is ugly."[1] His designs, while often experimental and conceptually driven, tend to have a romantic quality to them. He plays with notions of gender by using elements of menswear, such as high-waisted pleated trousers or jackets with a masculine cut. Yamamoto's Wedding collection (spring/summer 1999) reveals his fascination with volume, structure, and transformation. Consisting exclusively of garments designed for a bride and members of her wedding party—including ethereal black dresses for the newly widowed—the collection incorporates many of Yamamoto's signature elements: long languid silhouettes, cantilevered collars and necklines, and fluid dresses. Plastic whalebones—inserted in the hems of dresses, jackets, coats, and skirts cut from full circles of fabric to shape and stiffen garments—create gently sculptural forms that undulate with the wearer's movements. A key piece in the collection is a wedding dress with a simple bodice and a long hoopskirt. During the runway presentation, the model unzipped sections of her skirt to reveal hidden compartments from which she pulled accessories to complete her ensemble.

1 Yohji Yamamoto, in Jamie Huckbody, "Yohji Yamamoto: Perfection Is an Ugly Word," *i-D*, no. 219 (April 2002): 147.

WEDDING DRESS AND **PALANQUIN HAT** FROM COLLECTION, AUTUMN/WINTER 1998–99

above: INSTALLATION AT PALAZZO PITTI, FLORENCE, ITALY, 2005

left: VIEW OF PRESENTATION

WEDDING DRESS FROM COLLECTION, SPRING/SUMMER 1999, VIEWS OF PRESENTATION above: WEDDING DRESS FROM COLLECTION, SPRING/SUMMER 1999, FRONT AND BACK VIEWS

below: DRESSES FROM COLLECTION, SPRING/SUMMER 2006, FRONT AND BACK VIEWS

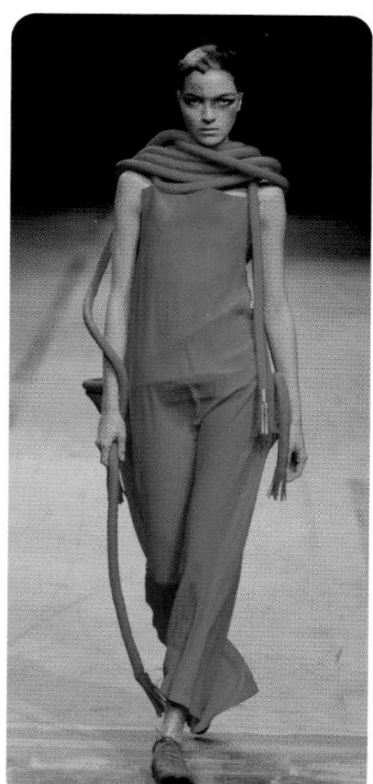

DRESS FROM COLLECTION, AUTUMN/WINTER 1996–97, FRONT AND BACK VIEWS

opposite, clockwise from top left:

ORANGE DRESS FROM COLLECTION, AUTUMN/WINTER 1996–97

CREAM COTTON DRESS FROM COLLECTION, SPRING/SUMMER 2000

GARMENTS FROM COLLECTION, AUTUMN/WINTER 2006–07

WOODEN DRESS FROM COLLECTION, AUTUMN/WINTER 1991–92

DINOSAUR DRESS FROM COLLECTION, SPRING/SUMMER 2006

J. MEEJIN YOON/MY STUDIO Boston and New York

J. Meejin Yoon, b. 1972, Seoul

J. Meejin Yoon's multidisciplinary practice MY Studio encompasses architecture, site-specific installations, and, on occasion, fashion design. Yoon's work falls between the conceptual and the concrete, and many of her small-scale conceptual designs enable her to test ideas that she may later incorporate into large-scale, realizable projects.

The Möbius (2005) and Defensible (2001) Dresses are one-of-a-kind conceptual projects undertaken by Yoon to explore form and performance. Made of white felt, the Möbius Dress takes the shape of a Möbius strip, a loop made by flipping one end of a rectangular strip and then connecting it to the opposite end. By cutting while following the contours of the strip two times around, three connected loops are formed. When the cut edges of the dress are zipped together, the garment encloses the body in a stiff A-line shape. When unzipped, the dress unfolds and its intertwining loops cascade to the floor. The Defensible Dress, equipped with sensor-activated latex-dipped "quills," reacts when it senses another person getting too close to its wearer. The quills thrust out and upward from the body to create what is essentially a protective interactive bustle.

MÖBIUS DRESS, 2005

VIEWS OF DRESS AND DEMONSTRATION OF MÖBIUS STRIP

overleaf: **DEFENSIBLE DRESS**, 2001

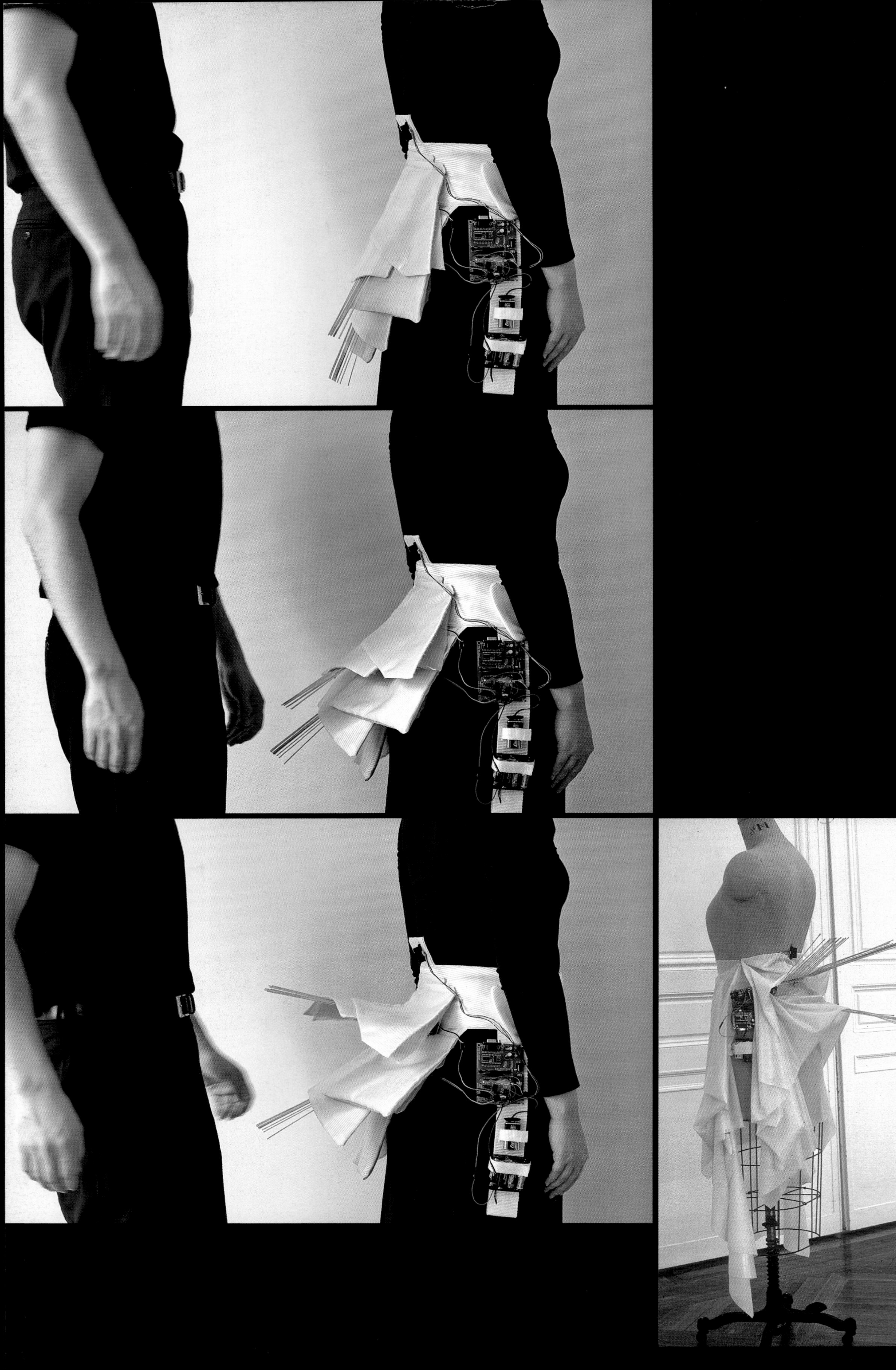

AFTERWORD
PROJECTS in the EXHIBITION
selected BIBLIOGRAPHY

In her introductory essay to this catalogue, Brooke Hodge lays out the conceptual and visual territory shared by the fashion designers and architects in "Skin + Bones: Parallel Practices in Fashion and Architecture." She concludes by imagining the "hybrid practices of the future," when the technical, material, and conceptual borders between fashion and architecture could all but dissolve. However, as "Skin + Bones" demonstrates, the future is here. Rippling folds, asymmetric bends, and uneven layering have become signature elements for practitioners within each domain. Certain preoccupations recur throughout the projects in the exhibition, despite the obvious differences in material, function, scale, and cost. There is an emphasis on the appearance of fragility, expressed in multiple, often transparent or translucent layers. These seemingly delicate layers, however, may actually be fabricated out of steel mesh or tempered glass or, in a garment, a sheer microfiber that resists tearing and repels stains. Layers—within both built and sewn structures—remain distinct and are repeated, sometimes extravagantly, for instance, in the work of Shigeru Ban. Witness also the seemingly endless tiers of shirtfronts and collars in Viktor & Rolf's autumn/winter 2003–04 One Woman Show collection. In both building and clothing designs, the generation of layers—whether wrought out of glass or silk georgette—suggests that there is strength in resilience. Fragility is first acknowledged, even embraced, then defied.

The repetition of edges is a strategy used sometimes by painters (Paul Cézanne, for example) to convey the difficulty of identifying with precision just exactly *where* the body and its clothing meet the spaces and objects around it. How does one distinguish the place where a person's back actually touches a chair? Where does a head end and a hat begin? What is the line between figure and ground, self and world? Junya Watanabe's autumn/winter 2000–01 Soirée (or Techno Couture) collection provides an equivocal answer to this question in the form of a dress that surrounds the body with a honeycombed pleated polyester organdy that almost entirely camouflages it while providing a visually dramatic shell.

Another shared quality that pervades both garment and building design in "Skin + Bones" is the difficulty of gaining immediate access to the interior of structures, whether intimate or monumental. Uneven layers and asymmetric planes often deflect attention from the entrance to a building, while spiraling seams, overlapping layers, and invisible fasteners obscure the ideal manner of donning a dress or coat, if in fact there is one. Indeed, parts are assembled in an unpredictable and potentially flexible way, as if the shape of a garment, or even a building, depended on the need to anticipate shifts of function. Yeohlee Teng's black-and-white *fil coupe* swirl skirt (autumn/winter 2001–02) becomes a cloak; Hussein Chalayan's chair slipcover becomes a dress (autumn/winter 2000–01). The wearer demands maximum adaptability, acknowledging, indeed affirming, the provisional nature of human habitation—whether of concrete or cloth.

Twenty-five years ago, fashion designers such as Giorgio Armani, Roberto Capucci, Gianfranco Ferré, Karl Lagerfeld, Miyake Issey, Claude Montana, Mariuccia Mandelli of Krizia, Stephen Manniello, Thierry Mugler, Ronaldus Shamask, Teng, Emmanuel Ungaro, and Gianni Versace—many of whom were included in my 1982 exhibition "Intimate Architecture: Contemporary Clothing Design" at the Hayden Gallery at the Massachusetts Institute of Technology—produced what might be called "architectonic" forms; however, their allusions to armor were more explicit. The layers that hovered around the body seemed impenetrable. The samurai was invoked, as was the protective gear of sports and ecclesiastical uniforms. Near-abstract faceted shapes—at times reminiscent of Russian Constructivist or Bauhaus theatrical designs—deflected the gaze from the organic qualities of the body. The designs that are at the heart of "Skin + Bones" are different. They are

46
LUCY ORTA
Refuge Wear–Habitent, 1992/93; aluminum-coated polyamide, polar fleece, telescopic aluminum poles, whistle, lantern, and transport bag; 59⁹⁄₁₆ x 59⁹⁄₁₆ x 59⁹⁄₁₆ inches; courtesy Galerie Anne de Villepoix

47
ANDREA ZITTEL
A–Z Living Unit, 1993; wood, steel, chair, electric lights, and various personal accoutrements; closed: 60 x 40 x 30 inches; open: 60 x 40 x 61 inches; Milwaukee Art Museum, gift of Contemporary Art Society

more flexible and adaptable, at times even playful. A virtue is made of the provisional. A skirt becomes a cloak; a slipcover a dress. A curtain becomes a wall, then a curtain again, if the inhabitant makes it so.

Writing in the aftermath of the London bombings during World War I, which left so many of the city's domestic interiors destroyed or cruelly exposed, Virginia Woolf wondered whether someday people might carry with them portable homes, like "snail shells." She speculated that they could "flirt out houses like little fans; and go on."[1] Woolf's premise was taken up quite literally by industrial designer Lucy Orta, whose Refuge Wear-Habitent (1992/93) is a silver tent "designed for displaced people who must carry their belongings and homes with them as they migrate within or between cities."[2] A number of young industrial designers and artists like Morena Ferrari and C. P. Company (Parka/Air Mattress, 2001), Michael Rakowitz (paraSITE homeless shelter, 1997), and Martín Ruiz de Azúa (Basic House, 1999) have produced both garments and portable shelters for the homeless, as well as for the contemporary individual who wants maximum protection and mobility. Prototypes of such designs were displayed in the 2005 Museum of Modern Art, New York, exhibition "Safe: Design Takes on Risk." (Incidentally, Teng has often remarked that she designs for the "urban nomad," who needs to roam around the city in clothing that can adapt to the multiple, often competing demands of the contemporary woman.)

The contingent nature of shelter for the body is also at the core of the practice of a number of young artists intent on subverting the boundaries between clothing forms and shelter, between art and life. Andrea Zittel conceived of *A–Z Administrative Services* (1991) to provide a life rendered utopian by design. Her portable Living Units (1993–94) contain all the essentials—sink, burners, toilet, bed, chair—most of which can be adapted to other functions. Zittel also designed a variety of clothing lines: the *A–Z Personal Uniforms* (1991–2002), a collection of minimalist dresses that can be worn for six months at a time (a solution for the artist/gallery assistant who needs elegance on a budget); and *A–Z Raugh Uniforms* (1998), made out of woven cloth torn from a bolt and wrapped and pinned to fit. Her more recent designs for *Fiber Form Uniforms* (2002) are made of washed and carded wool felted directly into the shape of a skirt or dress.[3]

South Korean artist Do-Ho Suh oscillates between clothing and building forms in his installations, confounding any simple division between them. In 2003, he suspended a full-scale replica of his New York apartment—hand-stitched in silken translucent blue nylon—from the ceiling of Lehmann Maupin Gallery in New York. *The Perfect Home II* appeared to float above the floor as visitors marveled at details such as light switches, radiators, and sinks. The shimmering nylon, suspended by a system of invisible metal poles and monofilament, trembled when visitors walked within its "walls," underscoring the porousness of every wall of a human environment, no matter how seemingly impenetrable. In Suh's installation for the 49th Venice Biennale, *Some/One* (2001), thousands of silver military dog tags lined the gallery floor, rising up and coalescing in the center to form the shape of a traditional Korean dress.

These days, artists, designers, and architects all practice within a culture that desires, indeed demands, *both* shelter and elegance. "Skin + Bones" demonstrates that the infinite variations on the theme of their conjunction are just beginning to be assessed.

48

1 Virginia Woolf, entry for 12 September 1935, in *A Writer's Diary*, ed. Leonard Woolf (New York: Harcourt, Brace, 1953), 246.
2 Lucy Orta, cited in Paola Antonelli, *Safe: Design Takes on Risk*, exh. cat. (New York: The Museum of Modern Art, 2005), 11.
3 See *Andrea Zittel: Critical Space*, exh. cat. (Houston: Contemporary Arts Museum; New York: New Museum of Contemporary Art; and Munich, Germany: Prestel Verlag, 2005), 66–134.

48
ANDREA ZITTEL
A–Z Personal Uniform, 1991–2002, installation at Andrea Rosen Gallery, New York, 2004

49
DO-HO SUH
The Perfect Home II, 2003; translucent nylon; 110 x 240 x 516 inches; collection of Lawrence B. Benenson, New York; installation at Lehmann Maupin Gallery, New York, 2003

49

PROJECTS IN THE EXHIBITION

AZZEDINE ALAÏA

BANDAGE DRESSES, 1985–91

VÊTEMENTS ÉPINGLÉS collection, spring/summer 1987

ZIPPER KNITS collection, spring/summer 1997

SHIGERU BAN ARCHITECTS

CURTAIN WALL HOUSE, Tokyo, 1993–95
Shigeru Ban, Yoko Nakagawa, and Shigeru Hiraki, project team; Hoshino Architect & Engineers, structural engineers; and Heisei Construction, general contractors

PAPER EMERGENCY SHELTERS for the United Nations High Commissioner for Refugees, Byumba Refugee Camp, Rwanda, 1995–99

JAPAN PAVILION, Expo 2000, Hannover, Germany, 1997–2000
Shigeru Ban, Nobutaka Hiraga, Shigeru Hiraki, and Jun Yashiki, project team; Frei Otto, consultant; Buro Happold, structural engineers; and Takenaka Europe, GmbH, general contractors

HUSSEIN CHALAYAN

BETWEEN collection, spring/summer 1998

ECHOFORM collection, autumn/winter 1999–2000

BEFORE MINUS NOW collection, spring/summer 2000

AFTERWORDS collection, autumn/winter 2000–01

PRESTON SCOTT COHEN

CORNERED HOUSE (unbuilt), Longboat Key, Florida, 1991
Charles Ray, client

TORUS HOUSE (unbuilt), Old Chatham, New York, 1998–2000
Eric Wolf, client; Alexandra Barker, Chris Hoxie, and Eric Olsen, project team; and Scott Cohen, Aaron D'Innocenzo, Darell Fields, and Judy Hodge, model team

TEL AVIV MUSEUM OF ART, Tel Aviv, 2003–projected 2008
Motti Omer, director and chief curator, client; Preston Scott Cohen, design; Amit Nemlich, project architect; James Forren, Isamu Kanda, and Tobias Nolte, project assistants; Nizan Inbar Projects Management Ltd., Ido Inbar CPM Construction Management Ltd., and Shlomo Cohen, project managers; YSS Consulting Engineers Ltd., structural engineers; M. Doron-I. Shahar & Co., Consulting Eng. Ltd., HVAC engineers; U. Brenner-A. Fattal Electrical & Systems Engineering Ltd., electrical engineers; and M. G. Acoustical Consultants Ltd., acoustics

COMME DES GARÇONS

BODY MEETS DRESS, DRESS MEETS BODY collection, spring/summer 1997

ADULT PUNK (DEMOLITION AND RECONSTRUCTION) collection, autumn/winter 1997–98

CLUSTERING BEAUTY collection, spring/summer 1998

FUSION collection, autumn/winter 1998–99

NEW ESSENTIAL collection, spring/summer 1999

EXCELLENT ABSTRACT collection, spring/summer 2004

NEIL M. DENARI ARCHITECTS

HIGH LINE 23 CONDOMINIUM TOWER, New York, 2005–projected 2007
Alf Naman Real Estate, client and developer; Neil M. Denari, design architect and architect of record; Duks Koschitz, project architect; Stefano Paiocchi, project designer; Carmen C. Cham, Alex Chew Kheng-Kai, Steven Epley, Craig Hoverman, Alexander Janowsky, Christian Kotzamanis, Eric Leishman, Philipp Traexler, Paola Vezzulli, and Joe Willendra, project team; Marc I. Rosenbaum, collaborating architect; Gruzen Samton Architects, consulting architects; and DeSimone Consulting Engineers, consulting engineers

DILLER SCOFIDIO + RENFRO

BAD PRESS: DISSIDENT HOUSEWORK SERIES, 1993–98
Elizabeth Diller and Ricardo Scofidio, principals; John Bachus, Brendan Cotter, and David Lindberg, project team

BLUR BUILDING, Media Pavilion, Swiss Expo 2002, Yverdon-les-Bains, Switzerland, 2002
Swiss Expo 2002, client; Elizabeth Diller and Ricardo Scofidio, principals; Dick Hebel, project leader; Charles Renfro and Eric Bunge, project team; Passera & Pedretti, collaborating engineers; Fujiko Nakaya, advisor; dbox, concept animation; Diller Scofidio + Renfro and Ben Rubio, EAR Studio, media; Mark Wasiuta, media associate; Christian Marclay, sound installation; Delux, Morphing Systems, and West 8, collaborators; and Bern Techdata, management

INSTITUTE OF CONTEMPORARY ART, Boston, 2002–06
Elizabeth Diller, Ricardo Scofidio, and Charles Renfro, principals; Flavio Stigliano, project leader; Eric Höweler, Jesse Saylor, and Deane Simpson, project team; Arup, collaborating engineers and lighting; Perry Dean Rodgers and Partners, associate architects; Fischer Dachs, theater consultants; Jaffe Holden Acoustics, acoustics; Seamus Henchy Associates, project management; and dbox and Matthew Johnson, animations

ALICE TULLY HALL RENOVATION, Lincoln Center, New York, 2005–projected 2008
Lincoln Center for the Performing Arts, client; Elizabeth Diller, Ricardo Scofidio, and Charles Renfro, principals; Gerard Sullivan and Ben Gilmartin, project leaders; Gerri Davis, Robert Donnelly, Frank Gesualdi, Stefan Gruber, Rainer Hehl, Eric Höweler, Michael Hundsnurscher, Gaspar Libedinsky, Ben Mickus, Filip Tejchman, Josh Uhl, and Florencia Vetcher, project team; Fox and Fowle Architects, associate architects; Ove Arup, structural and MEP engineers; and Hoxie/Hicks, animation

WINKA DUBBELDAM/ARCHI-TECTONICS

GREENWICH STREET PROJECT, New York, 2000–04
Take One LLC, developer; Winka Dubbeldam, principal in charge; David Hotson Architect, architect of record; Ana Sotrel, project architect; Tanja Bitzer, Amy Farina, Michael Hundsnurscher, Deborah Kully, and Bittor Sanchez, project team; Buro Happold, structural engineers; Israel Berger and Associates, Inc., curtain-wall consultants; Gabor Szakal Consulting Engineers, mechanical engineers; Shen, Milsom & Wilke, Inc., sound consultants; Barker Mohandas, elevator consultants; and York Hunter Construction Services, Inc., general contractors

EISENMAN ARCHITECTS

CHORA L WORKS: PROJECT FOR A GARDEN (unbuilt), Parc de la Villette, Paris, 1985–86
Peter Eisenman, Jacques Derrida with Renato Rizzi, architects; Thomas Leeser and Renato Rizzi, project architects; and Franco Alloca, Manou Ernster, Gerard de Gorter, Christian Kohl, Hiroshi Maruyama, and Paola Marzatico, assistants

MAX REINHARDT HAUS (unbuilt), Berlin, 1992–93
Advanta Management AG, client; Peter Eisenman, architect; Severud Associates, engineers; George Kewin, associate principal in charge; Richard Labonte, Edward Mitchell, and Lindy Roy, project architects; Armand Biglari, Brad Gildea, Norbert Holthausen, Gregory Luhan, Stefania Rinaldi, David Schatzle, and Jon Stephens, project team; Federico Beulcke, Mark Bretler, Andrew Burmeister, Robert Holten, Patrick Keane, Brad Khouri, Joseph Lau, Vincent LeFeuvre, Fabian Lemmel, John Maze, Steven Meyer, Debbie Park, Silke Potting, and Benjamin Wade, project assistants; Kurt Forster and Fritz Neumeyer, historians; Donnell Consultants, elevator consultants; and Hanna/Olin, landscape architects

ALBER ELBAZ FOR LANVIN

Collection, autumn/winter 2002–03

Collection, autumn/winter 2003–04

Collection, spring/summer 2005

Collection, autumn/winter 2006–07

FOREIGN OFFICE ARCHITECTS

YOKOHAMA INTERNATIONAL PORT TERMINAL, Yokohama, Japan, 1995–2002
The City of Yokohama Port & Harbor Bureau Construction Department, Osanbashi Passenger Vessel Terminal Maintenance Subdivision, client; Farshid Moussavi, Alejandro Zaera-Polo, Felix Bendito, Victoria Castillejos, Shokan Endo, Dafne Gil, Kensuke Kishikawa, Yasuhisa Kikuchi, Izumi Kobayashi, Jordi Mansilla, Kenichi Matsuzawa, Oriol Montfort, Tomofumi Nagayama, Xavier Ortiz, Lluis Viu Rebes, Jose Saenz, Keisuke Tamura, Santiago Triginer, Julian Varas, and Thomasine Wolfensberger, design team; Structure Design Group, Arup, structural engineers; PT Morimura & Associates, services engineers; Kado Lighting Design Laboratory, lighting; Nagata Acoustics Inc., acoustics; Akeno Fire Research Institute, disaster prevention consultants; Urban Traffic Engineering, traffic consultants; and Shimizu Corporation, Kajima Corporation, and Toda Corporation, general contractors

VIRTUAL HOUSE (unbuilt), 1997
Farshid Moussavi, Alejandro Zaera-Polo, Mónica Company, Kenichi Matsuzawa, Jordi Mansilla, Manuel Monterde, and Manuel Pérez, design team

BBC MUSIC CENTRE AND OFFICES, White City, London, 2003–projected 2006
Farshid Moussavi, Alejandro Zaera-Polo, Nerea Calvillo, Kelvin Chu Ka Wing, Kazuhide Doi, Eduardo Fernández-Moscoso, Laura Fernández, Kensuke Kishikawa, Friedrich Ludewig, Kenichi Matsuzawa, and Jordi Pagès i Ramón, design team; Adams Kara Taylor, structural engineers; Sandy Brown Associates, acoustics; Speirs and Major Associates, lighting; Davis Langdon & Everest, QS and project management; Ducks Sceno, theater consultants; and Cameron Taylor Brady, services engineers

FUTURE SYSTEMS

SELFRIDGES DEPARTMENT STORE, Birmingham, England, 1999–2003
Selfridges & Co., client; Jan Kaplicky, Amanda Levete, Søren Aagaard, Nerida Bergin, Sarah Jayne Bowen, Lida Caharsouli, Julian Flannery, Harvinder Gabhari, Dominic Harris, Nicola Hawkins, Matthew Heywood, Candas Jennings, Iain MacKay, Glenn Moorley, Andrea Morgante, Thorsten Overberg, Angus Pond, Jessica Salt, and Severin Soder, project team; Arup, structural, mechanical, fire protection, façade, and services engineers; Faithful + Gould, project managers; Boyden & Co., quantity surveyors; and Laing O'Rourke, contractors

FRANK GEHRY

GEHRY RESIDENCE, Santa Monica, California 1977–78/1991–94
Frank and Berta Gehry, clients; Frank Gehry, Paul Lubowicki, and Jon Drezner, project team

WALT DISNEY CONCERT HALL, Los Angeles, 1987–2003
Music Center of Los Angeles County, client; Frank Gehry, James M. Glymph, Craig Webb, Vano Haritunians, Terry Bell, Andrew Alper, Suren Ambartsumyan, Larik Ararat, Kamran Ardalan, Herwig Baumgartner, Pejman Berjis, Rick Black, Kirk Blaschke, Tomaso Bradshaw, Earle Briggs, Zachary Burns, John Carter, Padraic Cassidy, Vartan Chalikian, Tina Chee, William Childers, Rebeca Cotera, Jonathan Davis, Jim Dayton, Susannah Dickinson, Denise Disney, Jon Drezner, Nick Easton, Jeff Guga, David Hardie, James Jackson, Victoria Jenkins, Michael Jobes, Michael Kempf, Thomas Kim, Kurt Komraus, Gregory Kromhout, Naomi Langer, Meaghan Lloyd, Jacquine Lorange, Gary Lundberg, Michael Maltzan, Gerhard Mayer, Christopher Mazzier, Alex Meconi, Emilio Melgazo, George Metzger, Brent Miller, Julianna Morais, Rosemary Morris, Mathias Mortenson, Gaston Nogues, David Pakshong, Jay Park, Diego Petrate, Vytas Petrulis, Whit Preston, Michael Resnic, David Rodriguez, Christopher Samuelian, Michael J. Sant, Michael Sedlacek, Robert Seelenbacher, Matthias Seufert, Dennis Shelden, Bruce Shepard, Tadao Shimizu, Rick Smith, Eva Sobesky, Randall Stout, Suran Sumian, Thomas Swanson, John Sziachta, Tensho Takemori, Laurence Tighe, Hiroshi Tokumaru, Karen Tom, Jose Catriel Tulian, Dane Twichell, William Ullman, Monica Valtierra-Day, Mok Wai Wan, Eric Wegerbauer, Gretchen Werner, Adam Wheeler, Josh White, Tim Williams, Nora Wlin, Kristin Woehl, Yu-Wen Yang, Bryant Yeh, Brian Yoo, and Brian Zamora, project team; John A. Martin and Associates, structural engineers; Levine/Seegel Associates and

Consentini Associates Consulting Engineers, mechanical engineers; Frederick Russell Brown & Associates, electrical engineers; John A. Martin & Associates, structural engineers; Psomas and Associates, civil engineers; Gordon H. Smith Corporation, exterior wall consultants; Nagata Acoustics and Charles M. Salter Associates, acoustics; Theatre Projects Consultants, theater consultants; and M. A. Morenson, general contractor Engineering, Inc., structural engineers; Levine/Seegel Associates and Cosentini Associates, mechanical engineers; Frederick Russell Brown and Associates, electrical engineers; and HCB-Peck/Jones, general contractors

TESS GIBERSON

STRUCTURE 1 collection, autumn/winter 2003–04

ZAHA HADID ARCHITECTS

VITRA FIRE STATION, Weil am Rhein, Germany, 1990–94
Rolf Fehlbaum, Vitra International AG, client; Zaha Hadid, design; Patrik Schumacher, project architect; Patrik Schumacher and Signy Svalastoga, detail design; Nicola Cousins, David Gomersall, Edgar Gonzalez, Kar-Hwa Ho, Craig Kiner, Simon Koumjian, Daniel R. Oakley, Maria Rossi, Cristina Verissimo, Olaf Weishaupt, and Voon Yee-Wong, design team; Daniel Chadwick and Tim Price, models; and GPF & Assoziierte, drawings and building supervision

MAXXI NATIONAL CENTER OF CONTEMPORARY ARTS, Rome, 1997–projected 2007
Ministero per i Beni e le Attività Culturali, client; Zaha Hadid and Patrik Schumacher, design; Gianluca Racana, project architect; Ana M. Cajao, Fabio Ceci, Matteo Grimaldi, Paolo Matteuzzi, Mario Mattia, Maurizio Meossi, Luca Peralta, Barbara Pfenningstorff, Gianluca Ruggeri, Luca Segarelli, Anja Simons, Maria Velceva, and Paolo Zilli, design team; ABT, associate architects; Anthony Hunt Associates and OK Design Group, structural engineers; Max Fordham and Partners and OK Design Group, mechanical and electrical engineers; Equation Lighting, lighting; and Paul Gilleron Acoustic, acoustics

HERZOG & DE MEURON

RICOLA–EUROPE SA PRODUCTION AND STORAGE BUILDING, Mulhouse-Brunstatt, France, 1992–93
Ricola AG, client; Jacques Herzog, Pierre de Meuron, Annette Hammer, Andreas Maeder, and Ascan Mergenthaler, project team; Ingenieurbüro Andreas Zachmann, structural engineer; Kienast Vogt & Partner, landscape designers; Art et Industrie SARL, construction managers; and Marc Weidmann, silkscreen on polycarbonate panels

CENTRAL SIGNAL BOX, Basel, 1994–99
Schweizerische Bundesbahnen (Anlagen Management), client; Jacques Herzog, Pierre de Meuron, Harry Gugger, and Philippe Fürstenberger, project team; ARGE, Herzog & de Meuron, and Proplaning AG, general planning; Proplaning AG, structural engineers and construction managers; Selmoni AG, electrical engineers; Silzer Energieconsulting AG, HVAC engineers; Balduin Weisser AG, plumbing engineers; and Tecton AG, façade consultants

PRADA AOYAMA TOKYO EPICENTER, Tokyo, 2000–03
Prada (Prada Japan Co., Ltd.), client; Jacques Herzog, Pierre de Meuron, Luca Andrisani, Andreas Fries, Wolfgang Hardt, Yuko Himeno, Hiroshi Kikuchi, Stefan Marbach, Shinya Okuda, Daniel Pokora, Reto Redrocchi, Georg Schmid, and Mathis Tinner, project team; Takenaka Corporation, associate architects, general contractors, and fire safety design; Takenaka Coporation and WGG Schnetzer Puska (consultant), structural engineers; Takenaka Corporation and Waldhauser Engineering (HVAC consultant), mechanical and electrical engineers; Emmer Pfenninger Partner AG, façade consultants; Josef Gartner GmbH, curtain-wall subcontractor; and Arup, lighting

NATIONAL STADIUM, The Main Stadium for the 2008 Olympic Games, Beijing, 2002–projected 2007
National Stadium Co. Ltd., client; Herzog & de Meuron, architectural design; Jacques Herzog, Pierre de Meuron, Peter Karl Becher, Alexander Berger, Felix Beyreuther, Marcos Carreno, Xudong Chen, Simon Chessex, Massimo Corradi, Linxi Dong, Mia Hägg, Yichun He, Volker Helm, Claudia von Hessert, Yong Huang, Kasia Jackowska, Uta Kamps, Hiroshi Kikuchi, Martin Krapp, Hemans Lai, Emily Liang, Kenan Liu, Donald Mak, Stefan Marbach, Carolina Mojto, Thomas Polster, Christoph Röttinger, Roland Rossmaier, Luciano Rotoli, Mehrdad Safa, Roman Sokalski, Heeri Song, Christoph Weber, Tobias Winkelmann, Thomasine Wolfensberger, Pim van Wylick, Camillo Zanardini, and Xiaolei Zhang, project team; China Architectural Design & Research Group, Ove Arup & Partners Hong Kong Ltd., and Arup Sports, engineering and sports architecture; and Ai Weiwei, expert advisor

YOSHIKI HISHINUMA

BELLOWS DRESS collection, spring/summer 2000

CUBISM DRESS collection, autumn/winter 2001–02

INSIDE OUT 2WAY DRESS collection, spring/summer 2004

TOYO ITO

TOD'S OMOTESANDO BUILDING, Tokyo, 2002–04
Holpaf B.V., client; Toyo Ito, Takuji Aoshima, Takeo Higashi, Akihisa Hirata, Yasuaki Mizunuma, Kaori Shikichi, and Leo Yokota, design team; Structural Design Office OAK Inc., structural engineers; ES Associates, mechanical engineers; Light Design, Inc., lighting; Toyo Ito & Associates, Architects, furniture design; and Takenaka Corporation, general contractor

FORUM FOR MUSIC, DANCE & VISUAL CULTURE (unbuilt), Ghent, Belgium, 2004
City of Ghent, client; Toyo Ito & Associates, Architects (Toyo Ito, Taku Adachi, Florian Busch, Christoph Cellarius, Takeo Higashi, Akihisa Hirata, Takayasu Hirayama, Kento Sano, Shinichi Takeuchi, and Yuichi Yokokawa) and Andrea Branzi Architetto (Andrea Branzi, Eddy François, Giuseppe Galli, Daniele Macchi, and Hera van Sande), design team; Structural Design Office OAK, Inc., structural engineers; and Nagata Acoustics, theater design

MIKIMOTO GINZA 2, Tokyo, 2004–05
K. Mikimoto & Co., Ltd., client; Toyo Ito, Takeo Higashi, Takayasu Hirayama, and Yasuaki Mizunuma, design team; Taisei Corporation and Sasaki Structural Consultants, structural engineers; Taisei Corporation, mechanical engineers and contractor; and Taisei Corporation and Light Design Inc., lighting

JAKOB + MACFARLANE

PUZZLE HOUSE (unbuilt), 1996
Dominique Jakob and Brendan MacFarlane, architectural team

HOUSE H (unbuilt), Corsica, France, 2002
Dominique Jakob, Brendan MacFarlane, Florian Brillet, Jacques Cadhilac, and Gabrielle Evangelisti, architectural team

CITY OF FASHION & DESIGN, Paris, 2005–projected 2008
Dominique Jakob, Brendan MacFarlane, Sébastien Gamelin, Patrice Gardara, Petra Maier, and Atticus Manchego, architectural team

GREG LYNN FORM

BLOOM HOUSE, Venice, California, 2004–projected 2007
Jason and Jackilin Bloom, clients; Greg Lynn, Danny Bazil, Jackilin Bloom, Brian Ha, Brittney Hart, Chris Kabatsi, and Andreas Krainer, design team; Lookinglass Architecture & Design, architects of record; KPFF Consulting Engineers, structural engineers; Storms & Lowe, mechanical engineers; AGI Geo Technical, soils engineers; R. S. Engineering Company, Inc., survey engineers; Oliver Garrett Construction, Inc., general contractors; Kreysler & Associates, lantern fabricator; and Pacific Coast Installations, corian fabricator

SLAVIN HOUSE, Venice, California, 2004–projected 2008
Sylvia Lavin and Greg Lynn, clients; Greg Lynn, Danny Bazil, Jackilin Bloom, Deborah Chiu, Chris Kabatsi, Mo Lai, Florencia Pita, and Martin Sobota, design team; and Bollinger + Grohmann GmbH, structural engineers

ELENA MANFERDINI

Custom-Made Dress, 2006

MAISON MARTIN MARGIELA

Collection, autumn/winter 2000–01

Collection, spring/summer 2003

0 Artisanal collection, spring/summer 2005

Collection, autumn/winter 2006–07

ALEXANDER MCQUEEN

IRERE collection, spring/summer 2003

SCANNERS collection, autumn/winter 2003–04

IT'S ONLY A GAME collection, spring/summer 2005

WIDOWS OF CULLODEN collection, autumn/winter 2006–07

ENRIC MIRALLES BENEDETTA TAGLIABUE/EMBT ARQUITECTES

SANTA CATERINA MARKET, Barcelona, 1997–2005
Foment de Ciutat Vella S.A., client; Benedetta Tagliabue, principal; Igor Peraza, project director; Barbara Appolloni, Fabiàn Asunciòn, Sabine Bauchmann, Nils Becker, Josep Belles, Alicia Bramon, Joan Callis, Monica Carrera, Jorge Carvajal, Marta Cases, Ezequiel Cattaneo, Constanza Chara, Massimo Chizzola, Eugenio Cirulli, Lluís Corbella, Santiago Crespi, Marco Dario Chirdel, Raphael de Montard, Ane Ebbeskov Olsen, Stefan Eckert, Makoto Fukuda, Montse Galindo, Stephan Geenen, Loïc Gestin, Leonardo Giovannozzi, Tobias Gottschalk, Ute Grolz, Gianfranco Grondona, Fernanda Hannah, Annette Höller, Hirotaka Koizumi, Andrea Landell de Moura, Annie Marcela Henao, Francesco Jacques-Días, Stephanie Le Draoullec, Josep Miàs, Christian Molina, Francesco Mozzati, Barbara Oel Brandt, Mette Olsen, Adelaide Passetti, Joan Poca, Ignacio Quintana, Elena Rocchi, Dani Rosselló, Peter Sándor Nagy, Torsten Schmid, Torsten Skoetz, Silke Techen, Luca Tonella, Karl Unglaub, Jean François Vaudeville, Laura Valentini, Alejandra Vazquez, Maarten Vermeiren, Florencia Vetcher, Adrien Verschuere, and Thomas Wuttke, project team; Ricardo Flores and Eva Prats, special consultants; Robert Brufau, structural engineer; Jose Maria Velasco, roof engineer; Miquel Llorens, housing engineer; PGI, installations; and Ceramicas Cumella S.L., ceramic manufacturer

MIYAKE ISSEY

RHYTHM PLEATS, 1989; Pleats Please Issey Miyake line, 1992–present

A-POC JUPITER©, Miyake Design Studio, 2006

A-POC TRAMPOLINE AND GEMINI©, Miyake Design Studio in collaboration with Ripple Chair by Ron Arad for Moroso, 2005

MORPHOSIS

SUN TOWER, Seoul, 1994–97
Village Trading Company, Ltd., client; Thom Mayne, principal; Eul-Ho Suh, project manager; Dave Grant, Kim Groves, Kristina Loock, and Eui-Sung Yi, project designers; and Min-Seok Baek, Jay Behr, Mark Briggs, Neil Crawford, Towan Kim, Richard Koschitz, and Janice Shimizu, project team

NEUTELINGS RIEDIJK ARCHITECTEN

VEENMAN PRINTSHOP, Ede, The Netherlands, 1995–97
Veenman Printers, client; Willem Jan Neutelings, Michiel Riedijk, Willem Brujin, Dirk van den Heuvel, and Andy Woodcock, design team; Bureau Bouwkunde Rotterdam, technical design and building consultants; ABT Adviesbureau voor bouwtechniek, structural design; DWA Installatie-en energieadvies, building services engineers; West 8 Landscape Architects bv, landscape architects; Karel Martens, art designer; and K. Schippers, poet

CONCERT HALL (unbuilt), Bruges, Belgium, 1998
City of Bruges, client; Willem Jan Neutelings, Michiel Riedijk, Tania Ally, Marc De Bruijn, Dimitri Meessen, Arjan Mulder, Joost Mulders, Ute Schneider, Lennaart Sirag, Bas Suijkerbuijk, and Wessel Vreugdenhil, design team; Bureau Bouwtechniek bvba, technical design; Adviesbureau Peutz & Associates bv, acoustical engineers; Raadgevende Ingenieurs Prinssen en Bus bv, scenographic advisor; and Aronsohn Raadgevende Ingenieurs bv, structural engineers

ATELIERS JEAN NOUVEL

ARAB WORLD INSTITUTE, Paris, 1981–87
Institut du monde arabe, client; Scarif, owners' representative; Jean Nouvel, Gilbert Lezenes, Pierre Soria, and Architecture Studio, project team; JJ Raynaud, Antoinette Robain, and Adeline Rispail (museography), project managers; Jl Besnard, Pascal Debard, and Jm Reynier, architects; Cabinet Sery Bertrand, economist; Jacques Le Marquet, scenography; François Seigneur, interior design; Sa Zaidan, architectural advisor; Licht Design, museum lighting; Arcora, museum structure; A. Richert, landscape design; Michel Seban, scenography auditorium; and P. M. Jacot, north façade seriography

OFFICE dA

CASA LA ROCA (unbuilt), Caracas, 1995
Monica Ponce de Leon, Nader Tehrani, principals; Chris Arner, Vorapochana Ansvaneda, Jeffrey Asanza, Dan Bibb, Patricia Szu-Ping Chen, Natalie Maric, Gene Miao, Kazuyo Oda, Thamarit Suchart, Diego Toledo, Rusty Walker, and Apisek Wongvasu, design team

ZAHEDI HOUSE (unbuilt), Weston, Massachusetts, 1998
Monica Ponce de Leon, Nader Tehrani, principals; Jeffrey Asanza, Michael Autrey, Dan Bibb, Joelle Byrer, Patricia Szu-Ping Chen, Mario d'Artista, Kristen Giannattasio, Richard Lee, Jill Porter, Philip Smith, Lee Su, Thamarit Suchart, Kazuyo Oda, Mark Pasnik, and Diego Toledo, design team

HOUSE IN NEW ENGLAND, Boston, 2002–03
Monica Ponce de Leon, Nader Tehrani, principals; Hamad Al-Sultan, Tali Buchler, Albert Garcia, Kristen Giannattasio, Lisa Huang, and Elise Shelley, design team; Bill Bishop, structural engineers; Sun Engineers, mechanical engineers; Foresight Land Services, civil engineers; Peter Coxe Associates, lighting; Cutting Edge Systems Corporation, media and acoustical; Lou Boxer, general contractor; Race Mountain Tree Service, landscape; Manuel de Santaren, interior designer; and Johnson Engineering, plumbing

OFFICE FOR METROPOLITAN ARCHITECTURE/ REM KOOLHAAS

SEATTLE CENTRAL LIBRARY, Seattle, 1999–2004
Rem Koolhaas and Joshua Prince-Ramus, partners in charge; Meghan Corwin, Bjarke Ingels, Carol Patterson, Natasha Sandmeier, Mark von Hof-Zogrotzki, and Dan Wood, project architects; Keely Colcleugh, Rachel Doherty, Sarah Gibson, Laura Gilmore, Anna Little, John McMorrough, Kate Orff, Beat Schenk, Saskia Simon, Anna Sutor, Victoria Willocks with Florence Clausel, Thomas Dubuisson, Chris van Duijn, Erez Ella, Achim Gergen, Eveline Jürgens, Antti Lassila, Hanna Peer, Jao Costa Ribeiro, Kristina Skoogh, Sybille Waeltli, and Leonard Weil, project team; LMN, joint venture architects; Arup, structural engineers, fire, IT and A/V; Magnusson Kliencic Associates, civil engineers; Michael Yantis Associates, acoustics; Bruce Mau Design, environmental graphics; Dewhurst Macfarlane and Partners, façades; OMA/LMN and Inside-Outside, interiors; Inside-Outside, Jones & Jones, and Greenlee Nursery, landscape; and Kugler Tillotson Associates, lighting

NARCISO RODRIGUEZ

Collection, autumn/winter 2002–03

Collection, spring/summer 2003

Collection, autumn/winter 2003–04

Collection, spring/summer 2004

CHADO RALPH RUCCI

Haute couture collection, spring/summer 2003

Haute couture collection, autumn/winter 2003–04

Haute couture collection, autumn/winter 2004–05

KAZUYO SEJIMA + RYUE NISHIZAWA/SANAA

21ST CENTURY MUSEUM OF CONTEMPORARY ART, Kanazawa, Japan, 1999–2004
City of Kanazawa, client; Kazuyo Sejima and Ryue Nishizawa, principals; Keizo Eki, Shoko Fukuya, Erika Hidaka, Naoki Hori, Mizuki Imamura, Junya Ishigami, Kansuke Kawashima, Yoshifumi Kojima, Tetsuo Kondo, Koichiro Tokimori, and Toshihiro Yoshimura, project team; Sasaki Structural Consultants, structural engineers; ES Associates, mechanical engineers; P. T. Morimura & Associates, electrical engineers; and Takanaka, Hazama, Toyokura, Oka, Honjin, and Nihonkai, general contractors

GLASS PAVILION, TOLEDO MUSEUM OF ART, Toledo, Ohio, 2001–06
Toledo Museum of Art, client; Paratus Group, owner's representative; Kazuyo Sejima and Ryue Nishizawa, principals; Florian Idenburg, associate in charge; Takayuki Hasegawa, Toshi Oki, and Keiko Uchiyama, project architects; Mizuki Imamura, Junya Ishigami, Tetsuo Kondo, project team; Kendall Heaton Associates, executive architects; Guy Nordenson & Associates/SAPS, structural engineers; Cosentini Associates and Transsolar, mechanical engineers; Front Inc., glass consultants; and Arup and Kilt Planning, lighting

NANNI STRADA DESIGN STUDIO

SPORTMAX collection, autumn/winter 1971–72

IL MANTO E LA PELLE collection, 1973

PLI-PLÀ collection, 1993

YEOHLEE TENG

Collection, spring/summer 1992

Collection, autumn/winter 2005–06

Collection, spring/summer 2006

TESTA & WEISER

CARBON TOWER (unbuilt), 2001–04
Peter Testa and Devyn Weiser, principals; Ian Ferguson and Hans-Michael Foeldeak, project designers; Arup, consulting engineers; and 3D Systems Corporation, prototyping

CARBON FIBER REINFORCED TIMBER (CFRT) prototypes, 2005
Peter Testa and Devyn Weiser, principals; Ian Ferguson, project designer; ETH Zürich, consulting engineers; EMPA Zürich, materials science and testing; and 3D Systems Corporation, prototyping

M-BRANE series (unbuilt), 2006
Peter Testa and Devyn Weiser, principals; Joshua Mun and James Vincent, project team; and 3D Systems Corporation, prototyping

CARBON BEACH HOUSE (unbuilt), 2006
Peter Testa and Devyn Weiser, principals; Ian Ferguson, Sky Milner, Joshua Mun, and James Vincent, project team; and 3D Systems Corporation, prototyping

OLIVIER THEYSKENS FOR ROCHAS

Collection, autumn/winter 1999–2000

Collection, autumn/winter 2003–04

Collection, spring/summer 2004

ISABEL TOLEDO

Collection, spring/summer 1988

Collection, autumn/winter 1993–94

Collection, spring/summer 1995

Collection, autumn/winter 1997–98

Collection, spring/summer 1998

Collection, autumn/winter 2005–06

BERNARD TSCHUMI ARCHITECTS

PARC DE LA VILLETTE, Paris, 1982–98
French Government, Etablissement Public du Parc de la Villette, client; Bernard Tschumi, Renzo Bader, Thomas Balsly, Christian Biecher, Alexandra Billegas, Galen Cranz, Phoebe Cutler, Jean-Francois Erhel, Kathryn Gustafson, Ursula Kurz, Marie-Line Luquet, Steve McAdam, Luca Merlini, Jean-Pierre Nourry, Jon Olsen, Luca Pagnamenta, Didier Pasquier, Neil Porter, Alexandra Villegas, and William Wallis, project team

DRIES VAN NOTEN

Collection, autumn/winter 1997–98

VIKTOR & ROLF

RUSSIAN DOLL haute couture collection, autumn/winter 1999–2000

LONG LIVE THE IMMATERIAL, or BLUESCREEN, collection, autumn/winter 2002–03

ONE WOMAN SHOW collection, autumn/winter 2003–04

JUNYA WATANABE COMME DES GARÇONS

Collection, autumn/winter 1998–99

SOIRÉE, or TECHNO COUTURE, collection, autumn/winter 2000–01

Collection, spring/summer 2002

CLASSIC collection, autumn/winter 2004–05

VIVIENNE WESTWOOD

PUNK collection, 1977

PUNKATURE collection, spring/summer 1983

MINI-CRINI collection, spring/summer 1985

CUT AND SLASH collection, spring/summer 1991

WILKINSON EYRE ARCHITECTS

BRIDGE OF ASPIRATION, The Royal Ballet School, 2001–03
The Royal Ballet School, client; Jim Eyre, director in charge; Annette von Hagen, project architect; Keith Brownlie, Martin Knight, and Chris Wilkinson, design team; Flint & Neill Partnership, structural engineers; Buro Happold, environmental engineers; Benson Limited, main contractor; and Speirs and Major Associates, lighting

YOHJI YAMAMOTO

Collection, autumn/winter 1991–92

Collection, autumn/winter 1996–97

Collection, spring/summer 1999

Collection, spring/summer 2000

Collection, spring/summer 2006

J. MEEJIN YOON/MY STUDIO

DEFENSIBLE DRESS, 2001

MÖBIUS DRESS, 2005

selected BIBLIOGRAPHY

Addressing the Century: 100 Years of Art & Fashion. Exh. cat. London: Hayward Gallery, 1998. Texts by Judith Clark, Joanne Entwistle and Elizabeth Wilson, Caroline Evans, Ulrich Lehmann, Robin Muir, and Peter Wollen.

At the End of the Century: One Hundred Years of Architecture. Exh. cat. Los Angeles: The Museum of Contemporary Art; and New York: Harry N. Abrams, 1998. Texts by Zeynep Çelik, Jean-Louis Cohen, Beatriz Colomina, Jorge Francisco Liernur, Elizabeth A.T. Smith, Anthony Vidler, and Hajime Yatsuka.

Bolton, Andrew. *The Supermodern Wardrobe*. London: V&A Publications, 2002.

Brubach, Holly. *A Dedicated Follower of Fashion*. New York: Phaidon, 1999.

Castle, Helen, ed. *Fashion + Architecture*. London: Wiley-Academy, 2000. Special issue of *Architectural Design* 70, no. 6 (December 2000). Includes interviews with Jan Kaplicky and Rem Koolhaas.

Clark, Judith. *Spectres: When Fashion Turns Back*. London: V&A Publications; and Antwerp, Belgium: ModeMuseum, 2004. Texts by Christopher Breward and Caroline Evans.

Davis, Fred. *Fashion, Culture, and Identity*. Chicago: The University of Chicago Press, 1992.

Evans, Caroline. *Fashion at the Edge: Spectacle, Modernity and Deathliness*. New Haven, Connecticut: Yale University Press, 2003.

Fashion: The Collection of the Kyoto Costume Institute, A History from the 18th to the 20th Century. Cologne, Germany: Taschen, 2002.

Fashionation. Exh. cat. Stockholm: Moderna Museet, 2004. Texts by Magnus af Petersens and Salka Hallström Bornold. Includes Hussein Chalayan, Martin Margiela, Alexander McQueen, and Viktor & Rolf.

Fausch, Deborah, Paulette Singley, Rodolphe El-Khoury, and Zvi Efrat, eds. *Architecture: In Fashion*. New York: Princeton Architectural Press, 1994. Texts by Efrat, El-Khoury, Fausch, Leila Kinney, Erin Mackie, Mary McLeod, Singley, Val Warke, and Mark Wigley.

Forster, Kurt, ed. *Trajectories*. Vol. 1 of *Metamorph: 9th International Architecture Exhibition*. 3 vols. Venice, Italy: Fondazione La Biennale di Venezia; and New York: Rizzoli, 2004.

Frankel, Susannah. *Visionaries: Interviews with Fashion Designers*. London: V&A Publications, 2001. Includes interviews with Azzedine Alaïa, Hussein Chalayan, Rei Kawakubo, Martin Margiela, Alexander McQueen, Miyake Issey, Junya Watanabe, Vivienne Westwood, and Yohji Yamamoto.

Fraser, Kennedy. *The Fashionable Mind: Reflections on Fashion 1970–1981*. New York: Alfred A. Knopf, 1981.

Gill, Alison. "Deconstruction Fashion: The Making of Unfinished, Decomposing, and Re-assembled Clothes." *Fashion Theory* 2, no. 1 (February 1998): 25–50.

Golbin, Pamela. *Fashion Designers*. New York: Watson-Guptill Publications, 1999. Includes profiles on Azzedine Alaïa, Comme des Garçons, Miyake Issey, Vivienne Westwood, and Yohji Yamamoto.

Hitchcock, Henry-Russell, and Philip Johnson. *The International Style*. New York: W. W. Norton, 1996. Originally published in 1932.

Hollander, Anne. *Seeing Through Clothes*. Berkeley: University of California Press, 1993.

Horn, Marilyn J., and Lois M. Gurel. *The Second Skin: An Interdisciplinary Study of Clothing*. 3rd ed. Boston: Houghton Mifflin, 1981. Originally published in 1968.

Johnson, Philip, and Mark Wigley. *Deconstructivist Architecture*. Exh. cat. New York: The Museum of Modern Art, 1988. Includes Peter Eisenman, Frank Gehry, Zaha Hadid, Rem Koolhaas, and Bernard Tschumi.

Koda, Harold. *Extreme Beauty: The Body Transformed*. Exh. cat. New York: The Metropolitan Museum of Art, 2001.

Martin, Richard. "Destitution and Deconstruction: The Riches of Poverty in the Fashions of the 1990s." *Textile & Text* 15, no. 2 (1992): 3–12.

Quinn, Bradley. *The Fashion of Architecture*. Oxford, England: Berg, 2003.

Riley, Terence. *The International Style: Exhibition 15 and The Museum of Modern Art*. Exh. cat. New York: Rizzoli and Columbia Books of Architecture, 1992.

——. *The Un-Private House*. Exh. cat. New York: The Museum of Modern Art, 1999. Includes projects by Shigeru Ban, Preston Scott Cohen, Neil M. Denari, Diller + Scofidio, Winka Dubbeldam/Archi-Tectonics, Herzog & de Meuron, OMA/Rem Koolhaas, SANAA, and Bernard Tschumi.

——, ed. *Tall Buildings*. Exh. cat. New York: The Museum of Modern Art, 2003. Text by Guy Nordenson. Includes projects by Eisenman Architects, Foreign Office Architects, Gehry Partners, Office for Metropolitan Architecture/Rem Koolhaas, Greg Lynn FORM, and Jean Nouvel.

Rosa, Joseph. *Folds, Blobs + Boxes: Architecture in the Digital Era*. Exh. cat. Pittsburgh: Heinz Architectural Center Books, 2001. Includes Preston Scott Cohen, Neil M. Denari, Peter Eisenman, Foreign Office Architects, Frank Gehry, Jakob + MacFarlane, Greg Lynn, and Bernard Tschumi.

Rudofsky, Bernard. *Are Clothes Modern?* Chicago: Paul Theobald, 1947.

Sample: 100 Fashion Designers–010 Curators. London: Phaidon, 2005. Includes profiles on Alber Elbaz for Lanvin, Olivier Theyskens for Rochas, Viktor & Rolf, and Yohji Yamamoto's Y-3.

Sidlauskas, Susan. *Intimate Architecture: Contemporary Clothing Design*. Exh. cat. Cambridge, Massachusetts: MIT Committee on the Visual Arts, 1982. Includes Miyake Issey and Yeohlee Teng.

10 x 10_2: 100 Architects, 10 Critics. New York: Phaidon Press, 2005. Includes profiles on Jakob + MacFarlane, Office dA, and Wilkinson Eyre Architects.

Wilcox, Claire, ed. *Radical Fashion*. Exh. cat. London: V&A Publications. Texts by Judith Clark, Susannah Frankel, Amy de la Haye, Alistair O'Neill, Valerie Steele, and Wilcox; includes Azzedine Alaïa, Hussein Chalayan, Comme des Garçons, Alexander McQueen, Martin Margiela, Miyake Issey, Junya Watanabe, Vivienne Westwood, and Yohji Yamamoto.

Wilson, Elizabeth. *Adorned in Dreams: Fashion and Modernity*. Berkeley: University of California Press, 1988.

XXIème Ciel: Mode in Japan. Milan, Italy: Five Continents; and Nice, France: Musée des Arts asiatiques, 2003. Texts by Marie-Pierre Foissy, Akiko Fukai, Pamela Golbin, Yuniya Kawamura, Liz Larson, Patricia Mears, Pamela Ptak and Mears, and Antigone Schilling.

AZZEDINE ALAÏA

Baudot, François. *Alaïa*. New York: Universe Publishing and The Vendome Press, 1997.

Putman, Andrée, and François Baudot. "Azzedine Alaïa: Timeless Fashion." *Flash Art*, no. 204 (January–February 1999): 62–65. Interview with Alaïa.

SHIGERU BAN ARCHITECTS

McQuaid, Matilda. *Shigeru Ban*. London: Phaidon, 2003.

Mori, Toshiko, ed. *Immaterial/Ultramaterial: Architecture, Design, and Materials*. Cambridge, Massachusetts: Harvard Design School; and New York: George Braziller, 2002. Includes interview with Ban.

HUSSEIN CHALAYAN

Abbas, Remi. "Hussein Chalayan: Masked by Nature." *Blueprint*, no. 219 (May 2004): 94–97.

Chalayan, Hussein, ed. *No. C Magazine* (Artimo Foundation, Amsterdam) (2002).

Hussein Chalayan. Groningen, The Netherlands: Groninger Museum; and Rotterdam, The Netherlands: NAI Publishers, 2005. Texts by Caroline Evans, Suzy Menkes, Ted Polhemus, and Bradley Quinn.

Thompson, Henrietta. "Hussein Chalayan vs. Lucy Orta." *Blueprint*, no. 219 (May 2004): 128.

PRESTON SCOTT COHEN

Cohen, Preston Scott. *Contested Symmetries and Other Predicaments in Architecture*. New York: Princeton Architectural Press, 2001.

COMME DES GARÇONS

Kawakubo, Rei, ed. *Comme des Garçons*. Tokyo: Chikuma Shobo, 1986.

Koda, Harold. "Rei Kawakubo and the Aesthetic of Poverty." *Dress: Journal of the Costume Society of America* 11 (1985).

Sudjic, Deyan. *Rei Kawakubo and Comme des Garçons*. New York: Rizzoli, 1990.

Three Women: Madeleine Vionnet, Claire McCardell, and Rei Kawakubo. Exh. cat. New York: Fashion Institute of Technology, 1987.

NEIL M. DENARI ARCHITECTS

Denari, Neil M. *Gyroscopic Horizons*. New York: Princeton Architectural Press, 1999.

DILLER SCOFIDIO + RENFRO

Diller, Elizabeth, and Ricardo Scofidio. *Blur: The Making of Nothing*. New York: Harry N. Abrams, 2002.

Muschamp, Herbert. "Instant Inspiration: Just Add Water." *The New York Times*, 6 April 2001, E33.

Pogrebin, Robin. "Alice Tully, Could That Really Be You?" *The New York Times*, 13 November 2005, sec. 2, 40.

Scanning: The Aberrant Architectures of Diller + Scofidio. Exh. cat. New York: Whitney Museum of American Art, 2003. Texts by Aaron Betsky, Jordan Crandall, Edward Dimendberg, RoseLee Goldberg, K. Michael Hays, and Ashley Schafer. Interview with Diller and Scofidio by Laurie Anderson.

WINKA DUBBELDAM/ARCHI-TECTONICS

Dubbeldam, Winka. *Winka Dubbeldam: Architect (Con-Tex-Ture)*. New York: Princeton Architectural Press, 1996.

——. "(In-)Crease: Integral Architectures." "Extended Play" section, Arch'it website, architettura.supereva.com/extended/20010221/index.htm.

Speaks, Michael. "Design Intelligence, Part 11: Winka Dubbeldam—Archi-Tectonics." *A + U: Architecture and Urbanism* (November 2003): 190–97. Interview with Dubbeldam.

EISENMAN ARCHITECTS

Bédard, Jean-François, ed. *Cities of Artificial Excavation: The Work of Peter Eisenman, 1978–1988*. Exh. cat. Montréal: Canadian Centre for Architecture; and New York: Rizzoli, 1994. Texts by Alan Balfour, Yve-Alain Bois, Jean-Louis Cohen, Kurt W. Forster, K. Michael Hays, Arata Isozaki, and Fredric Jameson.

Kipnis, Jeffrey, and Thomas Leeser, eds. *Chora L Works: Jacques Derrida and Peter Eisenman*. New York: Monacelli Press, 1997.

ALBER ELBAZ FOR LANVIN

Hirschberg, Lynn. "The Classicist." *The New York Times Magazine* (25 September 2005): 32–37.

Horyn, Cathy. "Adieu to Paris with Lanvin and Saint Laurent." *The New York Times*, 8 March 2005, B11.

FOREIGN OFFICE ARCHITECTS

Foreign Office Architects. *The Yokohama Project: Foreign Office Architects*. Barcelona: Actar, 2002.

——. *Phylogenesis: FOA's Ark*. Exh. cat. Barcelona: Actar; and London: Institute of Contemporary Arts, 2004. Project descriptions; texts by Patrick Beaucé and Bernard Cache, Manuel De Landa, Jeffrey Kipnis, Sandra Knapp, Sanford Kwinter, Detlef Mertins, Fashid Moussavi and Alejandro Zaera-Polo, and Mark Wigley.

FUTURE SYSTEMS

Field, Marcus. *Future Systems*. London: Phaidon Press, 1999.

FRANK GEHRY

Dal Co, Francesco, and Kurt W. Forster. *Frank O. Gehry: The Complete Works*. New York: The Monacelli Press, 1998.

Ragheb, J. Fiona, ed. *Frank Gehry Architect*. Exh. cat. New York: Guggenheim Museum Foundation, 2001. Texts by Jean-Louis Cohen, Beatriz Colomina, Mildred Friedman, William J. Mitchell, and Ragheb.

TESS GIBERSON

Arakas, Irini. "Spring's Leading Ladies: Tess Giberson." *Vogue* (December 2004): 190.

ZAHA HADID ARCHITECTS

Dochantschi, Markus, ed. *Zaha Hadid: Space for Art*. Baden, Switzerland: Lars Müller Publishers, 2004. Texts by Charles Desmarais and Joseph Giovannini.

Noever, Peter, ed. *Zaha Hadid: Architektur/Architecture*. Exh. cat. Vienna: MAK; and Ostfildern-Ruit, Germany: Hatje Cantz Verlag, 2003. Texts by Noever, Patrik Schumacher, and Andreas Ruby.

Schumacher, Patrik, and Gordana Fontana-Giusti, eds. *Zaha Hadid: Complete Works*. 4 vols.: *Major and Recent Works*, *Projects Documentation*, *Process: Sketches and Drawings*, and *Texts and References*. New York: Rizzoli, 2004. Project descriptions; texts by Peter Cook, Fontana-Giusti, Andreas Ruby, and Schumacher.

HERZOG & DE MEURON

El Croquis, no. 84 (1997). Special issue on Herzog & de Meuron, 1993–97. Project descriptions; text by Jeffrey Kipnis; interview with Jacques Herzog by Kipnis.

El Croquis, nos. 109–10 (2002). Special issue on Herzog & de Meuron, 1998–2002. Project descriptions; text by William J. R. Curtis; interview with Jacques Herzog by Curtis.

Ursprung, Philip, ed. *Herzog & de Meuron: Natural History*. Exh. cat. Montréal: Canadian Centre for Architecture; and Baden, Switzerland: Lars Müller Publishers, 2002. Texts by Richard Armstrong, Carrie Asman, Gernott Böhme, Boris Groys, Georges Didi-Huberman, Kurt W. Forster, Jacques Herzog and Pierre de Meuron, Reinhold Hohl, Catherine Hürzeler, Petros Koumoutsakos, Robert Kudielka, Albert Lutz, Ulrike Meyer Stump, Christian Moueix, Peggy Phelan, Rebecca Schneider, Ursprung, Adolf Max Vogt, and Alejandro Zaera-Polo. Interviews with Herzog and de Meuron, Alfred Richterich, Thomas Ruff, Jeff Wall, and Rémy Zaugg by Ursprung.

YOSHIKI HISHINUMA

Webb, Martin. "Brave New World." *Metropolis* (Tokyo) website, metropolis.japantoday.com/tokyo/435/fashion.asp.

TOYO ITO

Cellarius, Christoph. "Twisting Vibrancies Flowing Through a Stimulating Atmosphere: The Making of Forum for Music, Dance and Visual Culture, Ghent, from Behind the Scenes." *A + U: Architecture and Urbanism* (June 2005): 80–107.

El Croquis, no. 123 (2004). Special issue on Ito, 2001–05. Project descriptions; interview with Toyo Ito by Koji Taki; text by Juan Antonio Cortés.

Hirata, Akihisa. "Ghent and Tod's: Coincidence of Opposites." *A + U: Architecture and Urbanism* (June 2005): 114–15.

Pollock, Naomi R. "Tod's Omotesando Building, Japan." *Architectural Record*, no. 6 (June 2005): 78–85.

JAKOB + MACFARLANE

"Jakob & MacFarlane: H House, Corsica, France 2002." *A + U: Architecture and Urbanism*, no. 390 (March 2003): 126–27.

GREG LYNN FORM

Lynn, Greg. *Animate Form*. New York: Princeton Architectural Press, 1999.

——, and Hani Rashid. *Architectural Laboratories*. Rotterdam, The Netherlands: NAI Publishers, 2002. Texts by Lynn, Rashid, and Mark C. Taylor; interview with Lynn by Max Hollein.

ELENA MANFERDINI

Chang, Jade. "Rococo A-Go-Go." *Metropolis* 23, no. 10 (June 2004): 46.

Kahn, Eve M. "Designer Labels: Elena Manferdini." *I.D.* 52, no. 3 (May 2005): 52–55.

MAISON MARTIN MARGIELA

Derycke, Luc, and Sandra Van de Veire, eds. *Belgian Fashion Design*. Antwerp, Belgium: Ludion, 1999.

Spindler, Amy M. "Coming Apart." *The New York Times*, 25 July 1993, 1.

ALEXANDER MCQUEEN

Roux, Caroline. "Fashion Makes a Statement." *Domus*, no. 865 (December 2003): 114–17.

ENRIC MIRALLES BENEDETTA TAGLIABUE/EMBT ARQUITECTES

El Croquis, nos. 100–01 (2000). Special issue on Miralles Taglibue, 1996–2000. Project descriptions; interview with Miralles by Emilio Tuñon and Luis Moreno Mansilla; texts by Rafael Moneo, Josep Quetglas, and Tagliabue.

Miralles, Enric, and Benedetta Tagliabue. *EMBT: Work in Progress*. Barcelona: Collegi d'Arquitectes de Catalunya, 2004.

MIYAKE ISSEY

Miyake, Issey. *Issey Miyake: Making Things*. Exh. cat. Paris: Fondation Cartier pour l'art contemporain; and Zürich: Scalo, 1999. Texts by Kazuko Sato; interview with Miyake by Hervé Chandès.

Saiki, Maggie K. *12 Japanese Masters*. New York: Graphis, 2002.

MORPHOSIS

Futagawa, Yoshio. "Thursday, April 28, 2005: 1 pm/Santa Monica, California—Interview with Thom Mayne." *GA Document*, no. 87 (August 2005): 8–17.

Morphosis. London: Phaidon Press, 2003. Text by Thom Mayne with Val Warke.

NEUTELINGS RIEDIJK ARCHITECTEN

El Croquis, no. 94 (1999). Special issue on Neutelings Riedijk Architecten, 1992–99. Project descriptions; texts by Maarten Delbeke, Willem Jan Neutelings, and Dirk van den Heuvel.

Neutelings Riedijk Architecten. *At Work: Neutelings Riedijk Architects*. Rotterdam, The Netherlands: 010 Publishers, 2004. Project descriptions.

ATELIERS JEAN NOUVEL

Jean Nouvel. Exh. cat. Paris: Éditions du Centre Pompidou, 2001. Texts by Chantal Béret, Jacques Lucan, Frédéric Migayrou, Nouvel, Jean-Paul Robert, Yehuda E. Safran, and Paul Virilio.

OFFICE DA

El-Khoury, Rodolphe. "Office dA's House Dressing." *Thresholds* (Cambridge, Massachusetts), no. 22 [fashion issue] (2001): 49–53.

OFFICE FOR METROPOLITAN ARCHITECTURE/REM KOOLHAAS

"The Making of a Library." *Metropolis* 24, no. 2 (October 2004): 97–115. Texts by Christopher Hawthorne, Paul Makovsky, Fred Moody, and Jacob Ward.

Office for Metropolitan Architecture. *S, M, L, XL*. New York: Monacelli Press, 1995.

NARCISO RODRIGUEZ

Holgate, Mark. "Narciso Rodriguez." *Vogue* (September 2005): 680.

Moore, Booth. "Designer Aims to Shine Without the Limelight." *Los Angeles Times*, 12 August 2003, E1.

RALPH RUCCI

Bissonnette, Anne. *Chado Ralph Rucci*. Exh. cat. Kent, Ohio: Kent State University Museum, 2005.

KAZUYO SEIJIMA + RYUE NISHIZAWA/SANAA

Pollock, Naomi R. "21st Century Museum, Japan." *Architectural Record*, no. 2 (February 2005): 88–97.

Sejima, Kazuyo, and Ryue Nishizawa. *Kazuyo Sejima + Ryue Nishizawa/SANAA Works 1995–2003*. Tokyo: TOTO Shuppan, 2003.

NANNI STRADA

Strada, Nanni. *Moda Design*. Milan, Italy: Editoriale Modo, 2002.

YEOHLEE TENG

Energetics: Clothes & Enclosures—Hamzah & Yeang and Yeohlee. Exh. cat. Berlin: Aedes East, 1998.

Major, John S., and Yeohlee Teng, eds. *Yeohlee: Work*. Victoria, Australia: Peleus Press, 2003. Texts by Paola Antonelli, Andrew Bolton, Richard Flood, Harold Koda, Marylou Luther, Richard Martin, Susan Sidlauskas, Valerie Steele, and Teng.

TESTA & WEISER

Beesley, Philip, and Sean Hanna. "Lighter: A Transformed Architecture." In Matilda McQuaid, *Extreme Textiles: Designing for High Performance*, 103–27. Exh. cat. New York: Cooper-Hewitt, National Design Museum, Smithsonian Institution; and Princeton Architectural Press, 2005.

Knecht, Barbara. "Brave New Solid-State, Carbon-Fiber World." *Architectural Record*, Innovation Supplement (October 2003): 36–41.

OLIVIER THEYSKENS FOR ROCHAS

Horyn, Cathy. "A Daring Stand at Rochas, Rare as a Paris Snowfall." *The New York Times*, 3 March 2005, B9.

ISABEL TOLEDO

Kane, Florence. "The Final Ten: Isabel Toledo." *Vogue* (November 2005): 364–65.

Toledo Toledo. New York: Visionaire Publishing, 2000. Texts by Alix Browne and Anne Bissonnette.

BERNARD TSCHUMI ARCHITECTS

Chaslin, François. "Bernard Tschumi: Parc de la Villette, Paris." *Domus*, no. 817 (July–August 1999): 8–17.

Tschumi, Bernard. "Disjunction: Essays Written Between 1984–1991." In Tschumi, *Architecture and Disjunction*, 171–259. Cambridge, Massachusetts: The MIT Press, 1994.

DRIES VAN NOTEN

Dries Van Noten: 01–50. Antwerp, Belgium: N. V. Van Noten Andries, 2004. Interview with the House of Van Noten by Alix Sharkey.

Tucker, Andrew. *Dries Van Noten: Shape, Print, and Fabric*. New York: Watson-Guptill, 1999.

VIKTOR & ROLF

Viktor & Rolf Haute Couture Book. Groningen, The Netherlands: Groninger Museum, 2000. Text by Amy Spindler.

Viktor & Rolf. Breda, The Netherlands: Artimo Foundation, 1999.

Viktor & Rolf, eds. *No. E Magazine* (Artimo Foundation, Amsterdam) (2003).

JUNYA WATANABE COMME DES GARÇONS

Ptak, Pamela, and Patricia Mears. "Junya Watanabe: Maître artisan." In *XXIème Ciel: Mode in Japan*, 101–11. Milan, Italy: Five Continents; and Nice, France: Musée des Arts asiatiques, 2003.

VIVIENNE WESTWOOD

Wilcox, Claire. *Vivienne Westwood*. Exh. cat. London: Victoria & Albert Publications, 2004.

WILKINSON EYRE ARCHITECTS

Hart, Sara. "Iconic Connections: Floral Street Bridge, London, England." *Architectural Record*, no. 6 (June 2004): 260–61.

——. "Architects Discover Bridge Design Can Be the Perfect Union of Art and Science." *Architectural Record*, no. 6 (June 2004): 279–86.

YOHJI YAMAMOTO

Aufzeichnungen zu Kleidern und Städten (A notebook on cities and clothes). Directed by Wim Wenders. Berlin: Road Movies Filmproduktion; and Paris: Centre Georges Pompidou, 1989.

Baudot, François. *Yohji Yamamoto*. New York: Assouline, 2005.

Kawamura, Yuniya. *The Japanese Revolution in Paris Fashion*. Oxford, England: Berg, 2004.

Sozzani, Carla, ed. *Yohji Yamamoto: Talking to Myself*. Göttingen, Germany: Steidl, 2002. Interview with Yamamoto by Kiyokazu Washida.

J. MEEJIN YOON/MY STUDIO

Kahn, Eve M. "Designer Labels: J. Meejin Yoon." *I.D.* 52, no. 3 (May 2005): 56–59.

ILLUSTRATION CREDITS

THE FOLLOWING LIST, KEYED TO PAGE NUMBERS, APPLIES TO IMAGES FOR WHICH CREDITS ARE DUE:

Courtesy MY Studio, pp. 1, 256–58; photo: © TESTA, pp. 2, 208–13; photo: © 2003 Todd Eberle, pp. 6, 20 bottom, 108–09, 125 bottom; courtesy Kyoto Costume Institute, photo: Takashi Hatakeyama, p. 10; courtesy MIT List Visual Arts Center, Cambridge, MA, photo: Herb Engelsberg, p. 11 left; courtesy AMO, p. 11 right; courtesy Yeohlee Teng, p. 12 right, photo: Irving Solero, p. 12 left; collection The Metropolitan Museum of Art, NY, gift of Yeohlee Teng, 1983, photo: Yeohlee Teng, p. 206 top; collection The Metropolitan Museum of Art, NY, gift of Yeohlee Teng, 1995, photo: Karen L. Willis/The Metropolitan Museum of Art, p. 206 bottom; courtesy Victoria & Albert Museum, London/Art Resource, NY, p. 13 bottom; artwork by Ludwig Mies van der Rohe © 2006 Artists Rights Society (ARS), NY/VG Bild-Kunst, Bonn, photo: Ezra Stoller © Esto, all rights reserved, p. 14 bottom left; photo: © Jacky Marshall, pp. 14 right column, 22–29, 188–89; courtesy Maison Martin Margiela, pp. 151–52, photo: Jonathan Hallam, p. 15 left, photo: Marina Faust, pp. 150 left, 153, photo: Ronald Stoops, p. 150 right; courtesy Gehry Partners, pp. 15 right, 30 right, 111 top; photo: © Balthazar Korab Ltd., p. 30 center; photo: © Tim Street-Porter/Esto, all rights reserved, p. 111 bottom; courtesy Hussein Chalayan, pp. 16–17 top, 60–65; courtesy Shigeru Ban Architects, pp. 16 bottom, 56–57; courtesy Atelier Manferdini, pp. 18, 148–49, photo: Deborah Bird, pp. 146–47; courtesy Kent State University Museum, photo: Anne Bissonnette, pp. 19 left, 192–93, 194 right, 195; courtesy Isabel Toledo, photo: Karen L. Willis, pp. 19 right, 219, photo: William Palmer, pp. 219 left, 219 top right, photo: Dan Lecca, p. 225 top row left, middle row left and center, bottom row left and right; courtesy Herzog & de Meuron, photo: © Margherita Spiluttini, pp. 20 top, 120–21, 122 top, 123, 125 bottom, 126 bottom; courtesy Comme des Garçons, pp. 240–43, photo: Paolo Roversi, pp. 20 left, 76–77, photo: Peter Lindbergh, pp. 33 left, 70–72, photo: Katerina Jebb, pp. 73, 272, photo: Yoshiko Seino, pp. 74–75; photo: Marleen Daniëls, pp. 21 right, 228–31; photo: Erich Lessing/Art Resource, NY, p. 31 left; courtesy Yohji Yamamoto, p. 31 top right, photo: Alessandro Ciampi, pp. 250–51 top, photo: Monica Feudi, pp. 251 bottom, 252–53, 254 left column top and center and right column, 255, photo: Thierry Chomel, p. 254 left column bottom; photo: Lynn Rosenthal, p. 32 left; artwork by Salvador Dalí © 2006 Salvador Dalí, Gala-Salvador Dalí Foundation/ Artists Rights Society (ARS), NY, photo: © 2006 Salvador Dalí Museum, Inc., p. 33 right; courtesy Conde Nast Archive, photo: © Hans Feurer (originally published in Vogue), p. 33 right; photo: © William Palmer, pp. 35–36; courtesy Susan Cianciolo, photo: Chikashi Suzuki, p. 37 left; courtesy Zaha Hadid Architects, pp. 39 right column, 114, 115 bottom, 116 right column; photo: © Christian Richters, pp. 115 top, 116 left column, 117–19, 172, 173 right and bottom left; photo: © Office for Metropolitan Architecture, pp. 41 top and center, 186 top, 187 top, photo: © Philippe Ruault, pp. 184, 186 bottom; photo: © Gerald Zugmann/ www.zugmann.com, p. 41 bottom left; courtesy Eisenman Architects, pp. 41 bottom right, 90–91, collection Centre Canadien d'Architecture/Canadian Centre for Architecture, Montréal, p. 92 right column center; collection Centre Canadien d'Architecture/Canadian Centre for Architecture, Montréal, p. 92 left and right column top and bottom; courtesy Studio Daniel Libeskind, p. 42; photo: © Peter Mauss/Esto, all rights reserved, p. 43; courtesy Bernard Tschumi Architects, pp. 44, 227 top right, photo: J. M. Monthiers, pp. 45, 227 top left and bottom, photo: Peter Mauss/Esto, p. 226; courtesy Azzedine Alaïa, p. 51 top and bottom, photo: Peter Lindbergh, p. 51 center; courtesy Shigeru Ban Architects, photo: © Hiroyuki Hirai, pp. 52–55, 58–59; courtesy Preston Scott Cohen, pp. 66–69; courtesy Neil M. Denari Architects, pp. 78–79; courtesy Diller Scofidio + Renfro, pp. 80–85, photo: Beat Widmer, pp. 86–87; photo: © 2006 floto + warner, pp. 88, 185, 187 bottom; courtesy Archi-Tectonics, p. 89; courtesy Lanvin, pp. 94–95; courtesy Foreign Office Architects, pp. 97 bottom, 100–03, photo: © Satoru Mishima, pp. 96–97 top, 98–99; courtesy Future Systems, pp. 104, 107 left, photo: © Richard Davies, pp. 105–06, 107 right; photo: © Thomas Mayer Archive, p. 110 top and bottom left; photo: Jonah Freeman, pp. 112–13; collection Centre Canadien d'Architecture/Canadian Centre for Architecture, Montréal, gift of Elise Jaffe and Jeffrey Brown, © Thomas Ruff, p. 122 bottom; courtesy and © Herzog & de Meuron, pp. 124, 125 top, photo: © 2000 Todd Eberle, p. 126 top, Herzog & de Meuron (primary designers) and Fong & Chan Architects (principal architects), photo: © 2005 Todd Eberle, p. 127; photo: © Guy Marineau, pp. 128–29; courtesy Toyo Ito & Associates, Architects, pp. 133 top row, 134, 135 left, 136 top and bottom, 137 bottom, photo: © Hisao Suzuki, pp. 132, 133 middle row, 135 right, 136 center, 137 top, 175; courtesy Jakob + MacFarlane, pp. 138–41; courtesy Greg Lynn FORM, pp. 142–45; courtesy Alexander McQueen, pp. 154–59; courtesy Enric Miralles Benedetta Tagliabue/EMBT, pp. 160, 161 bottom, photo: Alex Gaultier, p. 161 top; photo: © Duccio Malagamba, pp. 162–63; courtesy Miyake Design Studio, photo: © Raymond Meier, pp. 164–65, photo: Marcus Tomlinson, pp. 166–69; courtesy Morphosis, pp. 170–71; courtesy Neutelings Riedijk Architecten, p. 173 top left; photo: © Rob 't Hart, p. 174; courtesy Ateliers Jean Nouvel, pp. 176–77; courtesy Office dA, pp. 182–83, photo: John Horner, pp. 178, 180–81, photo: Nader Tehrani, p. 179; courtesy Chado Ralph Rucci, photo: Dan Lecca, p. 194 left; courtesy SANAA, pp. 196–97, 198 bottom, photo: © Shinkenchiku-sha, pp. 198 top, 199; courtesy Nanni Strada Design Studio, pp. 200–03; photo: © William Palmer, pp. 204, 205 right, 207, 218, 220–24; courtesy Rochas, pp. 214–17; courtesy Viktor & Rolf, photo: Peter Stigter, pp. 232–33, photo: Peter Kirby, pp. 234–35, photo: Peter Tahl, pp. 17 bottom, 236–39; photo: © Gavin Bond, p. 244 left; photo: © Arthur Elgort, pp. 244 right, 245; courtesy V&A Picture Library, pp. 246, 247 right; courtesy V&A Picture Library/Victoria and Albert Museum, p. 247 left; courtesy Wilkinson Eyre Architects, p. 249 second from top and bottom, photo: © Nick Wood, pp. 248, 249 top, photo: Peter Cook/VIEW, p. 249 second from bottom; photo: © Lucy Orta, artist, holds the first Rootstein Hopkins Chair at London College of Fashion for the University of the Arts, London, p. 260 left; courtesy Andrea Rosen Gallery, NY, reproduced by permission of the Milwaukee Art Museum, p. 260 right; courtesy Andrea Rosen Gallery, NY, photo: Oren Slor, p. 261 left; and courtesy of the artist and Lehmann Maupin Gallery, NY, p. 261 right.

Published on the occasion of the exhibition "Skin + Bones: Parallel Practices in Fashion and Architecture."

The Museum of Contemporary Art, Los Angeles
MOCA Grand Avenue
19 November 2006–5 March 2007

The National Art Center, Tokyo
6 June–13 August 2007

This publication is made possible through a generous grant from Carol and Jacqueline Appel.

"Skin + Bones: Parallel Practices in Fashion and Architecture" is made possible by generous support from The Ron Burkle Endowment for Architecture and Design Programs; the Sydney Irmas Exhibition Endowment; The MOCA Architecture & Design Council; Mondriaan Foundation, Amsterdam; Étant donnés: The French-American Fund for Contemporary Art; Dwell; Elise Jaffe + Jeffrey Brown; The Japan Foundation; and the Consulate General of the Netherlands.

89.9 KCRW is the Official Media Sponsor of MOCA.

Generous in-kind support is provided by Ralph Pucci International.

Additional in-kind support is provided by Yellow Book USA.

Director of Publications: Lisa Mark
Senior Editor: Jane Hyun
Editor: Elizabeth Hamilton
Administrative Assistant: Theeng Kok
Designer: Tracey Shiffman with Jenny Yee and Ari Young
Printer: Graphicom, Vicenza, Italy

This publication is typeset in Unit, a FontFont family with fifty-six styles, designed by information architect and type designer Erik Spiekermann and issued by FontShop in 2004.

First published in hardcover in the United States of America in 2006 by
Thames & Hudson Inc., 500 Fifth Avenue,
New York, New York 10110
thamesandhudsonusa.com

First published in the United Kingdom in 2006 by
Thames & Hudson Ltd, 181A High Holborn, London WC1V 7QX
www.thamesandhudson.com

LIBRARY OF CONGRESS CATALOG CARD NUMBER 2006901309

British Library Cataloguing-in-Publication Data
A catalogue record for this book is available from the British Library.

ISBN-13: 978-0-500-51318-7
ISBN-10: 0-500-51318-X

Printed and bound in Italy

page 1: **FUTURE SYSTEMS**, **SELFRIDGES DEPARTMENT STORE**, BIRMINGHAM, ENGLAND, 1999–2003, DETAIL
page 2: **TESTA & WEISER**, **CARBON FIBER REINFORCED TIMBER (CFRT) PROTOTYPES**, 2005, DETAILS OF MODELS
page 272: **COMME DES GARÇONS**, GARMENTS FROM **NEW ESSENTIAL** COLLECTION, SPRING/SUMMER 1999